PRAXIS® CORE ACADEMIC SKILLS FOR EDUCATORS
(5712, 5722, 5732)

Second Edition

NEW YORK

Cataloging-in-Publication Data is on file with the Library of Congress.

ISBN 978-1-61103-060-0

Printed in the United States of America

9 8 7 6 5 4 3 2 1

Second Edition

For more information on LearningExpress, other LearningExpress products, or bulk sales,
please write to us at:
    224 W. 29th Street
    3rd Floor
    New York, NY 10001

CONTENTS

CONTENTS

CHAPTER

1 ▶ ABOUT THE PRAXIS® CORE ACADEMIC SKILLS FOR EDUCATORS TESTS

CHAPTER SUMMARY
This chapter familiarizes you with the series of Praxis® Core Academic Skills for Educators tests, which are administered by the Educational Testing Service. You will learn the components of all three Core exams, how to register for the exams, how they are scored, and all about the computer-based testing format.

Welcome to your comprehensive review for the Praxis Core Academic Skills for Educators tests! This series of computer-based mathematics, reading, and writing exams tests your knowledge in these core subjects, and assesses your readiness to enter teacher education programs. As the name suggests, the content tested on these exams aligns with the Common Core State Standards.

This book offers complete review, practice, and preparation for the three Core exams:

- Core Academic Skills for Educators: Reading (5712)
- Core Academic Skills for Educators: Writing (5722)
- Core Academic Skills for Educators: Mathematics (5732)

Inside you will find a diagnostic test to assess your skill levels, comprehensive review of the academic content found on all three exams, and two practice exams to test what you have learned and to determine where you need more practice. At the end of the book, you will also find a link to an instantly scored online practice exam.

States Using the Praxis Series of Tests

Each state sets its own requirement for which tests you must take and what score will be accepted as passing. Information regarding specific state or organization requirements may change from time to time. For accurate, up-to-date information, refer to the official Praxis website at www.ets.org/praxis/about/core/ and your state's education department.

IMPORTANT CONTACT INFORMATION

ETS—*The Praxis Series*

P.O. Box 6051

Princeton, NJ 08541-6051

Website: www.ets.org/praxis

Phone: 609-771-7395, M–F 8 A.M. to 7:45 P.M. (EST) (except for U.S. holidays)

Phone for the Hearing Impaired: 609-771-7714

E-mail directly through the website at www.ets.org/praxis/contact

Before you begin your review, let's take a closer look at the Praxis Core exams.

What Is Covered on the Praxis Core Tests?

The Praxis Core tests are designed to see whether you have the academic skills to be an effective teacher. Each tests your basic skills in either Reading, Mathematics, or Writing.

Praxis Core at a Glance

CORE TEST	TEST CODE	NUMBER OF QUESTIONS	QUESTION TYPES	TIME ALLOWED
Reading	5712	56	Multiple-choice	85 minutes
Writing	5722	40 + 2	• 40 multiple-choice + two essays	40 minutes for multiple-choice questions; 30 minutes for each essay
Mathematics	5732	56	• Multiple-choice: some ask you to select one answer choice; some ask you to select one or more. • Numeric entry: no choices; type in your own answer.	85 minutes

As you can see, most of the questions on the Praxis Core tests, with the exception of the essay portion of the Writing test, are in multiple-choice format. The Mathematics test also features numeric entry questions, where you supply an answer without being given any choices. Each multiple-choice question has five answer choices and is worth one point. Because test scoring is based only on the number of items answered correctly, you are not penalized for incorrect answers on the Praxis Core tests—so be sure to fill in all the answer blanks rather than leaving difficult questions unanswered. Even a guess is better than leaving an answer blank!

Let's look at each test.

Reading

The Praxis Core Academic Skills for Educators: Reading test measures your ability to comprehend, analyze, and evaluate written information. The skills tested on the exam align with the Common Core State Standards for Reading, and emphasize the skills needed to thrive in a teacher preparation program.

You will be asked to read a number of passages (which may vary in length from a few sentences to 100 to 200 words) and then answer questions accompanying each that test your ability to comprehend what you have read. The genre and reading levels of the passages will vary. You will be tested only on your ability to understand and analyze the selection; you will not be required to have specific knowledge about the topics discussed in the passages.

You will have 85 minutes to read all the passages and answer the 56 multiple-choice questions on this exam. Here is a breakdown of the question types on the Praxis Core Reading test.

QUESTION TYPE	NUMBER OF QUESTIONS	PERCENTAGE OF TEST
Key Ideas and Details	17–22	35%
Craft, Structure, and Language Skills	14–19	30%
Integration of Knowledge and Ideas	17–22	35%

Chapter 4 provides more detailed coverage of these question types you will face, with examples of each.

Writing

The Praxis Core Academic Skills for Educators: Writing test is divided into two sections:

1. The first section consists of multiple-choice questions that require you to find and/or correct errors in standard English.
2. The second part asks you to write two 30-minute essays: an argumentative essay and a source-based essay.

The skills tested align with the Common Core State Standards for Writing. The multiple-choice section of the writing test is designed to measure your ability to use standard English correctly and effectively, and is divided into four parts: usage, sentence correction, revision in context, and research skills.

Usage questions test your knowledge of:

- structural and grammatical relationships
- mechanics
- idiom or word choice

Usage questions also test your ability to identify error-free sentences.

Sentence Correction questions test your ability to:

- select the best way to state a given phrase or sentence
- correct sentences with errors in grammar, mechanics, idioms, or word choice

Revision-in-Context questions test your skills in editing a passage to strengthen its word choice, flow, style, and organization.

Research Skills questions ask you to assess the credibility of sources, identify parts of a citation, and recognize parts of a passage that have been pulled from various sources.

The Essays

The essay portion of the Praxis Core Writing test is designed to evaluate your ability to express ideas clearly and effectively in standard written English under time constraints. You will be asked to write two different types of essays: an Argumentative essay and an Informative/Explanatory essay.

The **Argumentative** essay will ask you to draw from personal experiences and observation to support a position. To perform well on this essay, you will need to back up your point of view with examples—either from something you have read or seen, from your real life, or from a combination of both

The **Informative/Explanatory** essay will begin with two passages, which you should read before you begin. You will then be asked to take information from these two sources to answer a question presented by the prompt given.

The given topics present situations that are generally familiar to all educated people and do not require any specialized knowledge in a particular field. Although you will be posing an argument and drawing conclusions based on examples from personal experience or observation, you will not be graded on your opinion—you will be scored only on how effectively you are able to get across your ideas.

You will have 40 minutes to answer the 40 multiple-choice questions on this exam, and 30 minutes for each essay. Chapter 5 provides detailed information on how to approach both sections of the writing test.

Mathematics

The Praxis Core Academic Skills for Educators: Mathematics test measures your proficiency in math. Generally speaking, the test requires a competency at the high school or first-year college level. All the skills tested on the exam align with the Common Core State Standards for Mathematics. Here are the four main math content areas that will be tested:

Numbers and Operations
- order
- equivalence
- numeration and place value
- number properties
- operation properties

- computation
- estimation
- ratio, proportion, and percent
- numerical reasoning

Algebra and Functions
- equations and inequalities
- algorithmic thinking
- patterns
- algebraic representations
- algebraic reasoning

Geometry and Measurement
- geometric properties
- the xy-coordinate plane
- geometric reasoning
- systems of measurement

Statistics and Probability
- data interpretation
- data representation
- trends and inferences
- measures of center and spread
- probability

You will have 85 minutes to answer the 56 multiple-choice (one-answer and multiple-answer) and numeric entry questions on this exam. Here is a breakdown of the question types on the Praxis Core Mathematics test.

QUESTION TYPE	NUMBER OF QUESTIONS	PERCENTAGE OF TEST
Numbers and Operations	17	30%
Algebra	17	30%
Geometry and Measurement	11	20%
Statistics and Probability	11	20%

The lessons in Chapter 6 will give you more in-depth coverage of test content.

Please note: You *will* have access to an on-screen calculator for the duration of the Praxis Core Academic Skills for Educators: Mathematics test. Note that *no other* calculator use is allowed—you will not be able to bring a calculator from home. The calculator provided is simple and has four functions (+, −, ×, ÷).

The Computer-Delivered Test

Praxis Core Academic Skills for Educators tests are administered as computer-delivered tests in more than 300 locations throughout the United States. They are given frequently. You don't have to know much about computers to take these computer-based tests—each one begins with a tutorial on the use of the computer. You are encouraged to spend as much time as needed on the tutorial.

With the exception of the essay portion of the writing test and numeric entry mathematics questions, all questions are in multiple-choice format. The questions are presented on the computer screen, and you choose your answers by clicking in the oval next to the correct choice or choices (for multiple-answer math questions). For numeric entry questions, you will be asked to type your answer into the box or boxes provided.

The tests now have a special mark function, which allows you to mark a question that you would like to temporarily skip and come back to at a later time during the same section on the test. Test takers will have a review screen to see whether a question has been answered, not seen yet, or marked.

For the two essay questions, you will type your essay directly onto the screen in the space provided. If you are not comfortable with your typing skills, practice them in addition to making your way through this book. The 30 minutes provided for each essay cover your brainstorming, prep work, *and* typing in the essay.

These computer-based tests are designed to ensure fairness, because each test taker receives

- the same distribution of content.
- the same amount of testing time.
- the same test directions.
- the same tutorials on computer use.

REMINDER

Again, you may take the test only once a month, and no more than six times over the course of a year. This even applies to situations where you may have canceled your scores. If you violate this rule, your retest scores will not be reported, and your fees will not be refunded.

Scoring

Your official score report will be available online about two to three weeks after your test date. Your score report will also be sent to the recipients (for example, schools) you designated on your registration form.

The report shows a separate test score for each Praxis subject that you take. Reading and math test scores are based on the number of items answered correctly. There is no penalty for answering a question incorrectly. The writing test score is based on the number of multiple-choice questions answered correctly combined with the essay score, which is scored on a scale of 1 to 6.

Your score report will show your score, whether you passed, the raw points earned in each content category, and the range of possible scores. If you took any test previously within the past ten years, it will also show your highest scores on each test.

Can I Cancel My Scores?

These computer-based tests give you the option to cancel your scores at the end of your test session before viewing the scores (once you have viewed your computerized scores, you cannot cancel them). All score cancellations are permanent, and refunds are not given.

Passing Scores

Each state or institution determines its own passing score. The first thing you will want to do with your scores is to compare them to the passing scores set by your state. Along with your test scores, you will receive the *Understanding Your Praxis Scores* booklet that gives the passing scores for each state. The Praxis Series website (www.ets.org/praxis/states) also has a complete state-by-state listing of required tests and passing scores.

Retaking the Tests

If you don't pass one or more Praxis Core tests, you will be allowed to take them again. How many times or how often you may retake each test is determined by the policies of individual states or institutions. The ETS does mandate that you may take each of these tests only once per 30-day period and no more than six times in one year. Individual states may have further restrictions. Consult your scores from previous tests to see which areas require more study, so that you will pass the tests the next time you take them.

What to Bring to the Test

You will need your photo identification and your admission ticket. You may not bring calculators, cell phones, smartphones or any other electronic devices, pencils or pens, books, bags, scratch paper, or other people into the test room with you. The test administrator will designate an area where you may keep your personal belongings during the test.

On test day, allow plenty of time in the morning to get to your test location, especially if you are unfamiliar with the area where the test is given. You should arrive at least 30 minutes before your test to sign in, present your identification, and get yourself settled.

How Do I Register?

Usually you will need to register at least four weeks prior to the test date.

To register by mail, you must download and complete the appropriate Praxis Registration Form.

FEES FOR THE COMPUTER-BASED TESTS

Praxis Core Academic Reading:	$85
Praxis Core Academic Math:	$85
Praxis Core Academic Writing:	$85
Register to take two tests on the same day:	$125
Register to take three tests on the same day (combined test):	$135
Special Service Fees	
Extended registration:	$45
Test, test center, or test date change:	$30
Emergency registration:	$75
Telephone reregistration:	$35
File correction:	$40

Scores by phone:	$30 (per request)
Additional score reports:	$40 (per report)
Test surcharge (Nevada only):	$5
Score verification:	$40 (multiple choice); $55 (constructed response)

Approximately one week before your test date, you will receive a testing admission ticket by mail, which you will need to bring for entrance into the test. If you lose your ticket, do not receive it at least one week prior to your test day, or if there is an error on your ticket, contact ETS immediately.

You can also register online at www.ets.org/praxis. To register online, you will need a valid e-mail address, mailing address, and phone number. Order confirmations and test admission tickets will be e-mailed to your e-mail address—you will not be sent a paper admission ticket by postal mail when you register online. Print out the ticket provided for you online. Online registration is available only to those not needing special accommodations such as considerations for disabilities or Monday testing.

If you have previously created a Praxis account online, you can register by phone with a credit card. There will be a nonrefundable $35 surcharge for the transaction, in addition to the standard registration and test fees. To register by phone, call 800-772-9476, 8 A.M. to 7:45 P.M. (EST), Monday through Friday.

Emergency Registration
Those trying to register for a desired test date after the regular and late registration deadlines may still be able to take the test on that date by using the emergency registration service for an additional $75 fee. This service guarantees a seat at a test center. Emergency registration is not available for individuals needing special accommodations.

To Cancel or Reschedule Your Test
If you are absent the day of the test or arrive too late to take the test, you are not eligible for a refund. You may cancel or reschedule a test by logging into your Praxis account online, calling ETS at 1-800-772-9476, or completing and mailing a Change Request Form (see www.ets.org/praxis/ register/changes) to:

ETS—*The Praxis Series*
P.O. Box 6051
Princeton, NJ 08541-6051

You are eligible to receive a refund of 50% of your test fees if the change is received by ETS at least three days prior to the test date. Special service fees are nonrefundable. Registration deadlines are updated and posted on the website. Refunds are mailed approximately four to six weeks after receipt of your request. If you used a credit card to make a payment, the refund will be credited to your credit card account.

Special Arrangements

Special arrangements may be available for individuals with documented disabilities or for test takers whose primary language is not English (PLNE). Monday test dates are available to those who cannot take the test on a Saturday test date due to religious convictions or military orders. These accommodations may vary from state to state. You should contact the ETS long before the test date to make inquiries.

Nonstandard Testing Accommodations

If you have a documented disability, you may be able to receive nonstandard testing accommodations for the tests. Among a list of accommodations, you may qualify for

- extended test time.
- a test reader.
- a separate location.
- a Braille test.
- someone to record your answers.

Online, you will find the *Bulletin Supplement for Test Takers with Disabilities or Health-Related Needs*, which contains contact information, registration procedures, and special registration forms.

If you are requesting accommodations, you must register by mail. At least six weeks before the registration date, send your completed requests for testing accommodations to:

ETS Disability Services
P.O. Box 6054
Princeton, NJ 08541-6054

Where Do I Begin?

You have already taken the first step by reading this chapter and familiarizing yourself with the Praxis Series of tests. Perhaps you have even started researching to see which tests you need to take, when the tests are offered, and where you would like to take them. Now you should begin your study program: Start with "The LearningExpress Test Preparation System" (Chapter 2). This exclusive system gives you valuable test-taking techniques and will help you devise a study schedule that works best for you. If you stick with your study plan and concentrate on improving the areas in which you need help, you are sure to succeed. Good luck!

THE LEARNING-EXPRESS TEST PREPARATION SYSTEM

CHAPTER SUMMARY
The Praxis Series of tests can be challenging. A great deal of preparation is necessary for achieving top scores and advancing your career. The LearningExpress Test Preparation System, developed by leading experts exclusively for LearningExpress, offers strategies for developing the discipline and attitude required for success.

act: Taking the Praxis® Core Academic Skills for Educators Tests is not easy, and neither is getting ready for them. Your future career as a teacher depends on getting a passing score, but an assortment of pitfalls can keep you from doing your best. Here are some of the obstacles that can stand in the way of success:

- being unfamiliar with the exam format
- being paralyzed by test anxiety
- leaving your preparation to the last minute
- not preparing at all!
- not knowing vital test-taking skills: how to pace yourself through the exams, how to use the process of elimination, and when to guess
- not being in tip-top mental and physical shape
- messing up on test day by arriving late at the test site, having to work on an empty stomach, or feeling uncomfortable during the exams because the room is too hot or cold

What's the common denominator in all these test-taking pitfalls? One word: control. Who's in control, you or the exam?

Here's some good news: The LearningExpress Test Preparation System puts you in control. In nine easy-to-follow steps, you will learn everything you need to know to make sure that you are in charge of your preparation and your performance on the exams. Other test takers may let the tests get the better of them; other test takers may be unprepared or out of shape, but not you. You will have taken all the steps you need to take to get a high score on the Praxis Core Academic tests.

How It Works

Nine easy steps lead you through everything you need to know and do to get ready to master your exams. Each of the following steps includes both reading about the step and one or more activities. It's important that you do the activities along with the reading, or you won't be getting the full benefit of the system.

Step 1: Get Information	50 minutes
Step 2: Conquer Test Anxiety	20 minutes
Step 3: Make a Plan	30 minutes
Step 4: Learn to Manage Your Time	10 minutes
Step 5: Learn to Use the Process of Elimination	20 minutes
Step 6: Know When to Guess	20 minutes
Step 7: Reach Your Peak Performance Zone	10 minutes
Step 8: Get Your Act Together	10 minutes
Step 9: Do It!	10 minutes
Total	**3 hours**

We estimate that working through the entire system will take you approximately three hours, although it's perfectly okay if you work faster or slower. If you set aside an afternoon or evening, you can work through the whole LearningExpress Test Preparation System in one sitting. Otherwise, you can break it up, and do just one or two steps a day for the

next several days. It's up to you—remember, you are in control.

Step 1: Get Information

Time to complete: 50 minutes
Activity: Read Chapter 1, "About the Praxis® Core Academic Skills for Educators Tests."

Knowledge is power. The first step in the LearningExpress Test Preparation System is finding out everything you can about the Praxis Core tests. Once you have your information, the next steps in the LearningExpress Test Preparation System will show you what to do about it.

Part A: Straight Talk about the Praxis Core Tests

Why do you have to take rigorous exams, anyway? It's simply an attempt to be sure you have the knowledge and skills necessary to be a teacher.

It's important for you to remember that your scores on the Praxis tests do not determine how smart you are, or even whether you will make a good teacher. There are all kinds of things exams like these can't test, such as whether you have the drive, determination, and dedication to be a teacher. Those kinds of traits are hard to evaluate, while a test is easy to evaluate.

This is not to say that the exams are not important! The knowledge tested on the exams is knowledge you will need to do your job. And your ability to enter the profession you've trained for depends on passing. And that's why you are here—using the LearningExpress Test Preparation System to achieve control over the exams.

Part B: What's on the Tests

If you haven't already done so, stop here and read Chapter 1, which gives you an overview of the Praxis Core series of tests. Then, go online and read the most up-to-date information about your exam directly from the test developers at www.ets.org/praxis.

Step 2: Conquer Test Anxiety

Time to complete: 20 minutes
Activity: Take the "Test Anxiety Test."

Having complete information about the exams is the first step in getting control over them. Next, you have to overcome one of the biggest obstacles to test success: test anxiety. Test anxiety not only impairs your performance on the exams, but also keeps you from preparing. In Step 2, you will learn stress management techniques that will help you succeed. Learn these strategies now, and practice them as you work through the exams so that they will be second nature to you by exam day.

Combating Test Anxiety

The first thing you need to know is that a little test anxiety is a good thing. Everyone gets nervous before a big exam—and if that nervousness motivates you to prepare thoroughly, so much the better. It's said that Sir Laurence Olivier, one of the foremost British actors of the twentieth century, felt ill before every performance. His stage fright didn't impair his performance; in fact, it probably gave him a little extra edge—just the kind of edge you need to do well, whether on a stage or on an examination.

The Test Anxiety Test follows on page 14. Stop and answer the questions to find out whether your level of test anxiety is something you should worry about.

Stress Management Before a Test

If you feel your level of anxiety getting the best of you in the weeks before a test, here is what you need to do to bring the level down again:

- **Get prepared.** There's nothing like knowing what to expect and being prepared for it to put you in control of test anxiety. That's why you are reading this book. Use it faithfully, and remind yourself that you are better prepared than most of the people taking the test.
- **Practice self-confidence.** A positive attitude is a great way to combat test anxiety. This is no time to be humble or shy. Stand in front of the mirror and say to your reflection, "I am prepared. I am full of self-confidence. I am going to ace this test. I know I can do it." Record it and play it back once a day. If you hear it often enough, you will believe it.
- **Fight negative messages.** Every time someone starts telling you how hard the exam is or how it's almost impossible to get a high score, tune the person out or ask him or her to not speak negatively around you. Don't listen to the negative messages. Turn on your recorder and listen to your self-confidence messages.
- **Visualize.** Imagine yourself reporting for duty on your first day as a teacher or in your teacher training program. Visualizing success can help make it happen—and it reminds you of why you are doing all this work preparing for the exam.
- **Exercise.** Physical activity helps calm your body down and focus your mind. Besides, being in good physical shape can actually help you do well on the exam. Go for a run, lift weights, go swimming—and do it regularly.

Stress Management on Test Day

There are several ways you can bring down your level of anxiety on test day. They will work best if you practice them in the weeks before the test so that you know which ones work best for you.

- **Practice deep breathing.** Take a deep breath while you count to five. Hold it for a count of one, then let it out on a count of five. Repeat several times.

TEST ANXIETY TEST

You need to worry about test anxiety only if it is extreme enough to impair your performance. The following questionnaire will provide a diagnosis of your level of test anxiety. In the blank before each statement, write the number that most accurately describes your experience.

0 = Never
1 = Once or twice
2 = Sometimes
3 = Often

___ I have gotten so nervous before an exam that I simply put down the books and didn't study for it.

___ I have experienced disabling physical symptoms such as vomiting and severe headaches because I was nervous about an exam.

___ I have simply not shown up for an exam because I was afraid to take it.

___ I have experienced dizziness and disorientation while taking an exam.

___ I have had trouble filling in the little circles because my hands were shaking too hard.

___ I have failed an exam because I was too nervous to complete it.

___ **Total: Add up the numbers in the blanks.**

Your Test Anxiety Score

Here are the steps you should take, depending on your score. If you scored:

- **Below 3**, your level of test anxiety is nothing to worry about; it's probably just enough to give you that little extra edge.
- **Between 3 and 6**, your test anxiety may be enough to impair your performance, and you should practice the stress management techniques in this section to try to bring your test anxiety down to manageable levels.
- **Above 6**, your level of test anxiety is a serious concern. In addition to practicing the stress management techniques listed in this section, you may want to seek additional, personal help. Call your local high school or community college and ask for the academic counselor. Tell the counselor that you have a level of test anxiety that sometimes keeps you from being able to take an exam. The counselor may be willing to help you or may suggest someone else you should talk to.

- **Move your body.** Try rolling your head in a circle. Rotate your shoulders. Shake your hands from the wrist. Many people find these movements very relaxing.
- **Visualize again.** Think of the place where you are most relaxed: lying on the beach in the sun, walking through the park, or wherever. Now close your eyes and imagine you are actually there. If you practice in advance, you will find that you only need a few seconds of this exercise to experience a significant increase in your sense of well-being.

When anxiety threatens to overwhelm you right there during the exam, there are still things you can do to manage your stress level:

- **Repeat your self-confidence messages.** You should have them memorized by now. Say them quietly to yourself, and believe them!
- **Visualize one more time.** This time, visualize yourself moving smoothly and quickly through the test, answering every question right and finishing just before time is up. Like most visualization techniques, this one works best if you have practiced it ahead of time.
- **Find an easy question.** Find an easy question, and answer it. Getting even one question finished gets you into the test-taking groove.
- **Take a mental break.** Everyone loses concentration once in a while during a long test. It's normal, so you shouldn't worry about it. Instead, accept what has happened. Say to yourself, "Hey, I lost it there for a minute. My brain is taking a break." Put down your pencil, close your eyes, and do some deep breathing for a few seconds. Then you are ready to go back to work.

Try these techniques ahead of time, and see whether they work for you!

Step 3: Make a Plan

Time to complete: 30 minutes
Activity: Construct a study plan.

Maybe the most important thing you can do to get control of yourself and your exams is to make a study plan. Too many people fail to prepare simply because they fail to plan. Spending hours on the day before the exam poring over sample test questions not only raises your level of test anxiety, but it also is simply no substitute for careful preparation and practice over time.

Don't fall into the cram trap. Take control of your preparation time by mapping out a study schedule. On the following pages are two sample schedules, based on the amount of time you have before you take the Praxis Core Academic Skills for Educators Tests. If you are the kind of person who needs deadlines and assignments to motivate you for a project, here they are. If you are the kind of person who doesn't like to follow other people's plans, you can use the suggested schedules here to construct your own.

Even more important than making a plan is making a commitment. You have to set aside some time every day for study and practice. Try for at least 20 minutes a day. Twenty minutes daily will do you much more good than two hours on Saturday.

Don't put off your study until the day before the exam. Start now. A few minutes a day, with half an hour or more on weekends, can make a big difference in your score.

Schedule A: The 30-Day Plan for Praxis Core

If you have at least a month before you take the Praxis Core tests, you have plenty of time to prepare—as long as you don't waste it! If you have less than a month, turn to Schedule B.

TIME	PREPARATION
Days 1–4	Skim over any other study materials you may have. Make a note of areas you expect to be emphasized on the exam and areas you don't feel confident in. On Day 4, concentrate on those areas.
Day 5	Take the diagnostic pretest in Chapter 3.
Day 6	Score the pretest using the answers starting on page 40. Identify two areas that you will concentrate on before you take the first practice exam.
Days 7–10	Study one of the areas you identified as a weak point. Don't forget, there is a Reading Test Review in Chapter 4, a Mathematics Test Review in Chapter 5, and a Writing Test Review in Chapter 6. Review one of these chapters in detail to improve your score on the practice test.
Days 11–14	Study the other area you identified as a weak point. Don't forget, there is a Reading Test Review in Chapter 4, a Mathematics Test Review in Chapter 5, and a Writing Test Review in Chapter 6. Review one of these chapters in detail to improve your score on the first practice test.
Day 15	Take the first practice exam in Chapter 7.
Day 16	Score the practice exam. Identify one area to concentrate on before you take the next practice exam.
Days 17–21	Study the one area you identified for review. Again, use the Reading, Mathematics, and Writing Test Reviews for help.
Day 22	Take the second practice exam in Chapter 8.
Day 23	Score the test. Note how much you have improved!
Days 24–28	Study any remaining topics you still need to review. Use the review chapters for help.
Day 29	Take an overview of all your study materials, consolidating your strengths and improving on your weaknesses.
Day before the exam	Relax. Do something unrelated to the exam and go to bed at a reasonable hour.

Schedule B: The 10-Day Plan for Praxis Core

If you have two weeks or less before you take the exam, use this 10-day schedule to help you make the most of your time.

TIME	PREPARATION
Day 1	Take the diagnostic pretest in Chapter 3 and score it using the answers starting on page 40. Note which topics you need to review most.
Day 2	Review one area that gave you trouble on the pretest. Use the Reading Test Review in Chapter 4, the Mathematics Test Review in Chapter 5, and the Writing Test Review in Chapter 6. Review one of these chapters in detail to improve your score on the first practice test.
Day 3	Review another area that gave you trouble on the pretest. Again, use the Reading Test Review in Chapter 4, the Mathematics Test Review in Chapter 5, and the Writing Test Review in Chapter 6.
Day 4	Take the first practice exam in Chapter 7 and score it.
Day 5	If your score on the first practice exam doesn't show improvement on the two areas you studied, review them. If you did improve in those areas, choose a new weak area to study today.
Days 6–7	Continue to use the review chapters to improve some skills and reinforce others.
Day 8	Take the second practice exam in Chapter 8 and score it.
Day 9	Choose your weakest area from the second practice exam to review.
Day 10	Use your last study day to brush up on any areas that are still giving you trouble. Use the review chapters.
Day before the exam	Relax. Do something unrelated to the exam and go to bed at a reasonable hour.

Step 4: Learn to Manage Your Time

Time to complete: 10 minutes to read, many hours of practice!
Activity: Practice these strategies as you take the sample tests in this book.

Steps 4, 5, and 6 of the LearningExpress Test Preparation System put you in charge of your exams by showing you test-taking strategies that work. Practice these strategies as you take the sample tests, and then you will be ready to use them on test day.

First, take control of your time on the exams. It's a terrible feeling to know there are only five minutes left when you are only three-quarters of the way through a test. Here are some tips to keep that from happening to you:

- **Follow directions.** You should take your time making your way through the computer tutorial before the exam. Read the directions carefully and ask questions before the exam begins if there's anything you don't understand.
- **Pace yourself.** If there is a timer on the screen as you take the exam, keep an eye on it. This will help you pace yourself. For example, when one-quarter of the time has elapsed, you should be a quarter of the way through the test, and so on. If you are falling behind, pick up the pace a bit.
- **Keep moving.** Don't waste time on one question. If you don't know the answer, skip the question and move on. You can always go back to it later.
- **Don't rush.** Although you should keep moving, rushing won't help. Try to keep calm and work methodically and quickly.

Step 5: Learn to Use the Process of Elimination

Time to complete: 20 minutes
Activity: Complete the "Using the Process of Elimination" worksheet.

After time management, your next most important tool for taking control of your exam is using the process of elimination wisely. It's standard test-taking wisdom that you should always read all the answer choices before choosing your answer. This helps you find the right answer by eliminating wrong answer choices. And, sure enough, that standard wisdom applies to your exam, too.

You should always use the process of elimination on tough questions, even if the right answer jumps out at you. Sometimes the answer that jumps out isn't right after all. You should always proceed through the answer choices in order. You can start with answer choice **a**, and eliminate any choices that are clearly incorrect.

Even when you think you are absolutely clueless about a question, you can often use the process of elimination to get rid of one answer choice. If so, you are better prepared to make an educated guess, as you will see in Step 6. More often, the process of elimination allows you to get down to only two possibly right answers. Then you are in a strong position to guess. And sometimes, even though you don't know the right answer, you find it simply by getting rid of the wrong ones.

Try using your powers of elimination on the questions in the worksheet "Using the Process of Elimination." The questions aren't about teaching; they're just designed to show you how the process of elimination works. The answer explanations for this worksheet show one possible way that you might use the process to arrive at the right answer.

The process of elimination is your tool for the next step, which is knowing when to guess.

Use the process of elimination to answer the following questions.

1. Ilsa is as old as Meghan will be in five years. The difference between Ed's age and Meghan's age is twice the difference between Ilsa's age and Meghan's age. Ed is 29. How old is Ilsa?
   a. 4
   b. 10
   c. 19
   d. 24

2. "All drivers of commercial vehicles must carry a valid commercial driver's license whenever operating a commercial vehicle."

   According to this sentence, which of the following people need NOT carry a commercial driver's license?
   a. a truck driver idling his engine while waiting to be directed to a loading dock
   b. a bus operator backing her bus out of the way of another bus in the bus lot
   c. a taxi driver driving his personal car to the grocery store
   d. a limousine driver taking the limousine to her home after dropping off her last passenger of the evening

3. Smoking tobacco has been linked to
   a. increased risk of stroke and heart attack.
   b. all forms of respiratory disease.
   c. increasing mortality rates over the past 10 years.
   d. juvenile delinquency.

4. Which of the following words is spelled correctly?
   a. incorrigible
   b. outragous
   c. domestickated
   d. understandible

Answers

Here are the answers, as well as some suggestions as to how you might have used the process of elimination to find them.

1. d. You should have eliminated choice **a** right off the bat. Ilsa can't be four years old if Meghan is going to be Ilsa's age in five years. The best way to eliminate other answer choices is to try plugging them in to the information given in the problem. For instance, for choice **b**, if Ilsa is 10, then Meghan must be 5. The difference between their ages is 5. The difference between Ed's age, 29, and Meghan's age, 5, is 24. Is 24 two times 5? No. Then choice **b** is wrong. You could eliminate choice **c** in the same way and be left with choice **d**.

2. c. Note the word *not* in the question, and go through the answers one by one. Is the truck driver in choice **a** "operating a commercial vehicle"? Yes, idling counts as "operating," so he needs to have a commercial driver's license. Likewise, the bus operator in choice **b** is operating a commercial vehicle; the question doesn't say the operator has to be on the street. The limo driver in choice **d** is operating a commercial vehicle, even though it doesn't have a passenger in it. However, the driver in choice **c** is not operating a commercial vehicle, but his own private car.

3. **a.** You could eliminate choice **b** simply because of the presence of the word *all*. Such absolutes hardly ever appear in correct answer choices. Choice **c** looks attractive until you think a little about what you know—aren't fewer people smoking these days, rather than more? So how could smoking be responsible for a higher mortality rate? (If you didn't know that mortality rate means

the rate at which people die, you might keep this choice as a possibility, but you would still be able to eliminate two answers and have only two to choose from.) And choice **d** is plain silly, so you could eliminate that one, too. You are left with the correct choice, **a**.

4. **a.** How you used the process of elimination here depends on which words you recognized as being spelled incorrectly. If you knew that the correct spellings were *outrageous*, *domesticated*, and *understandable*, then you were home free.

YOUR GUESSING ABILITY

The following are ten really hard questions. You are not supposed to know the answers. Rather, this is an assessment of your ability to guess when you don't have a clue. Read each question carefully, as if you were expected to answer it. If you have any knowledge of the subject, use that knowledge to help you eliminate wrong answer choices.

1. September 7 is Independence Day in
   a. India.
   b. Costa Rica.
   c. Brazil.
   d. Australia.

2. Which of the following is the formula for determining the momentum of an object?
   a. $p = MV$
   b. $F = ma$
   c. $P = IV$
   d. $E = mc^2$

3. Because of the expansion of the universe, the stars and other celestial bodies are all moving away from each other. This phenomenon is known as
   a. Newton's first law.
   b. the big bang.
   c. gravitational collapse.
   d. Hubble flow.

4. American author Gertrude Stein was born in
   a. 1713.
   b. 1830.
   c. 1874.
   d. 1901.

5. Which of the following is NOT one of the Five Classics attributed to Confucius?
   a. *I Ching*
   b. *Book of Holiness*
   c. *Spring and Autumn Annals*
   d. *Book of History*

6. The religious and philosophical doctrine that holds that the universe is constantly in a struggle between good and evil is known as
   a. Pelagianism.
   b. Manichaeanism.
   c. neo-Hegelianism.
   d. Epicureanism.

7. The third chief justice of the U.S. Supreme Court was
   a. John Blair.
   b. William Cushing.
   c. James Wilson.
   d. John Jay.

8. Which of the following is the poisonous portion of a daffodil?
   a. the bulb
   b. the leaves
   c. the stem
   d. the flowers

9. The winner of the Masters golf tournament in 1953 was
   a. Sam Snead.
   b. Cary Middlecoff.
   c. Arnold Palmer.
   d. Ben Hogan.

10. The state with the highest per capita personal income in 1980 was
   a. Alaska.
   b. Connecticut.
   c. New York.
   d. Texas.

Answers

Check your answers against the following correct answers.

   1. c
   2. a
   3. d
   4. c
   5. b
   6. b
   7. b
   8. a
   9. d
   10. a

How Did You Do?

You may have simply gotten lucky and actually known the answer to one or two questions. In addition, your guessing was probably more successful if you were able to use the process of elimination on any of the questions. Maybe you didn't know who the third Chief Justice was (question 7), but you knew that John Jay was the first. In that case, you would have eliminated choice **d** and, therefore, improved your odds of guessing right from one in four to one in three.

According to probability, you should get two-and-a-half answers correct, so getting either two or three right would be average. If you got four or more right, you may be a really terrific guesser. If you got one or none right, you may be a really bad guesser.

Keep in mind, though, that this is only a small sample. You should continue to keep track of your guessing ability as you work through the sample questions in this book. Circle the numbers of questions you guess on as you make your guess; or, if you don't have time while you take the practice tests, go back afterward and try to remember which questions you guessed at. Remember, on a test with five answer choices, your chance of guessing correctly is one in five. So keep a separate "guessing" score for each exam. How many questions did you guess on? How many did you get right? If the number you got right is at least one-fifth of the number of questions you guessed on, you are at least an average guesser—maybe better—and you should always go ahead and guess on the real exam. If the number you got right is significantly lower than one-fifth of the number you guessed on, you would be safe in guessing anyway, but maybe you would feel more comfortable if you guessed only selectively, when you can eliminate a wrong answer or at least have a good feeling about one of the answer choices.

Remember, even if you are a play-it-safe person with lousy intuition, you are still safe guessing every time.

Step 6: Know When to Guess

Time to complete: 20 minutes
Activity: Complete the "Your Guessing Ability"
    worksheet.

Armed with the process of elimination, you are ready to take control of one of the big questions in test taking: Should I guess? The answer is: Yes. Some exams have what's called a "guessing penalty," in which a fraction of your wrong answers is subtracted from your right answers—the Praxis Series of tests does NOT work like that. The number of questions you answer correctly yields your raw score. So you have nothing to lose and everything to gain by guessing.

Step 7: Reach Your Peak Performance Zone

Time to complete: 10 minutes to read; weeks to
    complete!
Activity: Complete the Physical Preparation
    Checklist.

To get ready for a challenge like a big exam, you have to take control of your physical, as well as your mental, state. Exercise, proper diet, and rest will ensure that your body works with, rather than against, your mind on test day, as well as during your preparation.

Exercise

If you don't already have a regular exercise program going, the time during which you are preparing for an exam is actually an excellent time to start one. And if you are already keeping fit—or trying to get that way—don't let the pressure of preparing for an exam fool you into quitting now. Exercise helps reduce stress by pumping wonderful good-feeling hormones called *endorphins* into your system. It also increases the oxygen supply throughout your body, including

your brain, so you will be at peak performance on test day.

A half hour of vigorous activity—enough to raise a sweat—every day should be your aim. If you are really pressed for time, every other day is okay. Choose an activity you like and get out there and do it. Jogging with a friend always makes the time go faster, or take a radio.

But don't overdo it. You don't want to exhaust yourself. Moderation is the key.

Diet

First of all, cut out the junk. Go easy on caffeine and nicotine, and eliminate alcohol and any other drugs from your system at least two weeks before the exam. Promise yourself a treat the night after the exam, if need be.

What your body needs for peak performance is simply a balanced diet. Eat plenty of fruits and vegetables, along with protein and carbohydrates. Foods that are high in lecithin (an amino acid), such as fish and beans, are especially good "brain foods."

The night before the exam, you might carbo-load the way athletes do before a contest. Eat a big plate of spaghetti, rice and beans, or whatever your favorite carbohydrate is.

Rest

You probably know how much sleep you need every night to be at your best, even if you don't always get it. Make sure you do get that much sleep, though, for at least a week before the exam. Moderation is important here, too. Extra sleep will just make you groggy.

If you are not a morning person, and your exam will be given in the morning, you should reset your internal clock so that your body doesn't think you are taking an exam at 3 A.M. You have to start this process well before the exam. The way it works is to get up half an hour earlier each morning, and then go to bed half an hour earlier that night. Don't try it the other way around; you will just toss and turn if you go to bed early without having gotten up early. The next morning, get up another half an hour earlier, and so on. How long you will have to do this depends on how late you are used to getting up.

Step 8: Get Your Act Together

Time to complete: 10 minutes to read; time to complete will vary
Activity: Complete the Final Preparations worksheet.

You are in control of your mind and body, which means you are in charge of test anxiety, your preparation, and your test-taking strategies. Now it's time to take charge of external factors, like the testing site and the materials you need to take to the exam.

Find Out Where the Exam or Exams Are, and Make a Trial Run

Do you know how to get to the testing site? Do you know how long it will take to get there? If not, make a trial run, preferably on the same day of the week at the same time of day as you will be taking your test. Note, on the Final Preparations worksheet on the next page, the amount of time it will take you to get to the exam site. Plan on arriving 30 to 45 minutes early so you can get the lay of the land, use the bathroom, and calm down. Then figure out how early you will have to get up that morning, and make sure you get up that early every day for a week before the exam.

Gather Your Materials

The night before the exams, lay out the clothes you will wear and the materials you have to bring with you to the exam. Plan on dressing in layers; you won't have any control over the temperature of the examination room. Have a sweater or jacket that you can take off if it's warm. Use the checklist on the Final Preparations worksheet to help you pull together what you will need.

Don't Skip Breakfast

Even if you don't usually eat breakfast, do so on exam morning. A cup of coffee doesn't count. Don't eat doughnuts or other sweet foods, either. A sugar high will leave you with a sugar low in the middle of the exam. A mix of protein and carbohydrates is best: Cereal with milk and just a little sugar, or eggs with toast, will do your body a world of good.

Step 9: Do It!

Time to complete: 10 minutes, plus test-taking time
Activity: Ace the Praxis Core tests!

Fast-forward to exam day. You are ready. You made a study plan and followed through. You practiced your test-taking strategies. You are in control of your physical, mental, and emotional state. You know when and where to show up and what to bring with you. In other words, you are better prepared than most of the other people taking the exam. You are psyched.

Just one more thing. When you are finished with the exam, you will have earned a reward. Plan a celebration. Call up your friends and plan a party, or have a nice dinner for two—whatever your heart desires. Give yourself something to look forward to.

And then do it. Go into the exams full of confidence and armed with test-taking strategies you have practiced until they're second nature. You are in control of yourself, your environment, and your performance on the exam. You are ready to succeed. So do it. Go in there and ace the exam. And look forward to your future career as a teacher!

Getting to the Exam Site

Location of the exam site: _____

Date: _____

Departure time: _____

Do I know how to get to the exam site?   Yes ___   No ___

If no, make a trial run.

Time it will take to get to the exam site: _____

Things to Lay Out the Night Before

Clothes I will wear   _____

Sweater/jacket   _____

Watch   _____

Photo ID   _____

Other Things to Bring/Remember

_____

_____

_____

_____

_____

_____

_____

_____

_____

_____

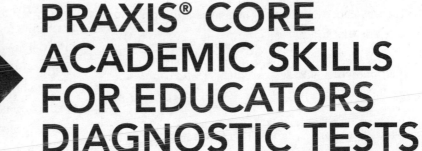

3 ▶ PRAXIS® CORE ACADEMIC SKILLS FOR EDUCATORS DIAGNOSTIC TESTS

CHAPTER SUMMARY

This is the first of the three full-length Praxis® Core Academic Skills for Educators tests based on the structure and difficulty level of the Reading, Writing, and Mathematics tests. Use these diagnostic tests to see how you would do if you were to take the Praxis Core tests today.

This chapter contains three diagnostic tests that mirror the Reading, Writing, and Mathematics Core exams. Although the actual tests you will take are computer-based, the question types for each exam are replicated here for you in the book.

As you take these diagnostic tests, do not worry too much about timing. The actual time you will be allotted for each exam is at the beginning of each test, but you should take these diagnostics in as relaxed a manner as you can to find out which areas you are skilled in and in which ones you will need extra work.

After you finish taking your tests, you should review the answer explanations. (Each individual test is followed by its own answer explanations.) See **A Note on Scoring** on page 407 to find information on how to score your exam.

Good luck!

Praxis® Core Academic Skills for Educators: Reading Diagnostic Test

Time: 85 Minutes

Directions: Read the following passages and answer the questions that follow.

Use the following passage to answer questions 1 through 7.

Gray wolves once roamed the Yellowstone area of the United States, but they were gradually displaced by human development and hunted by farmers and ranchers for preying on live-
5   stock. By the 1920s, wolves had practically disappeared from the Yellowstone area. They migrated north into the deep forests of Canada, where there was less contact with humans.

The disappearance of the wolves had
10 many consequences. Deer and elk populations—major food sources for the wolf—grew rapidly without their usual predator. These animals consumed large amounts of vegetation, which reduced plant diversity in the park. In the
15 absence of wolves, coyote populations also grew quickly. The coyotes killed a large percentage of the park's red foxes and completely eliminated the park's beavers.

By 1966, biologists asked the government
20 to consider reintroducing wolves to Yellowstone Park. They hoped that wolves would be able to control the population of the elk and coyote. Many ranchers and farmers opposed the plan because they feared that wolves would kill their
25 livestock or pets. Other people feared that the wolves would not be well protected in Yellowstone anymore.

The government spent nearly 30 years coming up with a plan to reintroduce the

30 wolves. Although the wolves are technically an endangered species, Yellowstone's wolves were classified as an "experimental" population. This allowed the government more control over the wolf packs. To counteract any potential resis-
35 tance, the government also pledged to pay ranchers for livestock killed by wolves. Today, the debate continues over how well the gray wolf is fitting in at Yellowstone. Elk, deer, and coyote populations are down, while beavers and
40 red foxes have made a comeback. The Yellowstone wolf project has been a valuable experiment to help biologists decide whether to reintroduce wolves to other parts of the country as well.

1. What is the main idea of the first paragraph of the passage?
   a. Gray wolves were unfairly treated by the ranchers and farmers.
   b. Canada provided a better habitat for gray wolves than Yellowstone.
   c. Gray wolves were displaced from their original homes by humans.
   d. Gray wolves were a threat to ranchers.
   e. It was important to reintroduce the gray wolves to Yellowstone.

2. According to the passage, why did biologists ask the government to reintroduce wolves in Yellowstone?
   a. to control the elk and coyote populations
   b. to restore the park's plant diversity
   c. to control the local livestock
   d. to protect the wolves from extinction
   e. to increase tourism revenue

3. In the sentence in lines 30 through 32, why does the writer include the word *technically?*
  a. to emphasize the legal definition of *endangered*
  b. to show that the government controls the wolves' status
  c. to explain why the wolves are endangered
  d. to highlight that the Yellowstone wolves are a special population
  e. to accentuate the scientific usage of the reintroduction

4. What is the most important organizing principle of the second paragraph of the passage?
  a. compare and contrast
  b. cause and effect
  c. chronological order
  d. order of importance
  e. classification

5. What is the implied main idea of the article?
  a. Yellowstone's wolf program was a mistake.
  b. The government is responsible for reintroducing wolves.
  c. Wolves are an important part of our national parks.
  d. Yellowstone's wolf program has been beneficial for the wolves and the park.
  e. It is important not to disrupt the delicate balance of life in nature.

6. Which statement, if it were true, would most significantly weaken the author's main argument?
  a. The government continues to monitor the populations of gray wolves, elks, and coyotes.
  b. The introduction of the gray wolf has increased the population diversity of the Yellowstone area.
  c. Yellowstone has been a protected area since its founding as a national park in 1872.
  d. The introduction of the gray wolf allowed scientists to consider reintroducing beavers to Yellowstone.
  e. The reintroduction of the gray wolf has resulted in the species suffering from a reduced genetic variability.

7. Which species endured the most similar experience to that of the gray wolves in Yellowstone?
  a. the polar bear, whose northern habitat is threatened by warming air temperatures and the resulting reduction of sea ice
  b. the possum, which was introduced in nonnative New Zealand in an effort to create a fur industry, but ended up overpopulating the land
  c. the muskox, which was hunted to extinction in Alaska by about 1900, but brought back to repopulate the land in the 1930s
  d. the moa, a series of large New Zealand birds that were hunted to extinction by about A.D. 1400.
  e. the housecat, whose introduction to Australia has resulted in the extinction of dozens of other species

Use the following statement and triple bar graph to answer question 8.

A sure sign of maturity is the realization that necessities are more important than luxuries.

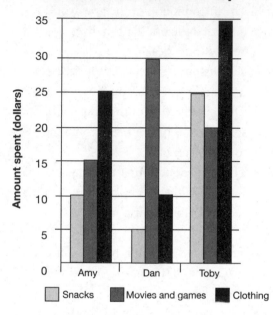

Purchases of Three Students in July

8. Which inference can be made using the information in the statement and the information in the graph?
   a. Amy is considerably older than Dan.
   b. Toby will spend more on clothing in August than Amy.
   c. Toby and Amy are probably more mature than Dan.
   d. Amy spent the same on clothing as she did on everything else in July.
   e. Toby's parents buy all of his snacks for him.

Use the following passage to answer questions 9 through 15.

In July 1969, *Apollo 11* Commander Neil Armstrong became the first man to step foot on the moon. Over the next several years, eleven more men walked on Earth's satellite. However, since
5   geologist Harrison Schmitt left the moon in December 1972, mankind has not returned.

10   The reasons why so much time has passed since a manned landing on the moon are clear. The financial costs of the trip are prohibitive, with estimates of a return costing about $100 billion. The moon's lack of atmosphere means that the lunar surface has no protection from cosmic rays' deadly radiation; astronauts put themselves in constant danger with any extended
15   trip to the moon. The dearth of other available resources, such as water, means that astronauts would have to carry their own resources roughly 400,000 kilometers. In short, there is little justifiable reason to take another jaunt to
20   the big rock in the sky. However, all this reasoning discounts the need for humans to continue to explore their universe. If men will someday step foot on Mars, they should first return to the moon—if only to practice for the consider-
25   ably lengthier and significantly more difficult trip to another planet.

9. In the context of the passage, *dearth* (line 15) can be replaced with which word to incur the smallest alteration in meaning?
   a. death
   b. scarcity
   c. importance
   d. abundance
   e. usefulness

10. According to the information in the reading selection, which inference can be made?
   a. A total of twelve men have walked on Earth's only natural satellite.
   b. The United States is planning a manned return to the moon.
   c. An astronaut cannot safely spend more than a week on the moon.
   d. There is no additional scientific knowledge to be gained from a return to the moon.
   e. A manned trip to Mars will be equally as hard as a manned trip to the moon.

11. Which sentence from the passage contains an opinion from the author?
a. "In July 1969 . . . the moon."
b. "Over the next . . . Earth's satellite."
c. "However, after geologist . . . not returned."
d. "The financial costs . . . $100 billion."
e. "If men will . . . another planet."

12. Which statement, if it were true, would most significantly strengthen the author's main argument?
a. The exploration of deeper space, including our outer solar system, is much more efficient if initiated from a space station instead of a satellite.
b. The lack of an atmosphere on the moon means that astronauts would need to carry or manufacture their own oxygen.
c. Since NASA sent its last astronaut to the moon in 1972, no other country has attempted a manned moon landing.
d. Helium-3, an incredibly rare and valuable resource on Earth that can be used as a fuel, is found in high quantities on the moon.
e. The government-run agency NASA retired its successful space shuttle program in 2011.

13. For which reason does the author most likely refer to the moon as a *big rock* (line 20)?
a. to downplay the importance of returning to the moon
b. to accentuate the massive size of Earth's only satellite
c. to provide an additional incentive for man to return to the moon
d. to describe the geological composition of the satellite
e. to use a metaphor to describe the attributes of the moon

14. Which word best describes the author's attitude toward a potential manned mission to the moon?
a. wasteful
b. scientific
c. dangerous
d. essential
e. timely

15. Which supporting detail best supports the author's main idea?
a. After Neil Armstrong, only eleven more men walked on Earth's satellite.
b. The financial costs of returning to the moon are excessive.
c. The moon has no atmosphere with which to shield astronauts from radiation.
d. Harrison Schmitt was the last man to walk on the moon in 1972.
e. A return to the moon is vital if mankind is ever going to venture to Mars.

Use the following statement and graph to answer question 16.

Endangered because of over-hunting, the gray wolf is becoming more common because of the concerted efforts of state agencies and local citizens.

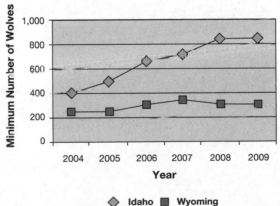

Wolf Population in Idaho and Wyoming, 2004–2009

16. Which inference can be made using the information in the statement and the information in the graph?

   a. The minimum wolf population in Idaho in 2002 was greater than 200.

   b. Groups in Wyoming are not working together to protect wolves effectively.

   c. By 2010, there were more than 1,000 wolves in Idaho.

   d. The wolf population decline in Wyoming was a result of poor weather.

   e. In 2004, there were fewer than 500 wolves in Idaho and Wyoming combined.

Use the following passage to answer questions 17 through 19.

Arguably the most famous feature on the most famous mountain on Earth, the Hillary Step is a narrow, nearly vertical 40-foot rock wall near the peak of Mt. Everest. Covered in snow and
5   ice at 28,750 feet, the Hillary Step presents the last great danger for climbers trying to reach the summit. Once conquered, it is only a few hundred feet of moderate climbing to the mountain's top at 29,028 feet—the planet's
10 highest point. Named for Edmund Hillary, one of the two climbers to first ascend it, the step now features a fixed rope for modern-day climbers to use; such an advantage was unavailable during Hillary's initial 1953 ascent, making
15 his achievement all the more venerable.

17. For which reason is the Hillary Step most likely the most famous feature on Mount Everest?

   a. The Hillary Step was named after the great climber Edmund Hillary.

   b. The Hillary Step acts as the final significant obstacle to the mountain's summit.

   c. The Hillary Step is one of the most difficult technical climbs in mountain climbing.

   d. Until 1953, the Hillary Step had not been successfully ascended.

   e. The highest point of the world is at the end of the Hillary Step.

18. In the passage, the word *venerable* most nearly means

   a. hazardous.

   b. technical.

   c. advantageous.

   d. victorious.

   e. admirable.

19. According to the information in the passage, it can be inferred that the Hillary Step

   a. is easier to ascend now than it used to be.

   b. is responsible for countless casualties on the mountain.

   c. requires several hours of climbing to pass.

   d. is at the highest point on planet Earth.

   e. has only been ascended by two climbers in its history.

Use the following passage pair to answer questions 20 through 25.

Passage 1
In recent years, the local minor league baseball team, the Dowshire Ducks, has become standard weekend entertainment for hundreds of families. On summer afternoons, the bleachers
5   in Hulldown Stadium are teeming with cheering fans. But it wasn't always so. Even ten years

ago, ticket sales were limited, and the team was largely ignored. The Ducks rarely won games or placed well in regional tournaments. The

10   arrival of manager Duncan Brin in 2004, however, started a new era of success and fame for the Ducks.

Passage 2

Before moving to the major leagues, baseball players do time in the minors. While minor league baseball does not come with the star status and multimillion-dollar salary of the majors, it provides players with the development and preparation they need to enter the big leagues. Minor leagues are not necessarily affiliated with Major League Baseball. Eight operate completely independently, and all function as independent businesses. The various minor leagues include the International League, the Pacific Coast League, the Mexican League, the Texas League, the California League, and the Mount Rainier Professional Baseball League. There are 28 minor leagues in all.

20. According to Passage 2, the minor leagues
   a. are more businesslike than the major leagues.
   b. are just as independently run as the major leagues.
   c. have teams that do not win as often as major league teams do.
   d. can serve as stepping stones to the major leagues.
   e. are important branches of the major leagues.

21. Which of the following statements best describes the relationship between the two passages?
   a. Passage 1 describes a cause and Passage 2 describes an effect.
   b. Passage 1 describes a specific aspect of Passage 2.
   c. Passage 1 presents a question and Passage 2 answers it.
   d. Passage 1 describes a method and Passage 2 shows how it is put to use.
   e. Passage 1 presents information that contradicts Passage 2.

22. Based on information in Passage 1 and Passage 2, what will most likely happen to the members of the Dowshire Ducks?
   a. They will become major league players.
   b. They will earn multimillion-dollar salaries.
   c. They will continue to develop their skills.
   d. They will eventually begin losing games again.
   e. They will continue to work with Duncan Brin.

23. Which sentence best summarizes the main idea of Passage 1?
   a. The Dowshire Ducks used to be an unsuccessful baseball team.
   b. Duncan Brin is the manager of the Dowshire Ducks.
   c. The Dowshire Ducks play in Hulldown Stadium.
   d. Manager Duncan Brin improved the status of the Dowshire Ducks.
   e. Going to see a Dowshire Ducks game is popular family entertainment.

24. Which organization best describes the structure of Passage 1?

  a. Details are provided through a series of contrasts, and then a main idea is provided.

  b. A main idea is provided, and then a series of supporting details is listed.

  c. A handful of comparisons are given, and then several dissimilarities are given.

  d. Definitions are given for several unknown terms, and then a main idea is given.

  e. A problem is posed, and then a series of potential solutions is discussed.

25. The word *teeming* in line 5 of Passage 1 could be replaced with which of the following words to result in the least change in meaning of the sentence?

  a. crowded

  b. rooting

  c. energized

  d. vacant

  e. teaming

Use the following passage to answer questions 26 through 29.

A cursory glance at a globe will reveal a fascinating observation: The continents of South America and Africa, separated by thousands of kilometers of open ocean, seem to fit together
5   like pieces of a jigsaw puzzle. The western edge of central South America, part of modern-day Brazil, juts out into the Atlantic Ocean at about the same latitude where the coast of northern Africa shrivels toward the east. The reason for
10   this geological phenomenon is not pure happenstance. Both massive land masses were once connected in a supercontinent called Gondwana, which also contained most of the land found today in India, Australia, and Antarctica,
15   about 200 million years ago. The process responsible for Gondwana splitting into the two separate continents in their current positions is called "continental drift." The significant hypothesis, put forth by
20   German geologist Alfred Wegener in 1915, states that parts of Earth's crust can shift over time above the planet's liquid core. A later theory of plate tectonics expanded on Wegener's discovery, conjecturing that Earth's continental
25   plates move in different directions and therefore affect the positions of the continents— including why South America and Africa seem to fit despite their locations on opposite ends of an ocean.

26. Which is the author's most likely purpose in describing the continents of South America and Africa as *pieces of a jigsaw puzzle* (line 5)?

  a. to contrast the significant difference between the land masses

  b. to describe the mystery of the continental shapes as a puzzle

  c. to minimize the geological importance of the continents

  d. to reinforce the corresponding physical relationship of the continents

  e. to illustrate the problems scientists faced in determining the causes of continental drift

27. The word *cursory* in line 1 could be replaced with which of the following words to result in the least change in meaning of the sentence?

  a. investigative

  b. superficial

  c. internal

  d. offensive

  e. cursive

28. Which statement, if it were true, would most significantly strengthen the author's main argument?
   a. Gondwana was once part of a much larger supercontinent called Pangaea.
   b. Fossils of the same type of plant have been found in parts of western Brazil and eastern Africa.
   c. The African island of Madagascar was once part of the supercontinent Gondwana.
   d. There are countless species of animals that exist in only South America or Africa but not in both continents.
   e. Ancient land bridges, now sunken, once connected the continents across the enormous oceans.

29. According to the passage, which inference can be made?
   a. Alfred Wegener developed the theory of plate tectonics.
   b. There was a time on planet Earth with no oceans.
   c. South America and Africa are roughly the same size.
   d. There is scant evidence that supports the "continental drift" theory.
   e. South America and Africa reside on different plates

Use the following passage pair to answer questions 30 through 32.

Passage 1
A sea spider, unlike the land animal that shares part of its name, does not spin a web to catch its food. Some sea spiders living thousands of feet underwater have developed an interesting technique to get their nourishment. Most sea spiders have eight legs—like land spiders—which they use to catch their food. The long

5

legs have feathers that trap random pieces of food that fall down to the depths of the ocean. Then the sea spider runs its legs across its mouth for a tasty meal.

10

Passage 2
Arachnophobia is one of the most common irrational fears. The term refers to a fear of arachnids, such as scorpions—and more commonly—spiders. People who suffer from arachnophobia can have very extreme reactions in the presence of spiders. They may scream, cry, or experience a panic attack. Sometimes a mere signifier, such as a cobweb or a drawing of a spider, is enough to provoke a reaction. While most species of spiders are not poisonous enough to pose an actual threat to people, they may trigger fears because of legs people often consider to be "creepy" or the erratic way they move.

30. According to Passage 2, the sight of a cobweb can be
   a. proof that spiders are rarely poisonous.
   b. the cause of a panic attack for a person with arachnophobia.
   c. a signifier that someone with arachnophobia is present.
   d. less creepy than the sight of a spider's legs.
   e. the most common trigger of fear in a person with arachnophobia.

31. Unlike the author of Passage 1, the author of Passage 2 describes
   a. a behavior.
   b. a survival technique.
   c. a reaction.
   d. a biological phenomenon.
   e. a physical trait.

32. What is the primary purpose of Passage 1?
   a. to tell about the similarities between land spiders and sea spiders
   b. to describe the unique eating habits of a type of sea spider
   c. to warn people to stay away from dangerous sea spiders
   d. to explain how a land spider uses a web to catch its food
   e. to describe the appendages of the sea spider

Use the following passage to answer questions 33 through 37.

One of Benjamin Franklin's better inventions was a stove called, appropriately, the Franklin stove. This invention improved the lives of countless homeowners in the eighteenth century and
5   beyond. Compared to the stoves that were used at the time of his invention, Franklin's stove made keeping a fire inside a home much less dangerous. His stove could burn less wood and
10   generate more heat than previous designs. This feature saved its users considerable amounts of money that would have been needed to buy wood.

As its inventor, Benjamin Franklin was
15   offered the right to patent his stove. That would have meant that only Franklin could have made and sold the useful stoves, making Franklin one of the richest men in the country. However, Franklin turned down the opportunity for the
20   patent, believing instead that the stove should be allowed to be used by anyone who wanted to use the safer and more efficient technology. In his autobiography, he wrote, "As we enjoy great advantages from the inventions of others, we
25   should be glad of an opportunity to serve others by any invention of ours; and this we should do freely and generously."

33. The primary purpose of the first paragraph of the passage is to
   a. tell about one particularly useful invention of Benjamin Franklin.
   b. point out that Benjamin Franklin was responsible for many great inventions.
   c. explain the physical process of how a stove works.
   d. tell all the ways that Benjamin Franklin made money from his stoves.
   e. compare a variety of stoves from early American history.

34. Which function best describes the function of the word *however* as it appears in line 17?
   a. to provide important physical descriptions of a critical development
   b. to provide several additional benefits for a life-saving invention
   c. to contrast the advantages of an invention with its potential drawbacks
   d. to compare the apparent usefulness of an invention with its extreme costs
   e. to contrast an inventor's altruistic motives from the potential for great wealth

35. The meaning of the word *right* in line 14, in context of the passage, most likely means
   a. correct.
   b. good health.
   c. turn.
   d. legal claim.
   e. exact.

36. Sentence 1 of the passage makes which of the following errors in logic?
   a. incomplete comparison
   b. circular reasoning
   c. fallacy of composition
   d. moral equivalence
   e. slippery slope

37. It can be inferred from the passage that the Franklin stove was
  a. expensive.
  b. dangerous.
  c. efficient.
  d. small.
  e. stylish.

Use the following passage to answer questions 38 through 41.

Most species on the planet exist solely within a relatively specific temperate zone on the planet. Polar bears live only within the most northern latitudes; iguanas are found only in tropical
5 locales; kangaroos are endemic only to the Australian continent. Human beings, known taxonomically as *Homo sapiens*, however, have been remarkably adept at populating the farthest corners of the planet—even those with extreme
10 environments. Alert, a Canadian community home to several permanent residents, is only about 500 miles from the North Pole; the Ethiopian community of Dallol has an average temperature of 94°F; La Rinconada, a Peruvian city
15 in the Andes Mountains, is nearly 17,000 feet above sea level. The ability of human beings to acclimate to their surroundings, no matter how unforgiving, is all the more impressive considering how few physical features of the species
20 allow it such adaptability.

38. Which detail from the passage most directly supports the author's main argument?
  a. Polar bears live only within the most northern latitudes.
  b. Human beings are known taxonomically as *Homo sapiens*.
  c. Kangaroos are endemic to the Australian continent.
  d. A Canadian community is about 500 miles from the North Pole.
  e. Iguanas are found only in tropical locales.

39. Which fact would the author most likely use to further strengthen his or her main argument?
  a. The Mariana Trench, the deepest known point on Earth, lies more than 36,000 feet below the surface of the ocean.
  b. The port city of Arica, Chile, receives an average annual rainfall of 0.03 inches.
  c. Penguins are found throughout the southern hemisphere, from the equator to the pole.
  d. The surface temperature on Venus is believed to exceed 700°F.
  e. Only about 30 percent of Earth's surface is covered by land.

40. Which role does the habitat of the kangaroo most significantly play in the context of the reading selection?
  a. to contrast with the habitat of the polar bear
  b. to demonstrate humanity's encroachment on animal territory
  c. to supply an additional extreme environment
  d. to illustrate mankind's limited reach in Australia
  e. to provide a contrast to humanity's spread

41. Which of the following situations is most similar to what is presented in the passage?
  a. Human beings domesticating polar bears.
  b. Iguanas living in northern latitudes
  c. Human beings colonizing the moon.
  d. Canadian communities relocating to the North Pole.
  e. Physical features evolving over time.

Use the following passage to answer questions 42 through 44.

In the long history of soccer, no single player has changed the game as much as Pelé. Born Edison Arantes do Nascimento in Brazil in 1940, Pelé played professional soccer for 20
5   years, including in four World Cups for his native Brazil. Toward the end of his career, he also played for a North American soccer league. Although he was well past his prime, Pelé helped to significantly increase American inter-
10   est in soccer. Counting his time in the American league, Pelé scored a total of 1,281 goals— the most goals scored by any professional soccer player. In fact, Pelé's athletic skills were so impressive that he was awarded the title
15   "Athlete of the Century" by the International Olympic Committee. By the time he retired, no one had helped increase the popularity of soccer more.

42. Which sentence from the passage presents an example of an opinion rather than a fact?
   a. "In the long . . . as Pelé."
   b. "Born Edison Arantes . . . native Brazil."
   c. "Toward the end . . . soccer league."
   d. "Counting his time . . . soccer player."
   e. "In fact, Pele's . . . Olympic Committee."

43. Which detail from the passage supports the main idea the least?
   a. Pelé was born Edison Arantes do Nascimento in Brazil in 1940.
   b. Pelé played professional soccer for 20 years, including in four World Cups.
   c. Pelé helped significantly to increase American interest in soccer.
   d. Pelé scored a total of 1,281 goals.
   e. Pelé earned the title "Athlete of the Century."

44. Which athlete is most similar to Pelé, based on the given information about him in the passage?
   a. Cristiano Ronaldo, a Portuguese soccer player who is the highest-paid soccer player in history
   b. Dilma Rousseff, the 36th president of Brazil and the first woman to hold the country's highest office
   c. Babe Ruth, who helped make baseball the most popular sport in America by breaking home run records
   d. Charles Haley, who was a member of five Super Bowl–winning football teams from 1986 through 1999
   e. Landon Donovan, who scored multiple goals in the 2010 World Cup for the American soccer team

Use the following passage to answer questions 45 and 46.

It is a statistical anomaly that Barack Obama is generally recognized as the 44th president of the United States, yet only 42 different people held the presidency before him. This is due to
5   the fact that Grover Cleveland served two non-consecutive terms in office, once from 1885 to 1889, and then again from 1893 to 1897. As the only president to serve non-consecutive terms, Cleveland is counted twice in the numbering of
10   the presidents and is therefore considered both the 22nd and 24th president of the United States. Given the resulting disparity, it would be more rational to number the presidents based solely on their first term, ignoring any second-
15   ary tenures that could complicate the sequence.

45. The author would most likely describe the current numbering system of the U.S. presidents as
  a. humorous.
  b. illogical.
  c. reverential.
  d. presidential.
  e. rational.

46. Which word has the closest meaning to *anomaly* as it appears in the passage?
  a. data
  b. irregularity
  c. representation
  d. conclusion
  e. indiscretion

Use the following passage to answer questions 47 through 52.

Sharks have layers of sharp teeth in their mighty jaws that allow them to cut through a fish's bones or a shellfish's hard shell. The shark will eat almost every creature found in
5   the ocean, from crabs and turtles to seals and penguins. If an animal is too big, a shark will simply tear it into smaller chunks before eating it. This ancient fish has been patrolling Earth's waters for more than 400 million years and can
10   now be found in all the planet's seas, from the surface to a depth of below a mile. Species of sharks can be massive, with a length of up to 46 feet, and some can be swift, with bursts of speed of up to 30 miles per hour.
15   Despite all the impressive physical characteristics of the shark that would make it seem especially treacherous to humans, on average fewer than 5 people in the world are killed each year by sharks—fewer than are killed by wasps
20   or lightning. By contrast, an estimated 100 million sharks are killed by fishermen each year. In

addition to this overfishing, sharks suffer from habitat loss due to coastal development and the impact of water pollution; some species
25   are facing severe population decline as a result. Many people share a groundless fear of shark attacks; perhaps they should instead be fearful of losing one of the planet's most remarkable creatures to extinction.

47. Which statement, if it were true, would most significantly strengthen the author's argument?
  a. The smallest shark in the world reaches only a length of about 8 inches when fully grown.
  b. Of the nearly 400 species of sharks in the world, only four have been known to be dangerous to humans.
  c. Swimming in a group is safer than swimming alone because sharks are less likely to attack an individual in a group.
  d. Other than humans, sharks have very few natural predators.
  e. The bull shark, known for its aggressive and often unpredictable nature, can often be found in shallow waters near beaches.

48. The author's attitude toward sharks could be best described as
  a. reverential.
  b. frightened.
  c. ambivalent.
  d. quarrelsome.
  e. cautionary.

49. According to the passage, which of the following is more dangerous to humans than sharks?
  a. water pollution
  b. other humans
  c. wasps
  d. the ocean
  e. coastal development

50. Which creature shares a similar relationship to humans as sharks to humans?
  a. killer whales, also called orcas, because they reside in all the oceans and lack natural predators
  b. frogs, because, despite their attractive appearance, they are among the most toxic animals on Earth
  c. caterpillars, because they go through a series of life stages during their complete metamorphosis
  d. deer, because they generally have a fear of humans and frequently will run away when approached
  e. snakes, because many people fear them despite the fact that very few species are venomous

51. Which detail from the passage would best support the idea that sharks should benefit from the protection of a conservation bill from Congress?
  a. More people are killed each year by wasps or lightning than by shark attacks.
  b. The shark will eat almost every creature found in the ocean.
  c. The shark can be found in all the planet's seas.
  d. Some species are facing severe population loss.
  e. Many people share a groundless fear of shark attacks.

52. Which sentence from the passage contains an opinion from the author?
  a. "Sharks have layers . . . hard shell."
  b. "The shark will . . . and penguins."
  c. "The ancient fish . . . a mile."
  d. "By contrast, an . . . each year."
  e. "Many people share . . . to extinction."

Use the following statement and double bar graph to answer question 53.

Public demand dictates the animal population of the local zoo.

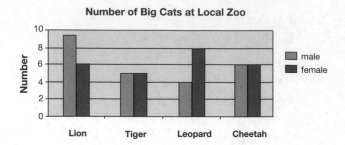

53. Which conclusion can be made from the information presented in the double bar graph?
  a. Lions are the most popular big cats at the local zoo.
  b. The zoo has an equal number of female cheetahs and lions.
  c. Tigers are more difficult to contain in captivity.
  d. The zoo has more male leopards than female leopards.
  e. The cheetah is the fastest animal on Earth.

Use the following passage to answer questions 54 through 56.

Although the Pacific island nation was populated by the Maori people more than 700 years earlier, the Dutchman Abel Tasman is generally credited with being the first European to dis-
5   cover New Zealand in 1642. Though Tasman described the place as "a very fine land," the Dutch did not continue their exploration of New Zealand; not until the Englishman James Cook captained a scientific voyage there in
10 1770 did another European visit New Zealand. In two subsequent voyages during the 1770s, Cook helped map the land and explore the

unexplored oceans around New Zealand.
Thanks to his thorough charting of the land
15 and his respectful treatment of the native
Maoris, Cook opened the door for further
explorers and navigators of New Zealand. Eventually, Europeans settled in the "fine land," setting up the country's first capital, Russell, with
20 the partnership of the Maoris in 1840.

54. Which organization best describes the structure of the passage?
   a. order of importance
   b. compare and contrast
   c. problem and solution
   d. classification
   e. chronological order

55. The passage is primarily focused on
   a. the means and methods for the exploration
   of New Zealand.
   b. the explorers Abel Tasman and James Cook.
   c. the initial European discovery of New
   Zealand.
   d. the first capital of New Zealand.
   e. the early history of New Zealand.

56. Which conclusion can be determined with certainty based on the information in the passage?
   a. The Maori people were living in New
   Zealand by A.D. 1000.
   b. The Dutch found no financial incentives to
   return to New Zealand.
   c. The Europeans and the Maori people have
   enjoyed a long, peaceful relationship.
   d. James Cook made significant scientific
   discoveries on his voyages to New Zealand.
   e. Russell is still the capital of New Zealand
   today.

Praxis® Core Academic Skills for Educators: Reading Diagnostic Test Answers and Explanations

1. c. This paragraph explains that wolves used to
live in the Yellowstone area until conflict
with humans caused them to disappear. The
wolves moved to Canada (choice **b**), and
were a threat to ranchers (choice **d**), but
these choices are too narrow and do not
reflect the main idea of the paragraph. You
can eliminate choices **a** and **e** because there
is nothing in the paragraph to suggest that
gray wolves were treated unfairly, or that it
was important to reintroduce them to
Yellowstone.

2. a. Biologists hoped that wolves would help balance the elk and coyote populations. Restor-
ing the park's plant diversity (choice **b**) was
a factor, but not the main motive. Ranchers
and farmers objected to the wolves killing
their livestock, so choice **c** can't be the reason
for reintroduction. And although the wolves
are technically endangered, the Yellowstone
wolves are governed by special, looser rules,
so choice **d** can be eliminated. There is no
evidence to suggest that wolves were reintroduced to increase tourism, so choice **e** is not
correct.

3. d. The phrase *although the wolves are techni-cally an endangered species* suggests that the Yellowstone wolves are going to be an exception. More specifically, the word *technically* tells us that the exception will be to their endangered status. It only suggests the legal definition of *endangered* (choice **a**), but does not explain it. Choice **b**, *that the government controls the wolves' status*, is a true statement, but it is not the best answer to the question. The statement also does not explain why the wolves are endangered (choice **c**) or how science is utilized during the reintroduction (choice **e**).

4. b. Paragraph 2 describes the outcome of the wolf's disappearance. Although the events occur in chronological order (choice **c**), they are organized to show cause and effect. There is no compare/contrast in the paragraph, and the events are not given in order of importance, so choices **a** and **d** are incorrect. The paragraph is also not broken down by classification, meaning that choice **e** is not correct either.

5. d. The author concludes the article by listing some of the positive effects of the wolf's return: beaver and red fox populations are being restored, and elk and coyote populations are balancing to normal levels. Thus the author must not believe that the program was a mistake, choice **a**. Choice **b** is not broad enough to encompass the main idea of the whole passage. Choices **c** and **e** are too general because the article only discusses Yellowstone Park and does not comment on the wolf's role in other national parks or about the disruption of life in general.

6. e. The author's argument is that the reintroduction of the gray wolf is beneficial. The only statement that provides a definitively negative result of the reintroduction would be the possibility of reduced genetic variability. The statements in choices **b** and **d** provide positive effects of the reintroduction, so they would strengthen the author's argument. The statements in choices **a** and **c** neither strengthen nor weaken the author's argument; because the information does not affect the argument, those choices cannot be correct.

7. c. Like the gray wolf, the muskox was driven to extinction within a particular geographic area, then it was reintroduced to those lands at a later date. The polar bear is threatened, but it has not been reintroduced, so choice **a** is not correct. The possum was introduced to New Zealand, causing environmental havoc, but it was not reintroduced there, so choice **b** is not correct. The moa was hunted to extinction centuries ago and never reintroduced, and the housecat has not itself been in any danger of extinction, so choices **d** and **e** are not correct.

8. c. The only inference that the statement and the graph support is that Toby and Amy are more mature than Dan. According to the statement, a sign of maturity is the realization that necessities are more important than luxuries. The only necessity covered in the graph is clothing. Both Amy and Toby spent more of their money on clothing than luxuries, such as snacks, movies, and games. However, one person is not necessarily more mature than another person because he or she is older, so the statement and graph do not support choice **a**. The data provided does not support choices **b** and **d**. Choice **e** is not true according to the information in the graph, because Toby spent a considerable amount of money on snacks.

9. b. One of the reasons against another moon landing is the unavailability of important resources. The word *dearth* is used to describe this unavailability, or *scarcity*. The word *death* is similar to *dearth* in spelling but has a very different meaning, so choice **a** is incorrect. The opposite meaning of *dearth* is *abundance*, so choice **d** is incorrect. The resources may be important or useful, but the word *dearth* does not suggest those meanings, so choices **c** and **e** are incorrect.

10. a. The selection begins with the statement that Neil Armstrong was the first man on the moon and then mentions that eleven other men have also walked on the moon, ending with Harrison Schmitt in 1972. Therefore, it can be inferred that a total of twelve men have walked on the moon. The passage states that an extended stay on the moon can pose a danger to astronauts, but because it does not give any specific timeframe, choice **c** cannot be correct. There is no evidence in the passage to support the statements in choices **b** or **d**, so they are incorrect. Choice **e** is disproven with the final sentence; a trip to Mars will be *significantly more difficult*, not *equally as hard*.

11. e. The final sentence of the passage suggests that man *should* return to the moon. This is an opinion in contrast with the facts presented earlier in the selection. The first three sentences of the passage provide verifiable facts about the early manned trips to the moon, so choices **a**, **b**, and **c** must be incorrect. The financial costs of a trip to the moon, even if this is just an estimate, can be verified, so choice **d** is not correct.

12. d. The author's main argument is that mankind *should* return to the moon, despite all the reasons against it. If a rare and valuable resource were available on the moon, that would be another incentive to return—thus strengthening the argument. Choices **a** and **b** are incorrect: If space travel were easier from a space station instead of from the moon or if the moon has no oxygen, then there would be more reasons against a return—thus weakening the argument. The statements in choices **c** and **e** provide additional information about space travel but are not particularly related to the argument about a return to the moon; therefore, they are not correct.

13. a. In the midst of listing reasons not to return to the moon, the author describes the satellite as a *big rock*. This expression refers to the moon as something uninteresting or unimportant. Therefore, the purpose is to downplay the importance of returning, despite the fact that the author is merely making a counterargument. The author's purpose in using the expression is not to describe the physical characteristics of the moon, thus eliminating choices **b**, **d**, and **e**. Furthermore, it does not serve to describe a reason to return, making choice **c** incorrect.

14. d. Despite spending much of the passage listing reasons not to return, the author ends the passage by listing his or her support for a return to the moon. Therefore, the correct answer choice will contain a word that supports a return, such as *essential* (choice **d**). Choices **a** and **c** contain negative adjectives, so they do not match the author's attitude. While a return may be *scientific* or *timely*, the author does not focus on the scientific benefits or the timeliness of a return, making **b** and **e** less-than-ideal choices.

15. e. The author's main idea is that man should return to the moon, if only to practice for further expeditions into space. The details in choices **a** and **d** do not relate significantly to the main idea, so they are not correct. The statements in choices **b** and **c** contradict the author's main idea and therefore do not support it.

16. b. According to the graph, the wolf population in Wyoming has not grown very much in the five-year period it details, and the statement indicates that population is dependent upon the concerted efforts of "state agencies and local citizens." Therefore, it is reasonable to conclude that Wyoming-based agencies and citizens are not working together to protect wolves effectively. The inferences in choices **a** and **c** cannot be supported because that information is not given by the graph, and neither of these choices take the statement into account. The statement contradicts choice **d**. Choice **e** is not true according to the graph; the line graph shows a total of more than 500 wolves in the two states in 2004.

17. b. The passage states that once the difficult Hillary Step is conquered, it is only a few hundred feet of moderate climbing to the mountain's top. Therefore, the step is the final significant obstacle to the mountain's summit. Because there are still several hundred feet to ascend after the Hillary Step, however, choice **e** cannot be correct. The statements in choices **a** and **d** do not explain why the step is so well known but instead provide some history for a physical feature of the mountain. The statement in choice **c** is not supported by the passage; while the Hillary Step is surely difficult, it is extreme to suggest that it is one of the most difficult technical climbs in mountain climbing.

18. e. The end of the passage accentuates the difficulties that Edmund Hillary faced in his initial ascent of Mount Everest; therefore, his climb must be respected; the best synonym for *venerable* is therefore *admirable*. The climb itself may have been *hazardous* or *technical*, but *venerable* is describing the achievement and not the climb, so choices **a** and **b** are not correct. The rope is *advantageous*, and the resulting climb may be *victorious*, but neither word can be used to replace *venerable* in the passage, making choices **c** and **d** incorrect.

19. a. The passage mentions the advantage of the fixed ropes that adorn the Hillary Step, a climbing advantage that was not always available; therefore, though it may still be difficult to ascend, it is easier than it used to be. There is no mention in the passage that the step is responsible for many deaths or requires several hours to pass (choices **b** and **c**). The passage does state, however, that there are several hundred feet above the step, making choice **d** incorrect. Hillary and his Sherpa first ascended the step together in 1953, but the passage does not suggest that they have been the only ones to ever do so, thus making choice **e** incorrect.

20. d. In Passage 2, the minor leagues interact with the major leagues by serving as stepping stones where players gain "the development and preparation they need to enter the big leagues." The passage explains very little about the business of minor leagues and makes no comparison with the business of major leagues, so it does not support choices **a** or **b**. If you selected choice **c**, you may have been confused by Passage 1, which describes a minor league team that did not win very much, but this question pertains to Passage 2 only. Passage 2 states that "Minor leagues are not necessarily affiliated with Major League Baseball," so choice **e** is not correct.

21. b. Passage 2 gives a brief overview of Minor League Baseball, and Passage 1 describes one specific minor league team. The other answer choices do not describe the relationship between the two passages accurately.

22. c. Passage 1 states that the Dowshire Ducks are a minor league team, and Passage 2 explains how baseball players develop in the minor leagues. Therefore, the most likely prediction is that the members of the Dowshire Ducks will continue to develop in the future. Choices **a** and **b** are unrealistic since they suggest that *all* members of the Dowshire Ducks will likely join the major leagues. Choices **d** and **e** fail to take Passage 2 into account.

23. d. The final sentence of the article states the main idea: Duncan Brin is responsible for the new success of the Dowshire Ducks baseball team. The sentences in choices **a**, **b**, **c**, and **e** only provide supporting details from the passage or other information that is not relevant to the main idea.

24. a. The beginning of the passage provides details about the Dowshire Ducks today, then contrasts those positive details with negative details with the team's past. The passage then concludes with the overall main idea. Because the passage does not begin with a main idea, a definition, or a problem, choices **b**, **d**, and **e** are not correct. While the passage provides a contrast between the past and present of the team, the organization is not entirely based on comparisons and contrasts, making choice **c** incorrect.

25. a. The word *teeming* is being used to describe the bleachers of a baseball stadium—specifically, how many cheering fans are in them. Therefore, the best word to replace *teeming* will likewise describe the size of the crowd. Although the word ends in *–ing*, *teeming* is an adjective; therefore, choices **b** and **e** do not contain proper words to use to replace *teeming* in the passage. The bleachers may be *energized* by the crowd, but the closest meaning of the word relates to the size of the crowd, not its energy, so choice **c** is not correct. *Vacant*, choice **d**, has the opposite meaning and is therefore incorrect as well.

26. d. The author follows the portrayal of the continents as puzzle pieces with a physical description of their shapes. Therefore, it is their physical relationship that he or she is most concerned with. The author's purpose is not to contrast the continents but rather to stress their connection, so choice **a** is incorrect. The purpose is also not to describe the mystery or minimize the importance of the continents, which means choices **b** and **c** are incorrect. There is nothing in the passage to suggest any problems scientists faced in determining the causes of continental drift, so choice **e** is also not correct.

27. b. The author uses the word *cursory* to suggest that it would not take much time to notice an obvious pattern in the globe's continental patterns. A replacement word, therefore, could be *brief, hurried,* or *superficial.* Choices **a** and **c** include words with an opposite meaning, so they cannot be correct. Choices **d** and **e** contain words that have little relation to the word *cursory* and are therefore incorrect as well.

28. b. The author makes the argument that the African and South American continents were once joined together. If the same plant was found to have lived on both continents, it would lend support to that argument. On the other hand, if species are unique to each continent alone, it would not strengthen the author's argument; therefore, choice **d** is not correct. The statements in choices **a** and **c** are largely irrelevant to the author's main idea, making those answer choices incorrect. The statement in choice **e** also does not reinforce the theory of continental drift, so it is not correct.

29. e. The final sentence of the passage states that different plates can move in different directions, resulting in the current positions of the continents. Therefore, it can be inferred that the African and South American continents exist on separate plates. Alfred Wegener developed the theory of "continental drift," but the theory of plate tectonics followed later; the passage does not suggest who proposed the theory of plate tectonics, but the statement in choice **a** cannot be inferred. Although there was no ocean between Africa and South America, that does not mean that Earth had no oceans; choice **b** is therefore incorrect. The passage does not compare the sizes of the continents, just their shapes, so choice **c** is incorrect. The passage also does not discuss the specific support for or against the continental drift theory, so choice **d** is not correct.

30. b. Passage 2 indicates that the sight of a cobweb and a panic attack can share a cause-and-effect relationship for people with arachnophobia ("Sometimes a mere signifier, such as a cobweb or a drawing of a spider, is enough to provoke a reaction"). The passage does not indicate that poisonous spiders do not make cobwebs, so choice **a** does not make sense. A person with arachnophobia would likely want to steer clear of cobwebs, so choice **b** does not make sense either. Although it is likely that someone with arachnophobia might consider cobwebs to be "creepy," the passage only describes spiders' legs this way and makes no comparison between cobwebs and spiders' legs, so choice **d** is not a good answer. Choice **e** is incorrect because Passage 2 indicates that the sight of an actual spider is the most common trigger for fear in a person with arachnophobia.

31. c. Only Passage 2 describes a reaction an animal provokes, which is the fear spiders provoke in people with arachnophobia. Passage 2 never describes how anyone reacts to sea spiders. Passage 1 describes the behavior of sea spiders, so choice **a** is incorrect. Passage 1 describes a survival technique (how sea spiders eat), and Passage 2 does not, so choice **b** is incorrect. Passage 2 deals with a psychological phenomenon, not a biological one (choice **d**). Both passages describe a physical trait (the legs of spiders), but the question asks you to identify something that *only* Passage 2 describes, so choice **e** is incorrect.

32. b. To find the primary purpose, you need to find the statement that best sums up what the entire passage is about. The best description of Passage 1's primary purpose is that it describes the unique eating habits of a type of sea spider (choice **b**). The passage mentions one similarity between land spiders and sea spiders—that both have eight legs—but this is not what the passage is mostly about, so choice **a** is not correct. The passage does not mention any warnings about sea spiders, so choice **c** is not correct. The statements in choices **d** and **e** are mentioned in the passage, but those statements are not the focus of the passage.

33. a. The first paragraph of this passage tells about one specific invention created by Benjamin Franklin: a stove called the Franklin stove. While Benjamin Franklin *was* responsible for many great inventions, the paragraph does not mention more of his inventions, so the statement in choice **b** is not the primary purpose. The paragraph does not tell much about how a stove works, so the statement in choice **c** is not the primary purpose either. The passage mentions that Franklin *could* have made a lot of money from his stoves (choice **d**), but he refused to patent it and so did not make money from the invention. The first paragraph compares stoves, but that is not the primary purpose of the paragraph, so choice **e** is not correct.

34. e. The word *however* separates the riches that Franklin could have received from his invention with his noble decision to share the stove's design. It is not being used to provide a physical description, provide additional benefits of the stove, contrast its advantages and drawbacks, or compare the apparent usefulness with its costs; therefore, choices **a**, **b**, **c**, and **d** are all incorrect.

35. d. Benjamin Franklin was the inventor of the Franklin stove. Therefore, according to the passage, he was offered *the right*, or permission, to patent his stove. Check the answer choices to see which word or phrase most closely fits the meaning of *right* in the given sentence. In fact, you can even test the terms in the answer choices by replacing the word *right* from the passage with them. Only *legal claim* (choice **d**) makes sense. While *right* may mean *correct*, *good health*, *turn*, or *exact* in other contexts, it refers to a legal claim in the context of the sentence. Therefore, choices **a**, **b**, **c**, and **e** are not correct.

36. a. Sentence 1 makes an incomplete comparison because it uses the word *better* without comparing two specific things. What was the Franklin stove *better* than? Choices **b**, **c**, **d**, and **e** are not logical errors present in sentence 1.

37. c. The passage mentions that the Franklin stove burned *less wood and generated more heat than previous designs*. This means it was very *efficient*, choice **c**. The price, size, or style of the stove was never mentioned in the passage, so it cannot be inferred that the Franklin stove was *expensive*, *small*, or *stylish*, choices **a**, **d**, or **e**. The Franklin stove was designed to be much safer than other stoves, so choice **b** is not true.

38. d. The author's main argument is that human beings are unique for their ability to live almost everywhere on the planet. The statement in choice **d** describes one human settlement near the North Pole, thus supporting the main idea. A statement about animals would not support the main argument as directly, so choices **a**, **c**, and **e** are not correct. Choice **b** is not correct because the taxonomy of the species is not directly related to the argument.

39. b. The author lists three human settlements with extreme conditions; a city that receives virtually no rainfall would also reinforce the argument that the human species has impressive adaptability skills. Facts about the Mariana Trench or Venus do not relate to places where human beings live, so choices **a** and **d** cannot be correct. Choice **c** is about penguins, so it cannot be correct either. Choice **e** would not reinforce the argument because it does not relate to the argument in any significant way.

40. e. The author lists three animals and their specific habitats. The author then contrasts those limited habitats to human beings' ability to live almost anywhere. Therefore, the role of mentioning the kangaroo's habitat is to contrast with humanity's spread. The role is not to contrast with the habitat of the polar bear; in fact, the habitat is similarly limited, so choice **a** is not correct. No mention is given of humanity's encroachment or limited reach, so choices **b** and **d** are not correct. The mention of the kangaroos in Australia does not provide an extreme environment, so choice **c** is not correct either.

41. c. The passage discusses how human beings adapt to the most inhospitable environments. The moon is an inhospitable environment that humans have visited, so the idea of humans colonizing the moon is very similar to the ideas in the passage. The domestication of dangerous animals (choice **a**) is never discussed in the passage. The passage suggests iguanas are not adaptable, and the passage never suggests that animals that are not adaptable are capable of becoming adaptable (choice **b**). The concept of an entire community relocating someplace else (choice **d**) is very different from any idea presented in the passage. The passage specifies that human beings have not evolved physical features that allow them to be adaptable, so **e** is not a good answer choice.

42. a. It cannot be proven that one player changed the game of soccer more than any other player. The other four choices provide statements that *can* be verified, such as the year and place of his birth (choice **b**), a league he played in (choice **c**), the number of goals he scored (choice **d**), and the fact that he was given a title from a large institution (choice **e**).

43. a. The main idea of the passage is that Pelé was an amazing soccer player who helped transform the sport. His name, place of birth, and year of birth do nothing to support that main idea. The fact that he played for 20 years, helped increase interest in the sport, scored 1,281 goals, and was called the "Athlete of the Century" all help support the main idea, so choices **b**, **c**, **d**, and **e** are not correct.

44. c. The passage focuses on Pelé's talent and his impact on the game of soccer. Because he transformed his sport in a similar way, Babe Ruth is most similar to Pelé. Cristiano Ronaldo and Landon Donovan are great soccer players, but because they did not change the sport like Pelé did, choices **a** and **e** are not correct. Dilma Rousseff is from Brazil, but she did not influence a sport like Pelé did, so choice **b** is not correct. Charles Haley was a successful athlete, but he likewise did not have a lasting impact on his sport, so choice **d** is incorrect.

45. b. The author lists the numbering system for the U.S. presidents, then provides a *more rational* numbering system. Therefore, he or she most likely believes that the current system is *illogical*. That is the opposite of *rational*, so choice **e** is incorrect. There is no indication in the passage that he or she believes the numbering system to be *humorous*, *reverential*, or *presidential*, so choices **a**, **c**, and **d** are incorrect as well.

46. b. An *anomaly* is an abnormality or *irregularity*, which makes choice **b** the best option. The words in answer choices **a**, **c**, **d**, and **e** do not make sense in the context of the passage and do not share a close meaning to *anomaly*.

47. b. The author's chief argument is that, despite the public perception, sharks are not especially dangerous to humans. If only 1% of shark species were dangerous to humans, that would strengthen the argument. The statements about sharks in choices **a** and **d** are not relevant to the author's argument, so are not correct. The statement in choice **c** provides a potential way to avoid a shark attack, but it does nothing to either weaken or strengthen the author's argument. The statement in choice **e**, however, would make sharks seem more dangerous to people, thereby weakening the author's argument. Choice **e** is therefore incorrect.

48. a. The author describes the shark as *massive*, *swift*, and *impressive*, then refers to it as *one of the planet's most remarkable creatures*. Therefore, he or she is treating the shark with *reverence* (choice **a**). The author explains that the fear is largely unwarranted, so choices **b** and **d** are not correct. The author has a strong positive opinion about sharks, so the attitude would not be best described as *ambivalent*, choice **c**. The author's attitude toward sharks would not be best described as *cautionary*, though perhaps that would describe his or her attitude toward the protection of sharks; therefore, choice **e** is not the best answer.

49. c. According to the passage, wasps kill more humans every year than sharks do. The passage only discusses water pollution (choice **a**) in terms of its danger to sharks; its danger to humans is never mentioned. Similarly, the passage only discusses the danger of humans (choice **b**) and coastal development (choice **e**) to sharks. The dangers of the ocean (choice **d**) are never mentioned in the passage.

50. e. The author points out that many people are afraid of sharks even though sharks do not pose a great danger to them. Similarly, many people fear snakes, even though most snakes are not dangerous. Therefore, choice **e** represents the most similar relationship that sharks share with humans. Killer whales may share some attributes with sharks, but they do not have a similar relationship to humans, so choice **a** is not correct. People do not fear frogs or caterpillars, making choices **b** and **c** incorrect. Deer may fear people, but people do not have an unnatural fear of deer, so choice **d** is not the best choice.

51. d. The detail that best supports the idea of a conservation bill would show that the shark's population numbers are declining; this is best shown in choice **d**. The details listed in choices **b** and **c** describe the shark in some way but do not directly support the idea for the protection of the shark; therefore, these choices cannot be correct. The details in choices **a** and **e** might provide a reason to not want to kill sharks, but they do not provide great support to show that sharks are deserving of our protection.

52. e. An opinion cannot be supported by concrete evidence and represents the author's personal beliefs. When the author suggests that people should *be fearful of losing one of the planet's most remarkable creatures*, he or she is providing an opinion. Each of the other sentences listed in answer choices **a, b, c,** and **d** contain facts because they can be supported with concrete evidence. Even though an estimate, such as the one in choice **d,** cannot be verified precisely, the estimate itself can still be a fact.

53. a. According to the statement, public demand dictates the animal population of the local zoo. Since there are more lions than any other big cat at the local zoo, you can conclude that they are the most popular big cats with the public. The graph contradicts choice **b.** The conclusions in choice **c** cannot be proven or disproven by the data in the graph because the graph does not represent the difficulty of keeping a particular big cat in captivity. The graph shows that the zoo has eight female leopards and only four male leopards, so choice **d** is incorrect. While the statement in choice **e** may seem correct, it cannot be concluded from the information in the graph; in fact, the cheetah is not as fast as many birds. Regardless, choice **e** cannot be supported, so it cannot be correct.

54. e. The passage begins with the first European explorer to reach New Zealand and then describes some of the important milestones in the country's history until its formation of a capital in 1840. Because the information is given in order of the year the events occurred, the passage is in chronological order. The information is not provided in terms of most important to least important, so choice **a** is not correct. The passage also does not use a compare/contrast or problem/solution structure, so choices **b** and **c** are not correct. A classification structure would organize the passage into specific categories; because the passage does not do this, choice **d** is incorrect.

55. e. Because the passage describes the initial populating of New Zealand through the formation of its first capital, it focuses mostly on the early history of the country, choice **e.** While it describes the exploration, it does not focus primarily on why and how the exploring was done, making choice **a** incorrect. The passage mentions Abel Tasman and James Cook as important explorers of New Zealand, but the passage is mostly about New Zealand itself and not any specific explorer; therefore, choice **b** is not the correct answer. While the passage mentions the initial European discovery of New Zealand and its first capital, those are only details that support the primary purpose. Therefore, choices **c** and **d** are also not correct.

56. a. The first sentence of the passage states that the Maori people populated New Zealand more than 700 years before Abel Tasman visited New Zealand. Therefore, the Maoris must have been living in New Zealand before A.D. 1000. The passage states that the Dutch did not seek to return to New Zealand, but it did not suggest why, meaning that the statement in choice **b** cannot be concluded with certainty. While James Cook treated the Maoris with respect and visited New Zealand on a scientific voyage, there is no evidence to support the statements in either choice **c** or choice **d** with absolute certainty. Likewise, while Russell was the New Zealand capital in 1840, it cannot be concluded from the passage that it is still the country's capital. In fact, Wellington is the current capital, so choice **e** is incorrect.

Praxis® Core Academic Skills for Educators: Writing Diagnostic Test

Part I: Multiple-Choice
Time: 40 Minutes

Directions: Choose the letter for the underlined portion that contains a grammatical error. If there is no error in the sentence, choose **e**.

1. My <u>mother</u> is a <u>teacher</u> <u>and who</u> also has
       a   b   c

   <u>been a principal</u>. <u>No error</u>
       d   e

2. After <u>Pele's</u> final soccer <u>game, in</u> which he had
         a   b

   played for both <u>teams, players</u> from both
                c

   squads carried him off the field on <u>their</u>
                               d

   shoulders. <u>No error</u>
           e

3. In his speeches to the <u>crowds</u>, President Obama
                  a

   referred to ideals expressed by President <u>Lincoln</u>
                                 b

   about renewal, <u>continuity</u>, and <u>national unity</u>.
                c   d

   <u>No error</u>
      e

4. <u>When</u> the casting agent called out her name,
     a

   <u>she walked</u> rather <u>hesitant</u> to the front of the
       b   c

   stage and stood <u>there</u> shaking. <u>No error</u>
                d   e

5. The <u>principal's</u> decision at last <u>Monday's</u>
       a   b

   teacher conference is sure to have an <u>affect</u> on
                                c

   all the <u>students</u> in the junior high school.
           d

   <u>No error</u>
     e

6. At <u>first</u> the <u>Plains Indians</u> <u>traded</u> with the
       a   b   c

   travelers on the <u>Santa Fe Trail</u>. <u>No error</u>
               d   e

7. As you read <u>them</u>, remember that this story
           a

   <u>is intended to be</u> a source of entertainment and
           b

   that <u>nothing</u> in it is <u>factual</u>. <u>No error</u>
       c   d   e

8. <u>As soon as</u> we stepped off of the water taxi,
       a

   <u>which</u> pulled away from the <u>dock, leaving</u> both
       b   c

   of us standing <u>in a puddle of</u> river water.
                  d

   <u>No error</u>
     e

9. Nokomis <u>is</u> <u>Hiawathas</u> gracious grandmother,
          a   b   c

   and Minnehaha is his beautiful <u>wife</u>. <u>No error</u>
                         d   e

10. Corporate educators will often <u>use</u> analogies
                        a

    and metaphors <u>from</u> sports <u>describing</u> business
                b   c

    <u>decisions</u> and goals. <u>No error</u>
        d   e

11. The used car had been treated <u>bad</u> by <u>its</u>
                                        a   b
previous <u>owner, but</u> the people at the car
              c
dealership <u>worked hard</u> to fix it up like new.
                  d
<u>No error</u>
    e

12. Wolfgang <u>Amadeus</u> Mozart <u>began playing</u>
                    a   b
music <u>on</u> a pianolike instrument called a
        c
clavier. <u>No error</u>
  d   e

13. <u>Neither</u> the soldiers <u>nor</u> the sergeant <u>was</u> sure
        a   b   c
of <u>their</u> location. <u>No error</u>
      d   e

14. <u>As the popularity</u> of professional lacrosse
        a
<u>continues</u> to grow, more and more companies
    b
are <u>investing</u> thousands of <u>dollars</u> to become
        c   d
primary sponsors so they can get their brand
names in front of television viewers. <u>No error</u>
                                          e

15. <u>During</u> the first act of the play, I <u>begun</u> to ask
        a   b
<u>myself</u> why I spent my hard-earned money on
    c
tickets <u>to</u> such a flop. <u>No error</u>
        d   e

16. A <u>captain</u> sailing a ship from <u>New York Harbor</u>
          a   b
to <u>San Francisco Bay</u> can shave 7,872 miles off
      c
his <u>or</u> her trip by cutting through the Panama
      d
Canal. <u>No error</u>
            e

Directions: Choose the best replacement for the underlined portion of the sentence. If no revision is necessary, choose **a**, which always repeats the original phrasing.

17. <u>The novel *The Grapes of Wrath* written by John Steinbeck in 1939 won the Pulitzer Prize in 1940.</u>
   a. The novel *The Grapes of Wrath* written by John Steinbeck in 1939 won the Pulitzer Prize in 1940.
   b. The novel *The Grapes of Wrath*, written by John Steinbeck, in 1939 won the Pulitzer Prize, in 1940.
   c. The novel *The Grapes of Wrath* written by John Steinbeck, in 1939 won the Pulitzer Prize, in 1940.
   d. The novel, *The Grapes of Wrath*, written by John Steinbeck in 1939, won the Pulitzer Prize in 1940.
   e. In 1940, John Steinbeck's 1939 novel, *The Grapes of Wrath*, won the Pulitzer Prize.

18. <u>I myself called the ambulance after the man fell and hurt himself.</u>
   a. I myself called the ambulance after the man fell and hurt himself.
   b. I called the ambulance after the man fell and hurt himself myself.
   c. I, myself, called the ambulance after the man fell and hurt himself.
   d. I called the myself ambulance after the man fell and hurt himself.
   e. Myself I called the ambulance after the man fell and hurt himself.

19. The CEO wished <u>to insure the stockholders that their investment would be spent wisely.</u>
   a. to insure the stockholders that their investment would be spent wisely.
   b. that the stockholders would be insured of investment wisely spent.
   c. in assuring the stockholders, that their investment would be wisely spent.
   d. to assure the stockholders that he would spend their investment wisely.
   e. to assure and promise the stockholders of his intentions to spend their investment wisely.

20. <u>I, even though she is my closest friend, am not going to have time to visit her this summer.</u>
   a. I am not going to have time to—even though she is my closest friend—visit her this summer.
   b. Even though she is my closest friend, I am not going to have time to visit her this summer.
   c. I am not, even though she is my closest friend, going to have time to visit her this summer.
   d. I am not going to have time, even though she is my closest friend, to visit her this summer.
   e. I am not, even though she is my closest friend, going to have time to visit her this summer.

21. The Beatles were <u>a big hit in America like England</u>.
   a. a big hit in America like England.
   b. as well a big hit in England as they were in America.
   c. as big a hit in America as they were in England.
   d. just as big a hit in America than in England.
   e. a big hit as well as in both England and America.

22. Reverend Martin Luther King, Jr. helped organize the famous 1963 March on Washington, <u>which drew</u> hundreds of thousands of civil rights supporters from all over the United States.
   a. which drew
   b. it drew
   c. but it drew
   d. that it drew
   e. and drawing

23. NASA scientists confirmed <u>that the Mars rover's signal was lost for more than 24 hours.</u>
   a. that the Mars rover's signal was lost for more than 24 hours.
   b. that the Mars rover's signal were lost for more than 24 hours.
   c. that the Mars rovers' signal were lost for more than 24 hours.
   d. that the Mars rovers' signal was lost for more than 24 hours.
   e. for more than 24 hours that the Mars rover lost its signal.

24. Evelyn has a multifaceted fitness regimen: <u>she swims laps, plays baseball, the weight machines, and runs.</u>
   a. she swim laps, plays baseball, the weight machines, and runs.
   b. she swims laps, plays baseball, lifts weights, and runs.
   c. she swim laps, plays baseball, she lift weights, and runs.
   d. swimming laps, baseball, lifting weights, and running.
   e. swims laps, plays baseball, lifting weights, and running.

25. Miles Davis, <u>a twentieth-century American trumpeter, is well known and renowned for creating</u> important improvisational jazz techniques.
   a. a twentieth-century American trumpeter, is well known and renowned for creating
   b. an American trumpeter who lived and played in the twentieth century, is well known for the creation of
   c. renowned and prominent, was known as a twentieth-century American trumpeter for creating
   d. he is an American trumpeter well known and renowned for creating
   e. a twentieth-century American trumpeter, is well known for creating

26. When the mayor took office, his plan was to bolster the economy, clean up the subways, <u>and reducing the crime rate.</u>
   a. and reducing the crime rate.
   b. and reduced the crime rate.
   c. and reduce the crime rate.
   d. and reduction of the crime rate.
   e. and to reduce the rates of unlawful illegal criminal activities.

27. The entire staff signed the salary increase petition before <u>we submit it</u> to the board.
   a. we submit it
   b. one submits them
   c. you submit them
   d. we will submit it
   e. we submitted it

28. I am so <u>grateful the time</u> you put into the project.
   a. grateful the time
   b. grateful to the time
   c. grateful for the time
   d. grateful on the time
   e. grateful with the time

29. Which of the following would be the most credible source to use while researching an essay about climate change?
   a. a post titled "What I'm Doing to Stop Climate Change" on a blog called Stop Climate Change Now!!!
   b. an article titled "The Big Climate Change Lie" on a website called Climate Truth.com
   c. an article titled "Climate Change" published on a website called Wikipedia.com
   d. a graph titled "Global Temperature Changes 1990–2015" published on a website called EPA.gov
   e. an article titled "Is the Earth's Climate Changing?" published in an issue of *National Geographic Magazine* from 1972

30. The most effective way to begin a research project is to
   a. outline the essay's introduction, body, and conclusion.
   b. select the topic that interests you personally.
   c. cite all the sources you plan to use.
   d. eliminate every unreliable resource.
   e. read the assignment very carefully.

Directions: Choose the letter for the underlined portion of the citations that contains an error. If there is no error in the citation, choose **e.**

31. Book citation:
   <u>Roach</u>, Mary. <u>*Packing for Mars: The Curious*</u>
      a   b
   Science of Life in the Void. <u>W.W. Norton &</u>
                                         c
   <u>Company, Inc., 2010.</u> <u>Print.</u> <u>No error.</u>
            d   e

32. Web page citation:

Mayor's Press Office. "Mayor Emanuel and the
      a   b

Chicago Department of Public Health Launch
PlayStreets 2015" *City of Chicago.* N.p., June 11,
                                           c

2015. Web. June 28, 2015. No error.
      d   e

Use the following passage to answer questions 33 through 36.

(1) In the summer of 1919, the Cleveland Indians and the New York Yankees were two of the strongest teams in baseball's American League, but one team stood head and shoulders above the rest: the Chicago White Sox. (2) The Chicago White Sox, called the White Stockings until 1902, were owned by an ex-ballplayer named Charles Comiskey. (3) Between the years of 1900 and 1915, the White Sox had won the World Series only once, and Comiskey was determined to change that. (4) In 1915, he purchased the contracts of three of the most promising stars in the league. (5) Comiskey only had to wait two years for his plan to come to fruition; the 1917 White Sox, playing in a park named for their owner, won the World Series. (6) Two years later they had the best record in all of baseball, a sport played with a bat and a ball, and were on their way to the World Series again.

(7) Baseball players' salaries in that era were much different than the exorbitant paychecks of today's professional athletes. (8) Often, ballplayers would have second careers in the off-season because of the mediocrity of their pay. (9) To make matters worse, war-torn 1918 was such a horrible year for baseball attendance that many owners cut player salaries for the following season. (10) So, it is said in all of baseball there was no owner as parsimonious as Charles Comiskey. (11) In 1917, he reportedly promised every player on the White Sox a bonus if they won the American League Championship. (12) After winning the championship, they returned to the clubhouse to receive their bonus—a bottle of inexpensive champagne. (13) Unlike other owners, Comiskey also required the players to pay for the cleaning of their uniforms. (14) The White Sox had the best record in baseball, but "they were paid the least, were the most discontented, and wore the dirtiest uniforms."

33. In context, which is the best revision of sentence 2 (reproduced sentence 2 follows)?

> The Chicago White Sox, called the White Stockings until 1902, were owned by an ex-ballplayer named Charles Comiskey.

a. (As it is now)
b. An ex-ballplayer named Charles Comiskey owned the Chicago White Sox, called the White Stockings until 1902.
c. Called the White Stockings until 1902, the Chicago White Sox were owned by an ex-ballplayer named Charles Comiskey.
d. The Chicago White Sox, until 1902 called the White Stockings, were owned by an ex-ballplayer named Charles Comiskey.
e. Until 1902, the Chicago White Sox were called the White Stockings and owned by an ex-ballplayer named Charles Comiskey.

34. In context, which is the best revision of sentence 6 (reproduced sentence 6 follows)?

> Two years later they had the best record in all of baseball, a sport played with a bat and a ball, and were on their way to the World Series again.

a. (As it is now)

b. Two years later they had the best record in all of baseball, a sport, and were on their way to the World Series again.

c. Two years later they had the best record in all of baseball, a sport played with a bat, and were on their way to the World Series again.

d. Two years later they had the best record in all of baseball and were on their way.

e. Two years later they had the best record in all of baseball and were on their way to the World Series again.

35. In context, which revision to sentences 9 and 10 (reproduced sentence 9 follows) is most needed?

> To make matters worse, war-torn 1918 was such a horrible year for baseball attendance that many owners cut player salaries for the following season. So, it is said in all of baseball there was no owner as parsimonious as Charles Comiskey.

a. Replace "So" with "However".

b. Replace "year" with "time".

c. Replace "attendance" with "crowd".

d. Replace "following" with "next".

e. Replace "parsimonious" with "thrifty".

36. In context, which is the best revision to sentence 14 (reproduced sentence 14 follows)?

> The White Sox had the best record in baseball, but "they were paid the least, were the most discontented, and wore the dirtiest uniforms."

a. (As it is now)

b. The White Sox had the best record in baseball, but "they were paid the least, were the most discontented, and wore the dirtiest uniforms." Buchanan 234

c. The White Sox had the best record in baseball, but "they were paid the least, were the most discontented, and wore the dirtiest uniforms." (Buchanan 234)

d. The White Sox had the best record in baseball, but it was said "they were paid the least, were the most discontented, and wore the dirtiest uniforms."

e. "The White Sox had the best record in baseball, but they were paid the least, were the most discontented, and wore the dirtiest uniforms."

Use the following passage to answer questions 37 through 40.

(1) Music abounds with a vast variety of extraordinary kinds: classical, blues, pop, rock, country, and all their more specific subcategories. (2) Yet no form of music thrills my soul as jazz does. (3) The music's visceral powers are self-evident, but the innate qualities of jazz are not the only reason I find it intoxicating. (4) It is also a form of music with a rich and truly fascinating history of its own.

(5) Jazz developed from its early roots in slave spirituals and the marching bands of New Orleans into the predominant American musical style by the 1930s. (6) In this era, jazz musicians played a lush, orchestrated style known as swing. (7) Played in large ensembles, also called big

bands, swing filled the dance halls and night-clubs. (8) Once considered risqué, jazz was made more accessible to the masses with the vibrant, swinging sounds of these big bands, whose musicians improvised from the melody to create original performances. (9) Then came bebop. (10) In the mid-1940s, jazz musicians strayed from the swing style and developed this more improvisational method. (11) That's how jazz was transformed from popular music to an elite art form that I totally dig if you know what I mean.

37. In context, which revision to sentence 1 (reproduced sentence 1 follows) is most needed?
    Music abounds with a vast variety of extraordinary kinds: classical, blues, pop, rock, country, and all their more specific subcategories.
    a. Replace "abounds with" with "has".
    b. Replace "Music" with "It".
    c. Replace "kinds" with "genres".
    d. Replace "specific" with "general".
    e. Replace "all" with "every".

38. In context, which revision to sentence 3 (reproduced sentence 3 follows) is most needed?
    The music's visceral powers are self-evident, but the innate qualities of jazz are not the only reason I find it intoxicating.
    a. (As it is now)
    b. The innate qualities of jazz are not the only reason I find it intoxicating.
    c. The music's visceral powers are self-evident.
    d. The music's visceral powers are self-evident the innate qualities of jazz are not the only reason I find it intoxicating.
    e. The music's visceral powers are self-evident—the heart-pounding rhythms, the unfettered emotion, the superlative musicianship—but the innate qualities of jazz are not the only reason I find it intoxicating.

39. In context, which revision to sentence 9 (reproduced sentence 9 follows) is most needed?
    Then came bebop.
    a. (As it is now)
    b. Then came a form of jazz that came to be known by the jazz term *bebop*.
    c. Bebop is a type of jazz that followed at a later date.
    d. What came next; bebop came next.
    e. In the mid-1940s, bebop came.

40. In context, which revision to sentence 11 (reproduced sentence 11 follows) is most needed?
    That's how jazz was transformed from popular music to an elite art form that I totally dig if you know what I mean.
    a. (As it is now)
    b. That's how jazz was transformed from popular music to an elite art form and I totally love jazz.
    c. That's how jazz was transformed from popular music to an elite art form that exploits cross rhythms, complex inversions, and a variety of scale incarnations that include Lydian, Dorian, and Phrygian modes.
    d. That's how jazz was transformed from popular music to an elite art form that resonates with me as no other genre does.
    e. That's how jazz was transformed from popular music to an elite art form that I totally dig.

Part IIa: Argumentative Essay

Time: 30 Minutes

Carefully read the essay topic that follows. Plan and write an essay that addresses all points in the topic. Make sure that your essay is well organized and that you support your central argument with concrete examples. Allow 30 minutes for your essay.

School boards often discuss books that should be included in a reading curriculum, like *To Kill a Mockingbird* or *The Adventures of Huckleberry Finn*. Some think that these books should not only be part of the curriculum, but also be required reading for students. Is there a book that you feel should be required reading for everyone? Choose a book you think should be required reading and write an essay persuading your audience to read this book. Be sure to support your position with logical arguments and specific examples.

Part IIb: Source-Based Essay

Time: 30 Minutes
Directions

The following assignment requires you to use information from two sources to discuss the most important concerns that relate to a specific issue. When paraphrasing or quoting from the source, cite each source used by referring to the author's last name, the title, or any other clear identifier. Allow 30 minutes for your essay.

Assignment
Read the two passages carefully and then write an essay in which you identify the most important concerns regarding the reformation of the French government in the revolutionary year of 1789 and explain why they are important. Your essay must draw on information from both of the sources. In addition, you may draw on your own experiences, observations, or reading. Be sure to cite the sources, whether you are paraphrasing or directly quoting.

The French Revolution was a period of social and political upheaval in France from 1789 to 1799 that developed from the dissatisfaction of the lower classes with the privileges and wealth of the upper classes and the church establishment in Paris (encouraged by the American Revolution). The Estates General, comprised of the clergy, the nobility, and the common people, met in May of 1789 at the invitation of King Louis XVI to seek solutions to the unrest of the populace. The following decree was one of the documents produced after that historic meeting, and the subsequent document was British essayist Edmund Burke's response to the proceedings in 1790.

Source 1

Decree Abolishing the Feudal System Passed in the National Assembly, August 11, 1789

The National Assembly hereby completely abolishes the feudal system. It decrees that, among the existing rights and dues . . . all those originating in or representing real or personal serfdom shall be abolished. . . .

The president of the [French National] Assembly shall be commissioned to ask . . . the recall of those sent to the galleys or exiled, simply for violations of the hunting regulations, as well as for the release of those at present imprisoned for offenses of this kind, and the dismissal of such cases as are now pending.

All manorial courts are hereby suppressed without indemnification. But the magistrates of these courts shall continue to perform their functions until such time as the National Assembly shall provide for the establishment of a new judicial system.

Tithes of every description, as well as the dues which have been substituted for them . . . are abolished. . . .

The sale of judicial and municipal offices shall be abolished forthwith. Justice shall be dispensed for free. Nevertheless the magistrates at present holding such offices shall continue to exercise their functions and to receive their emoluments until the Assembly shall have made provision for indemnifying them. . . .

All citizens, without distinction of birth, are eligible to any office or dignity, whether ecclesiastical, civil, or military; and no profession shall imply any descent in rank. . . .

Source 2

From Edmund Burke, Reflections on the French Revolution (1790)

You might, if you pleased, have profited of our example and have given to your recovered freedom a correspondent dignity. Your privileges, though discontinued, were not lost to memory. . . . In your old states you possessed that variety of parts corresponding with the various descriptions of which your community was happily composed; you had all that combination and all that opposition of interests; you had that action and counteraction which, in the natural and in the political world, from the reciprocal struggle of discordant powers, draws out the harmony of the universe. These opposed and conflicting interests which you considered as so great a blemish in your old and in our present constitution interpose a salutary check to all precipitate resolutions. They render deliberation a matter, not of choice, but of necessity; they make all change a subject of compromise, which naturally begets moderation. . . .

You had all these advantages in your ancient states, but you chose to act as if you had never been molded into civil society and had everything to begin anew. You began ill, because you began by despising everything that belonged to you. You set up your trade without a capital. If the last generations of your country appeared without much luster in your eyes, you might have passed them by and derived your claims from a more early race of ancestors. Under a pious predilection for those ancestors, your imaginations would have realized in them a standard of virtue and wisdom beyond the vulgar practice of the hour; and you would have risen with the example to whose imitation you aspired. Respecting your forefathers, you would have been taught to respect yourselves. You would not have chosen to consider the French as a people of yesterday, as a nation of lowborn servile wretches until the emancipating year of 1789.

Praxis® Core Academic Skills for Educators: Writing Diagnostic Test Answers and Explanations

1. c. This sentence contains faulty coordination. Using the conjunction *and* in this sentence creates an illogical link between the dependent and independent clauses. To make the sentence grammatically correct, you must delete *and*.

2. e. Because there are no grammatical, idiomatic, logical, or structural errors in this sentence, choice **e** is the best answer.

3. e. Because there are no grammatical, idiomatic, logical, or structural errors in this sentence, choice **e** is the best answer.

4. c. The verb *walked* should be modified by an adverb, not an adjective. The adverb *hesitantly* should replace the incorrect adjective *hesitant*.

5. c. Here, the word *affect* is used incorrectly as a noun. *Affect* is a verb meaning to influence. As a noun, *effect* means result, which is how it is used in this sentence.

6. a. This sentence is missing a comma after the introductory element, *At first*.

7. a. This sentence has an agreement problem. The plural pronoun *them* does not agree with the singular noun *story*. Therefore, *them* should be replaced by the singular pronoun *it*.

8. b. This is not a complete sentence because it has no subject. To correct this problem, the word *which* should be replaced by the word *it*, which then becomes the subject of the sentence.

9. b. Use the apostrophe to show possession. Place the apostrophe before the *s* to show singular possession—*Hiawatha's*.

10. c. The gerund *describing* is incorrect in this sentence. The infinitive *to describe* should be used.

11. a. The verb *treated* should be modified by an adverb. *Bad* is an adjective and is used incorrectly; it should be replaced by the adverb *badly*.

12. e. Because there are no grammatical, idiomatic, logical, or structural errors in this sentence, choice **e** is the best answer.

13. d. This sentence contains a pronoun error between *soldiers*, *sergeant*, and *their*. When antecedents are connected with a *neither . . . nor* phrase, the pronoun should agree with the closer antecedent. In this sentence, the two antecedents are *soldiers* and *sergeant*. Because sergeant is the antecedent closer to the pronoun, the pronoun should be singular—either *his* or *her*—not the plural *their*.

14. e. Because there are no grammatical, idiomatic, logical, or structural errors in this sentence, choice **e** is the best answer.

15. b. The error is in the verb formation of *begin*. The sentence requires the past tense of the verb. To correct this error, the past participle *begun* should be replaced with the past tense *began*.

16. e. Because there are no grammatical, idiomatic, logical, or structural errors in this sentence, choice **e** is the best answer.

17. e. This is the choice that arranges the three clauses for clarity and properly places the commas between them.

18. a. This sentence uses the intensive pronoun *myself* to emphasize the fact that the speaker called for an ambulance. The intensive pronoun should be placed directly after the pronoun it is intensifying, which is *I* in the case of this sentence. It does not need commas to offset it. Only the original sentence places the intensifying pronoun correctly, so choice **a** is correct.

19. d. The word *insure* is incorrect in this sentence. The word that should be used here to make the sentence clear and logical is *assure*, and the correct case is the infinitive (*to assure*).

20. b. The phrase *even though she is my closest friend* is misplaced in the sentence. A phrase should not be dropped in the middle of a clause. It needs to be offset from the clause distinctly, as it is in choice **b**. The other choices all make the error of dropping the phrase into the clause at various points.

21. c. The comparison in this sentence between America and England requires a parallel *as . . . as* structure. Choice **c** establishes the proper comparison and creates the only sentence that is clear and logical.

22. a. The other choices create either faulty subordination or a comma splice.

23. a. This is the only choice that uses correct possession and the correct verb tense. Because *signal* is a singular noun, it needs a singular verb (*was*). Choice **e** implies that the scientists were in the act of confirming for 24 hours.

24. b. The second clause of this sentence requires a parallel construction (verb noun, verb noun, verb noun). Conjugate the verbs so they are in the same tense: *swims laps*, *plays baseball*, and therefore *lifts weights*. *Runs* can stand by itself. Choice **b** is the only one in which all four elements are parallel.

25. e. This is the only choice that maintains the structure and meaning of the sentence without a redundancy.

26. c. The item in the underlined portion of the sentence should be parallel with the rest of the sentence. Only choice **c** has the appropriate parallel construction. Choices **a**, **b**, **d**, and **e** break the parallel flow of the sentence with the use of *reducing*, *reduced*, *reduction*, and *to reduce*. Choice **e** is also wordy and redundant.

27. e. This is the correct choice because there is agreement in verb tense between *signed* and *submitted*, and there is agreement between the noun *petition* and the pronoun *it*.

28. c. This sentence should contain the prepositional idiom *grateful for* since the speaker is grateful *something* (*the time you put into the project*) happened. Choice **b**, *grateful to*, should only be used if the speaker is expressing gratitude to a person. Choices **d** and **e** are not proper prepositional idioms.

29. d. Government websites indicated with the domain name .gov are generally trustworthy sources, and a graph designating how the global temperature has changed over a 25 year period would likely be relevant to an essay on climate change. However, blogs (choice **a**) and websites with the domain name .com (choices **b** and **c**) are less reliable since anyone can post on them regardless of credentials. Furthermore, the title "What I'm Doing to Stop Climate Change" is too personal, and the title "The Big Climate Change Lie" suggests bias. Both of these indicate that they are unreliable sources. While *National Geographic Magazine* (choice **e**) is generally a reliable source, an issue from 1972 is very outdated. The most credible sources are up-to-date.

30. e. The very first step of a research project involves reading the assignment very carefully to ensure you choose the best topic for the particular assignment. You would not start outlining the essay (choice **a**) until after you have selected a topic and performed research. Since you would perform both of those steps after reading the assignment carefully, choices **b** and **d** are incorrect. Citing sources (choice **c**) is part of the research process that happens after reading the assignment carefully.

31. c. The city of publication should appear directly before the name of the publisher in a book citation such as this one. Section **c** should read: *Packing for Mars: The Curious Science of Life in the Void.* New York: W.W. Norton & Company, Inc.,. The other sections of this citation are written and formatted correctly.

32. e. There are no errors in the way this web page is cited.

33. b. The original sentence is written in the passive voice, which is not the clearest and strongest way to word a sentence. Choice **b** uses the active voice to correct this error.

34. e. The complex language used in the majority of this passage indicates that it was written for an educated, adult audience. However, sentence 6 patronizes that audience by explaining something about baseball (it is *a sport played with a bat and a ball*) that most educated adults know. Choice **e** corrects this error by removing the phrase altogether. Choice **d** makes the error of removing too much information, so the reader does not know to where the team was on its way.

35. a. The transitional word *so* should precede the effect of a cause, but sentence 10 contains positive information that contrasts the negative information in sentence 9. Therefore, *However*, which signals a contrast, is the best transitional word to use between the sentences. Choice **b** replaces a specific word with a less specific one without improving the sentences. Choice **c** would render the sentence unclear. Choices **d** and **e** replace words with their synonyms, which does not improve the sentences.

36. c. The quotation marks around the phrase *they were paid the least, were the most discontented, and wore the dirtiest uniforms* indicates that it is a quotation from a source. Therefore, the writer needs to use in-text

citation to attribute the quotation and avoid plagiarism. Choice **c** uses in-text citation properly. While choice **d** would be adequate if the writer of the quotation was unknown, choice **c** indicates the name of that writer is known, so it is the better answer choice.

37. c. The word *genres* refers to different styles of music more precisely than *kinds* does. The topic should be clear in the first sentence of an essay, and replacing "Music" with It" (choice **b**) would make that topic unclear. Choice **d** makes the mistake of replacing a perfectly fitting word with its antonym. Choice **e** would create a grammatically incorrect sentence.

38. e. Sentence 3 would be stronger with some examples to support the statement that *The music's visceral powers are self-evident.* Choice **e** provides some of those examples. Choice **b** removes the clause that makes those examples necessary, but it deprives the passage of a strong transition between sentence 2 and sentence 3. Similarly, choice **c** deprives the passage of a strong transition from sentence 3 to sentence 4. Choice **d** lacks the examples needed and is a run-on sentence.

39. a. Sentence 9 is short but it is grammatically correct, containing a subject (*bebop*) and a verb (*came*). It also provides some variety since most of the passage's sentences are relatively long. Choices **b** and **c** are unnecessarily wordy. Choice **d** is constructed awkwardly. Choice **e** uses the phrase *In the mid-1940s*, which is also used in sentence 10. This choice would not provide the needed variety.

40. d. While this essay is not excessively formal, the phrase *that I totally dig if you know what I mean* is still too informal. Choice **d** is more in keeping with the style and tone of the passage. Choice **c** uses an excess of technical language unusual for this particular essay.

Sample Responses for the Argumentative Essay

Following are sample criteria for scoring an Argumentative essay.

A score 6 writer will

- create an exceptional composition with a clear thesis that appropriately addresses the audience and given task.
- organize ideas effectively and logically, include very strong supporting details, and use smooth transitions.
- present a definitive, focused thesis and clearly support it throughout the composition.
- include vivid details, clear examples, and strong details to support the key ideas.
- exhibit an exceptional level of skill in the usage of the English language and the capacity to employ an assortment of sentence structures.
- build essentially error-free and varied sentences that accurately convey intended meaning.

A score 5 writer will

- create a commendable composition that appropriately addresses the audience and given task.
- organize ideas, include supporting details, and use smooth transitions.
- present a thesis and support it throughout the composition.
- include details, examples, and supporting text to enhance the themes of the composition.
- generally exhibit a high level of skill in the usage of the English language and the capacity to employ an assortment of sentence structures.
- build mostly error-free sentences that accurately convey intended meaning.

A score 4 writer will

- create a composition that satisfactorily addresses the audience and given task.

- display satisfactory organization of ideas, include adequate supporting details, and generally use smooth transitions.
- present a thesis and mostly support it throughout the composition.
- include some details, examples, and supporting text that typically enhance most themes of the composition.
- exhibit a competent level of skill in the usage of the English language and the general capacity to employ an assortment of sentence structures.
- build sentences with several minor errors that generally do not confuse the intended meaning.

A score 3 writer will

- create an adequate composition that basically addresses the audience and given task.
- display some organization of ideas, include some supporting details, and use mostly logical transitions.
- present a somewhat underdeveloped thesis but attempt to support it throughout the composition.
- exhibit an adequate level of skill in the usage of the English language and a basic capacity to employ an assortment of sentence structures.
- build sentences with some minor and major errors that may obscure the intended meaning.

A score 2 writer will

- create a composition that restrictedly addresses the audience and given task.
- display little organization of ideas, have inconsistent supporting details, and use very few transitions.
- present an unclear or confusing thesis with little support throughout the composition.
- include very few details, examples, and supporting text.

- exhibit a less than adequate level of skill in the usage of the English language and a limited capacity to employ a basic assortment of sentence structures.
- build sentences with a few major errors that may confuse the intended meaning.

A score 1 writer will

- create a composition that has a limited sense of the audience and given task.
- display illogical organization of ideas, include confusing or no supporting details, and lack the ability to effectively use transitions.
- present a minimal or unclear thesis.
- include confusing or irrelevant details and examples, and little or no supporting text.
- exhibit a limited level of skill in the usage of the English language and little or no capacity to employ basic sentence structure.
- build sentences with many major errors that obscure or confuse the intended meaning.

Sample 6 Argumentative Essay

Most people know who Frankenstein is—or at least they think they do. Because of the way Mary Shelley's brilliant 1818 novel was adapted to film, most Americans think that Frankenstein is a towering, scar-faced monster who brings terror wherever he goes. In Shelley's novel, however, the real monster is Victor Frankenstein, the scientist who is the monster's creator. In her story of how Victor Frankenstein creates the monster and what he does after the monster comes to life, Shelley conveys several timeless messages about the dangers of science, the consequences of isolation, and the importance of being a good parent. It is a novel that everyone should read.

In the story, Frankenstein, eager for glory, wants to discover the "elixir of life" so that he can have the power to bring the dead back to life. He wants to create a new race of superhuman beings and wants them to worship him like a god. He wants to unlock the secrets of nature and use that power for his own selfish goals.

Shelley's novel warns us that we must be careful what we do with science—how we apply the knowledge we discover. For when Frankenstein does discover the elixir of life, and when he does create a superhuman being, he creates a creature that is beyond his control. The creature is more powerful and more intelligent than Victor Frankenstein, and the creature engineers Frankenstein's demise.

Shelley's novel also warns us about the consequences of isolation. Frankenstein's creation is so revolting and dangerous in part because Frankenstein works completely alone. He becomes so absorbed with his project that he completely blocks out family and friends. He stops communicating with others and works secretly; he does not consult with anyone about his project, both because he knows that what he is doing is wrong, and because he wants all the glory. But because he does not work with others, and because he loses touch with his community of family and friends, he also loses touch with his responsibility to other human beings. When the creature comes to life, Frankenstein runs away, abandoning his creation even though he knows the creature might harm others.

This abandonment brings us to the novel's third timeless message: the importance of being a good parent. Frankenstein creates a living being and then abandons him because he is an "ugly wretch." He totally ignores his responsibility to the creature, who is born as innocent as a child, even though he is the size of a giant. The creature is abhorred by everyone he meets, and because no one has ever shown him love, he learns to hate. And the person he comes to hate most is the father who abandoned him. Shelley's message is clear: You are responsible for what you create, and if you are a parent, you must love your child, whatever his or her appearance.

In our age of cloning and genetic engineering, of scattered communities and neighbors who don't know each other's names, of abandoned children and neglectful parents, Shelley's book may have more importance than ever. But it is not just the message that makes this book great. It is also a great read, powerful and suspense-filled. Will Frankenstein capture the creature?

Will he create a "bride" for the monster? Will Walton, the ship captain who records Frankenstein's story, learn from Frankenstein's tale? Shelley's Frankenstein should be required reading for everyone.

Comments on the Sample Argumentative Essay That Received a Score of 6

The author has created an exceptional composition with a clear thesis that is both definitive and focused. This essay successfully addresses the issue at hand with an effective, logical organization. The supporting details are correct and relevant. Stylistically, it uses smooth transitions, excellent examples, and clear and vivid details. The key ideas are readily apparent and explored throughout the essay through skillful prose and a variety of sentence structures. The author displays a clear mastery of the subject and of the English language, and uses clear, correct sentences.

Sample 4 Argumentative Essay

Frankenstein isn't who most people think he is—a monster. The real Frankenstein is the scientist who brings the monster to life. The confusion comes from the fact that many rely on the movie version of the story, rather than the original book by Mary Shelley. Frankenstein should be required reading for a number of reasons. It teaches some important lessons, which are maybe even more important today than they were in Shelly's time (the 1800s.)

One lesson is about how to use science. Dr. Frankenstein in the story discovers how to bring a dead person back to life. But everything goes wrong after the creature wakes up. What was supposed to be a great thing that would bring Frankenstein glory and make him a master creator instead brought him and many other people all kinds of terrible horror. I think Mary is telling us to be very careful how we use science.

She also is telling us in this story to stay close to others. Frankenstein makes the creature by himself. While working on the monster; he doesn't talk to anyone, and no one in the university knows what he's up to.

He's so obsessed that he doesn't consider what will happen once this giant creature comes to life. He doesn't think about being responsible to and for the creature.

Another lesson is that we need to be good parents. Frankenstein is like the creature's father and mother. He created him, and he needs to take care of him. But he doesn't, he just runs away. That's when the horror begins. The creature is hated by everyone and his life is really sad.

There are many other important lessons to be learned from Frankenstein, including the need to learn from other's mistakes. Walton, a ship captain, learns the story from Frankenstien, and then writes about it in letters to his sister. The reader is left wondering if Walton will understand the messages of Frankenstein's story and live his life differently as a result.

Another message is the need to tell the truth, and the consequences of not doing so. Victor Frankenstein knows that the monster strangled his brother, but he does not want to tell anyone. Even when an innocent girl is accused of the crime, he keeps his silence. The girl is found guilty and executed as a result of his unwillingness to tell the truth. Shelley's Frankenstein is filled with important lessons, and I think it should be required reading for everyone.

Comments on the Sample Argumentative Essay That Received a Score of 4

The author has created a serviceable composition. The thesis is readily perceived and adequately, if not spectacularly, defended. This essay addresses the issue at hand, and is sufficiently organized. Details are correct, if vague. Stylistically, it is somewhat awkward and clichéd; sentence structures are stilted and tend to repeat, and the essay goes point-by-point in a fairly rote way. Still, the key ideas are readily apparent. The author displays adequate knowledge of the subject and mastery of the English language. The essay, for the most part, is grammatically and orthographically correct, even though it dips into personal opinion instead of objectively dealing with the subject.

Sample 1 Argumentative Essay

Every school has a required reading list. They are filled with "the classics." Classics are books thought to be important by teachers. Some books leave the list, and others are added. But for the last century, many books have stayed the same. Some of them probably shouldn't be considered classics, but they remain on the list. Others are great books that are enjoyed by millions of people. One of these books is Mary Shelly's Frankenstien.

It is the story of a monster. Many people think the monster's name is Frankenstien, but this is really the name of the doctor who creates him. This is due to the 1931 movie version of the novel, which starred Boris Karloff. The movie was directed by James Whale. It was based on a play of the Shelly book. When people hear the name Frankenstien, they think of Boris Karloff.

In the book, Victor Frankenstien makes the monster out of dead body parts. Then he makes the monster come to life. But then he abandons the childlike monster and trouble starts. Everyone hates the monster, and he starts to hate, too. There is also a story about a sailor named Walton. He writes letters to someone in his family. They are about the story of Frankenstien. Frankenstine deserves to be on the list of classics.

Comments on the Sample Argumentative Essay That Received a Score of 1

The essay is wholly insufficient. There is no clear thesis, and the author has difficulty staying on topic, spending a great deal of space on irrelevant details. The prose is graceless and clunky. The essay also says little about the book itself, about which the author apparently doesn't have much knowledge. There are numerous spelling and grammatical errors. In all, the essay fails to fulfill the assignment.

Sample Responses for the Source-Based Essay

Following are sample criteria for scoring a source-based essay.

A score 6 writer will

- create an exceptional composition explaining why the topic is important and support the explanation with specific references to both sources.
- organize ideas effectively and logically, include well chosen information from both sources, and link the two sources in the discussion.
- exhibit an exceptional level of skill in the usage of the English language and the capacity to employ an assortment of sentence structures.
- build essentially error-free and varied sentences that accurately convey intended meaning.
- cite both sources when quoting or paraphrasing.

A score 5 writer will

- create a commendable composition that explains why the concerns are important and support the explanation with specific references to both sources.
- organize ideas effectively and logically, include information from both sources, link the two sources, and use smooth transitions.
- generally exhibit skill in the usage of the English language and the capacity to employ variety in sentence structures.
- build mostly error-free sentences that accurately convey intended meaning.
- cite both sources when quoting or paraphrasing.

A score 4 writer will

- create a composition that satisfactorily explains why the concerns are important and support the explanation with specific references to both sources.

- use information from both sources to convey why the concerns discussed in the sources are important.
- display satisfactory organization of ideas, include adequate details, and link the two sources.
- exhibit a competent level of skill in the usage of the English language and the general capacity to employ an assortment of sentence structures.
- build sentences with several minor errors that generally do not confuse the intended meaning.
- cite both sources when quoting or paraphrasing.

A score 3 writer will

- create an adequate composition that basically addresses the audience and given task but conveys the importance of the concerns in only a limited way.
- use information from only one source or inadequately from both sources to convey why the concerns discussed in the sources are important.
- display some organization of ideas and include some supporting details.
- exhibit an adequate level of skill in the usage of the English language and a basic capacity to employ an assortment of sentence structures.
- build sentences with some minor and major errors that may obscure the intended meaning.
- cite sources when quoting or paraphrasing.

A score 2 writer will

- fail to explain why the concerns are important.
- use information from only one source poorly or fail to convey why the concerns discussed in the sources are important.
- display little organization of ideas, have inconsistent supporting details, and fail to link the two sources.
- demonstrate a less than adequate level of skill in the usage of the English language and a limited capacity to employ a basic assortment of sentence structures.

- build sentences with a few major errors that may confuse the intended meaning.
- fail to cite sources when quoting or paraphrasing.

A score 1 writer will

- display illogical organization of ideas, include confusing or no supporting details, and fail to adequately address the concerns raised by the sources.
- include confusing or irrelevant details and examples, and few or no supporting references.
- exhibit a limited level of skill in the usage of the English language and little or no capacity to employ basic sentence structure.
- build sentences with many major errors that obscure or confuse the intended meaning.

Score 6 Essay

When the representatives of the Third Estate declared themselves the National Assembly on June 13, 1789, the period of radical social change known as the French Revolution began. Chief among the grievances of the Third Estate, composed of commoners, were the traditional rights and privileges of the nobility known collectively as the "feudal system." The philosophes of the French Enlightenment had long blamed these rights and privileges for France's economic and social backwardness; moreover, they struck progressive thinkers as patently unfair and contrary to the natural equality of all men.

The National Assembly specifically targeted the special legal privileges enjoyed by the nobility and clergy. First of all, the condition of serfdom (that is, the legal status of being bound to the land) was abolished. The nobility's right to administer private justice, a right remaining from the Middle Ages, was revoked; thereafter, the law was to be administered impartially by professional civil servants beholden to none. In the same vein, the sale of judicial offices was interdicted, ending the corruption and cronyism related to this system, as well as the nobility's effective immunity to prosecution.

Tithes, or private taxes paid to lords and the Church, were likewise abolished, as was the nobility's exclusive right to hunt game; wild animals were henceforth to be regarded as public property and not the privilege of a few. Prisoners sent to row the galleys for the crime of poaching were to be freed. Finally, the National Assembly opened the way to true meritocracy ("All citizens, without distinction of birth, are eligible to any office or dignity") and removed the prohibitions for the nobility to practice any trade save going into the military ("no profession shall imply any descent in rank. . . .").

Edmund Burke, a British conservative, harshly critiqued the National Assembly's actions. Hearkening back to the Glorious Revolution of 1688, Burke, while not denying that there had been abuses of power, questioned the wholesale overthrow of the class system in France. Rather, says Burke, it would have been better to restore ancient liberties while keeping the structure of society intact: "You might, if you pleased, have profited of our example and have given to your recovered freedom a correspondent dignity. Your privileges, though discontinued, were not lost to memory." Rather, the French sought to refashion society from whole cloth: "You had all these advantages in your ancient states, but you chose to act as if you had never been molded into civil society and had everything to begin anew. You began ill, because you began by despising everything that belonged to you." By keeping to traditional forms, this reformation of government, in Burke's opinion, could forge a productive future and avoid anarchy. Specifically, Burke says that a balance of powers is necessary for a truly democratic society: "you had that action and counteraction which, in the natural and in the political world, from the reciprocal struggle of discordant powers, draws out the harmony of the universe." However, the National Assembly chose to place everything under the control of itself. Unfortunately, the course chosen by the National Assembly would not only destroy the organs of government and "the reciprocal struggle of discordant powers," but strip the nation of all respect for social forms and dismantle civil society

itself: "Respecting your forefathers, you would have been taught to respect yourselves. You would not have chosen to consider the French as a people of yesterday, as a nation of lowborn servile wretches until the emancipating year of 1789." Burke was correct in that France, deprived of its social structure as an anchor, quickly descended into anarchy and the Terror; however he neglected one critical point: Feudalism and the elite stranglehold on the economy had by and large disappeared from England by 1688, whereas they remained present in France. No progress could be made without first dismantling this system.

Comments on the Sample Source-Based Essay That Received a Score of 6

This is an outstanding essay. The author has clearly explained why the topic is important, referencing both sources, and clearly, effectively, and logically organized the ideas shown therein. The author has linked these ideas together into a thematic essay on the subject of the actions of the French National Assembly and Edmund Burke's reaction to them and has additionally brought in a great deal of outside information. The use of the English language is exemplary, with a wide variety of error-free sentences that clearly convey the intended meaning. Both sources are sufficiently and accurately cited.

Score 4 Essay

Every nation needs a government. However, people often disagree on how the nation is to be governed. One great disagreement in history took the form of the French Revolution. In the French Revolution, the National Assembly tried to abolish feudalism. First, they did away with real and personal serfdom. A serf is a sort of peasant. Also, those who were sent to the galleys for the crime of hunting were set free. They also did away with the manorial courts and forbid anyone to sell jobs in the justice system. The National Assembly also tried to erase the class system by saying that "All citizens, without distinction of birth, are eligible to any office or dignity." They also said that anyone could do any job by saying that "no profession shall imply any descent in rank."

Edmund Burke did not think this was a good idea. He thought that they the French were throwing out the baby with the bathwater. By throwing out the foundations of their society, the French were inviting disorder. Burke thinks that they should have retained their ancient structures and rights but reformed them. Instead, they failed to respect their heritage. He says that, "Respecting your forefathers, you would have been taught to respect yourselves." Instead the French disrespected their heritage and their traditional forms of government. This eventually led to anarchy.

Comments on the Sample Source-Based Essay That Received a Score of 4

This composition satisfactorily explains why the concerns in the topic are important and supports the explanation with specific information and references to both sources. However, the author is able to deploy information from both sources to discuss the source, but is not entirely clear on the historical background or able to bring in outside information. The essay is satisfactorily organized and uses adequate details. The author's use of English is competent, with some variety in sentence structures. Errors are minor, and do not interfere with general understanding.

Score 1 Essay

The French Revolution tries to abolish the feudal system and win the French independence from England like America had. The government had a very unfair way of life in France at the time. They thought instead slaves should be freed and people who had been caught hunting should be set free from the gallaries. As the second writer said, they were leading a very disrespectful way of life at the time. The French did not respect themselves or their history. Disresepct is a bad thing and no basis for a system of government.

Also, the government office buildings should not be sold to people because they belong to all of the people. All people can have dignity and buy an office building if they want. This would give them control over the government. Edward Burk was a French politican who agreed with this. He thought that the French people should go ahead and free themselves from their bad rulers.

I feel that feudalism is no way to govren a countrey. As can be seen, this eventually in France led to the rise of Adolf Hitler and a disaster for the French people.

Comments on the Sample Source-Based Essay That Received a Score of 1

This essay displays an illogical organization of ideas and badly mismanages supporting details. The author shows no understanding of the sources or issues involved. What details he or she brings in are irrelevant and inaccurate. She or he also fails to adequately address the concerns raised by the sources. The level of English usage is poor, at best, and confuses the intended meaning.

Praxis® Core Academic Skills for Educators: Mathematics Diagnostic Test

Time: 85 Minutes

Directions: Choose the best answer to each of the following questions.

1. Which of the following is equal to $\sqrt{600} = \underline{\quad\quad}$?
   a. $10\sqrt{6}$
   b. $6\sqrt{10}$
   c. 60
   d. $10\sqrt{60}$
   e. $60\sqrt{10}$

Use the following graph to answer question 2.

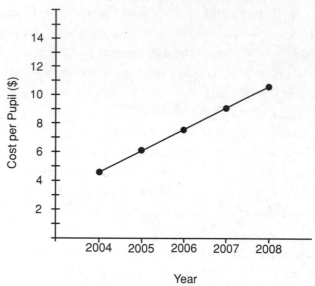

Cost of Field Trip Transportation

2. Based on the graph, if the current trend continues, what will be the approximate cost per pupil for field trip transportation in 2010?
   a. $10.50
   b. $11.50
   c. $12.00
   d. $13.00
   e. $13.50

3. Which of the following has numerical value *greater than* 1? Select all that apply.
   a. $(0.7)^2$
   b. 0.7π
   c. $\frac{0.7}{7}$
   d. $\frac{7}{0.7}$
   e. $\sqrt{0.7}$

Use the following figure to answer question 4.

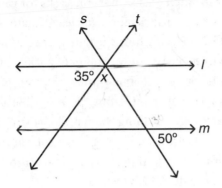

4. In the figure, line *l* is parallel to line *m*. What is the measure of the angle labeled *x*?

  a. 15 degrees

  b. 35 degrees

  c. 50 degrees

  d. 85 degrees

  e. 95 degrees

5. In Sunnyside, a special lottery is held for the elementary student who will attend the county's invention contest. There are 100 fifth graders, 150 fourth graders, and 200 third graders who qualified for the lottery. Each fifth grader's name is placed in the lottery three times, each fourth grader's name is placed twice, and each third grader's name is placed once. If one name is picked at random, what is the probability that a fifth grader's name will be chosen?

  a. $\frac{1}{8}$

  b. $\frac{2}{9}$

  c. $\frac{2}{7}$

  d. $\frac{3}{8}$

  e. $\frac{1}{2}$

6. If $f(x) = -2x^2 + 8x - 4$, which of the following are true? Indicate *all* that apply.

  a. ☐ The maximum value of $f(x)$ is –4.

  b. ☐ The graph of $f(x)$ opens downward.

  c. ☐ The graph of $f(x)$ has no *x*-intercept.

  d. ☐ $f(x)$ is not a one-to-one function.

  e. ☐ The endpoints of the graph point in different directions.

7. Petra earns $10.40 per hour for the first eight hours that she works each day, and she earns time and a half for each hour after that. If she works an average of 9.5 hours per day, how much does she earn in a five-day workweek?

  a. $83.20

  b. $106.60

  c. $416.00

  d. $533.00

  e. $790.40

8. Rowan wears black socks and white socks. The number of pairs of white socks Rowan has is six less than three times the number of pairs of black socks he has. If *b* represents the number of pairs of black socks Rowan has, which of the following expressions represents the number of pairs of white socks he has?

  a. $3b - 6$

  b. $6 - 3b$

  c. $3(b - 6)$

  d. $-3b - 6$

  e. $-6b + 3$

9. Which of the following geometric figures would be appropriate to use to model a tree trunk?
   a. cube
   b. cylinder
   c. square pyramid
   d. cone
   e. sphere

10. Parker spends eight hours a day in the office. If $\frac{5}{12}$ of her workday is spent answering e-mails, how much time does she spend doing other things?
    a. 4 hours and 40 minutes
    b. 5 hours and 20 minutes
    c. 3 hours and 20 minutes
    d. 4 hours and 20 minutes
    e. 5 hours and 40 minutes

11. Four congruent squares are joined together to form one large square. If the perimeter of one of the original squares was $8x$ units, what is the perimeter of the new, large square?
    a. $16x$ units
    b. $20x$ units
    c. $24x$ units
    d. $32x$ units
    e. $64x$ units

12. Maddie's soccer team used three different colors for their socks: maroon socks for tournaments, gold socks for away league games, and white socks for home league games. Maddie owns two pairs of tournament socks, three pairs for away league games, and four pairs for home league games, but she is terrible about matching or folding them and just stuffs them all into a drawer. If she grabs a sock at random from her sock drawer, what is the probability that it will NOT be white?
    a. $\frac{5}{9}$
    b. $\frac{4}{9}$
    c. $\frac{2}{3}$
    d. $\frac{7}{9}$
    e. $\frac{5}{18}$

13. Kevin was half the age of his father 20 years ago. Kevin is 40. How old is Kevin's father?
    a. 50 years
    b. 60 years
    c. 70 years
    d. 80 years
    e. 100 years

14. A certain probability model suggests that when a certain typical 6-sided die is rolled, the probability of it landing with the 2-side up is $\frac{1}{6}$. Select all of the following statements that are true.
    a. It is possible to roll 10 consecutive 2s.
    b. It is impossible to roll the die 50 times and get only three 2s.
    c. In the long run, you expect to have the die land on a 2 one-sixth of the time.
    d. It is possible to roll the die 12 times and get two 2s, and to roll it another 12 times and get five 2s according to this model.
    e. If you roll 8 consecutive 2s, the probability model must be invalid.

15. Which of the following numbers is greatest?

    a. $\frac{7}{12}$

    b. $\frac{5}{7}$

    c. 0.079

    d. 0.63

    e. 0.0108

16. In the United States, the yearly average is 15 births for every 1,000 people. Which of the following proportions can be used to determine x, the total number of births expected in one year if the population is 301,000,000?

    a. $\frac{15}{10} = \frac{x}{301,000,000}$

    b. $\frac{15}{1,000} = \frac{301,000,000}{x}$

    c. $\frac{1}{15} = \frac{x}{301,000,000}$

    d. $\frac{1}{15} = \frac{301,000,000}{x}$

    e. $\frac{15}{1,000} = \frac{x}{301,000,000}$

17. During the semester break, Marcus can wax the floors of five classrooms in an hour. Josie can wax the floors of four classrooms in an hour. If Marcus works for three hours and Josie works for two hours, what percentage of the 50 classrooms will be waxed?

    a. 23%

    b. 44%

    c. 46%

    d. 52%

    e. 56%

18. A pole that casts a 15-foot-long shadow stands near an 8-foot-high stop sign. If the shadow cast by the sign is 3 feet long, how tall is the pole?

    a. $5\frac{5}{8}$ feet

    b. 28 feet

    c. 30 feet

    d. 40 feet

    e. 45 feet

Use the following figure to answer question 19.

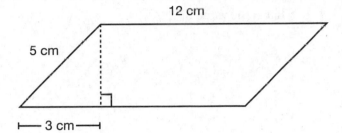

19. Find the area of the parallelogram.

    a. 48 cm^2

    b. 60 cm^2

    c. 72 cm^2

    d. 90 cm^2

    e. 240 cm^2

20. Which of the following is the solution set for the inequality $-2 \le -(2 + 4x) < 3$?

    a. $\{x | -1 < x \le \frac{1}{4}\}$

    b. $\{x | -\frac{1}{4} < x \le 1\}$

    c. $\{x | -4 < x \le 1\}$

    d. $\{x | -\frac{1}{4} < x \le -1\}$

    e. $\{x | +1 < x \le -\frac{1}{4}\}$

21. Each teacher at Main Street School teaches at least three classes and at most five classes per day. Each of the classes is 40 minutes in length. Which of the following statements must be true?

    a. The average class time for the teachers at the school is 160 minutes per day.

    b. The teachers have an average of four classes per day.

    c. Each teacher has between 120 and 200 minutes of class time per day, inclusive.

    d. Choices **a** and **c** only.

    e. Choices **a**, **b**, and **c**.

22. If x and y are the hundreds and tens digits, respectively, of the quotient $13{,}595{,}036 \div 338$, what is the value of y^{-x}?

   a. 0

   b. $\frac{1}{9}$

   c. −6

   d. 9

   e. $\frac{1}{8}$

23. If three more than one-fourth of a number is three less than the number, what is the value of the number?

   a. $\frac{3}{4}$

   b. 4

   c. 6

   d. 8

   e. 12

24. According to recent statistics of a certain region of the United States, 5,000,000 students who took an aptitude test scored less than a perfect score, and 8,000 earned a perfect score. What is the ratio of students who earned a perfect score to the students who did not earn a perfect score?

   a. 1:624

   b. 1:625

   c. 1:626

   d. 625:1

   e. 626:1

25. A photo with dimensions $1\frac{3}{8}$ inches $\times\, 2\frac{3}{4}$ inches is to be enlarged so that the longer dimension is 8 inches. Assuming the sides remain proportional, what will be the length of the shorter side?

   a. $\frac{121}{4}$ inches

   b. 6 inches

   c. 3 inches

   d. 4 inches

   e. $5\frac{1}{4}$ inches

26. Jacqueline was $\frac{1}{3}$ as young as her grandmother 15 years ago. If the sum of their ages is now 110, how old is Jacqueline's grandmother?

     ┌─────────────┐
     │   │
     └─────────────┘

27. A major city recently endured a snowstorm that left a total of eight inches of snow. If it snowed at a constant rate of three inches every two hours, how much snow had fallen in the first five hours of the storm?

   a. 3 inches

   b. 3.3 inches

   c. 5 inches

   d. 7.5 inches

   e. 8 inches

28. In isosceles triangle VIC, $\angle V$ is the vertex. If $\angle V$ is three times as large as each of the base angles, then what is the sum of one of the base angles and the vertex angle?

   a. 142°

   b. 36°

   c. 72°

   d. 108°

   e. 60°

29. What are the x-intercepts of $f(x) = 12x^2 + 5x - 2$?

    a. $(-\frac{1}{4},0)$ and $(\frac{2}{3},0)$

    b. $(4,0)$ and $(-\frac{3}{2},0)$

    c. $(\frac{1}{4},0)$ and $(-\frac{2}{3},0)$

    d. $(0,\frac{1}{4})$ and $(0,-\frac{2}{3})$

    e. $(0,-2)$

30. Consider the following scatterplot that depicts the relationship between the variables X and Y:

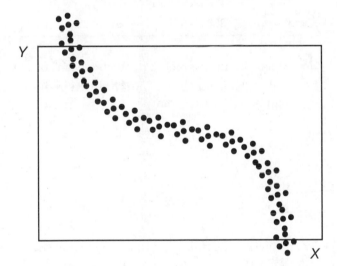

Which of the following statements are true?

    I. This data is negatively correlated.

    II. The correlation is strong in this data set.

    III. The best fit curve is a straight line.

    a. I only

    b. II and III only

    c. I and II only

    d. III only

    e. I, II, and III

31. Which of the following is NOT equal to a whole number?

    a. $5\frac{2}{3} - \frac{28}{6}$

    b. 1.1×0.1

    c. $1\frac{7}{8} \div \frac{3}{8}$

    d. 16×0.5

    e. 200% of $\frac{3}{2}$

32. If R is divisible by 4, S is divisible by 5, and B is divisible by 3, then any multiple of RBS must be divisible by all the following EXCEPT

    a. 6.

    b. 8.

    c. 10.

    d. 12.

    e. 15.

33. Which of the following collections of data, if any, has a mean of 44 and a variance of 0?

    I. 44, 44, 44, 44, 44, 44

    II. 44, 44, 0, 44, 44

    III. −44, −44, −44, 176, 176

    a. I only

    b. II only

    c. III only

    d. I and II

    e. I, II, and III

34. The Huntington Cottage Grove Inn charges $1.50 for the first minute of an outgoing call and 60¢ for every additional minute of the call. If Terry makes a call for m minutes, which of the following equations accurately represents the cost of the call in terms of c dollars?

    a. $c = 60(m) + 1.50$

    b. $c = 0.60(m) + 1.50$

    c. $c = 0.60(m - 1) + 1.50$

    d. $m = 0.60(c - 1) + 1.50$

    e. $c = 60(m - 1) + 1.50$

35. A box is filled with 20 different shaped solids, consisting of 10 spheres, 6 tetrahedra, and 4 cubes. Two solids are chosen at random, one after the other without replacement. What is the probability that neither is a cube?

a. $\frac{16 \times 15}{20}$

b. $\frac{16}{20} \times \frac{15}{20}$

c. $\frac{15}{20} \times \frac{15}{20}$

d. $\frac{16}{20} \times \frac{16}{20}$

e. $\frac{16}{20} \times \frac{15}{19}$

Use the following table to answer question 36.

CITY OF HULE 911 CALL FREQUENCY		
MONTH	911 CALLS	POLICE DISPATCHED
May	213	66
June	194	70
July	257	61
August	267	79
September	279	70
October	308	68

36. What was the average (arithmetic mean) of 911 calls in Hule for the six months listed in the table?

a. 262

b. 253

c. 308

d. 79

e. 69

37. Which of the following is(are) factors of the number $3^3 \times 5 \times 7^2$? Select all that apply.

a. 9

b. 25

c. 10

d. 21

e. 45

38. If $x + y < 10$ and $x - y > 12$, which of the following pairs could be the values of x and y? Indicate *all* such pairs.

a. □ (10,–3)

b. □ (6,–4)

c. □ (12,–4)

d. □ (8,–6)

e. □ (10,–2)

39. If a, b, and c represent distinct real numbers, which of the following equations must be true?

a. $a \times b = b \times c$

b. $a + (b \times c) = ab \times ac$

c. $a(b + c) = ab + ac$

d. $ab + bc = b(a \times c)$

e. $a \times b + c = (a + b) \times (b + c)$

40.

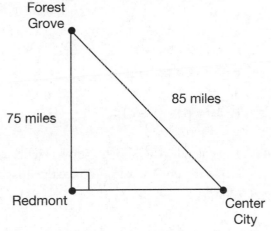

Forest Grove

85 miles

75 miles

Redmont

Center City

Note: Figure not drawn to scale.

Pierre's usual route between Center City and Forest Grove is 85 miles long, as shown in the diagram. Because of construction, he must now take a detour through Redmont first before driving the 75 miles between Redmont and Forest Grove. How much longer is the detoured route than his regular route between Center City and Forest Grove?

a. 10 miles

b. 30 miles

c. 40 miles

d. 75 miles

e. 115 miles

41. Simplify the following expression: $\dfrac{(-2)^3 \cdot 4^{-2}}{(-4)^2 \cdot 2^{-3}}$

a. 4

b. $-\dfrac{1}{4}$

c. $\dfrac{1}{4}$

d. −4

e. −1

42. Joe has exactly 720 hours until his vacation begins. How many days are there before his vacation begins?

a. 30

b. 60

c. 72

d. 144

e. 17,280

43. An administrative assistant can file 26 forms per hour. If 5,600 forms must be filed in an eight-hour day, how many assistants must you hire for that day?

a. 24 assistants

b. 25 assistants

c. 26 assistants

d. 27 assistants

e. 28 assistants

44. The times it took 17 fourth-grade students to finish a 50-yard dash are recorded. The mean time was 15 seconds and the mode time was 18 seconds. The judge subtracted 3 seconds from everyone's time to make the comparison to the seventh-grade times fair. Which of the following is a true statement regarding the data set consisting of the fourth-grade scores?

a. The mean and median decrease by 3 seconds, but the mode remains the same.

b. The mean, median, and mode all decrease by 3 seconds.

c. The mode and mean decrease by 3 seconds, but the median remains the same.

d. Only the mode will decrease by 3 seconds.

e. The mean, median, and mode remain unchanged.

45. Two trains are heading toward each other. One train travels due east at 35 miles per hour, and the other train travels due west at 15 miles per hour. If the two trains start out 2,100 miles apart, how long will it take them to meet?

a. 30 hours

b. 42 hours

c. 60 hours

d. 105 hours

e. 140 hours

46. A rectangular yard is 30 feet wide. The length of the yard is $\frac{4}{3}$ the width. If Jeannie wants to hang a clothing line diagonally across the yard, how many feet of line will Jeannie need?

a. 35 feet

b. $\sqrt{70}$ feet

c. 50 feet

d. 70 feet

e. 40 feet

47. During the spring bowling season, a bowler achieves the following scores: 116, 100, 104, 104, 114, 109, and 109. The bowler's three best scores are averaged for her final score on the season. What is her final score?

48. Factor this expression completely: $5x^3 - 20x^2 - 60x$

a. $x - 6$

b. $5x(x - 6)(x + 2)$

c. $5x(x^2 - 4x - 12)$

d. $5x(x - 4)(x + 3)$

e. $5x(x + 10)(x - 6)$

49. The triangle ABC shown below is reflected across the line $y = x$ to produce the image $A'B'C'$.

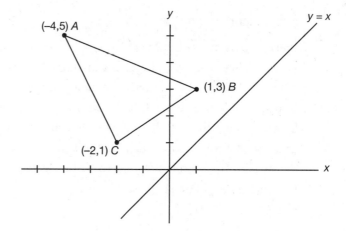

What are the coordinates of C'?

a. $(-2,1)$

b. $(2,-1)$

c. $(2,1)$

d. $(1,-2)$

e. $(-2,-1)$

50. Solve the following equation for x: $\frac{10}{x} + \frac{8}{x} = 3$
   a. 6
   b. 4
   c. 3
   d. 2
   e. None of the above.

51. A sand pile is in the form of a right circular cone. If the radius of the circular base is 10 feet and the volume is 600π cubic feet, what is the height of the pile?
   a. _____
   b. _____
   c. _____
   d. _____
   e. _____

52. Let x be a positive integer and consider the following data set:
$$\{x + 2, x + 4, x - 4, x - 3, x + 6\}$$
Which of the following statements is true?
   I. The mode is $x - 4$
   II. The median is $x + 2$
   III. The mean is $x + 1$
   a. II only
   b. I, II, and III
   c. I and II only
   d. III only
   e. II and III only

53. Suppose that a random variable X has the following probability distribution:

x	–2	0	1	3	4
$P(X = x)$	$\frac{1}{6}$	$\frac{1}{4}$	$\frac{1}{8}$	$\frac{5}{24}$	$\frac{1}{4}$

What is the expected value of X? Enter your answer as a simplified improper fraction in the space provided.
   a. _____
   b. _____
   c. _____
   d. _____
   e. _____

54. If $H = 2w$ and $G = 3w - 1$, then what will the value of $5H - 4G$ be in terms of w?
   a. $-2w + 4$
   b. $-2w - 4$
   c. $2w + 4$
   d. $2w$
   e. $-2w$

55. After three days, a group of hikers on a biology field trip discovers that they have used $\frac{2}{5}$ of their food supplies. They need enough food to make a round trip. At this rate, how many more days can they go forward before they have to turn around?
   a. 0.75 days
   b. 1.5 days
   c. 3.75 days
   d. 4.5 days
   e. 7.5 days

56. What is the area, in square units, of the following figure drawn on the coordinate grid?

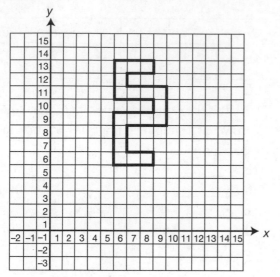

a. 13 square units

b. 12 square units

c. 18 square units

d. 24 square units

e. 38 square units

Praxis® Core Academic Skills for Educators: Mathematics Diagnostic Test Answers and Explanations

1. a. Observe that $\sqrt{600} = \sqrt{10 \cdot 10 \cdot 6} = 10\sqrt{6}$.

2. e. The cost of a field trip increases by approximately $1.50 each year. Because the cost per pupil in 2008 is $10.50 per pupil, the cost in 2009 will be approximately $10.50 + 1.50 = $12.00 and the cost in 2010 will be $12.00 + 1.50 = $13.50.

3. b and d. For **b**, observe that $0.7\pi \approx 0.7(3.14) = 2.20$, which is greater than 1. For **d**, observe that $\frac{7}{0.7} = \frac{70}{7} = 10.0$, which is greater than 1.

4. e. Because lines l and m are parallel, there are a number of angle relationships that allow you to solve for x. As shown in the following figure, the angle labeled 35° and its corresponding angle are congruent. In addition, the angle vertical to, or across from, the angle labeled 50° is also 50°.

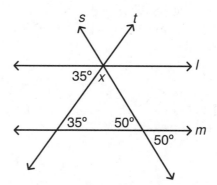

The two newly labeled angles and the angle labeled x are three interior angles of a triangle, so subtract the sum of the two known angles from 180 to solve for x: $180° - (50° + 35°) = 180° - 85° = 95°$.

5. d. To determine the probability that a fifth grader's name will be chosen, you must determine the total number of fifth graders' names that are in the lottery and divide this number by the total number of names in the lottery. Because each fifth grader's name is placed in the lottery three times, there are $3 \times 100 = 300$ fifth-grade names. Likewise, there are $2 \times 150 = 300$ fourth-grade names and $1 \times 200 = 200$ third-grade names in the lottery. The probability that a fifth grader's name will be chosen is $\frac{300}{300 + 300 + 200} = \frac{300}{800} = \frac{3}{8}$.

6. b and d. $f(x)$ is a quadratic function, and its graph is a parabola that opens downward and that may be intercepted by horizontal lines at two points. It is therefore not a one-to-one function. The vertex is $(-2,4)$, so its maximum is 4, not -4. Moreover, it intersects the x-axis because its vertex is above the x-axis and it opens downward.

7. d. First, calculate her earnings for one day: $10.40 times 8 hours per day is equal to $83.20. For any amount of time she worked over 8 hours, she earns time and a half, or 1.5 times her regular pay. This is equal to $10.40 \times 1.5 = \$15.60$ per hour worked overtime. Because she worked $1\frac{1}{2}$ hours overtime on average, this is equal to $15.60 \times 1.5 = $23.40 overtime pay per day. Therefore, her total pay per day is equal to $83.20 + $23.40 = $106.60. Multiply this amount by 5 days per week to get her weekly pay: $106.60 \times 5 = \$533.00$.

8. a. The variable b represents the number of pairs of black socks Rowan has. The number of pairs of white socks is equal to six less than three times b. Three times b can be written as "$3b$," and six less than $3b$ can be written as $3b - 6$, so choice **a** is correct.

9. b. The cross-sections of a tree trunk parallel to the ground are roughly congruent and circular. As such, a cylinder would be appropriate to use to model a tree trunk.

10. a. Since there are 60 minutes in an hour, multiply the 8-hour workday by 60 to get a total of 480 minutes. To find $\frac{5}{12}$ of 480, multiply $\frac{5}{12} \times 480 = 200$. So, Parker spends 200 minutes, or 3 hours and 20 minutes, answering e-mails. 3 hours and 20 minutes subtracted from 8 hours is 4 hours and 40 minutes.

11. a. The perimeter of each small square is $8x$ units; therefore, the length of one side of each small square is $\frac{8x}{4} = 2x$ units. Because the new, large square is comprised of two sides from each of the four squares (the remaining four sides are now within the large square), the perimeter of the new, large square is equal to $4(2x + 2x) = 4(4x) = 16x$ units.

12. a. Because Maddie has 9 pairs of socks in total, there are 18 socks in her drawer. Four pairs, or 8 socks, are white, which means that 10 socks are not white. The chance of her selecting a nonwhite sock at random is $\frac{10}{18}$, which reduces to $\frac{5}{9}$.

13. b. Kevin is 40, so 20 years ago he was $40 - 20 = 20$ years old. At that time in the past, Kevin's father was twice his age, so his father was 40 then. Therefore, Kevin's father is $40 + 20 = 60$ years old now.

14. a, c, and d. For **a**, the model suggests a *long run* likelihood of getting a 2. No definitive conclusion can be drawn from just 10 rolls of the die. Choice **c** is the very definition of probability. For **d**, the model suggests a *long run* likelihood of getting a 2. Such rolls are independent of each other and certainly can come out this way and not contradict the model.

15. b. Change the fractions to decimals by dividing: $\frac{7}{12} = 7 \div 12 \approx 0.583$, and $\frac{5}{7} = 5 \div 7 \approx 0.713$. Change all the numbers to decimals with the same number of digits after the decimal point: 0.5830, 0.7130, 0.0790, 0.6300, 0.0108. The decimal 0.7130 is the greatest, which corresponds to $\frac{5}{7}$.

16. e. To set up a proportion, put the number of births in the numerator and the corresponding total number of people in the denominator:

$$\frac{births}{total\ \#\ of\ people} = \frac{15}{1,000} = \frac{x}{301,000,000}$$

17. c. First, find the total number of floors they can wax in the specified time. This is found by multiplying the rate of work for each person by the amount of time spent working by each. Marcus waxes five floors an hour for three hours, or 15 floors; Josie waxes four floors an hour for two hours, or eight floors. Together, they wax 23 floors. Because there are 50 classrooms total, the percentage of classrooms whose floors are waxed is $\frac{23}{50} = 0.46$, which is equal to 46%.

18. d. This problem is modeled with two similar right triangles: the smaller one has a height of 8 and a shadow of 3. The larger one has a height of h and a shadow of 15. Setting up a proportion of height over shadow and then cross-multiplying gives:

$$\frac{height}{shadow} = \frac{8}{3} = \frac{h}{15}$$

$$3h = 120$$

$$h = 40\ feet$$

19. a. In order to find the area of the parallelogram, first find the height. The vertical, dashed line is the height, and it also forms a right triangle on the left side. Because two sides of this triangle are given, use the Pythagorean theorem to find the length of the missing side: $a^2 + b^2 = c^2$. In this case, $a = 3$, $c = 5$, and $b =$ the height. Substitute: $3^2 + b^2 = 5^2$. Evaluate the exponents: $9 + b^2 = 25$. Subtract 9 on both sides of the equation: $9 - 9 + b^2 = 25 - 9$; $b^2 = 16$. Therefore, $b = 4$. (The triangle is a 3–4–5 right triangle.) To find the area of the parallelogram, multiply the base of the figure by the height: $12 \times 4 = 48\ cm^2$.

20. a. To solve this inequality, simplify the expression in the middle. Then, isolate x in the middle by adding 1 and dividing by –4; when dividing by –4, make certain to switch the inequality signs.

$$-2 \leq 1 - (2 + 4x) < 3$$

$$-2 \leq -1 - 4x < 3$$

$$-1 \leq -4x < 4$$

$$\frac{1}{4} \geq x > -1$$

So, the solution set is $\{x \mid -1 < x \leq \frac{1}{4}\}$.

21. c. The words *at least* and *at most* in the first sentence indicate that a teacher at this school teaches between three and five classes, inclusively. Because the actual number of teachers at the school is not known, the average number of classes and the average time spent teaching cannot be determined. Therefore, it can only be concluded that each teacher has from three to five classes at 40 minutes each, for a total class time between 120 and 200 minutes per day, inclusive.

22. b. The quotient is 40,230. So, the hundreds digit is $x = 2$ and the tens digit is $y = 3$. As such, $y^{-x} = 3^{-2} = \frac{1}{9}$.

23. d. This question translates into the equation $\frac{1}{4}x + 3 = x - 3$. First, subtract $\frac{1}{4}x$ from both sides of the equation: $3 = x - \frac{1}{4}x - 3$. Multiply both sides by 4: $12 = 4x - x - 12$. Combine like terms: $12 = 3x - 12$. Add 12 to both sides: $24 = 3x$. Divide both sides by 3: $8 = x$.

24. b. The ratio is *number of perfect scores:number of non-perfect scores*. This unreduced ratio is 8,000:5,000,000 or 8:5,000. Because 5,000 divided by 8 equals 625, this ratio then becomes 1:625.

25. d. Let s be the length of the shorter side in the enlarged photo. Since the lengths are proportional, we have the following:

$$\frac{1\frac{3}{8} \text{ inches}}{2\frac{3}{4} \text{ inches}} = \frac{s \text{ inches}}{8 \text{ inches}}$$

Solving for s, we have

$$\frac{1\frac{3}{8} \text{ inches}}{2\frac{3}{4} \text{ inches}} = \frac{s \text{ inches}}{8 \text{ inches}}$$

$$\frac{1\frac{3}{8} \text{ inches}}{2\frac{3}{4} \text{ inches}} = \frac{s \text{ inches}}{8 \text{ inches}}$$

$$\frac{(1\frac{3}{8} \text{ inches})(8 \text{ inches})}{2\frac{3}{4} \text{ inches}} = s \text{ inches}$$

$$\frac{\frac{11}{8} \times 8}{\frac{11}{4}} \text{ inches} = s \text{ inches}$$

$$(\tfrac{11}{8} \times 8 \times \tfrac{4}{11}) \text{ inches} = s \text{ inches}$$

$$s = 4 \text{ inches}$$

26. The correct answer is **75**. This uses two algebraic equations to solve for the age. Jacqueline (J) and her grandmother (G) have a sum of ages of 110 years. Therefore, $J + G = 110$. Jacqueline was $\frac{1}{3}$ as young as her grandmother 15 years ago. Therefore, $J - 15 = \frac{1}{3}(G - 15)$. Solve the first equation for J and substitute that value into the second equation: $J = 110 - G$; $(110 - G) - 15 = \frac{1}{3}(G - 15)$. This simplifies to $95 - G = \frac{1}{3}G - 5$. Add G and 5 to each side: $100 = \frac{4}{3}G$. Multiply each side of the equation by $\frac{3}{4}$ to get $G = 75$.

27. d. First, find the rate of snowfall per hour. Because it snowed at a constant rate of three inches every two hours, divide $\frac{3 \text{ inches}}{2 \text{ hours}}$ to get a rate of 1.5 inches per hour. The question asks for the amount of snow that fell in the first five hours, so multiply 1.5 inches per hour × 5 hours = 7.5 inches.

28. a. The sum of the interior angles of a triangle is 180°. Because the vertex angle is 3 times as large as each of the base angles, let the measure of the vertex angle be $3b$ and each of the base angles measure b. Solve the equation $3b + b + b = 180°$; $5b = 180°$; $b = 36°$. Therefore, the base angles will each equal 36° and the vertex will be $3 \times 36° = 108°$. The sum of one base angle and the vertex is $36° + 108° = 142°$.

29. c. Factor the expression and then set each factor equal to zero to get the x-coordinates of the x-intercepts.

$f(x) = 12x^2 + 5x - 2 = (4x - 1)(3x + 2)$

The right side equals zero when $x = \frac{1}{4}$ and $-\frac{2}{3}$. So, the x-intercepts are $(\frac{1}{4}, 0)$ and $(-\frac{2}{3}, 0)$.

30. c. Statement I is true because the best fit line to this data set has a negative slope. Statement II is true because the points are relatively packed close together (and hence would be close to the best fit line); in such case, the correlation is said to be strong. Statement III is not true since the best fit curve is a cubic, which is nonlinear.

31. b. Observe that $1.1 \times 0.1 = 0.11$, which is not a whole number.

32. b. Because R is divisible by 4, S is divisible by 5, and B is divisible by 3, then any multiple of RBS must be divisible by $4 \times 5 \times 3 = 60$. Any number that is divisible by 60 will also be divisible by 6, 10, 12, and 15, because these are all factors of 60. The only number listed that is not a factor of 60 is 8.

33. a. Anytime all the data points are the same, the mean equals the common value and the variance (average distance from the mean) is zero, so statement I is true. Statement II is false because the mean is not 44 because you must divide the sum by the number of data points, which is 5. You cannot ignore the 0. Also, the variance is not zero because all of the points are measurable distances from the mean. The only time the variance can be zero is if all data points equal the mean. Statement III is false because the mean is 44, but the variance is not zero because all of the points are measurable distances from the mean. The only time the variance can be zero is if all data points equal the mean.

34. c. Because the first minute is charged only the $1.50 fee and not the 60¢ fee, when calculating the charges for the m minutes, m must be reduced by one before multiplying by the 60¢ per minute charge. It is also critical to write 60¢ in decimal terms, as 0.60. Therefore, $0.60(m - 1)$ represents what Terry will be charged for all his minutes *after* his first minute. Since his first minute costs $1.50, add this to $0.60(m - 1)$ to get the total price, c.

35. e. For the first choice, there are 16 solids in the box that are NOT cubes. Hence, the probability of choosing a solid that is not a cube is $\frac{16}{20}$. Now, for the second choice, the number of solids in the box from which we can choose has been reduced by 1, and so have the non-cubes. Specifically, for the second choice, there are 15 non-cubes in the collection of 19 solids. So, the probability that the second choice is a non-cube is $\frac{15}{19}$. Thus, to get the probability that neither is a cube, we multiply these two probabilities to obtain $\frac{16}{20} \times \frac{15}{19}$.

36. b. Add up the number of 911 calls for every month, and then divide by the number of months. The total number of calls was $213 + 194 + 257 + 267 + 279 + 308 = 1,518$. Divide 1,518 by 6 months to get 253.

37. a, d, e. For A, a factor of a whole number must divide it evenly. Since $9 = 3^2$ and 3^3 is known to be a factor, 9 must also be a factor. For D, since both 3 and 7 are factors of the whole number, their product $3 \cdot 7 = 21$ is also a factor. For E, since $9 = 3^2$ and 5 are both factors of the whole number, their product $3^2 \cdot 5 = 45$ is also a factor.

38. **a, c, and d.** The easiest way to do this problem is to backsolve. Since each pair of numbers in the answer choices represents possible values of x and y, just substitute the x and y values in each choice into the two inequalities. Only these three pairs satisfy both inequalities.

39. **c.** Choice **c** represents the distributive property of multiplication over addition. This property can be checked by substituting numbers for a, b, and c. For example, if $a = 3$, $b = 4$, and $c = 5$, the equation would become $3(4 + 5) = 3 \times 4 + 3 \times 5$. The equation simplifies to $3(9) = 12 + 15$, which becomes $27 = 27$. Because both sides are equal, the equation is true. Each of the other choices would not be true if different numbers were substituted in for a, b, and c.

40. **b.** The length of the regular route is the hypotenuse of a right triangle. The length of the detour is the sum of the legs of the right triangle. Use the Pythagorean theorem ($a^2 + b^2 = c^2$, or $\text{leg}^2 + \text{leg}^2 = \text{hypotenuse}^2$) to find the length of the missing side of the triangle: $x^2 + 75^2 = 85^2$. Evaluate the exponents: $x^2 + 5,625 = 7,225$. Subtract 5,625 from each side of the equation: $x^2 + 5,625 - 5,625 = 7,225 - 5,625$; $x^2 = 1,600$. Take the square root of each side of the equation: $x = 40$. Because the distance between Center City and Redmont is 40 miles and the distance between Redmont and Forest Grove is 75 miles, the length of the detour is $40 + 75 = 115$ miles. To find how much longer the detour is, subtract $115 - 85 = 30$ miles.

41. **b.** First, take all terms with a negative exponent in the numerator to the denominator, and vice versa. Then, simplify all exponent terms and cancel like factors, as follows:
$$\frac{(-2)^3 \cdot 4^{-2}}{(-4)^2 \cdot 2^{-3}} = \frac{(-2)^3 \cdot 2^3}{(-4)^2 \cdot 4^2} = \frac{(-8) \cdot 8}{(16) \cdot 16} = -\frac{1}{4}$$

42. **a.** This is a conversion problem. Use the fact that there are 24 hours in one day to solve the problem. Remember, converting from a smaller unit to a larger unit requires division: 720 hours ÷ 24 hours per day = 30 days.

43. **d.** Multiply: 26 forms × 8 hours = 208 forms per day per assistant. Divide the total number of forms that need to be filed by the number of forms one assistant can file per day: $5,600 \div 208 \approx 26.9$. You can't hire 0.9 of an assistant, so you have to round up and hire 27 assistants for the day.

44. **b.** We shall refer to the data set obtained by subtracting 3 from each score the *new data set*. Subtracting 3 from each point in the data set shifts all of the points to the left three units (along a number line). As such, the median of the new data set must move three units to the left as well. After all, it is the ninth element of the arranged data set. So, the median is decreased by 3 seconds.

45. **b.** Because they are traveling toward each other, the trains' combined rate of travel is 35 miles per hour + 15 miles per hour = 50 miles per hour. Because *distance = rate × time, time =* $\frac{distance}{rate}$. Divide the rate of travel into the total distance that the trains need to go: 2,100 miles ÷ 50 miles per hour = 42 hours.

46. c. Because the length is $\frac{4}{3}$ as long as the width, the length will be $\frac{4}{3} \times 30 = 40$ feet. A rectangular yard of 30 feet by 40 feet cut by a diagonal will give two congruent right triangles.

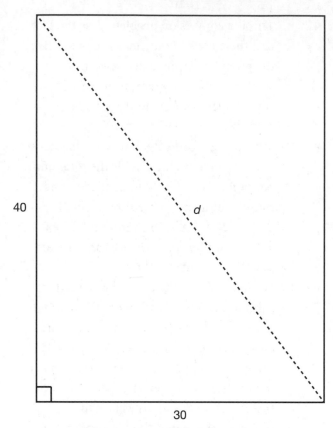

Because this is a right triangle, you can use the Pythagorean theorem, $a^2 + b^2 = c^2$, to solve for the diagonal, where a and b are legs and c is the hypotenuse, or diagonal. In this case, you can use d as your hypotenuse, and plug 30 in for a, and 40 in for b:

$a^2 + b^2 = d^2$

$30^2 + 40^2 = d^2$

$900 + 1{,}600 = d^2$

$2{,}500 = d^2$

$\sqrt{2{,}500} = \sqrt{d^2}$

$50 = d$, so the hypotenuse d equals 50 feet.

47. **The correct answer is 113.** The bowler's three best scores are the highest three scores. These are 116, 114, and 109. To find the average, divide the sum of these three scores by 3: $\frac{116 + 114 + 109}{3} = \frac{339}{3} = 113$.

48. b. The greatest common factor in this expression is $5x$. Factoring this term out gives $5x(x^2 - 4x - 12)$. The expression inside the parentheses can also be factored to arrive at the complete factored expression $5x(x - 6)(x + 2)$.

49. d. To obtain the points of the image when reflecting a figure over the $y = x$ line, you simply switch the x- and y-coordinates. Doing so for point C yields the point $(1, -2)$.

50. a. First, notice that the fractions can be added because they have the same denominators: $\frac{10}{x} + \frac{8}{x} = \frac{18}{x}$. The equation is now $\frac{18}{x} = 3$. Multiply both sides by x to remove the fraction: $18 = 3x$. Finally, divide both sides by 3 to isolate the variable: $x = 6$.

51. **18 feet.** The volume of a right circular cone with radius r and height h is given by the formula $V = \frac{1}{3} \pi r^2 h$. Substituting $r = 10$ and $V = 600\pi$ yields the equation $\frac{1}{3} \pi \cdot 100h = 600\pi$. Solving for h gives 18.

52. e. I is not true, as the mode is not $x - 4$, as this value only occurs once, just like every other value in this set. II is true, because when you order the values from least to greatest, the middle value is $x + 2$. III is true because the mean is the sum of the values divided by the number of values. Here the sum is $5x + 12 - 7 = 5x + 5$. The number of values is 5, so the mean is $x + 1$.

53. $\frac{17}{12}$. To compute the expected value of such a random variable, multiply x times $P(X = x)$ and sum all of them. Doing so yields:

$(-2)(\frac{1}{6}) + 0(\frac{1}{4}) + 1(\frac{1}{8}) + 3(\frac{5}{24}) + 4(\frac{1}{4}) = \frac{17}{12}$.

54. a. Substitute the expressions given for H and G into $5H - 4G$, then distribute while remembering to also distribute the minus sign: $5(2w) - 4(3w - 1) = 10w - 4(3w) - 4(-1)$ (Here the negative must stay with the 4 when it is distributed) $= 10w - 12w - (-4)$ $= -2w + 4$.

55. a. First, determine how long the entire hike can be, based on the rate at which the hikers are using the total amount of their supplies: $\frac{\frac{2}{5}}{3} = \frac{1}{x}$, where 1 is the total amount of supplies and x is the number of days for the whole hike. By cross-multiplying, you get $\frac{2}{5}x = 3$. Multiply each side of the equation by $\frac{5}{2}$ to get $x = \frac{5}{2} \times 3 = \frac{15}{2} = 7\frac{1}{2}$ days for the length of the entire hike, which includes the trip back. Because half of $7\frac{1}{2}$ is $3\frac{3}{4}$, or 3.75, the hikers could go forward for 3.75 days altogether before they would have to turn around. They have already hiked for three days, so $3.75 - 3 = 0.75$ (days) is the amount of time they can now go forward before they have to turn around.

56. c. The area enclosed by the figure is the total number of unique squares within the shape. Starting at the top and counting down to the bottom, there are 18 unique squares. So, the area is 18 square units.

4 ▶ PRAXIS® CORE ACADEMIC SKILLS FOR EDUCATORS: READING TEST REVIEW

CHAPTER SUMMARY

Reading comprehension is an important skill to have in life and on tests. This chapter covers the most essential reading and reading comprehension strategies for success. You will learn to become an active reader, to understand the difference between main ideas and supporting ideas, and to recognize information that is implied, but not stated, in a passage. You will also strengthen your understanding of how texts are structured and crafted and how to integrate information between paired passages and passage/visual representation combinations.

Developing strong reading comprehension skills is crucial for success as a prospective teacher. The Praxis® Core Academic Skills for Educators: Reading test measures your ability to understand written passages and demonstrate insight about what you have read. The exam contains passages of varying lengths: paired passages totaling about 200 words, long passages of about 200 words, shorter passages of approximately 100 words, and short statements of a few sentences. Some passages will also include visual representations, such as graphs, charts, and tables. One or more multiple-choice questions follow each passage or statement. You will be asked to answer 56 multiple-choice questions in 85 minutes.

The topics presented in the passages reflect a range of subjects, from art, science, politics, and history to real-life situations. Although you do not need any specialized knowledge or a background in the subject to answer the questions, you do need to show that you can extract information from the passage. Some questions will focus on the explicit information offered in a passage: its main purpose, supporting details, and organization. Other questions will ask you to interpret and evaluate what is presented in the passage—its underlying message, arguments, and logic.

For questions that refer to long and short passages on the exam, you will view a split screen on your computer, with the reading passage displayed on the left-hand side and a question on the right-hand side. For questions that refer to short statements, you will see both the statement and the question appear in the same screen. In all cases, you will view one question at a time and select your response by clicking the oval next to your preferred answer.

Reading Question Types

Some of the questions on the Core Reading test focus on the information presented in a passage, while others deal with *how* the information is presented. The questions fall into three basic categories: Key Ideas and Details (about 35% of the test questions); Craft, Structure, and Language Skills (about 30% of the test questions); and integration of Knowledge and Ideas (about 35% of the test questions).

Key Ideas and Details

Key Ideas and Details questions ask you to identify an author's purpose for writing a passage and how facts and details help to support a passage's main theme. They focus on what is explicitly presented within a passage—the people, places, things, and ideas—and how they all work to support the message the author hopes to get across.

Craft, Structure, and Language Skills

This question type asks you to look at the mechanics of a reading passage—how it is written, and how the author's word choice and sentence and paragraph structure inform his or her meaning and tone. For example, Craft, Structure, and Language Skills questions will ask you to determine the meaning of vocabulary words within the context of a passage or to identify whether a specific sentence is a fact or an opinion. These questions focus on how a passage is written and constructed.

Integration of Knowledge and Ideas

This question type tests your ability to analyze arguments within a passage, across paired passages, and across passage/visual representation combinations to draw conclusions based on the information presented. You will be asked to dig deeper into the passages to extract evidence for an author's point of view, to determine why and how the evidence adds or subtracts from the main argument, and how the ideas and attitudes of authors of paired passages are different or the same.

Now that you have a better idea of what to expect on the Praxis Core Reading test, you can begin to review some reading comprehension skills and test-taking strategies. By honing these skills, you will be better equipped to understand the passages presented and excel on the exam.

Reading Skill Builders

Reading may seem like a passive activity—after all, you are just sitting and looking at words on a page. However, to improve your reading comprehension you need to *read actively*, which means you need to interact with the text. Incorporate the following active-reading techniques into your study plan for the Praxis Core Reading test. You can practice each time you read a magazine, newspaper, or book, sharpening your reading comprehension skills using these strategies:

■ **Skim ahead.** Scan the text before you read. Look at how the text is organized: How is it broken into sections? In what order are the topics presented? Note key words and ideas that are highlighted in boldface type or in bulleted lists.

- **Jump back.** Review the text after you read. By looking at summaries, headings, and highlighted information, you increase your ability to remember information and make connections between ideas.
- **Look up new words.** Keep a dictionary on hand as you read. Look up unfamiliar words and list them with their definitions in a notebook or make flash cards. To help you remember new words, connect them to something in your life or previous reading. Make a point to use new words in your writing and conversation. By increasing your vocabulary, you build your reading comprehension.
- **Highlight key ideas.** As you read, highlight or underline key terms, main ideas, or concepts that are new to you. Be selective—if you highlight too much of the text, nothing will stand out for you on the page. (If you don't own the book, use a notebook to jot down information.)
- **Take notes.** Note taking can help you remember material, even if you never look at your notes again. That's because it's a muscle activity, and using your muscles can actually aid your memory. Record your questions, observations, and opinions as you read. Write down the main idea of the passage, the author's point of view, and whether you agree with the author.
- **Make connections.** When you connect two ideas, you improve your chances of remembering the material. For example, if you are reading about a current political race, you may note how it is similar to or different from past elections. How have circumstances changed? You may also connect the topic to your own experience: How did you feel about the past election versus the current race?

Key Ideas and Details

The main idea and the details that support it are the most essential elements of any piece of writing.

Therefore, the ability to understand the main idea and its supporting details are the most essential reading comprehension skills. Sometimes these supporting details will be stated explicitly in the text. Sometimes you will need to detect clues for ideas that are merely implied in the text. By mastering the following skills for comprehending key ideas and details in writing, you will be on your way to building the abilities you will need to perform well on the Praxis Core Reading test.

Locate the Main Idea

When standardized reading tests ask you to find the main idea of a passage, they are asking you to determine an overall feeling or thought that a writer wants to convey about a subject. To find the main idea, think about a **general statement** that brings together all the ideas in a paragraph or passage.

Main idea questions might take on one of the following formats:

- *The passage is primarily concerned with. . . ?*
- *What is the author's main purpose in this passage?*
- *Which of the following would be the best title for this passage?*

The passages on the Praxis Core Reading test often follow a basic pattern of **general idea → specific idea**. In other words, a writer states her main idea (makes a general claim about her subject) and then provides evidence for it through specific details and facts. Do you always find main ideas in the first sentence of the passage? The answer is *no*; although a first sentence may contain the main idea, an author may decide to build up to her main point. In that case, you may find the main idea in the last sentence of an introductory paragraph, or even in the last paragraph of the passage.

Read the following paragraph and answer the practice question that follows.

Experts say that if you feel drowsy during the day, even during boring activities, you haven't had enough sleep. If you routinely fall asleep within five minutes of lying down, you probably have severe sleep deprivation, possibly even a sleep disorder. *Microsleep*, or a very brief episode of sleep in an otherwise awake person, is another mark of sleep deprivation. In many cases, people are not aware that they are experiencing microsleeps. The widespread practice of "burning the candle at both ends" in Western industrialized societies has created so much sleep deprivation that what is really abnormal sleepiness is now almost the norm.

Source: National Institute of Neurological Disorders and Stroke, National Institutes of Health, www.ninds.nih.gov.

What is the main point of this passage?

a. If you fall asleep within five minutes every time you lie down, you are sleep deprived.

b. If you experience enough microsleeps, you can attain the sleep you need to function.

c. Sleep deprivation is a pervasive problem in the United States and other Western nations.

d. If trends in sleep deprivation continue, our society will experience grave consequences.

e. Sleep deprivation is responsible for approximately 100,000 car accidents each year.

Choice **a** is a true statement, but too specific to be a main idea. Choice **b** is a false statement. Choice **d** is a speculative statement that is not implied in the passage, and choice **e** is a detail or fact that the information in the paragraph does not support. Only choice **c** represents a general or umbrella statement that covers all the information in the paragraph. Notice that in the sample passage, the author does not present the main idea in the first sentence, but rather builds up to the main point, which is expressed in the last sentence of the paragraph.

Find Essential Facts and Supporting Details

Some of the key ideas and details questions on the Praxis Core Reading test will ask you to identify a paraphrase or rewording of supporting details. To answer these questions successfully, you will need to be able to locate specific information in the passage, such as a fact, figure, or name. Here are some examples of supporting details questions:

- *According to the passage, how many people in the United States have Type II diabetes?*
- *The passage states that a lunar eclipse occurs when . . . ?*
- *Which of the following is NOT mentioned as one of the reasons for the Cuban Missile Crisis?*

How can you distinguish a main idea from a supporting idea? Unlike main ideas, supporting ideas present facts or **specific information**. They often answer the questions *what? when? why?* or *how?*

How can you locate a supporting detail in a passage that is 200 words long? One thing you don't have to do is memorize the passage. The Praxis test does not require you to have perfect recall. Instead, it measures your ability to read carefully and know where to look for specific information.

Here are some tips for finding supporting details.

- **Look for language clues.** Writers often use transitional words or phrases to signal that they are introducing a fact or supporting idea. As you read, keep your eye out for these common phrases:

for example	for instance	in particular
in addition	furthermore	some
other	specifically	such as

- **Focus on key words from the question.** Questions often contain two or three important words that signal what information to look for in the passage. For example, a question following a passage about the American car industry reads, "The passage states that *hybrid automobiles* work best if. . . ." The key words are *hybrid automobiles* and *best*. They tell you to look for a sentence that contains the phrase *hybrid automobiles* and describes an optimal situation. Instead of rereading the passage, *skim* through the paragraphs looking for the key word. Keep in mind that the passage may use a slightly different wording than the key word. As you scan, look for words that address the same idea.

- **Pay attention to the structure of the passage.** Take note of how the passage is organized as you read. Does the author begin with or build to his main point? Is information presented chronologically? Where does the author offer evidence to back up his main point? Understanding how a passage is structured can help you locate the information you need. Read on for more about common organizational models.

Read the following paragraph, focusing on its main idea and the details that support the main idea. Then, answer the practice questions that follow.

(1) The history of microbiology begins with a Dutch haberdasher named Antoni van Leeuwenhoek, a man of no formal scientific education. (2) In the late 1600s, Leeuwenhoek, inspired by the magnifying lenses used by drapers to examine cloth, assembled some of the first microscopes. (3) He developed a technique for grinding and polishing tiny, convex lenses, some of which could magnify an object up to 270 times. (4) After scraping some plaque from between his teeth and examining it under a lens, Leeuwenhoek found tiny squirming

creatures, which he called "animalcules." (5) His observations, which he reported to the Royal Society of London, are among the first descriptions of living bacteria.

1. What inspired Leeuwenhoek's invention of the microscope?
   a. his training in science
   b. the great microbiologists of his era
   c. the lenses used by the practitioners of his profession
   d. the desire to observe bacteria
   e. the common practice of teeth scraping

The correct answer is choice **c**. The second sentence provides the supporting detail to answer this question. Leeuwenhoek, a haberdasher, was *inspired by the magnifying lenses used by drapers to examine cloth*. One of the key words from the question—*inspired*—leads you to the location of the detail in the passage. Choice **a** is refuted by a detail presented in the line *a man of no formal scientific education*. Choice **b** is untrue because the first sentence of the passage states that *the history of microbiology begins with* Leeuwenhoek. Choice **d** is also incorrect because Leeuwenhoek did not know what he would discover under his microscope. Choice **e** is a silly choice used as a distracter.

2. In which sentence does the author give Leeuwenhoek's description of living bacteria?
   a. sentence 1
   b. sentence 2
   c. sentence 3
   d. sentence 4
   e. sentence 5

The correct answer is choice **d**. You can find Leeuwenhoek's description of bacteria in sentence 4: *tiny squirming creatures, which he called "animalcules."* You may have been tricked into selecting choice e because of its repetition of the phrase *descriptions of living bacteria*, from sentence 5. Be sure to always refer back to the passage when answering a question—do not rely on your memory. Choice **e** is incorrect because it does not refer to Leeuwenhoek's own description, but rather the significance of his observation. This question highlights the importance of taking note of where crucial details are located in a passage. Again, do not try to memorize or learn facts or details, but have an idea about where to find them.

Drawing Inferences: Reading between the Lines

Making inferences is something we do every day. A stranger at the supermarket may say, "I am buying steaks, which I'll cook tonight, but my wife makes dinner three nights a week." Though he did not state any of this explicitly, you can conclude that the man and his wife share household duties and that they are not vegetarians. You can draw these conclusions by making inferences based on what the man said:

EXPLICITLY STATED CLUE	LOGICAL INFERENCE
1. . . . I'll cook tonight, but my wife makes dinner three nights a week.	1. The man and his wife share household duties.
2. I am buying steaks, which I'll cook tonight . . .	2. The man and his wife are not vegetarians.

However, one might make incorrect inferences from ideas that are not based on explicitly stated clues:

EXPLICITLY STATED CLUE	ILLOGICAL INFERENCE
1. . . . I'll cook tonight, but my wife makes dinner three nights a week.	1. The man cooks four nights a week. (Maybe the man and his wife order take-out food one or more nights a week.)
2. I am buying steaks, which I'll cook tonight . . .	2. Steaks are the only meat the man and his wife eat. (Although they are eating steaks this night, there is no reason to believe this is the only kind of meat they eat.)

Often, the Praxis Core Reading test will ask you to make an inference, or draw a logical conclusion, about what you read. Here are some examples of questions that may be asked about drawing inferences:

- *Which of the following inferences may be drawn from the information presented in the passage?*
- *It can be inferred from the passage that Charles Darwin's most important contribution to science was which of the following?*
- *Which of the following is an unstated assumption the author of the passage makes?*

Read the following paragraph and answer the practice question that follows.

(1) The impact that drilling for oil, vehicular carbon emissions, and livestock and vegetable farming has on the environment is well documented and well known. (2) However, many people do not consider how the clothing on their backs is changing our world. (3) Clothing companies that produce large volumes of product can have a highly consequential impact on the environment as well. (4) Cotton is a crop that requires excessive water. (5) The tanning

process for creating leather produces vast amounts of hazardous waste. (6) For example, 20 to 80 cubic meters of chromium-polluted water is a by-product of tanning a single ton of leather.

3. Which of the following inferences may be drawn from the information presented in the passage?
   a. Oil drilling is having a more serious impact on the environment than livestock farming is.
   b. Clothing companies often violate the guidelines of the Environmental Protection Agency.
   c. Irresponsible cotton farming is currently causing serious droughts throughout the world.
   d. Cotton farming produces dangerous amounts of hazardous waste materials.
   e. Environmentally conscious consumers should be mindful of the clothing they purchase.

The correct answer is choice **e**. The main idea of the passage is that clothing production can have destructive consequences for the environment, so it is logical to conclude that people who care about the environment should be mindful that they are purchasing clothing from environmentally conscious companies. Choice **a** makes a comparison based on information not present in the passage. Choices **b** and **c** make assumptions based on information not present in the passage. Choice **d** confuses the harmful effects of cotton farming with those of leather production.

Building a Case: Details and Ideas Inform an Argument

The purpose of certain pieces of writing is to argue either in favor of or against something. The writer builds her case by selecting relevant details to support it. The individuals, events, and ideas cited in a text must support its overall idea. On the Praxis Core Reading test, you will have to identify how an author uses these elements to support her argument, and you will have to be aware of how they interact with each other.

THE ELEMENTS

Individuals: the people involved in the topic
Events: what happens
Ideas: what it all means

Example
In 1958, Jack Kilby began working for the Texas Instruments electronics company. That year, he constructed an electronic circuit from a piece of semiconductor material the size of a fingernail. Kilby's microchip completely revolutionized the electronics field.

Let's identify the important elements in the preceding paragraph:

Individuals: Jack Kilby
Events: invention of the microchip
Ideas: Kilby's invention revolutionized the electronics field.

Notice how each element of the paragraph interacts: Kilby is responsible for the invention of the microchip. His invention revolutionized an industry. Each element supports the paragraph's main idea, which is that Jack Kilby's invention of the microchip revolutionized the electronics field.

Read the following paragraph and answer the practice question that follows.

(1) In 1968, Native American activists George Mitchell, Dennis Banks, and Clyde Bellecourt united to found the American Indian Movement (AIM). (2) The movement aimed to combat the rampant unemployment, unacceptable housing, and other hurdles Native Americans faced in their homeland. (3) To push their cause, the founders of AIM established the K–12 Heart of the Earth Survival School in 1971 and mounted a protest march christened the Trail of Broken Treaties in Washington, D.C. (4) There they occupied the Bureau of Indian Affairs, the government office that was supposed to be supporting the rights of Native Americans but had failed terribly in the eyes of AIM. (5) In an effort to stop the organization, the FBI and CIA entered into a violent confrontation with AIM in the Wounded Knee community of South Dakota. (6) A 71-day siege followed, and though two people were killed in the fighting and 1,200 were arrested, the confrontation at Wounded Knee had the positive affect of drawing attention to the Native American movement.

4. Why does the author mention Clyde Bellecourt in the passage?
    a. He was the most important Native American activist.
    b. He founded the K–12 Heart of the Earth Survival School.
    c. He was responsible for introducing George Mitchell to Dennis Banks.
    d. He helped draw attention to the Native American movement.
    e. He led the FBI confrontation against AIM at Wounded Knee.

The correct answer is choice **d**. The main idea of the passage is that AIM's efforts drew attention to the Native American movement, and as a co-founder of that organization, Clyde Bellecourt had an important effect on that outcome. The author does not suggest that Bellecourt was any more important than his partners George Mitchell or Dennis Banks, so choice **a** is not the correct answer, nor does the author indicate that Bellecourt introduced his partners to each other, which eliminates choice **c**. Although Bellecourt co-founded AIM, and AIM founded the K–12 Heart of the Earth Survival School, this is merely one detail in a passage with a more important overall idea, so **b** is not the best answer choice. Bellecourt was a member of AIM, not a member of the FBI, so choice **e** is wrong.

Craft, Structure, and Language Skills

After identifying the most essential elements of a text—its main idea, explicitly and implicitly stated supporting details—and how these elements interact with each other, it is necessary to look deeper into how that text is constructed. Words are the hardware writers use to build texts, and just as a carpenter must select the correct hardware to build a physical structure, so writers must choose the right words to craft solid texts. The ability to recognize how a writer chooses and uses words is a key facet of effective reading comprehension. It will help you to understand a writer's point of view and his or her opinion about the topic in question, distinguish between facts and opinions, and recognize organizational patterns. Understanding these elements will help you to evaluate how reliable an authority a writer is and whether or not his argument could be made stronger with additional information. Examining language closely will also help you to build your own vocabulary by identifying and using context clues to learn the meanings of unfamiliar words.

What Do You Think? Determining the Author's Attitude

Some texts are written in a completely neutral tone; encyclopedia entries, for example, primarily are concerned with conveying concrete facts and details about a wide variety of topics. Other texts intend to sway the reader to believe a certain opinion. These are argumentative texts. Some writers are very forthcoming about their opinions, stating them in no uncertain terms. Other writers are cagier about imparting their opinions. To determine a writer's underlying assumptions or attitude, you need to look for clues in the context of the passage. One revealing clue to the writer's meaning is his word choice.

Word choice, also called diction, is the specific language the writer uses to describe people, places, and things. Word choice includes these forms:

- the particular words or phrases a writer uses
- the way words are arranged in a sentence
- the repetition of words or phrases for effect
- the inclusion of particular details

Consider how word choice affects the following sentences:

    a. Lesson preparation benefits a teacher's performance in the classroom.

    b. Lesson preparation improves a teacher's performance in the classroom.

The only difference between the two sentences is that sentence **a** uses *benefits*, and sentence **b** uses *improves*. Both sentences state that lesson preparation has a positive influence on a teacher's performance in the classroom. However, sentence **a** is stronger because of the words the writer chose: to *benefit* means *to be useful or advantageous*, whereas to *improve* means *to enhance in value*. The writer of sentence **b** believes that preparation is not only useful; it actually increases a teacher's effectiveness. The writer doesn't have to spell this out for you, because his word choice makes his position clear.

Denotation and Connotation

Even words with similar dictionary definitions (**denotations**) can have different suggested meanings (**connotations**). Consider the different implied meanings of the following word pairs:

- slim/thin
- perilous/dangerous
- rich/wealthy

Although they are nearly synonyms, these word pairs suggest varying degrees and have subtle differences in their effect. The word *slim* suggests fitness and grace. *Thin* is more neutral, or possibly negative, implying someone may be too skinny to be healthy. *Perilous* suggests a greater threat of harm than the term *dangerous*: It has a more ominous connotation and implies a more life-threatening situation. The subtle difference between *rich* and *wealthy* is, again, one of degree: *rich* implies having more than enough to fulfill normal needs; *wealthy* suggests an established and elevated societal class.

Style

Just as word choice can alert you to a writer's underlying message, so can other aspects of a writer's style. **Style** is the distinctive way in which a writer uses language to inform or promote an idea. In addition to word choice, a writer's style consists of three basic components:

1. sentence structure
2. degree of detail or description
3. degree of formality

When you read a magazine, newspaper, or book, consider how the writer uses sentences. Does the writer use short, simple sentences or long, complex ones packed with clauses and phrases? Writers use different **sentence structures** to create different effects: They may make short declarative statements in order to persuade readers or long descriptions to create a flow that pleases the reader.

Degree of detail refers to how specific an author is in describing something. For example, a writer may use a general term (*dog, beach, government*) or specific terms (*German shepherd, Crane's Beach, British Parliament*). In evaluating the strength of a writer's argument, consider whether terms are too general to provide adequate evidence.

Degree of formality refers to how formal or casual the writer's language is. Technical jargon or terminology is an example of formal language. Colloquial phrases and slang are examples of casual language. Writers create distance and a sense of objectivity when they use formal language, whereas slang expresses familiarity. The degree of formality a writer uses should be appropriate to his purpose and message. For example, a business missive that uses slang is likely to put off its audience, whereas a novel aimed at teenage readers may use slang to appeal to its audience.

Euphemism and Dysphemism

Writers also reveal their attitude toward a subject through the use of euphemism or dysphemism. Here is a quick definition of the terms:

- **euphemism:** a neutral or positive expression used in place of a negative one
- **dysphemism:** a negative expression substituted for a neutral or positive one

A euphemism is the substitution of an agreeable description of something that might be unpleasant. In contrast, a dysphemism is an offensive, disagreeable, or disparaging expression that describes something neutral or agreeable.

For example, a student who fails a test might use a euphemistic statement when reporting the grade to her parents:

"I didn't do very well on the test."

The student might feel more comfortable using a dysphemism when talking to her classmates:

"I bombed that test. I tanked!"

Another example might be the sentence "I've been fired." A euphemism for this statement is "I've been let go," whereas a dysphemism for the statement is "I've been axed."

Emotional Language

When writers want to persuade a reader of something, they may rely on emotional language. **Emotional language** targets a reader's emotions—fears, beliefs, values, prejudices—instead of appealing to a reader's reason or critical thinking. Just as advertising often uses emotional language to sell a product, writers use emotional appeals to sell an idea. Here are five techniques to look out for as you read:

1. **Bandwagon.** The basic message of a bandwagon appeal is that "everyone else is doing something, so you should, too." It appeals to the reader's desire to join the crowd or be on the winning team. Examples from advertising include: "Americans buy more of our brand than any other brand," or "the toothpaste picky parents choose."
2. **Common man.** In this approach, writers try to convince a reader that their message is just plain, old, common sense. Colloquial language or phrases and well-known jokes are examples of this technique.
3. **Generalities.** In this approach, writers use words or phrases that evoke deep emotions and carry strong associations for most people. By doing so, a writer can appeal to readers' emotions so that they will accept her message without evaluating it. Generalities are vague so that

readers supply their own interpretations and do not ask further questions. Examples of generalities are *honor*, *peace*, *freedom*, or *home*.

4. **Labeling or name-calling.** This method links a negative label, name, or phrase to a person, group, or belief. Name-calling can be a direct attack that appeals to hates or fears, or it can be indirect, appealing to a sense of ridicule. Labels such as *communist* or *terrorist* can evoke deep emotions. Others can be negatively charged, depending on the situation: *yuppie*, *slacker*, *reactionary*.

5. **Testimonial.** In advertising, well-known athletes promote a range of products, from cereal to wristwatches. Likewise, a writer may use a public figure, expert, or other respected person to endorse an idea or support the writer's argument. Because readers may respect or admire the person, they may be less critical and more willing to accept an idea.

TONE MAKES MEANING

You can detect a writer's tone—his mood or attitude as conveyed through language—from his choices about point of view, language use, and style. Praxis Core test questions will sometimes ask you to evaluate and summarize a writer's tone. When you read material in preparation for the exam, always think about the tone of each passage. Here are some common words that describe tone:

cheerful	apologetic	sarcastic
complimentary	critical	playful
hopeful	humorous	authoritative
gloomy	ironic	indifferent

Practice

Read the following passage and answer the practice questions. Consider the writer's choice of words, style, and point of view and how they affect the message presented in the text.

Jane Austen died in 1817, leaving behind six novels that have since become English classics. Most Austen biographers accept the image of Jane Austen as a sheltered spinster who knew little of life beyond the drawing rooms of her Hampshire village. They accept the claim of Austen's brother, Henry: "My dear sister's life was not a life of events."

Biographer Claire Tomalin takes this view to task. She shows that Jane's short life was indeed tumultuous. Not only did Austen experience romantic love (briefly, with an Irishman), but her many visits to London and her relationships with her brothers (who served in the Napoleonic wars) widened her knowledge beyond her rural county, and even beyond England. Tomalin also argues that Austen's unmarried status benefited her ability to focus on her writing. I believe that Jane herself may have viewed it that way. Although her family destroyed most of her letters, one relative recalled that "some of her [Jane's] letters, triumphing over married women of her acquaintance, and rejoicing in her freedom, were most amusing."

5. In order to evaluate the validity of the author's claim that Austen's marital status helped her writing, it would be helpful to know which of the following?
   a. why the author mentions the biographer Claire Tomalin
   b. how single women were regarded in Austen's time period
   c. whether marriage would actually prevent a woman from writing during Austen's era
   d. the reliability of the source of the quotation at the end of the passage
   e. more details about Austen's tumultuous life

The correct answer is choice **d**. This evaluation question asks you to consider the evidence used to support the author's claim that Jane Austen viewed her unmarried status as a benefit to her writing. Because the author employs a quotation from one of Austen's relatives to back up her claim, it would be helpful to know more about the source. A greater degree of detail and description (which relative? can the relative be considered reliable?) would strengthen the author's argument.

6. What word best describes the tone of the passage?
   a. somber
   b. critical
   c. apathetic
   d. appreciative
   e. playful

The correct answer is choice **b**. To determine the tone of the passage, you need to look at the author's point of view, style, and word choice. Because the author's style and word choice are not formal, you can eliminate choice **a**, *somber*. Her style and word choice are not overly casual, either, so you can strike choice **e**, *playful*. The author uses the third-person point of view for most of the passage, signaling that the passage is attempting to be objective. Because the author uses the first-person point of view to make a claim, you can infer that the author is not *apathetic* (choice **c**) about her subject. Although the author may indeed be *appreciative* (choice **d**) about her subject, her word choice does not support this.

One Thing Leads to Another: Transitional Words and Phrases

Every part of a well-constructed text works together to present strong ideas. This includes the way each idea leads into the next one. Transitional words and phrases help ideas to progress logically and words to flow. Take a look at the following example:

"I'm not a fan of sports. I love tennis."

As written, the second sentence seems to contradict the first one. Someone who is not a sports fan doesn't seem like the kind of person who would like the sport of tennis. However, if tennis is the exception to the person's general dislike of sports, then a simple transitional word would make the second idea connect to the first one more logically.

"I'm not a fan of sports, *but* I love tennis."

The transitional word *but* indicates that tennis is the exception to the person's general dislike of sports. It also helps the words flow better by joining two short, choppy sentences to create a single longer, fluid sentence.

Here are samples of common transitional words and phrases:

additionally	but
also	however
after all	instead
and	rather
finally	nevertheless
in addition	nonetheless
neither	on the contrary
nor	on the other hand
or	still
secondly	yet
meanwhile	for example
simultaneously	furthermore
subsequently	in other words
then	in the same way
while	as a result
although	consequently
at the same time	therefore
besides	thus

Practice

Read the following passage and answer the practice question.

Jackson Pollock's discovery of liquid paint while participating in an experimental art workshop in 1936 had seismic effects on his work and art history in general. Pollock used the pourable paint in revolutionary ways, dripping it onto canvasses directly, without the aid of brushes. The resulting pieces eschewed conventional imagery in favor of colors and patterns that seemed to move. Some critics dismissed Pollock's "action paintings" as "random," "meaningless," and "in bad taste," yet his work helped liberate art from the conventions of both imagery and technique. Consequently, the artist inspired a new generation of artists to explore the multitudinous possibilities of creation.

7. Which key word from the passage helps the transition from Pollock's revolutionary techniques to the negative reactions his work sometimes provoked?
a. and
b. directly
c. dismissed
d. yet
e. consequently

The correct answer is choice **d.** The transitional word *yet* indicates that the effects Pollock's paintings had on the art world often contradicted the criticism his art received. Although *and* (**a**) and *consequently* (**e**) are transitional words, the author does not use either to connect Pollock's revolutionary techniques to the negative reactions his work sometimes provoked. Neither *directly* (**b**) nor *dismissed* (**c**) are transitional words.

All About Organization

Now let's look closer at how transitional words and phrases indicate how a passage is organized overall. Organization questions on the Praxis Core Reading test ask you to identify how a passage is structured. You need to be able to recognize organizational patterns, common transitional phrases, and how ideas relate within a passage. Understanding the structure of a passage can also help you locate concepts and information, such as the main idea or supporting details. Here are some examples of organization questions:

- *Which of the following best describes the organization of the passage?*
- *This passage is most likely taken from a . . . ?* (newspaper column, textbook, etc.)
- *The phrase* the contrast in meaning and tone *refers to the contrast between . . . ?*
- *Why is the word* indescribably *used in sentence 4?*

To organize their ideas effectively, writers rely on one of several basic organizational patterns.

Chronological order arranges events by the order in which they happened, from beginning to end. Textbooks, instructions and procedures, essays about personal experiences, and magazine feature articles may use this organizing principle. Passages organized by chronology offer language cues—in the form of transitional words or phrases—to signal the passage of time and link one idea or event to the next. Here are some of the most common chronological transitions:

first, second, third, etc.	before	after	next	now
then	when	as soon as	immediately	suddenly
soon	during	while	meanwhile	later
in the meantime	at last	eventually	finally	afterward

Order of importance organizes ideas by rank instead of by time. Instead of describing what happened next, this pattern presents what is most, or least, important. The structure can work two ways: Writers can organize their ideas either by increasing importance (least important idea → most important idea) or by decreasing importance (most important idea → least important idea).

Newspaper articles follow the principle of decreasing importance; they cover the most important information in the first sentence or paragraph (the *who*, *what*, *when*, *where*, and *why* about an event). As a result, readers can get the facts of an event without reading the entire article. Writing that is trying to persuade its readers or make an argument often uses the pattern of increasing importance. By using this structure, a writer creates a snowball effect, building and building on her idea. "Saving the best for last" can create suspense for the reader and leave a lasting impression of the writer's main point.

Just as a chronological arrangement uses transitions, so does the order of importance principle. Watch for the following common transitional words and phrases:

first and foremost	most important	more important	moreover
above all	first, second, third	last, but not least	finally

Comparison and contrast arranges two things or ideas side by side to show the ways in which they are similar or different. This organizational model allows a writer to analyze two things and ideas and determine how they measure up to one another. For example, this description of the artists Pablo Picasso and Henri Matisse uses comparison and contrast:

The grand old lions of modernist innovation, Picasso and Matisse, originated many of the most significant developments of twentieth-century art [comparison]. However, although they worked in the same tradition, they each had a different relationship to painting [contrast]. For example, Picasso explored signs and symbols in his paintings, whereas Matisse insisted that the things represented in his paintings were merely things: The oranges on the table of a still life were simply oranges on the table [contrast].

Writers use two basic methods to compare and contrast ideas. In the **point-by-point** method, each aspect of idea A is followed by a comparable aspect of idea B, so that a paragraph resembles this pattern: ABABABAB. In the **block method**, a writer presents several aspects of idea A, followed by several aspects of idea B. The pattern of the block method looks like this: AAAABBBB.

Again, transitions can signal whether a writer is using the organizing principle of comparison and contrast. Watch for these common transitions:

TRANSITIONS SHOWING SIMILARITY

similarly	in the same way	likewise
like	in a like manner	just as
and	also	both

TRANSITIONS SHOWING DIFFERENCE

but	alternatively	yet
however	on the contrary	in contrast
conversely	whereas	unlike

Cause and effect arranges ideas to explain why an event took place (cause) and what happened as a result (effect). Sometimes one cause has several effects, or an effect may have several causes. For example, a historian writing about World War I might investigate several causes of the war (assassination of the heir to the Austro-Hungarian throne, European conflicts over territory and economic power), and describe the various effects of the war (10 million soldiers killed, weakened European powers, enormous financial debt).

Key words offer clues that a writer is describing cause and effect. Pay attention to these words as you read:

WORDS INDICATING CAUSE

because	created by
since	caused by

WORDS INDICATING EFFECT

therefore	so
hence	consequently
as a result	

A writer might also describe a **contributing** cause, which is a factor that helps to make something happen but can't make that thing happen by itself. On the opposite end of the spectrum is a **sufficient** cause, which is an event that, by itself, is strong enough to make the event happen. Often an author will offer her opinion about the cause or effect of an event. In that case, readers must judge the validity of the author's analysis. Are the author's ideas logical? Does she support her conclusions?

Read the following excerpt and answer the practice question.

When Rosa Parks refused to give up her seat to a white person in Montgomery, Alabama, and was arrested in December 1955, she set off a train of events that generated a momentum the Civil Rights movement had never before experienced. Local civil rights leaders were hoping for such an opportunity to test the city's segregation laws. Deciding to boycott the buses, the African-American community soon formed a new organization to supervise the boycott, the Montgomery Improvement Association (MIA). The young pastor of the Dexter Avenue Baptist Church, Reverend Martin Luther King, Jr., was chosen as the first MIA leader. The boycott, more successful than anyone hoped, led to a 1956 Supreme Court decision banning segregated buses.

Source: Excerpt from the Library of Congress, "The African American Odyssey: A Quest for Full Citizenship."

8. The author implies that the action and arrest of Rosa Parks directly resulted in
   a. the 1956 Supreme Court decision banning segregated buses.
   b. Martin Luther King, Jr.'s ascendancy as a civil rights leader.
   c. the formation of the Civil Rights movement in Montgomery, Alabama.
   d. the bus boycott in Montgomery, Alabama.
   e. the birth of a nationwide struggle for civil rights.

The correct answer is choice **d.** According to the passage, Rosa Parks's action directly inspired local civil rights leaders to institute the Montgomery bus boycott. Although Rosa Parks's action may have been a contributing factor to King's emergence as a civil rights leader (choice **b**) and the Supreme Court's later decision to ban segregated buses (choice **a**), it was not the *direct* cause of these events, according to the passage. Choice **c** is incorrect because the passage makes clear that a local civil rights movement already existed and was not the result of Rosa Parks's refusal to give up her bus seat. Likewise, choice e is incorrect. Rosa Parks may have furthered the national Civil Rights movement, but she was not its direct cause.

Point of View

One strategy that writers use to convey their meaning to readers is through point of view. **Point of view** is the person or perspective through which the writer channels her information and ideas. It determines who is speaking to the reader. Depending on the writer's intentions, she may present a subjective point of view (a perspective based on her own thoughts, feelings, and experiences) or an **objective** one (one that discounts the writer's personal feelings and attempts to offer an unbiased view). Understanding the point of view of a passage will help you answer questions that ask you to identify an author's assumptions or attitude. Here are three approaches to point of view.

First-person point of view expresses the writer's personal feelings and experiences directly to the reader using these pronouns: *I, me, mine, we, our, us.* The first person creates a sense of intimacy between the reader and writer because it expresses a subjective point of view.

This excerpt from Walt Whitman's *Leaves of Grass* provides an example of first-person perspective:

> As I ponder'd in silence,
> Returning upon my poems, considering, lingering long,
> A Phantom arose before me with distrustful aspect,
> Terrible in beauty, age, and power,
> The genius of poets of old lands,
> As to me directing like flame its eyes,
> With finger pointing to many immortal songs,
> And menacing voice, What singest thou? it said,
> Know'st thou not there is but one theme for ever-enduring bards?

Second-person point of view is another personal perspective in which the writer speaks directly to the reader, addressing the reader as *you.* Writers use the second person to give directions or to make the reader feel directly involved with the argument or action of their message. The following excerpt from Mark Twain's *The Adventures of Huckleberry Finn* uses the second person.

> The widow rung a bell for supper, and you had to come to time. When you got to the table you couldn't go right to eating, but you had to wait for the widow to tuck down her head and grumble a little over the victuals, though there warn't really anything the matter with them— that is, nothing only everything was cooked by itself.

Third-person point of view expresses an impersonal point of view by presenting the perspective of an outsider (a third person) who is not directly involved with the action. Writers use the third person to establish distance from the reader and present a seemingly objective point of view. The third person uses these pronouns: *he, him, his; she, her, hers; it, its;* and *they, them, theirs.* Most Praxis Core passages are written in the third person. The following is an example of the third-person perspective.

> The Sami are an indigenous people living in the northern parts of Norway, Sweden, Finland, and Russia's Kola Peninsula. Originally, the Sami religion was animistic; that is, for them, nature and natural objects had a conscious life, a spirit.

The Roles of Ideas, References, and Information in Arguments

Most writing presents reasonable opinions based on fact: A writer asserts her opinion and supports it with facts or other evidence. A writer can use different types of evidence to build an argument—some forms of proof are more reliable than other types. On the Praxis Core Reading test you will determine the roles that ideas, references, and information play in an author's discussion or argument. When you read, look for the forms of evidence listed here and consider how accurate each might be.

observations	experiments
interviews	personal experience
surveys and questionnaires	expert opinions

Now read the following passage and answer the practice question.

> Laughter is always the laughter of a group. It may, perchance, have happened to you, when seated in a railway carriage, to hear travelers relating to one another's stories which must

have been comic to them, for they laughed rapturously. Had you been one of their company, you would have laughed like them; but, as you were not, you had no desire whatsoever to do so. However spontaneous it seems, laughter always implies a kind of complicity with other laughers, real or imaginary. How often has it been said that the fuller the theater, the more uncontrolled the laughter of the audience! On the other hand, how often has the remark been made that many comic effects are incapable of translation from one language to another, because they refer to the customs and ideas of a particular social group!

Source: Excerpt from *Laughter: An Essay on the Meaning of the Comic* by Henri Bergson.

9. What role does the author's anecdote about the travelers in the railway carriage serve in the passage's central argument?
   a. It demonstrates through personal experience that laughter is an isolated phenomenon.
   b. It illustrates how the specific customs and ideas of his or her society dictate what is and what is not funny.
   c. It accentuates that an individual apart from an intended audience may lack a necessary connection to find humor in a situation.
   d. It shows the significant impact of proximity on a humorous situation.
   e. It demonstrates that laughter is an inexplicably spontaneous event.

The correct answer is choice **c**. The author shows support for the statement in choice **c** in the anecdote about the group of laughing travelers on the railway; because you were not part of the group and were apart from the intended audience, you lacked a connection and did not find the humor funny. The final sentence in the text ("many comic effects are incapable of translation from one language to another . . .") supports the role listed in choice **b**, but the railway anecdote does not relate specifically to the customs and ideas of a society. The statement provided in choice **a** is contradicted throughout the passage and therefore could not be correct. Because the author is not using the anecdote to show that laughter is spontaneous or that proximity affects the humor, choices **d** and **e** are incorrect.

Fact versus Opinion

Just because something is in print does not mean that it is fact. Most writing contains some bias—the personal judgment of a writer. Sometimes a writer's beliefs inadvertently affect how he or she writes about a topic. In other cases, a writer deliberately attempts to shape the reader's reaction and position. For example, a writer may present only one perspective about a subject or include only facts that support his or her point of view. Critical and inferential questions on the Praxis Core Reading test will ask you to judge the strengths or weaknesses of an author's argument. You will be required to distinguish between fact and opinion, and to decide whether the supporting details or evidence effectively back up the author's main point.

To separate fact from opinion, consider these differences:

- A **fact** is a statement that a reliable source can verify.
- An **opinion** is a statement about the beliefs or feelings of a person or group.

When determining whether a statement is factual, consider whether a source gives researched, accurate information. The following is an example of a factual statement the recent national census supports:

> The U.S. population is growing older—in fact, adults over age 85 are the fastest-growing segment of today's population.

Opinions reflect judgments that may or may not be true. Opinions include speculation or predictions of the future that cannot be proven at the present time. The following statement represents an opinion—it offers a belief about the future. Other people may disagree with the prediction:

> Many believe that the population boom among elderly Americans will create a future health-care crisis.

Language clues can alert you to a statement that reflects an opinion. Look for these common words that introduce opinions:

likely	should/could	say
possibly	think	charge
probably	believe	attest

Read the following passage and answer the practice question.

> Despite an innocuous appearance that brings to mind an oversized pig or water-dwelling cow, the hippopotamus is capable of great viciousness. Short legs and hefty bodies (on average, adults weigh in the neighborhood of 3,000 lbs.) do not slow the hippo, which can run up to 19 miles per hour in short spurts. That weight, coupled with tusks that may measure more than a foot long and a generally aggressive attitude, makes for an unexpected danger. People would be wise to steer clear of the beasts, and though young hippos might fall prey to the lions, crocodiles, and hyenas with which they share their habitat, full-grown hippos are more likely to be the aggressors in confrontations with such notoriously deadly animals.

10. Which description of a hippopotamus best represents a statement of opinion rather than a fact?

   a. It looks like an oversized pig or water-dwelling cow.

   b. It is often aggressive to lions, hyenas, and crocodiles.

   c. It can weigh in the neighborhood of 3,000 pounds.

   d. It is capable of running 19 miles per hour in short spurts.

   e. It has tusks that may measure more than a foot long.

The correct answer is choice **a**. A statement of opinion is a statement that cannot be proven with facts; not everyone may agree that a hippopotamus looks like a pig or a cow, so choice **a** is merely an opinion. However, it can be scientifically proven that the hippo is aggressive to predators (choice **b**), weighs around 3,000 lbs (choice **c**), can run 19 miles per hour in short spurts (choice **d**), and has tusks that measure more than a foot long (choice **e**). These statistics are all facts, not opinions.

Strategies for Vocabulary Questions

Vocabulary questions ask you to determine the meaning of a word as it is used in the passage. An effective way to build your vocabulary is to read a wide range of challenging materials in your spare time. At the college and career levels, you might try reading fine literature or scientific journals to broaden your knowledge of words. When you encounter an unfamiliar word or phrase, look it up in the dictionary or a reliable online source. Then try using it in written or spoken sentences three times throughout the day.

   During the Praxis Core Reading test, you cannot use a dictionary to check the meaning of new words. However, you can use a number of strategies to figure out what a word means. Here are some examples of vocabulary questions:

- *Which of the following words, if substituted for the word* indelible *in the passage, would introduce the least change in the meaning of the sentence?*
- *The word* protest *in the passage could best be replaced by . . . ?*
- *Which of the following is the best meaning of the word* experience *as it is used in the passage?*

Vocabulary questions measure your word power; moreover, they also evaluate an essential reading comprehension skill—your ability to determine the meaning of a word from its context. The sentences that surround the word offer important clues about its meaning. For example, see whether you can figure out the meaning of the word *incessant* from this context:

> The incessant demands of the job are too much for me. The responsibilities are endless!

11. The word *incessant* most nearly means

   a. inaccessible.

   b. difficult.

   c. unceasing.

   d. compatible.

   e. manageable.

The correct answer is choice **c**. The second sentence, *The responsibilities are endless*, restates the phrase in the first sentence, *incessant demands*. This restatement, or elaboration, suggests the meaning of *incessant*: continuing or following without interruption.

   If the context of an unfamiliar word does not restate its meaning, try these two steps to figure out what the word means:

1. **Is the word positive or negative?** Using the context of the passage, determine whether the unfamiliar word is a positive or negative term.

If a word is used in a positive context, you can eliminate the answer choices that are negative. In the preceding example, you can guess that the word *incessant* is used negatively. The phrase *too much for me* suggests that the demands of the job are overwhelming and negative. Thus, you can eliminate choices **d** and **e** because they represent positive terms.

2. **Replace the vocabulary word** with the remaining answer choices, one at a time. Does the choice make sense when you read the sentence? If not, eliminate that choice. In the previous example, choice **a**, *inaccessible*, simply does not make sense in the sentence. Choice **b**, *difficult*, is too general to be a likely synonym. Only choice **c**, *unceasing*, makes sense in the context.

Imaginative Expression: Figurative Language

Looking up words in a dictionary is not always an effective way to understand how writers use them. Sometimes writers use words **figuratively**. Instead of using words literally, they use words in less precise yet more descriptive and imaginative manners for artistic reasons. Take a look at the following examples:

Literal: The headlights lit up the night.

This sentence requires no decoding to understand its meaning, yet it is not the most interesting way to describe what the headlights did.

Figurative: The headlights were like a pair of low-hanging stars scorching away the blackness.

Here the writer uses more imaginative language to let the reader know that the headlights lit up the night. He compares the headlights to stars, which are known for their brightness. He also states that they scorched "away the blackness," which suggests that the headlights replaced the blackness of night with bright light.

There are several common forms of figurative language:

Simile: a comparison of two unlike things, using the words "like" or "as" (examples: "The headlights were like a pair of low-hanging stars." "The headlights were as bright as stars.")

Metaphor: a comparison of two unlike things *without* the words "like" or "as" (example: "The headlights were low-hanging stars.")

Personification: The attribution of human characteristics to inanimate objects (example: "The headlights glared at me with scorn"— headlights cannot feel the human emotion of scorn.)

Hyperbole: a colorful exaggeration ("The headlights were brighter than a gamma ray burst"—while headlights might seem very bright, there are no headlights that are as bright as a gamma ray burst, which is the brightest thing in our universe.)

Paradox: a statement that seems sensible but leads to a conclusion that *seems* senseless (example: "The headlights were so bright that I could not see anything."—headlights are supposed to help you to see, so the idea that they prevented someone from seeing anything seems senseless.)

Synecdoche: a part of something is used to represent the whole (example: "The headlights bore down on me"—headlights alone would not bear down on someone; they need to be attached to a car.)

Euphemism: replacing a harsh, insulting, or unpleasant word or phrase with a milder substitute (example: "After his car skidded off the road and hit a tree, the driver expired."—in this sentence, the term *expired* is a euphemism for the harsher word *died*.)

Idiom: A commonly used figurative phrase with a fixed meaning. While the meanings of other forms of figurative language may be determined by their contexts, idioms require a degree of familiarity to understand. You cannot be expected to familiarize yourself with every known idiom before taking the Praxis Core Reading test, but some of the most common idioms are:

IDIOM	MEANING
A penny for your thoughts.	What are you thinking?
Add insult to injury.	To make matters worse.
At the drop of a hat.	Instantly.
Back to the drawing board.	It is time to start over again.
Barking up the wrong tree.	Searching in the wrong spot.
Beat around the bush.	Delay or avoid addressing the subject.
Bite off more than you can chew.	Take on too difficult or large a job.
Can't judge a book by its cover.	Appearances are deceiving.
Costs an arm and a leg.	Is very expensive.
Hit the nail on the head.	Reach the exact correct conclusion.
Hit the sack.	Go to bed.
Kill two birds with one stone.	Accomplish two tasks at the same time.
Let the cat out of the bag.	Disclose information or secrets.
Piece of cake.	Easy.
Pull the wool over someone's eyes.	Deceive.
Under the weather.	Sick.

Practice

"My son is the light of my life."

12. What figure of speech is used in this sentence?
   a. hyperbole
   b. idiom
   c. euphemism
   d. personification
   e. paradox

This sentence contains the common idiom *light of my life*, meaning *the brightest or happiest thing in my life*, so the answer is choice **b**. The phrase also qualifies as a metaphor since it compares *son* to *life*, but *metaphor* is not an answer choice in this question. The sentence does not make an exaggeration, so *hyperbole* (choice **a**) is not the correct answer. It does not use the phrase *light of my life* to replace a harsh statement—in fact, this is a loving statement—so choice **c** is incorrect. Personification (choice **d**) attributes human characteristics to something non-human, but this phrase does the opposite of that (comparing the human *son* to the non-human *light*). It does not use language to reach a seemingly illogical conclusion, so the sentence does not contain a paradox (choice **e**) either.

"The music was light, golden streams of honey."

13. The phrase *was light, golden streams of honey* means the music was

a. too harsh and bright.

b. very indistinct.

c. unfamiliar but pleasant.

d. more like food than music.

e. delicate and sweet.

In this sentence, the phrase *was light, golden streams of honey* is used metaphorically to indicate delicacy (as indicated by *light*) and sweetness (as indicated by *honey*, a food known for its sweetness), so the correct answer is **e**. Although *light* may suggest bright, the rest of the metaphor does not suggest harshness, so **a** is not the best choice. No aspect of the metaphor implies the music is indistinct (choice **b**) or unfamiliar (choice **c**). Choice **d** takes the phrase too literally.

Integration of Knowledge and Ideas

So far, all of the reading skills discussed in this book have focused on individual texts. However, the Praxis Core Reading test also assesses your ability to comprehend information across multiple materials. For some questions, you will synthesize information across pairs of reading passages. For others you will examine how data in visual representations—charts, tables, and graphs—enhances your understanding and comprehension of accompanying reading passages. You will also think about how information in a passage might relate to ideas beyond the printed page.

For the most part, the skills involved in integrating information and ideas across paired passages and passage/visual representation combinations are very similar to those you already have studied in this book. These questions will expect you to identify supporting details, draw inferences, compare and contrast, and assess arguments. However, you will also be expected to think beyond the provided texts and visual representations to consider how these materi-

als might reflect or be put to use in situations beyond the material provided in the Praxis Core Reading test. To answer such questions, you will have to draw on the experiences and knowledge you accumulated before ever opening this book.

Get the Picture: Visual Representations

After reading and answering questions pertaining to standard reading comprehension passages, you may feel as though you've been thrown a curve ball the first time you encounter a chart, table, and graph on the Praxis Core Reading test. Don't fret, though, because such visual representations will function very similarly to any detail or idea you read in any standard reading passage. Just think of these charts, tables, and graphs as additional supporting details to deepen your understanding of the accompanying passages' main ideas.

Visual representations differ from standard supporting details because they present quantitative information, which is anything that can be represented in numbers, such as amount, time, proportion, and score. Three types of visual representations are:

Charts: Represent quantitative data with bars, lines, and pie pieces.

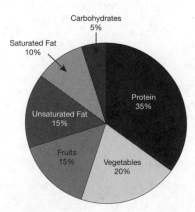

Consumption for a Balanced Diet

Tables: Represent quantitative data in headed columns and/or rows.

MONTHLY HOUSEHOLD ENERGY BILL COST FOR 2014	
MONTH	COST
January	$142.84
February	$156.75
March	$135.10
April	$120.19
May	$ 99.65
June	$101.19
July	$124.77
August	$122.97
September	$101.31
October	$ 88.12
November	$101.34
December	$111.48

Graphs: Represent quantitative data with points and/or lines on a grid.

U.S. Population Growth in the First Decade of the 21ˢᵗ Century

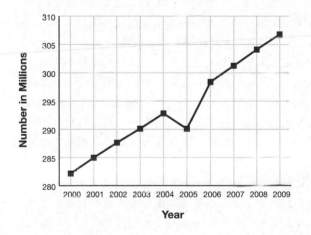

To answer the questions that accompany passage/visual representation pairs, you will draw on the main idea, inference, interpretation, and analytical skills you've learned in the earlier sections of this book. Practice now by reading the following passage and answering the questions that follow.

While few would argue that Alfred Hitchcock created his most enduring works in Hollywood, he had a very prolific filmmaking career in his home country before making his most celebrated classics: *Rear Window, Vertigo, North by Northwest, Psycho,* and *The Birds.* In fact, he made a staggering 23 films in Great Britain in the brief 15-year span before coming to the states to adapt Daphne du Maurier's Rebecca for producer David O. Selznick in 1939. Only a few of Hitchcock's British films are well-known among casual cinema buffs (*The Lady Vanishes, The 39 Steps, The Man Who Knew Too Much*), yet his early work displays the same mastery of suspense, editing, and audience-friendly experimentation that defined his definitive work.

ALFRED HITCHCOCK'S FILMS 1935–1945		
RELEASE YEAR	**FILM**	**NATION OF PRODUCTION**
1935	*The 39 Steps*	Great Britain
1935	*Secret Agent*	
1936	*Sabotage*	
1938	*Young and Innocent*	
1938	*The Lady Vanishes*	
1939	*Jamaica Inn*	
1940	*Rebecca*	
1940	*Foreign Correspondent*	United States
1941	*Mr. and Mrs. Smith*	
1941	*Suspicion*	
1942	*Saboteur*	
1943	*Shadow of a Doubt*	
1944	*Lifeboat*	
1945	*Spellbound*	

14. The main purpose of the table is to
   a. provide a filmography spanning Alfred Hitchcock's entire career.
   b. prove that Alfred Hitchcock actually made his most enduring work in Great Britain.
   c. show that Hitchcock's British films were not adaptations of books as his American ones were.
   d. indicate how moving from Great Britain to the United States affected Hitchcock's work.
   e. outline Alfred Hitchcock's work immediately before and after he came to the United States.

The correct answer is choice **e**. This table shows the names of the films Alfred Hitchcock made in the years immediately before and after he came to the United States. The passage indicates that Hitchcock was making films in Great Britain for fifteen years before coming to the United States and mentions films that are not included in the table, so the films it contains do not encompass his entire filmography (choice **a**). Although the table includes films Hitchcock made in Great Britain that the author of the passage describes as "well-known," its limited number of films does not support the idea that he made his most enduring movies in Great Britain (choice **b**). The passage states that Hitchcock's first American film was an adaptation, but neither the passage nor the table indicate whether any of his other films were adaptations of books (choice **c**). This table only includes the names, years, and geographical origins of Hitchcock's films; it does not provide enough information to draw any conclusions about how the move from Great Britain to the United States affected his work (choice **d**).

15. Which conclusion about Hitchcock's career is best supported in the table above?

    a. Hitchcock was much more prolific when he was working in his home country than he was after coming to the United States.

    b. Hitchcock did not begin making his most celebrated classics as soon as he came to the United States.

    c. Hitchcock's first films made in the United States are generally regarded as artistic failures.

    d. Hitchcock did not create a memorable or successful film before he made *The 39 Steps* in 1935.

    e. Hitchcock's main reason for coming to the United States was to work with his idol, David O. Selznick.

The correct answer is choice **b**. None of the films the author defines as Hitchcock's "most celebrated classics"—*Rear Window*, *Vertigo*, *North by Northwest*, *Psycho*, and *The Birds*—were made during his first five years in the United States. Therefore, the reader can draw the conclusion that he did not instantly begin making his most celebrated films as soon as he came to the United States. According to the table, Hitchcock only made one more film in his first five years in the United States than he did in the five years before he arrived, so it is an exaggeration to conclude that he was "much more prolific" in the United States than he was in Great Britain (choice **a**). While Hitchcock did not make any of the films the author defines as his "most celebrated classics" immediately upon coming to the United States, there is no reason to believe his early American films were "artistic failures" (choice **c**), nor is it reasonable to conclude the same about the films that preceded the ones in this chart (choice **d**). Neither the passage nor the table implies that Selznick was Hitchcock's idol (choice **e**).

Examining Claims

Some essays intend to inform the reader by imparting concrete facts, ideas, and details. Others are written to put forth opinions. These are argumentative essays. Even though the author's personal opinion about a topic is the driving force behind an argumentative essay, that opinion will not be very convincing if the author does not provide reliable facts, ideas, and details to support her or his stance. Those facts, details, and ideas will be most convincing if they come from reliable sources the author identifies in the essay so the reader knows the author did not merely making up those claims. On the Praxis Core Reading test, you will analyze claims to evaluate how they support central arguments and whether or not they are logical.

Identifying Relationships

The most essential way to evaluate a claim in an argumentative essay is to figure out how it relates to the other ideas in the piece. Accomplishing this task requires some critical thinking on your part, but it also requires you to remember some essential types of relationships:

- **Cause and effect**, in which one idea is the result of another
  Example: Constantly running an air conditioner [**cause**] during the summer may make you more comfortable, but you should be prepared for the elevated electricity bills that will follow [**effect**].
- **Problem and solution**, in which one idea resolves another
  Example: The rising cost of gasoline is causing the cost of produce to rise as well [**problem**], so planting a garden in your own backyard may be a cost-effective alternative [**solution**].
- **Contrasting views**, in which one view contradicts another
  Example: As the education provided in public schools continues to come under fire, many

parents are shouting that private schooling is the only option [**view**]. However, the exorbitant tuitions of private schools clearly leave them less viable options than public schools for most families [**contrasting view**].

- **Supporting evidence**, in which one idea supports another

  Example: The dire effects of climate change are already more than detectable in the United States [**main idea**], as the recent droughts on the west coast are making troublingly clear [**supporting evidence**].

- **Explanation**, in which one idea explains or defines another

  Example: A cell phone is indispensible in this age of constant communication [**idea**] because it enables you to respond to messages no matter where you are [**explanation**].

On the Praxis Core Reading test, you will identify the relationship among ideas within individual reading passages and across paired passages. Here are some examples of identifying the relationship among ideas questions:

- *Which of the following statements best describes the relationship between the two passages?*
- *Unlike the author of Passage 2, the author of Passage 1 mentions . . .*
- *Which of the following specific strategies mentioned by the author of Passage 1 is exemplified in Passage 2?*

Analyzing the Evidence

Now that you know the various ways ideas relate to each other in argumentative essays, you can start thinking about the effectiveness of those relationships. No just any example, viewpoint, or detail supports a claim. It has to be relevant and taken from a reliable source.

Relevant details pertain directly to the main idea of an argumentative essay. They do not go off on tangents. Sometimes the relevance of a detail will not be immediately apparent; it will be clear only after reading the essay in full. However, poorly constructed arguments may include details that have little or nothing to do with the topic. Irrelevant details weaken an argument by softening its focus. They may even cause readers to question the reliability of the relevant details.

A detail does not have to be inaccurate to be irrelevant. For example, it is true that Alaska is the northernmost state in the United States, yet that detail has little relevance to an argument in favor of a particular candidate for the mayor of Anchorage, Alaska. Irrelevant information can also play a deliberately deceitful role in arguments if the author includes it to deceive the reader or confuse him with information that seems relevant but is not.

> **Example:** I have never trusted the Green Party, because I've never liked the face of a Green Party candidate.

The explanation in this statement may *seem* relevant since it refers to the topic of the Green Party, yet the writer's superficial assessments of the looks of Green Party candidates has nothing to do with the *complete* main idea: *the trustworthiness of Green Party candidates*. This detail is irrelevant and weakens the writer's argument that the Green Party is untrustworthy.

Claims cited from unreliable sources may also weaken an argument.

> **Examples of reliable sources:**
> newspapers
> up-to-date encyclopedias
> scholarly articles
> books published by university presses
> government websites (those with the
>   domain .gov)
> educational institution websites (those with the
>   domain .edu)

Examples of unreliable sources:
blogs
Wikipedia
online forums
excessively biased articles
magazines and books published before the
    most recent data was collected
books published by vanity presses

To be able to evaluate the reliability of evidence, the reader needs to know the source from which it was cited.

- As famed physicist Stephen Hawking wrote in his *A Brief History of Time*, humankind did not properly understand the electron until Paul Dirac proffered a groundbreaking theory in 1928.
- The number of Americans at risk for diabetes is now up to 86 million (American Medical Association).

Even if a claim taken from an unreliable source is true, it may weaken the overall argument since the reader may not trust its truthfulness. The strongest claims are completely relevant to the topic and cited from trustworthy sources. Keeping this in mind will help you to answer questions about whether evidence strengthens, weakens, or is relevant to arguments on the Praxis Core Reading test. Examples of these kinds of questions include:

- *Which of the following, if true, would most weaken the implied argument?*
- *The passage supports which of the following claims?*

Determining Logical Assumptions

A strong argument must be rooted in logic. Logic is the scientific process behind inference and arguments. A logically sound argument can be tested in the same way that any sound scientific principle can be. This test is known as a **syllogism**, and it comprises three key components: the major premise, the minor premise, and the conclusion. Greek philosopher Aristotle invented this concept when he posed this logical sequence:

All men are mortal. (**major premise**)
Socrates is a man. (**minor premise**)
Therefore, Socrates is mortal. (**conclusion**)

This syllogism is logical because the minor premise can be tested against the major premise. However, Aristotle would have made an illogical assumption had his syllogism read:

All men are mortal.
Socrates is mortal.
Socrates is a man.

Indeed, Socrates was a man, but this statement still makes the error of assuming that only men are mortal. What about women? What about animals? Since you will have to determine the logical assumptions upon which arguments and conclusions are based on the Praxis Core Reading test, you should become familiar with some of the common ways in which writers make assumptions that logic does not support.

Ad hominem, a personal attack on anyone whose opinion is opposite of yours (**example:** You might not agree with me if you're a fool.)
Circular reasoning, a claim that is the same as its conclusion (**example:** Gluttonous people suffer poor health because they eat too much.)
Fallacies of composition, which assume that what is true of the part is true of the whole (**example:** That song is beautiful, so the album it's on must be great.)
Hasty generalization, a thoughtless jump to a conclusion (**example:** I saw a photo of that house, so I know I would love to live there.)
Incomplete comparison, a mock comparison that fails to include one of the items being compared (**example:** This soft drink is better.)

Moral equivalence, a comparison between a minor wrong and a major wrong (**example:** Losing my glasses was like receiving a death sentence.)

Post hoc ergo, which mistakes a sequence of events for a cause and effect relationship (**example:** The phone rang after I turned on the lamp, so turning on the lamp must have caused the phone to ring.)

Slippery slope, assuming one act will inevitably lead to another (**example:** If I invite him over this weekend, he'll want to come over every weekend.)

Drawing Conclusions

The skill of making inferences was discussed earlier in this book. Making inferences is often confused with drawing conclusions, but they are not the same thing. While making inferences requires you to refer to *explicitly stated details and facts* in a text to reach a conclusion, drawing conclusions does not. You may recall the example used to illustrate making inferences:

A stranger at the supermarket may say, "I am buying steaks, which I'll cook tonight, but my wife makes dinner three nights a week."

Explicitly Stated Clue

1. . . . *I'll cook tonight, but my wife makes dinner three nights a week.*
2. *I am buying steaks, which I'll cook tonight . . .*

Logical Inference

1. The man and his wife share household duties.
2. The man and his wife are not vegetarians.

Now, what if you also noticed that the man was buying broccoli. He might not say "I'm cooking steaks and broccoli for dinner" explicitly, but the fact that he is cooking dinner tonight may make you draw the conclusion that he will be serving broccoli with the steaks tonight. You *could* be wrong, but it would be a fairly logical next step after his purchase of the broccoli. When answering drawing conclusions questions on the Praxis Core Reading test, the process of elimination is an important method for determining the most logical conclusion.

At the supermarket, you meet a man who is purchasing broccoli and who says he is cooking dinner that night. Therefore you might conclude that he

a. is cooking broccoli for dinner.
b. is going to give the broccoli away.
c. purchased the broccoli by mistake.
d. is saving the broccoli for a later date.
e. considers broccoli his favorite vegetable.

The correct answer is choice **a.** Any of the conclusions described in the answer choices *could* be true, but considering the information provided—the man is buying broccoli and he is cooking dinner that night—the one that makes the most sense is choice **a.**

Now read the following passage and answer the practice questions testing your ability to examine claims.

Commuting to an office was once the workforce norm, but communication technologies such as e-mail and Skype have made working from home a desirable and common option for an increasingly large number of today's workers. Working from home—or telecommuting—has a number of benefits that working in an office simply does not offer. The time clock does not rule telecommuters, forcing them to complete their duties between nine and five. Telecommuters can perform their duties according to their own schedules. Plus, they don't have to work with managers breathing down their necks or with potentially distracting coworkers. It's no surprise that 47% of telecommuters are "very satisfied" with their work situations, as opposed to the paltry 27% of traditional commuters who are "very satisfied" with theirs. Job satisfaction is not just a boon to the worker; it also benefits the employer, because when workers are happier with their jobs, they are more productive. Furthermore, when they do not have to punch out at 5:00 P.M., Monday through Friday, employees are more likely to work late nights or weekends until their projects are completed.

16. Which of the following statements best describes the relationship between telecommuting and job satisfaction?

   a. Telecommuting is a problem and job satisfaction is a solution.

   b. Telecommuting is a cause and job satisfaction is an effect.

   c. Telecommuting is an idea and job satisfaction is supporting evidence.

   d. Telecommuting is an idea and job satisfaction is an explanation.

   e. Telecommuting is a view and job satisfaction is a contrasting view.

17. In order to evaluate the validity of the author's claim regarding the percentage of telecommuters who are "very satisfied" with their jobs, it would be most helpful to know which of the following?

   a. the companies that employ these telecommuters

   b. the names of the people polled

   c. how many people are "somewhat satisfied"

   d. the source of the statistic

   e. the definition of "very satisfied"

18. Which off the following is an unstated assumption the author of the passage makes?

   a. Skype is a more useful communication technology than e-mail is.

   b. Working from home did not exist before communication technologies such as Skype and e-mail.

   c. Companies should ban traditional commuting altogether.

   d. Traditional commuters will go home at 5:00 even if they have work to complete.

   e. There are no benefits to spending one's day with coworkers.

19. Which of the following conclusions can be made from the passage?

   a. Companies that make telecommuting an option for their employees are likelier to be successful than ones that don't.

   b. Traditional commuting will likely cease to exist sometime in the near future.

   c. Companies that rely on traditional commuters will have to make the work day longer to compete with ones that allow telecommuting.

   d. Telecommuting has a negative impact on the economy, because it means the sale of fewer cars and less gasoline.

   e. Office managers at companies that do not allow telecommuting are incapable of increasing office productivity.

Answers

16. b. In this passage, telecommuting and job satisfaction share a cause-and-effect relationship, because job satisfaction is the result of telecommuting. That means telecommuting is the opposite of a problem (choice **b**). Since telecommuting and job satisfaction share a complementary, not contrasting, relationship, choice **e** can be eliminated.

17. d. Statistics are hard to trust if the reader does not know from where the statistics were taken. For all the reader of this passage knows, the author could have taken these statistics from an unreliable blog or even made them up himself. Including the source of the statistics would help the reader to evaluate their validity. Knowing the names of the people polled (choice **b**), the companies for which they work (choice **a**), or how many people were "somewhat satisfied" (choice **c**) would have little bearing on the validity of these statistics. The term "very satisfied" is fairly self-explanatory, so **e** is not the best answer choice.

18. d. The author makes the point that telecommuters who do not have to punch a time clock at 5:00 are likely to work past that time, with the implication that this is different from how traditional commuters approach their work. So, you can conclude that the author probably assumes traditional commuters will go home at 5:00 even if they have work to complete. However, the author never implies a comparison between Skype and e-mail (choice **a**) or suggests that working from home did not exist before communication technologies such as these (choice **b**), which is untrue anyway. Although the author clearly favors telecommuting over traditional commuting, choice **c** is an extreme assumption. The same can be said of choice **e**, even though the author mentions one downside of sharing an office with coworkers.

19. a. The author explains that telecommuters are more satisfied with their jobs and more productive than traditional commuters, which should result in a company with less employee turnover and greater output than those that do not allow telecommuting. So, it is fairly logical to conclude that companies

that make telecommuting an option for their employees are likelier to be successful than ones that don't, even though the author does not cite any explicit evidence to support this conclusion. However, it is extreme to conclude that traditional commuting is likely to cease to exist altogether (choice **b**), since many jobs simply cannot be done from home. The author does not suggest that companies with employees who do not telecommute will have to make the work day longer (choice **c**), nor is there any discussion of the impact of telecommuting on the economy at all (choice **d**). Although the author mentions a downside of office managers, choice **e** is still an extreme conclusion to draw.

Thinking between and outside the Boxes

We looked at the relationships between ideas in passages and visual representations and within individual passages. Now you will learn how you will have to synthesize ideas between and beyond paired passages on the Praxis Core Reading test.

The paired passages are never combined randomly on the test. They will always share a common component, whether it is a similar theme, idea, attitude, or approach. However, since the two passages are still distinct from each other, they will never be completely alike. Recognizing the similarities and differences between paired passages is the essence of answering the questions that follow them. You should also be able to comprehend how one passage develops on the ideas of the other and how the two authors' attitudes or approaches are similar or different. Recognizing relationships, comparing and contrasting, and comprehending an author's attitude should already be in your skill set if you've read the previous sections in this chapter. You only have to apply them to a pair of passages instead of a single text.

Example

Passage 1

Urban development is running out of control in our fair city. Developers eyeball every last patch of land as a potential cash source. Never mind that there might be trees on the spot. Their only goal is to build, build, build, regardless of whether or not the community even has the resources to support the increased population new properties attract. Where will these people park their cars? How much will they overtax our already overtaxed public transportation systems? Of course, these are the concerns of my community's citizens, not the concerns of the developers who seek to exploit our land.

Passage 2

It has become almost fashionable to decry the building and extending of properties in our community. Developers are constantly portrayed as greed-motivated, immoral monsters. However, isn't a populated community a strong community? Is there a touch of fear in the complaints about "over-development"—the fear of new neighbors, the fear of sharing? Critics of development use terms like "my community," as if the community is these individuals' private, personal property. The community belongs to us all: we who have lived here for years and we who have arrived recently. Isn't a welcoming spirit the essence of America?

Here are two passages about the same topic—urban development—yet each author has an entirely different, even contrasting, opinion on the topic. It is also clear that Passage 2 is a reaction to Passage 1, not because it is placed second in this particular sequence, but because it refers to details in Passage 1, such as the author's use of the phrase "my community." What other connections between the two passages can you discern?

What's Next?

You will also think about what happens beyond the end of the given texts to make predictions about similar situations that may occur. Consider Passage 1 in the precious section again. Its author opposes "out of control" urban development in his city. Based on his ideas and attitude, what might he do next if, for example, a developer buys a grassy area in his neighborhood and earmarks it as the location of a high-rise apartment building? Maybe he will attend a town hall meeting to voice his displeasure with the situation. Maybe he will organize a protest of the construction. These are both reasonable predictions, considering the given circumstance and the author's opposition to urban development.

What's Beyond?

The Praxis Core Reading test also tests your ability to apply ideas in texts to situations other than those described within them. Returning once again to Passage 1, we know that the author has strong opinions about urban development. We know that he values nature, because he implies that areas containing nothing more than trees should not be turned into construction sites. So, what is the likeliest way he would react if he heard that loggers plan to raze a forest in a completely different area of the world? This is a situation totally separate from the one he describes in Passage 1, yet there is enough information in that passage to conclude that he would be opposed to loggers razing that forest. This is an example of the kind of outside-the-box thinking you will have to perform in order to answer questions that require you to apply ideas presented in a reading selection to other situations.

Now read the paired passages and answer the practice questions that follow.

Passage 1

Can advertising be art? Perhaps that depends on your definition of art, because many critics draw the distinction that anything created primarily for financial gain cannot be art and warrants no further consideration, and financial gain is the inciting factor in the creation of all advertisements. However, this does not necessarily mean that the execution cannot still be quite artful. In fact, some of the most challenging artists of our time—including experimental filmmaker David Lynch—have worked in advertising. This fact alone may not be revelatory since even the finest artists have to pay their bills, but the fact that Lynch's experimental touch has extended to his work in advertising suggests that advertising is not immune to true artistry.

Passage 2

In 1971, an executive named Bill Backer working for the McCann-Erickson agency created a landmark moment in television. The commercial he created for Coca-Cola found people of all races and nationalities united on a hilltop to sing a message of peace and unity. Granted, this advertisement in which people set aside their differences to voice their desire to "buy the world a Coke" was created to sell soft drinks, but to ignore the deeper importance of it would be incredibly shortsighted. Consider that just a few years earlier, Caucasian and African American people were not even allowed to stand side by side in an ad. Despite what cynics might say, this advertisement was not just about selling soda—it was a significant reflection of America's evolving attitudes about race.

20. The authors of the passages agree that
   a. advertising does not have to be motivated by consumerism.
   b. advertising is capable of being genuine art.
   c. advertising can have effects beyond consumerism.
   d. advertising is most effective when controlled by true artists.
   e. advertising has made a monumental impact on the world.

21. Based on information in the passages, what would most likely happen if an advertisement featured a brand-new technological innovation?
   a. Critics would rethink their negative opinions of advertising.
   b. It would immediately be used in a major motion picture.
   c. More fine artists would consider taking jobs in advertising.
   d. It would be copied in a number of other advertisements.
   e. Some critics would not recognize it because of where it appeared.

Answers

20. c. The author of Passage 1 discusses how advertising is capable of being art, while the author of Passage 2 discusses an advertisement that displayed how America's attitudes about race were changing. Both passages show how advertising can have effects beyond consumerism. However, both authors acknowledge that consumerism is always the main motivation behind any advertisement, so choice a is incorrect. Only Passage 1 addresses the topic of art, so choices b and d can be eliminated. Neither passage suggests that advertising can have a monumental impact on the world (choice e).

21. e. Both authors agree that some critics dismiss advertising outright, so it is likely that those critics would not recognize the value of the innovation simply because it appeared in an advertisement. Such critics, who are immovable about the artistic possibilities of advertising, are not likely to rethink their opinions because of one innovation (choice **a**). While it is very possible that the innovation might be used in a motion picture (choice **b**) or other advertisements (choice **d**), neither passage contains details that support this conclusion. The passages do not support choice **c** either.

Test-Taking Tips

Now that you have reviewed the components that will help you understand and analyze what you read, you are ready to consider some specific test-taking strategies. The following techniques will help you read the Praxis Core passages quickly and effectively and answer the multiple-choice questions strategically, so that you can boost your score.

Reading passages for a standardized test is different from reading at home. For one thing, you have a time limit. You have 85 minutes to complete 56 questions. This means that you have about 90 seconds to answer each question! And the time you spend reading each passage detracts from the time you have to answer questions. Here are some basic guidelines for keeping you moving through the test in a time-efficient way:

- **Spend no more than two minutes on a question.** Circle difficult questions and return to them if you have time.
- **Skim and answer short passages quickly.** Short passages have only one or two questions, so you should move through them with speed. Give yourself a bit more time for long passages that are followed by four or more questions.
- **Guess, if necessary.** The Praxis Core Reading test does not penalize you for wrong answers. Make sure to answer each question, even if you think you might return to it later.
- **Target the first part of the passage.** The first third of many reading passages is packed with essential information. Often you can answer main-idea questions based on the information contained at the start of a passage. Likewise, for longer passages of 200 words, you will often find what each paragraph is about from its first two sentences.
- **Locate details, but don't learn them.** Detail-heavy portions of passages can be dense and difficult to read. Don't spend precious time rereading and absorbing details—just make sure you know where to find them in the passage. That way, you can locate a detail if a question asks about it.

Eliminating Wrong Answers

Test makers use "distracters" in test questions that can confuse you into choosing an incorrect answer. Familiarizing yourself with some of the common distraction techniques that test makers use will increase your chances of eliminating wrong answers and selecting the right answer.

- **The choice that does too little.** This distracter type often follows main-idea questions. The answer choice makes a true statement, but it is too narrow or too specific to be a main idea of the passage. It zeros in on select elements or supporting ideas of a passage instead of expressing a main idea.
- **The choice that does too much.** This distracter also relates to main-idea questions. Unlike the type just discussed, this answer choice goes too far beyond the scope of the passage. It may be a true statement, but the information in the text cannot support it.

- **The close, but not close enough, choice.** This type of answer is very close to the correct answer, but is wrong in some detail.
- **The off-topic choice.** Test takers often find this answer choice the easiest to spot and eliminate. It may have nothing at all to do with the passage itself.
- **The irrelevant choice.** This option uses language found in the text—elements, ideas, phrases, or words—but does not answer the question correctly. These distracters are tricky because test designers bait them with a good deal of information from the passage.

- **The contradictory choice.** This answer may in fact be opposite or nearly opposite to the correct answer. If two of the answer choices seem contrary to each other, there is a good chance that one of these choices will be correct.
- **The choice that is too broad.** This distracter relates to supporting detail questions. Although it may be a true statement, it is too general and does not address the specifics the question is looking for.

TYPES OF READERS

How you approach a reading passage may show what kind of reader you are. Each of the approaches listed here has some merit. When you practice reading passages as part of your study plan, experiment with some of these different styles to see what works best for you.

- The **concentrator** reads the passage thoroughly before looking at the questions. By concentrating on the passage, you can locate answers quickly if you don't already know the answer.
- The **skimmer** skims the passage before looking at the questions. Once you understand how the passage is arranged, you can go back and find the answers.
- The **cautious reader** reads the questions and answer choices first. Because you know what questions to expect, you can be on the lookout as you read the passage.
- The **game player** reads the questions first and answers them by guessing. By guessing the answers, you become familiar with the questions and can recognize the answers when you read the passage.
- The **educated guesser** reads the questions first, but not the answers. When you find the answer in the passage, you can quickly look among the answer choices for the right one.
- The **efficiency expert** reads the questions first, looking for key words that indicate where an answer is located. By doing this, you can skim the passage for answers instead of reading the whole passage.

Look Out for Absolutes

Reading comprehension questions that use words that represent absolutes should alert you to the likely presence of clever distracters among the answer choices. Two or more answers may be close contenders—they may reflect language from the passage and be true in general principle, but not true in all circumstances. Beware of these commonly used absolutes in reading questions:

best	most closely	always	all
primarily	most nearly	never	none

Five-Step Approach to Answering Reading Questions

If the task of quickly reading and understanding dense passages is too daunting, here is a quick approach that you can use. Feel free to adapt it to your style or change the order of the steps, but try to incorporate each of the five steps somewhere in your process.

Step 1—Preview

To get an idea of the content and organization of a passage, begin by skimming it. With practice, you will quickly discern topic sentences and key adjectives. Often, the first two sentences in a paragraph are topic sentences—they will tell you what a paragraph is about. If the passage is several paragraphs long, read the first and last sentence of each paragraph. You can't depend 100% on this technique, though; use your judgment to determine whether a sentence is truly a topic sentence.

Step 2—Skim the Questions

Quickly take in the question or questions that follow a passage, marking important words and phrases. Don't bother reading the multiple-choice answers. You simply want to gather clues about what to look for when you read.

Step 3—Read Actively

Although you do not want to memorize or analyze the passage, you do need to read it. Look for information that applies to the questions you skimmed. Identify topic sentences, main ideas, or phrases that reveal the author's point of view. Check for important names, dates, or difficult words. Note transitions and phrases, such as *however, most importantly, but,* or *except,* that help you to follow the author's direction or the organization of the passage.

As you read, ask yourself some of the following questions:

- *What is the main theme or idea in the passage?*
- *What is the author's purpose or goal?*
- *How do ideas in the passage relate to the main idea?*
- *What is the tone or mood of the passage? Informative? Critical? Playful?*
- *How is the passage structured?*

Step 4—Review the Passage

After actively reading the passage, take a few seconds to look over the main idea, the topic sentences, or other elements you have marked. Ask yourself what you have just read. Your goal is not to understand the passage thoroughly, but rather to get the gist of it. Quickly summarize it in your own words.

Don't get hung up on difficult phrasing or technical elements in the passage that you might not even need to know. Instead of focusing on absorbing specific details, just know the location of details in the passage. Remember, you can refer back to the passage several times while answering the questions. Focus on identifying the general direction, main ideas, organization, purpose, and point of view of the passage, rather than learning details.

Step 5—Answer the Questions

Now it's time to answer the questions. Base your answers only on what is stated and implied in the passage. Some answer choices will try to trick you with information that is beyond the scope of the passage. Read all five multiple-choice answers before rushing to choose one. Eliminate as many choices as possible. If you eliminate three of the answer choices, reach your decision quickly between the remaining two. After you have timed yourself working with the practice tests in this book, you will have a good idea of your time limitations.

Using the Five-Step Approach

This practice applies the five-step approach to a sample passage. You may want to review the five-step approach before you begin.

Sample Passage

Read the following passage to answer questions 1 and 2.

In his famous study of myth, *The Hero with a Thousand Faces*, Joseph Campbell writes about the archetypal hero who has ventured outside the boundaries of the village and, after many trials and adventures, has returned with the boon that will save or enlighten his fellows. Like Carl Jung, Campbell believes that the story of the hero is part of the collective unconscious of all humankind. He likens the returning hero to the sacred or tabooed personage described by James Frazier in *The Golden Bough*. Such an individual must, in many instances of myth, be insulated from the rest of society, "not merely for his own sake but for the sake of others; for since the virtue of holiness is, so to say, a powerful explosive which the smallest touch can detonate, it is necessary in the interest of the general safety to keep it within narrow bounds."

There is much similarity between the archetypal hero who has journeyed into the wilderness and the poet who has journeyed into the realm of imagination. Both places are dangerous and full of wonders, and both, at their deepest levels, are journeys that take place in the kingdom of the unconscious mind, a place that, in Campbell's words, "goes down into unsuspected Aladdin caves. There not only jewels but dangerous jinn abide. . . ."

1. Based on the passage, which of the following best describes the story Campbell's returning hero and Frazier's sacred or tabooed personage will likely tell?
   a. a radically mind-altering story
   b. a story that will terrify people to no good end
   c. a warning of catastrophe to come
   d. a story based on a dangerous lie
   e. a parable aimed at establishing a religious movement

2. Which of the following is the most accurate definition of the word *boon* as it is used in the passage?
   a. present
   b. blessing
   c. charm
   d. prize
   e. curse

Let's follow the five-step approach to walk through these questions.

Preview

Read the first sentence of each paragraph: "In his famous study of myth . . ." and "There is much similarity. . . ." Because of the length of the sentences in each paragraph, you may or may not wish to read the ending sentences in each one. Underline the topic sentences.

Skim the Questions

Now, skim the questions and mark them.

■ Based on the passage, which of the following best describes the story that will likely be told by

Campbell's returning hero and Frazier's sacred or tabooed personage? An important word in this question is *story*. Also note the use of the absolute, *best*. This means that more than one answer choice may be true, but only one is the *best* answer. Circle or mark these terms. You may also notice that this is an inference question; it asks you to infer something based on the information of the passage.

■ Which of the following is the most accurate definition of the word *boon* as it is used in the passage? This is a vocabulary question that measures your literal comprehension. The most important elements in this question are *definition* and *boon*. Mark these words. Again, note that the question asks for the *most accurate* definition —more than one answer choice may apply, but only one offers the best answer.

Read Actively

Now, read actively, marking the passage. The following marked passage provides examples of which things you might choose to circle or underline in the passage:

> In his famous study of myth, *The Hero with a Thousand Faces*, Joseph Campbell writes about the archetypal hero who has ventured outside the boundaries of the village and, after many **trials** and **adventures**, has returned with the boon that will **save** or **enlighten** his fellows. Like Carl Jung, Campbell believes that the story of the hero is part of the collective unconscious of all humankind. He likens the returning hero to the **sacred or tabooed personage** described by James Frazier in *The Golden Bough*. [**comparison here**] Such an individual must, in many instances of myth, be insulated from the rest of society, "not merely for his own sake but for the sake of others; for since the virtue of holiness is, so to say, a powerful explosive which the smallest touch can detonate, it is necessary

in the interest of the general safety to keep it within narrow bounds."

> There is much similarity between the archetypal hero who has journeyed into the wilderness and the poet who has journeyed into the realm of imagination. [**comparison here**] Both places are **dangerous** and **full of wonders**, and both, at their deepest levels, are journeys that take place into the kingdom of the **unconscious mind**, a place that, in Campbell's words, "goes down into unsuspected Aladdin caves. There not only jewels but dangerous jinn abide. . . ."

Like many reading comprehension passages, the sample text features topic sentences that begin each paragraph. Then, the paragraphs become detail-heavy. Although you may have marked different terms in the sample passage, you should underscore the word *boon* in the first sentence because it applies to the second question. The information you need in order to infer the answer to the first question (the story that Campbell's hero and Frazier's sacred or tabooed personage are likely to tell) is also contained in the first paragraph. The quotation at the end of the first paragraph is dense and somewhat difficult to read and understand. Don't bother rereading difficult parts of a passage—in this case, you can answer the questions without completely comprehending the quotation.

Your system of marking this passage may vary. You may underline topic sentences, circle words that cue important details, or put a star beside words that indicate the author's attitude or purpose. The important thing is to mark the passage in a way that will help you answer the questions.

Depending on the answers you are seeking, you may jot down notes or make observations as you read:

■ Regarding the main idea, it seems that the author is proposing that the act of creating is similar to the journey undertaken by Campbell's mythic hero—both make a kind of passage and return with a vital message for others. (This would apply to a question that asks you to summarize the main idea.)

- The passage uses comparison to describe Campbell's study of myth: It compares Jung and Campbell, Campbell and Frazier, and the hero and the poet. (This would apply to a question about the organization of the passage.)
- The author cites quotes by Campbell to support the main idea. (This would apply to an evaluation question in which you are asked to look at the strengths and weaknesses of the author's argument.)
- The tone of the passage is measured and analytical. (This would apply to a question about the author's attitude or point of view.)

Review the Passage

Take a few seconds to summarize in your own words what the passage is about. Look again at how you have marked the passage.

The passage is about Joseph Campbell's mythic hero and how his journey and his return home relate to the experience of a poet.

Answer the Questions

Look again at question 1:

1. Based on the passage, which of the following best describes the story that Campbell's returning hero and Frazier's sacred or tabooed personage will likely tell?
   a. a radically mind-altering story
   b. a story that will terrify people to no good end
   c. a warning of catastrophe to come
   d. a story based on a dangerous lie
   e. a parable aimed at establishing a religious movement

The passage states that the hero's tale will *save and enlighten* his fellows, but that it will also be *dangerous*. Choice **a** is the best answer. You can infer from the information of the passage that such a story would surely be radically mind-altering. Choice **b** is directly contradicted in the passage. If the hero's tale would terrify people to no good end, it could not possibly be enlightening. There is nothing in the passage to imply that the tale is a warning of catastrophe, a dangerous lie, or a parable (choices **c**, **d**, and **e**).

Now, look again at question 2:

2. Which of the following is the most accurate definition of the word *boon* as it is used in the passage?
   a. present
   b. blessing
   c. charm
   d. prize
   e. curse

Even if you don't know the dictionary definition of the word *boon*, you can determine its meaning from the context of the passage. You can determine that *boon* is a positive term, because the passage states that the hero's boon will save or enlighten his fellows. Therefore, you can eliminate choice **e**, *curse*, which is negative. You can also guess from the context of the passage that a boon is likely to be intangible, and thus not a concrete *present*, *charm*, or *prize* (choices **a**, **c**, and **d**). Choice **b** offers the most accurate definition of *boon*, which is a timely benefit, favor, or blessing.

Now, take the skills you have learned or honed in this review and apply them to Reading Practice Exam I.

5 ▶ PRAXIS® CORE ACADEMIC SKILLS FOR EDUCATORS: WRITING TEST REVIEW

CHAPTER SUMMARY

Good writing skills are essential to success as a teacher. To be effective both in the classroom and with your colleagues, it's important to be able to communicate ideas clearly and accurately in written English. This chapter reviews the elements of good writing: basic grammar, sentence structure, verb and pronoun agreement, and idiomatic expressions.

The Praxis Core Writing test is divided into two parts. The first part presents multiple-choice questions that measure your ability to identify errors in grammar or sentence structure, and to recognize the correct use of standard written English. You will be given 40 minutes to answer 40 multiple-choice questions. The second part asks you to write two short essays: an **argumentative essay** that takes a stance on a given prompt and uses personal observation and experiences to back it up, and an **informative/explanatory essay** that provides two sources to read, then asks you to use information from both to comment on an issue. You will be given 30 minutes to complete each essay.

The writing topics are designed so that you do not need any specialized knowledge to respond to the prompt. However, you will need to demonstrate that you can organize and support your thoughts effectively in writing. You will be given 30 minutes to create a clear, well-developed essay. The essay portion of the writing test is not designed to showcase creative writing; rather, it focuses on your ability to follow the rules of English grammar, avoid common errors, take a stance on an issue, provide quality examples to make a point, use a piece of writing to cite information from sources, and more.

Multiple-Choice Questions

In the first part of the writing test, you will not do any writing at all. Rather, you will answer multiple-choice questions that measure your knowledge of the basics of grammar, sentence construction, and appropriate word choice, and also your ability to locate errors.

Usage Questions

In these questions, you need to be able to identify errors and oddities in sentences. You will be presented with a sentence that has four underlined words, phrases, or punctuation marks. You will choose the underlined portion that is incorrect. Some sentences are correct. In that case, you would select "No error," choice **e**. None of the sentences has more than one error. Here are some examples:

1. Acid rain <u>looks</u>, feels, even tastes <u>like</u> clean
          a   **b**

    rainwater, but it actually <u>contain</u> high levels
                                      c

    of pollutants. <u>No error</u>
          d   **e**

2. <u>In science fiction</u>, writers <u>have</u> the opportunity
          a   **b**

    <u>to explore</u> and imagine what the world <u>will be</u>
          c   **d**

    like in the future. <u>No error</u>
                            e

Answers
1. **c.** The problem in this sentence is noun and verb agreement. The pronoun *it* (referring to the subject *acid rain*) is singular, so the verb should be singular as well—*contains*.
2. **e.** Because this sentence contains no grammatical, idiomatic, logical, or structural errors, the correct answer is choice **e**.

The underlined words or phrases do not correspond with a list of answer choices **a–e**. Instead, you simply click on your answer choice to highlight it. To alter your highlight, click on another underlined word or phrase in the sentence. If there are no problems in the sentence, click on "No error." Here is an example of what you will see on your computer screen:

> <u>Less</u> teachers attended the conference <u>this year</u>, even though <u>it offered</u> <u>more</u> workshops and seminars. <u>No error</u>

Answer

<u>**Less**</u> teachers attended the conference <u>this year</u>, even though <u>it offered</u> <u>more</u> workshops and seminars. <u>No error</u>

The first underlined choice contains a grammatical error. The modifier *less* describes singular nouns that represent a quantity or degree. The modifier *fewer* would be correct in this context—it describes plural nouns, or things that can be counted.

Sentence Correction

In these questions, you will demonstrate your ability to recognize and correct awkward sentence constructions and other grammatical elements. You will be shown a sentence with one part of it underlined. You will be asked to select one of five possible ways to rephrase the underlined part. Choice **a** always repeats the original phrasing, whereas choices **b**, **c**, **d**, and **e** suggest changes to the underlined portion. Choose the phrasing that creates the most effective sentence with wording that is clear, exact, and without awkwardness or redundancy. If you think the original phrasing is better than the suggested alternatives, select the first answer choice. Here are some examples of this question type.

1. Lee Iacocca, the son of Italian immigrants, <u>worked arduously</u> to reach the top rungs of the Ford Motor Company corporate ladder.
   a. worked arduously
   b. worked arduous
   c. did worked arduously
   d. has work arduously
   e. had worked arduous

2. <u>As an employee, one is eligible</u> for the benefits we worked to attain, including health insurance, life insurance, and a retirement plan.
   a. As an employee, one is eligible
   b. We the employees are either eligible
   c. The employee is eligible
   d. Either the employee is eligible
   c. As employees, we are eligible

Answers

1. a. The sentence does not have any problems in its structure or meaning. Both the verb tense and the use of the adverb *arduously* are correct. Choices **b** and **e** incorrectly use the adjective *arduous*. Options **c** and **d** use the correct adverb but have incorrect verb forms.

2. e. The problem with the original sentence is pronoun agreement. The underlined part of the sentence uses the singular pronoun *one*, which agrees with its singular antecedent *employee*. However, the plural pronoun *we* is used later in the sentence. To make a sentence with pronoun agreement, you must look for a choice that contains the pronoun we and the plural of *employee*.

Research Skills

In these questions, you will recognize the correct and most effective ways to perform research. You will be expected to identify the correct format for citing research sources in bibliographies and within the text of an essay. Such questions will feature citations with underlined portions labeled **a**, **b**, **c**, and **d**. Choice **e** will read <u>no error</u>, which you will select if portions **a**, **b**, **c**, and **d** are all formatted correctly. You will also assess the relevance and credibility of sources for particular research tasks. Each brief question is followed by five possible answer choices. Here are some examples of this question type.

1. The following is a citation of a web page.
   <u>Wilcox, Christie.</u> <u>Thinking Inside The Box:</u>
       a   b
   <u>Insights Into One Of The World's Deadliest</u>
   <u>Venoms.</u> *Discover Magazine.com.* *Discover*
                                     c
   <u>*Magazine*, June 2, 2015.</u> <u>Web. July 20, 2015.</u>
                                     d

   <u>No error</u>
   e

2. Which is the main purpose of cross-checking research?
   a. to make the bibliography more extensive
   b. to present contrasting ideas about a topic
   c. to think more seriously about the topic
   d. to confirm the credibility of research
   e. to prove there is no such thing as an irrefutable fact

Answers

1. b. The segment of the citation labeled **b** is the title of the article, which needs to be placed within quotes to be formatted properly. The rest of the citation is formatted correctly.

2. d. Cross-checking is the method of checking information in more than one source. Information that appears in more than one source is likelier to be credible. While the additional sources checked must be cited in the bibliography, which does make the bibliography more extensive, this is not the main reason for cross-checking, so **a** is not the best answer choice. Discovering contrasting ideas about a topic (choice **b**) might be a consequence of cross-checking, but this is not the main purpose of cross-checking. Likewise, cross-checking might help writers to think more seriously about a topic (choice **c**), but this is not the main purpose of it either. Choice **e** is simply untrue.

Revision-in-Context

In these questions, you will edit and revise passages to strengthen their development, organization, word choice, tone, style, and grammar. You will learn more about these skills in the essay writing section of this book. You will be presented with a passage with numbered sentences, some of which may contain errors. There are three types of revision-in-context questions.

The first type of question repeats a particular sentence from the passage and asks you to choose the best revision of that sentence. Answer choices **a**, **b**, **c**, **d**, and **e** suggest changes to the underlined portion. In some cases, you will have the option of selecting *As it is now*, which will always be choice **a**. Choose this option if the sentence is already correct as it is.

The second type of question also repeats a particular sentence from the passage and asks you to choose the revision most needed. However, none of the words in the repeated sentences are underlined, and the five answer choices are directions for replacing or changing words in the sentences. You will select the direction that best improves the sentence.

The third type of question briefly asks you to select the best addition to the passage from five possible choices.

Here are some examples of these three question types.

(1) Placement on the endangered species list is not a certain death sentence. (2) Animals that the International Union for Conservation of Nature (IUCN) designate "endangered" sometimes increase their population and are removed from the list. (3) <u>Therefore</u>, this does not mean that those animals and the ones that coexist with them face an easy transition. (4) For example, they are reaching numbers that may see them removed from the endangered species list sometime in the near future, but their environment has changed in their absence. (5) On return, northern elephant seals may seem more like pests than triumphant survivors as they crowd beaches, attract sharks closer to shores, and deplete fish supplies to the chagrin of fishermen.

1. In context, which is the best version of the underlined portion of sentence 3 (reproduced below)?

<u>Therefore</u>, this does not mean that those animals and the ones that coexist with them face an easy transition.

   a. (As it is now)
   b. However,
   c. In fact,
   d. In effect,
   e. So,

2. In context, which revision to sentence 4 (reproduced below) is most needed?

For example, they are reaching numbers that may see them removed from the endangered species list sometime in the near future, but their environment has changed in their absence.

   a. Replace *For example* with *For certain*.
   b. Change *numbers* to *population*.
   c. Replace *they* with *northern elephant seals*.
   d. Change *list* to *this*.
   e. Replace *absence* with *nonappearance*.

3. In context, which sentence provides the best conclusion to the paragraph?
   a. Therefore, conservationists must stop trying to help animals get off the endangered species list.
   b. In conclusion, animals that have come back from being endangered and the ones that coexist with them do not face an easy transition.
   c. While some view this as a "downside" of the reinvigoration of endangered species, conservationists consider it a small price for those species' survival.
   d. Fortunately, there are ways that conservationists can plan better for the return of animals that were once included on the endangered species list.
   e. Gray seals, however, are found in areas with cold currents in and around the North Atlantic Ocean, and prefer to live in places where people are scarce.

Answers

1. b. Sentence 3 introduces a negative idea (*formerly endangered animals and the ones that coexist with them do not face an easy transition*) that contrasts the positive idea of sentence 2 (*endangered animals sometimes increase their population and are removed from the endangered species list*). Choice **b**, *However*, is the only transitional word that indicates contrast. Choices **a**, **d**, and **e** would only be used if sentence 3 was an effect of a cause in sentence 2. Choice **c**, *In fact*, would only be used if sentence 3 supported an idea in sentence 2.

2. c. Sentence 4 introduces the animal used as an example of a returning species in this passage. The reader should know which animal is being used as an example as soon as it is introduced, and the vague pronoun *it* makes this unclear.

3. c. Concluding sentence **c** puts the ideas in this passage into perspective without veering off topic. Choice **a** is an extreme, abrupt, and sloppily worded conclusion. Choice **b** is a weak concluding statement because it merely rewords sentence 3 slightly. Choice **d** introduces a new idea, but a concluding statement needs to wrap up the ideas already present in a passage. Choice **e** veers off topic, which is a discussion of the difficult transition animals face when returning from endangerment and not a general discussion of different kinds of seals.

Now that you are familiar with the format of the writing test, you are ready to review some of the rules and patterns of English grammar, sentence structure, idioms, and word usage. This review will aid you in both parts of the writing test: the multiple-choice section and the essay section. The last part of this chapter covers the essay portion of the test in more detail: the kinds of writing prompts that you can expect, test-taking strategies, and essential information for organizing and creating clear, well-supported essays.

Grammatical Relationships

For the multiple-choice section of the Praxis Core Writing test, you must be able to identify problems in the relationships between the parts of a sentence. You need to be on the lookout for the incorrect use of adjectives and adverbs, subject-verb agreement, noun-noun agreement, pronoun agreement, and verb tenses.

Adjectives and Adverbs

Adjectives and adverbs add spice to writing—they are words that describe, or modify, other words. However, adjectives and adverbs describe different parts of speech. Adjectives modify nouns or pronouns, whereas adverbs modify verbs, adjectives, or other adverbs.

> We enjoyed the *delicious* <u>meal</u>.
> The chef <u>prepared</u> it *perfectly*.

The first sentence uses the adjective *delicious* to modify the noun *meal*. In the second sentence, the adverb *perfectly* describes the verb *prepared*. Adverbs are easy to spot—most end in *-ly*. However, some of the trickiest adverbs do not end in the typical *-ly* form. The following are problem modifiers to look out for in the Praxis Core Writing test:

Good/Well—Writers often confuse the adverb *well* with its adjective counterpart, *good*. Ellie felt *good* about her test results. (*Good* describes the proper noun, *Ellie*.) Ruben performed *well* on the test. (*Well* modifies the verb, *performed*.)

Bad/Badly—Similarly, writers confuse the function of these two modifiers. Remember to use the adverb *badly* to describe an action. Henry felt *bad* after staying up all night before the exam. (*Bad* describes Henry.) Juliet did *badly* in her first classroom presentation. (*Badly* describes the verb form, *did*.)

Fewer/Less—These two adjectives are a common pitfall for writers. To distinguish between them, look carefully at the noun modified in the sentence. *Fewer* describes plural nouns, or things that can be counted. *Less* describes singular nouns that represent a quantity or a degree.
The high school enrolls *fewer* students than it did a decade ago.
Emilia had *less* time for studying than Maggie does.

Adjectives that follow verbs can also cause confusion. Although an adjective may come after a verb in a sentence, it also may describe a noun or pronoun that comes before the verb. Here is an example:

> The circumstances surrounding Shakespeare's authorship seemed strange. (The adjective, *strange*, describes the subject, *circumstances*.)

Take special note of modifiers in sentences that use verbs that deal with the senses: *touch*, *taste*, *look*, *smell*, and *sound*. Here are some examples of sentences that use the same verb, but different modifiers:

> Sarah felt sick after her performance review. (The adjective, *sick*, modifies *Sarah*.)
> The archaeologist felt carefully through the loose dirt.
> (The adverb, *carefully*, modifies *felt*.)

The judge looked skeptical after the witness testified.
(The adjective, *skeptical*, modifies *judge*.)
The judge looked skeptically at the flamboyant lawyer.
(The adverb, *skeptically*, modifies *looked*.)

Verb Tense

A verb is the action word of a sentence; it describes what the subject is doing:

The chef cooks. (**subject**: *chef*; **verb**: *cooks*)
The dog barks. (**subject**: *dog*; **verb**: *barks*)
The tree grows. (**subject**: *tree*; **verb**: *grows*)

The correct verbs for particular sentences always depend on when those sentences take place. The above examples all take place in the **present**, but sentences may also take place in the **past**:

The chef *cooked*.
The dog *barked*.
The tree *grew*.

. . . or the future:

The chef *will cook*.
The dog *will bark*.
The tree *will grow*.

Verb tense should be consistent. If a sentence describes an event in the past, its verbs should all be in the past tense.

Incorrect: *When Kate visited Japan, she sees many Shinto temples.*
The first clause of this sentence takes place in the past (When Kate *visited* Japan), yet the second clause indicates a present action (she *sees* many Shinto temples).

Correct: When Kate visited Japan, she saw many Shinto temples.
In this sentence, both clauses take place in the past tense.

Try this practice question:

1. Earlier this year, Hyundai <u>announces</u> the
   _a
   <u>introduction</u> of Android Auto software in its
   _b
   new Sonata automobiles, which <u>indicates</u> how
   _c
   computer technology <u>is affecting</u> every aspect
   _d
   of our lives. <u>No error</u>.
   _e

The correct answer is choice **a**. The phrase *Earlier this year* indicates the action took place in the past, so the following verb should be in the past tense: *announced*. While Hyundai's announcement took place in the past, what it indicates and its effects are relevant in the present, so neither *indicates* nor *is affecting* are errors.

Subject-Verb Agreement

They goes together, or *they go together*? You probably don't even have to think about which subject goes with which verb in this clause—your ear easily discerns that the second version is correct. Subject-verb agreement is when the subject of a clause matches the verb in *number*. Singular nouns take singular verbs; plural nouns take plural verbs. However, some instances of subject-verb agreement are tricky. Look out for the following three problem areas on the writing test.

Phrases Following the Subject—Pay close attention to the subject of the sentence. Do not let phrases that may follow the subject mislead you. These phrases may confuse you into selecting a verb that does not agree with the subject. Try this practice question:

1. Betty Friedan's 1963 book, <u>an exposé</u> of
   a
   domesticity <u>that challenged</u> long-held
   b
   American attitudes, <u>remain</u> an <u>important</u>
   c   d
   <u>contribution</u> to feminism. <u>No error</u>
   e

The correct answer is choice **c**. The singular subject, *book*, needs a singular verb, *remains*. Don't let the plural noun *attitudes*, part of a phrase that follows the subject, confuse you.

Subjects Following the Verb—Be sure to locate the subject of the sentence. Test makers use subjects that come after the verb to confuse you. Sentence constructions that begin with *there is* or *there are* signal that the subject comes after the verb.

2. Although the Australian government protects the Great Barrier Reef, <u>there is environmental factors that continue to threaten</u> the world's largest coral reef ecosystem.
   a. there is environmental factors that continue to threaten
   b. there are fewer environmental factors that continue to threaten
   c. there are environmental factors that continue to threaten
   d. there are environmental factors that continued to threaten
   e. there is environmental factors that would continue to threaten

The correct answer is choice **c**. The plural subject *factors* requires a plural form of the verb, *are*. The verb *continue* is in the correct tense in the original sentence, so choices **d** and **e** are incorrect. The addition

of the adjective *fewer* in choice **b** does not make sense in the sentence.

Special Singular Nouns—Some words that end in *s*, such as *measles*, *news*, *checkers*, *economics*, *sports*, and *politics*, are often singular despite their plural form because we think of them as one thing. Watch for collective nouns—nouns that refer to a number of people or things that form a single unit. These words, such as *audience*, *stuff*, *crowd*, *government*, *group*, and *orchestra*, need a singular verb.

3. That <u>rowdy</u> group of drama students <u>were</u>
   a   b
   labeled "the anarchists" <u>because</u> they took over
   c
   the university president's office <u>in a protest</u>
   d
   against the dress code. <u>No error</u>
   e

The correct answer choice is **b**. The collective noun *group* is the singular subject of the sentence. Notice how the position of the prepositional phrase of *drama students* following the subject is misleading.

Noun-Noun Agreement

Nouns are words that represent the people, places, things, or concepts that are the focal points of all sentences, and they interact with other words in those sentences. Verbs describe what nouns do. Adjectives describe how nouns are. Nouns also interact with other nouns in sentences, and therefore, those nouns must agree in terms of number and gender.

Number refers to whether a noun is singular or plural.
Example: *Biscuit and Gracie are the names of my sister's dogs.*
This sentence refers to two animals (*Biscuit* and *Gracie*), so the writer uses the plural form of dog—*dogs*—to refer to them. Therefore, the

nouns are in agreement in terms of number in this sentence. They would not be in agreement if it read *Biscuit and Gracie are the names of my sister's dog.*

Gender refers to whether a noun applies to a male or female.
Example: *Ms. Anthony is the woman who teaches my art class.*
We know the subject of this sentence is female because of the female title *Ms.* Therefore, the nouns are in agreement in terms of gender in this sentence. They would not be in agreement if it read *Ms. Anthony is the man who teaches my art class.*

Just as you would when answering questions about subject-verb agreement, be mindful of special singular nouns that end in *s* but only indicate one thing.

Incorrect: *Measles are the only major illnesses I suffered as a child.*
Although *Measles* ends with an *s*, it is a singular noun.
Correct: *Measles is the only major illness I suffered as a child.*

4. The Smiths is the families that moved into
     ‾‾‾‾‾‾‾‾ a ‾‾‾‾‾‾‾‾‾‾ b

that house on Sycamore Avenue last year.
‾‾‾‾‾‾‾‾ c ‾‾‾‾‾‾‾‾ d

No error.
‾‾‾‾‾‾ e

The correct answer choice is **b.** The collective noun *The Smiths* only refers to one family, so the second underlined segment should read *the family.*

Pronoun Agreement

Pronouns are words that take the place of a noun or another pronoun, called an **antecedent.** Just as subjects and verbs must agree in number, and nouns must agree with other nouns that relate to them,

pronouns and their antecedents must match in **number** as well. If an antecedent is singular, the pronoun must be singular. If an antecedent is plural, the pronoun must be plural.

SINGULAR	PLURAL
she, he, it	they
her, him, it	them
her, hers, his, its	their, theirs
herself, himself, itself	themselves

Pronouns also need to agree in terms of person. **Person** refers to the speaker's point of view. A text written in the first person is told from the writer's point of view and must use **first person pronouns** (*I, me, my, mine*). A text written in the second person addresses the reader directly and must use **second person pronouns** (*you, your, we, us, our, ours, yours,* etc.). A text written in the third person discusses someone or something other than the narrator or the reader and must use **third person pronouns** (*he, she, it, hers, his, its, them, their, that, those*).

Finally, pronouns need to match their antecedent in case. **Case** refers to a word's grammatical relationship to other words in a sentence. A pronoun that takes the place of the subject of a sentence should be in the **nominative case** (*I, we, he, she, they*), whereas a pronoun that takes the place of the object in a sentence should be in the **objective case** (*me, us, him, her, them*). Here are some examples.

Matteo is funny, but *he* can also be very serious. (subject)
Bernadette hired Will, and she also fired *him.* (object)

In most cases, you will automatically recognize errors in pronoun agreement. The phrase *Me worked on the project with him* is clearly incorrect. However, some instances of pronoun agreement can be tricky. Review these common pronoun problems:

- **Indefinite pronouns** such as *each, everyone, anybody, no one, one,* and *either* are singular.
  <u>Each</u> of the boys presented *his* science project.
- **Two or more nouns that *and* joins** use a plural pronoun.
  <u>Andy Warhol and Roy Lichtenstein</u> engaged popular culture in their art.
- **Two or more singular nouns that *or* joins** use a singular pronoun.
  <u>Francis or Andrew</u> will lend you *his* book.
- **He or she?** In speech, people often use the pronoun *they* to refer to a single person of unknown gender. However, this is incorrect—a singular antecedent requires a singular pronoun.
  <u>A person</u> has the right to do whatever *he* or *she* wants.

The following table lists some pronouns that are commonly confused with verb contractions or other words. Watch out for these errors in the multiple-choice questions.

CONFUSING WORD	QUICK DEFINITION
its	belonging to it
it's	it is
your	belonging to you
you're	you are
their	belonging to them
they're	they are
there	refers to where an action takes place
whose	belonging to whom
who's	who is or who has
who	refers to people
that	refers to things
which	introduces clauses that are not essential to the information in the sentence and do not refer to people

Try this practice sentence-correction question:

5. A child who is eager to please will often follow <u>everything that their parents say</u>.
   a. everything that their parents say.
   b. everything which their parents say.
   c. everything that his or her parents say.
   d. most everything that their parents say.
   e. everything that their parents said.

Choice **c** is the correct answer. The antecedent, *a child*, is singular. Even though you don't know the gender of the child, the possessive pronoun should be *his or her* in order to agree in number.

Pronoun Problem—Unclear Reference

When a pronoun can refer to more than one antecedent in a sentence, it is called an unclear, or ambiguous, reference. Ambiguous pronoun references also occur when there is no apparent antecedent. Look carefully for this common error in the Praxis Core Writing test—a sentence may read smoothly, but it may still contain an unclear reference. Look at this practice usage question:

7. A regular feature in American newspapers <u>since</u> the early nineteenth century, <u>they</u> use
       a   b
   satirical humor to <u>visually</u> comment <u>on a</u>
                          c   d
   current event. <u>No error</u>
                      e

The answer is choice **b**. Who or what uses satirical humor? You don't know how to answer, because the pronoun *they* does not have an antecedent. If you replace *they* with *political cartoons*, the sentence makes sense.

Using Intensive Pronouns for Emphasis

Writers use intensive pronouns (*myself, yourself, herself, himself, itself, ourselves, yourselves, themselves*) when referring to the subject of a sentence. Intensive pronouns do not serve essential functions in a sentence; they are merely present for extra emphasis.

> The president *himself* will make the speech.

In this sentence, the intensive pronoun *himself* is used to emphasize the president's importance, and therefore, the speech's importance (*The president will not assign the speech to his vice president. He is going to make it himself!*). The intensive pronoun should be placed directly after the pronoun it is intensifying or at the end of the clause.

Here are some more examples of intensive pronoun use:

> Did you *yourself* make the phone call?
> I *myself* prefer the other brand.
> She *herself* made an appearance at the show.
> I frosted the cake *myself*.

Notice how the intensive pronoun can be removed from each sentence without affecting the grammar. For example, *Did you make the phone call* still makes grammatical sense without the intensive pronoun *yourself*. However, the *meanings* would change slightly because there would be less emphasis on each sentence's subject; these sentences would be less *intense*. On the Praxis Core Reading test, you will be expected to recognize errors in the use of intensive pronouns. Try this practice question:

6. The children painted this mural <u>itself</u>.
   a. itself.
   b. herself.
   c. himself.
   d. ourselves.
   e. themselves.

Choice **e** is the correct answer. The intensive pronoun in this sentence should refer to the children, not the mural. The intensive pronoun *themselves* applies to the children correctly because it indicates their plural

number. The intensive pronoun *ourselves* also refers to a plural subject, but choice **d** is incorrect because the speaker of this sentence is not one of the children who painted the mural. Otherwise, the sentence would read *We children painted this mural ourselves.*

Structural Relationships

When you speak, you may leave your sentences unfinished or run your sentences together. Written expression makes a more permanent impression than speech. In writing, sentence fragments, run-on sentences, misplaced modifiers, and dangling modifiers are structural problems that obscure the meaning of a sentence. The parts of sentences need to have a clear relationship to each other in order to make sense. This section reviews common errors in sentence structure that will appear on the Praxis Core Writing test, including comparison mistakes, incorrect use of independent and subordinate clauses, and nonparallel sentence construction.

Clauses and Phrases

Sentences are made up of clauses and phrases. In fact, a sentence can be made up of nothing more than a single **clause**. A clause is a group of words that contains a subject and a verb.

> I am going to stay awake.

The preceding sentence makes sense all by itself, so it is an **independent clause**. However, not all clauses can stand alone.

> Although I am sleepy, I am going to stay awake.

The first part of this sentence, *Although I am sleepy*, contains the subject *I* and the verb *am*, but it cannot stand on its own because the conjunction *Although* does not connect to anything. It is a **subordinate clause** that needs the independent clause *I am going to stay awake* to make sense.

Like a dependent clause, a **phrase** cannot stand on its own. However, unlike any kind of clause, it does not contain a subject and verb combination.

Despite my sleepiness, I am going to stay awake.

In this sentence, *Despite my sleepiness* is a phrase. It does not contain a subject or verb and does not make sense on its own.

There are several ways to place phrases and clauses in a sentence. The following variation on the previous sentence is also correct:

I am going to stay awake despite my sleepiness.

However, a writer can render a sentence unclear and awkward by dropping a phrase within a clause. Read the following awkward variations on the original sentence:

I am going to, despite my sleepiness, stay awake.
I am going to stay, despite my sleepiness, awake.
I am going, despite my sleepiness, to stay awake.

Now try this practice question:

7. To be honest, I have never completely under-stood James Joyce's highly experimental novel *Ulysses.*
   a. To be honest, I have never completely understood
   b. I have never, to be honest, completely understood
   c. To be, I have never completely understood, honest
   d. I have never completely, to be honest, understood
   e. I have, to be honest, never completely understood

Choice **a** is the correct answer. There is a clear distinction between the phrase *To be honest,* and the independent clause that follows in this version of the sentence. The other answer choices make the mistake of dropping the phrase within the independent clause *I have never completely understood James Joyce's highly experimental novel* Ulysses. Doing so would result in a very awkward and unclear sentence.

More about Clauses

When a sentence contains two clauses that are linked in a logical way, they are **coordinated**. A conjunction (*as, after, although, because*) joins subordinate clauses with the independent clause to complete a thought or idea. Problems occur when conjunctions are misused in a way that makes a sentence obscure and lacking in meaning. Notice how, in the first example, the conjunction *because* creates a confusing and illogical premise—whereas in the second example, the conjunction *although* sets up a contrast between the two clauses that makes sense.

Unclear: Because he was late again, the teacher let him off with just a warning.
Correct: Although he was late again, the teacher let him off with just a warning.

Another type of mistake is when a sentence has two or more subordinate clauses but no independent clause. This is a problem with **subordination**. Here is an example:

Incorrect: Since the Industrial Revolution took place, because people have increased the concentration of carbon dioxide in the atmosphere by 30% by burning fossil fuels and cutting down forests.

The previous sentence contains two subordinate clauses: the conjunction *since* introduces the first, and the conjunction *because* introduces the second. By removing *because*, you create an independent clause, and the sentence makes sense. Try the following practice question.

8. When European settlers <u>arrived</u> in North
            a

America <u>in the fifteenth century,</u> <u>where</u> they
         b   **c**

<u>encountered</u> diverse Native American cultures.
   d

<u>No error</u>
   e

The correct answer is choice **c.** If you remove the subordinating conjunction *where*, the second subordinating clause becomes an independent clause.

Sentence Fragments

All inventory at reduced prices! Spectacular savings for you! Although pithy and popular with advertisers, sentence fragments are incomplete sentences that do not accurately communicate an idea. To be complete, a sentence needs more than punctuation at its end— it needs a subject and an active verb. A common fragment error that you will see on the Praxis Core Writing test is the use of the *-ing* form of a verb without a helping verb.

> *Incorrect:* Emily sitting on the sofa, wondering what to do next.
> *Correct:* Emily was sitting on the sofa, wondering what to do next.

Another common type of sentence fragment is a **subordinate clause** that stands alone. To review, clauses are groups of words that have a subject and a verb. An **independent clause** is one that stands alone and expresses a complete thought. Even though a subordinate clause has a subject and a verb, it does not express a complete thought. It needs an independent clause to support it.

To identify a sentence fragment or a subordinate clause on the Praxis Core Writing test, look for the following joining words, called **subordinating conjunctions**. When a clause has a subordinating conjunction, it needs an independent clause to complete an idea.

after	because	once	though	when
although	before	since	unless	where
as, as if	if	that	until	while

Examples
The Canada goose that built a nest in the pond outside our building.
As if the storm never happened, as if no damage was done.

In the first example, removing the connector *that* would make a complete sentence. In the second example, the subordinate clauses need an independent clause to make logical sense: *As if the storm never happened, as if no damage was done, Esme remained blithely optimistic.* Try to locate the sentence fragment in the following practice question.

9. <u>One participant</u> of the Civil Rights movement
     a

<u>explained</u> that <u>in the heated atmosphere</u> of the
   b   **c**

1960s, <u>sit-in protests effective enough</u> to draw
          d

the attention of the nation. <u>No error</u>
               e

The correct choice is **d.** In this question, the independent clause has a subject (*one participant*) and a verb (*explained*). However, the subordinate clause beginning with the connector *that* needs a verb to make sense. Adding the verb *were* completes the thought and fixes the fragment: *that in the heated atmosphere of the 1960s, sit-in protests were effective enough to draw the attention of the nation.*

Run-On Sentences

"Planning ahead and studying for a test builds confidence do you know what I mean?" In speech, you may run your sentences together, but if you do so in writing, you will confuse your reader. In a run-on sentence, two independent clauses run together as one sentence without proper punctuation or conjunctions to separate them.

There are four ways to correct a run-on sentence. Study how each of the four fixes changes the following run-on sentence.

Example
We stopped for lunch we were starving.
1. **Add a period.** This separates the run-on sentence and makes two simple sentences.
    We stopped for lunch. We were starving.
2. **Add a semicolon.**
    We stopped for lunch; we were starving.
3. **Use a coordinating conjunction** (*and, but, or, for, nor, yet, so*) to connect the two clauses.
    We were starving, so we stopped for lunch.
4. **Use a subordinating conjunction** (see the preceding page for a list of subordinating conjunctions). By doing this, you turn one of the independent clauses into a subordinating clause.
    Because we were starving, we stopped for lunch.

On the Praxis Core Writing test, be sure to watch for another common form of run-on sentence: the comma splice. A **comma splice** incorrectly uses a comma to separate two independent clauses.

Incorrect: Jacob bought the groceries, Lucy cooked dinner.

You can repair a comma splice in two ways: add a conjunction after the comma, or replace the comma with a semicolon.

Correct: Jacob bought the groceries, and Lucy cooked dinner.
OR
Jacob bought the groceries; Lucy cooked dinner.

Try this practice question.

10. *Citizen Kane*, Orson Welles's first full-length film, <u>is considered an American classic, however it did not manage</u> to garner the 1941 Academy Award for best picture.
    a. is considered an American classic, however it did not manage
    b. is considered an American classic. However, it did not manage
    c. is considered an American classic however it did not manage
    d. is considered an American classic however. It did not manage
    e. is considered an American classic because it did not manage

Choice **b** is correct. This original sentence is a run-on because the word *however* is used as if it were a conjunction. The words *however*, *therefore*, and *then* are not conjunctions, but rather a special kind of adverb that expresses a relationship between two clauses. Called **conjunctive adverbs**, these words cannot join two independent clauses the way a conjunction does. To repair this kind of run-on or comma splice, you can make two sentences (the way that choice **b** does). Another option for fixing the original sentence is to separate the two main clauses with a semicolon and set the adverb off from the rest of the clause with a comma. Note that you can move the adverb around in its clause without changing the meaning of the sentence.

■ *Citizen Kane*, Orson Welles's first full-length film, is considered an American classic; however, it did not manage to garner the 1941 Academy Award for best picture.

- *Citizen Kane*, Orson Welles's first full-length film, is considered an American classic; it did not manage, however, to garner the 1941 Academy Award for best picture.

Parallel Structure

When a sentence has a parallel structure, its words and phrases follow the same grammatical structure. Parallel structure makes sentences easier to read and helps express ideas clearly. Parallel construction is important in sentences that make lists or describe a series of events. Each part of the list or series must be in the same form, or part of speech, as the others.

Not Parallel:	Every day, I went to school, worked part-time, and was exercising. (Two verbs are in the past tense; one is a past participle.)
Parallel:	Every day, I went to school, worked part-time, and exercised.
Not Parallel:	We are looking for a teaching assistant who is smart, reliable, and will come on time. (Two characteristics are adjectives, whereas the third consists of a verb phrase.)
Parallel:	We are looking for a teaching assistant who is smart, reliable, and punctual.

Parallel construction is also crucial when a sentence uses a two-part, or correlative, conjunction. Like all conjunctions, **correlative conjunctions** join two ideas in a sentence. Unlike the standard use of conjunctions such as *and*, *but*, *because*, and *however*, correlative conjunctions need two or more conjunctions to get the job done. These pairs include:

both/and (**Example:** *Both* my father *and* my mother attended this high school.)

either/or (**Example:** You're *either* interested in what I am saying *or* you are not.)

whether/or (**Example:** I am going to your party *whether* it rains *or* it doesn't.)

not only/but also (**Example:** *Not only* is she a painter *but* she is *also* a sculptor.)

neither/nor (**Example:** I am *neither* a baseball player *nor* a basketball player.)

Review the following examples to see how to maintain parallel construction in sentences with correlative conjunctions.

The author <u>not only raised several important questions</u>, but she also <u>made a convincing argument</u>. (Notice how the phrases following the *not only/but also* pattern are in the same form. Each has a verb in the past tense and a noun.)

The contract dispute was the result of a breakdown both <u>in communication</u> and <u>of the town's budgetary crisis</u>. (Here the words following the *both/and* pattern are in the form of prepositional phrases.)

Practice answering this sentence correction question:

11. Expressing yourself clearly and effectively in writing means knowing the basic mechanics of language, eliminating ambiguity, choosing the right words, <u>and correct punctuation</u>.
    a. and correct punctuation.
    b. or correct punctuation
    c. and use correct punctuation.
    d. and having used correct punctuation.
    e. and using correct punctuation.

12. A report by the Bureau of Economic Analysis revealed that the economy neither shrank nor <u>is surging</u> over the past year.
   a. is surging
   b. surging
   c. surged
   d. surges
   e. surge

Answers

11. e. Choice **e** is correct because it follows the grammatical pattern of the sentence—a list of phrases beginning with **gerunds** (a gerund is a noun created from the *-ing* form of a verb).

12. c. Choice **c** is correct because it follows the past-tense grammatical pattern of the sentence, which is apparent in the past-tense verb *shrank* that follows *neither*, the first word in the correlative-conjunction pair *neither/nor*.

Misplaced Modifiers

Modifiers are phrases that describe nouns, pronouns, and verbs. In a sentence, they must be placed as closely as possible to the words they describe. If they are misplaced, you will end up with a sentence that means something other than what you intended. The results can be comical, but the joke may be on you!

Misplaced Modifier:	My uncle told me about feeding cows in the kitchen. (Why are there cows in the kitchen?)
Correct:	In the kitchen, my uncle told me about feeding cows.

Misplaced Modifier:	A huge python followed the man that was slithering slowly through the grass. (Why was the man slithering through the grass?)
Correct:	Slithering through the grass, a huge python followed the man. OR A huge python that was slithering slowly through the grass followed the man.

Most of the misplaced modifier problems on the Praxis Core Writing test are **dangling modifiers**. Dangling modifiers are phrases, located at the beginning of a sentence and set off by a comma, that mistakenly modify the wrong noun or pronoun. To be correct, modifying phrases at the beginning of a sentence should describe the noun or pronoun (the subject of the sentence) that directly follows the comma.

Dangling Modifier:	Broken and beyond repair, Grandma threw the serving dish away. (Why was Grandma broken?)
Correct:	Grandma threw away the serving dish that was broken and beyond repair.

Try the following sentence correction question.

13. A federal government subsidy, <u>students can get help financing their post-secondary education through the Federal Work-Study Program.</u>
    a. students can get help financing their post-secondary education through the Federal Work-Study Program.
    b. since students finance their post-secondary education through the Federal Work-Study Program.
    c. to students who need help financing their post-secondary education.
    d. financing a post-secondary education is possible through the Federal Work-Study Program.
    e. the Federal Work-Study Program helps students finance their post-secondary education.

The correct answer is choice **e**. In the original sentence, the modifying phrase incorrectly describes the subject *students*. In choice **d**, the modifying phrasing incorrectly describes *financing*. Choices **b** and **c** are subordinate clauses, and, therefore, incorrect. Only choice **e** answers the question "What is a federal government subsidy?" in a way that makes sense.

Idioms and Word Choice

Idioms—words, phrases, or expressions used in everyday language—make up a large part of English. If your native language is not English, the use of idioms may challenge you. That is because idioms often have unusual grammatical structures or a meaning that does not make sense if you simply add up the standard meanings of each individual word. Native English speakers recognize most idioms *by ear*—the words just sound right. The Praxis Core Writing test will require you to identify both the proper use of idioms and correct word choice.

Prepositional Idioms

Prepositions are words that express the relationship in time or space between words in a sentence. They are generally short words such as *in, on, around, above, between, beside, by, before,* or *with* that introduce prepositional phrases in a sentence. The Praxis Core Writing test covers the idiomatic use of prepositions—word combinations that often go together. Review and familiarize yourself with this list of common prepositional idioms.

according to	conscious of	in the near
afraid of	consist of	future
anxious	depend on	knowledge of
about	equal to	next to
apologize for	except for	of the opinion
(something)	fond of	on top of
apologize to	from now on	opposite of
(someone)	from time to	prior to
approve of	time	proud of
ashamed of	frown on	regard to
aware of	full of	related to
blame (someone) for	glance at/ through	rely on
blame (something) on	grateful for (something)	respect for responsible for
bored with	grateful to	satisfied with
capable of	(someone)	similar to
compete with	in accordance	sorry for
complain about	with	suspicious of
composed of	incapable of	take care of
concentrate on	in conflict	thank (someone) for
concerned with	inferior to	tired of
congratulate on	insist on	with regard to
	interested in	
	in the habit of	

Keep your ear attuned to the use of prepositional idioms in this practice usage question.

14. The <u>period of</u> intellectual development known
     _a

as the Renaissance <u>corresponded toward</u> a time
          _b

of political stability <u>in Western Europe</u>.
             _c

<u>No error</u>
 _d

The answer is choice **b**. The word combination *corresponded toward* is simply not idiomatic. When followed by a thing, such as a time period, either *corresponded with* or *corresponded to* are the correct prepositional idioms. When followed by a person, use *correspond with*.

Wrong Word Use

Using the wrong word in a sentence can make a writer look silly and undermine his or her reliability. This may seem like an obvious statement, but you may be surprised to learn how often writers misuse words. In fact, some misuses of language are so common that they have entered conventional English. For example, the common phrase *Begging the question* means *assuming the first point made*, which is a form of circular reasoning. However, the phrase is more commonly misused to mean *raising the question*. Similarly, the word *literally*, which means *actually*, is often misused to mean its opposite: *figuratively*. If someone is capable of saying, "It was so hot that I literally melted," you can be sure that person is misusing the word *literally*!

On the Praxis Core Writing test, you will be expected to use words correctly even if the majority of writers and readers have informally accepted their misuses. Here is a select list of frequently misused words:

WORD	INCORRECT DEFINITION	CORRECT DEFINITION
bemused	amused	confused
enormity	enormousness	evil
fortuitous	fortunate	unintentional
ironic	coincidental	the opposite of what is expected
nauseous	to feel sick to the stomach	to cause sick feelings
nonplussed	unmoved	confused
obsolete	old	no longer produced
peruse	to skim	to study
plethora	many	excessive
redundant	repetitive	excessive
travesty	a tragedy	a mockery
ultimate	best	final

Commonly Confused Words

A misused word can significantly alter the meaning of a sentence. The following list contains some commonly confused words. If you find some that you frequently confuse, study them and practice using them in a sentence correctly.

CONFUSING WORD	QUICK DEFINITION
accept except	recognize, receive excluding
affect (verb) effect (noun) effect (verb)	to influence result to bring about
all ready already	totally prepared by this time
allude elude illusion	make indirect reference to evade unreal appearance
all ways always	every method forever
among between	in the middle of several in an interval separating (two)

assure	to make certain (assure someone)
ensure	to make certain
insure	to make certain (financial value)
beside	next to
besides	in addition to
complement	match
compliment	praise
continual	constant
continuous	uninterrupted
disinterested	no strong opinion either way
uninterested	don't care
elicit	to stir up
illicit	illegal
eminent	well known
imminent	pending
farther	beyond
further	additional
incredible	beyond belief, astonishing
incredulous	skeptical, disbelieving
loose	not tight
lose	unable to find
may be	something could possibly be
maybe	perhaps
overdo	do too much
overdue	late
persecute	to mistreat
prosecute	to take legal action
personal	individual
personnel	employees
precede	go before
proceed	continue
proceeds	profits
principal (adjective)	main
principal (noun)	person in charge
principle	standard
stationary	still, not moving
stationery	writing material
than	in contrast to
then	next
to	on the way to
too	also
weather	climate
whether	if

Redundancy and Wordiness

You may be asked to identify redundant or wordy language. Your ability to write concisely and clearly will also be an important part of the essay portion of the test. To eliminate unnecessary repetitions or excessive wordiness, look for words that add no new information to a sentence.

Redundant: Due to the fact that the circumstances of the case were sensitive in nature, the proceedings were kept confidential.

Correct: Because the circumstances of the case were sensitive, the proceedings were kept confidential.

Redundant: Charles returned back to his room at 10 A.M. in the morning.

Correct: Charles returned to his room at 10 A.M.

Mechanics

Knowing the mechanics of language means getting down to basics—the rules of punctuation and capitalization. Punctuation marks are standardized marks that clarify meaning for your reader and serve as traffic signs that direct the reader to pause, connect, stop, consider, and go. Although you have most likely studied and learned many of the basic rules of punctuation and capitalization, this section covers some common problem areas that may appear on the Praxis Core Writing test, including the misuse of commas, semicolons, colons, apostrophes, and capitalization.

Commas

Commas create pauses, clarify meaning, and separate different parts of a sentence. The comma splice is a common misuse of the comma—review this problem on page 156. For the Praxis Core Writing test, remember the six basic rules for using commas, outlined here.

Use a comma

1. to separate independent clauses joined by a coordinating conjunction, such as *and*, *but*, *nor*, *so*, *for*, or *or*. Use a comma before the conjunction.

> My instinct was to solve the problem slowly and deliberately, *but* we only had a week before the deadline.

2. to set off nonessential clauses. A nonessential clause is one that can be removed from a sentence without changing its meaning.

> My friend Rebecca, who is active in the local labor union, is a fifth-grade teacher.

3. to set off words or phrases that interrupt the flow of thought in a sentence.

> The certification program, *however,* works well for me.
> Elena Alvarez, *my adviser and mentor,* was present at the meeting.

4. to set off an introductory element, such as a word or phrase that comes at the beginning of a sentence.

> *Thrilled by the results*, Phin presented the study to his colleagues.

5. to set apart a series of words in a list. Usually, a conjunction precedes the last item in a list. Although a comma is not necessary before the conjunction, it is preferred that you use one.

> *Micah, Jose, and Sam* attended the conference.
> *Micah, Jose and Sam* attended the conference.

6. to separate elements of dates and addresses. Commas are used to separate dates that include the day, month, and year. Dates that include just the month and year do not need commas. When the name of a city and state are included in an address, set off both with commas.

> Margaret moved to *Portsmouth, New Hampshire*, for the job.
> Maco came to Greensboro on *June 15, 2004*, right after she graduated from the program.
> Maco came to Greensboro in *June 2004* after she graduated from the program.

Semicolons

You may be asked to recognize errors involving the use of semicolons on the Praxis Core Writing test. Review how to use this mark correctly in the following three guidelines and examples.

1. **Use a semicolon to link independent clauses** that are not joined by a conjunction.
   Stephen King used the pen name Richard Bachman for his novel *The Running Man*; he used his own name for *It*.

2. **Use a semicolon to link independent clauses** that contain commas, even if the clauses are joined by a conjunction.
   At the arboretum, I photographed a hawthorn, which is a small tree; an arbovitae, which is a medium-sized tree; and a red pine, which is a very large tree.

3. **Use a semicolon to link independent clauses** connected with a conjunctive adverb, such as *however*, *therefore*, *then*, *thus*, or *moreover*.
   The meteorologist predicted rain for today; however, it is very sunny.

Apostrophes

Apostrophes are used to show possession, contractions, and so on. Consider these eight rules for using apostrophes:

1. **Add *'s* to form the singular possessive, even when the noun ends in *s*:**
   Mr. Summers's essay convinced me.

2. **Add *'s* to plural words not ending in *s* to show possession.**

> The *children's* ability to absorb foreign language is astounding.
> The workshops focus on working women's needs.

3. **Add *'* to plural words ending in *s* to show possession.**

> The *students'* grades improved each semester

4. **Add *'s* to indefinite pronouns that show ownership.**

> *Everyone's* ability level should be considered

5. **Never use apostrophes with possessive pronouns.**

> This experiment must be yours.

6. **Use *'s* to form the plurals of letters, figures, and numbers, as well as expressions of time or money.**

> Mind your *p's* and *q's*.

7. **Add *'s* to the last word of a compound noun, compound subject, or name of a business or institution to show possession.**

> The *president-elect's* speech riveted the audience.
> *Gabbie and Michael's* wedding is in October.
> *The National Science Teachers Association's* meeting will take place next week.

8. **Use apostrophes to show that letters or words are omitted in contractions.**

> Abby *doesn't* (does not) work today.
> *Who's* (who is) on first?

Capitalization

Capitalization is necessary both for specific words and to start sentences and quotations. The following are six instances when capitalization is needed:

1. the first word of the sentence
2. proper nouns (names of specific people, places, and things)

3. the first word of a complete quotation, but not a partial quotation
4. the first, last, and any other important words of a title
5. languages
6. the pronoun *I*, and any contractions made with it

Sometimes, knowing when to capitalize a word is tricky. Look for these trouble spots:

- **Compass directions**, such as east or west, are not capitalized unless they refer to a specific geographical region.
  > The American Civil War was fought between the *North* and the *South*.
- **Family relationships** are not capitalized when a pronoun precedes them.
  > I met *my mother* for lunch.
  > *Uncle Russ* agreed to babysit, so that I could meet *Mother* for lunch.
- **Seasons and parts of the academic year** are not capitalized.
  > I'll register for the course this *fall*.
- **Words modified by proper adjectives** are not capitalized unless they are part of a proper name.
  > Jacob recommended the *Italian restaurant* in his neighborhood.

Practice answering this usage question.

15. When Thomas Jefferson sent explorers Lewis and Clark into the West, he patterned their
    <u>a</u>

    mission on the <u>Enlightenments'</u> scientific
    <u>b</u>

    methods: to observe, collect, document, and
    <u>c</u>   <u>d</u>

    classify. <u>No error</u>
    <u>a</u>

The answer is choice **b**. As a proper noun, the *Enlightenment* is correctly capitalized; however, the apostrophe is misplaced. To show possession, add *'s* to a singular noun. The *West* is correctly capitalized because it refers to a geographical region of the United States.

Research Skills

Research is necessary for any informative essay. Writers who rely only on what they already know, or on their personal opinions, will not compose the most thorough or convincing essay. Writers need to support their stockpile of knowledge and opinions with relevant details culled from reliable sources. Writers who show readers that they can back up their ideas and information are more trustworthy than those who do not. Therefore, it is important for writers to consult reliable sources while performing research, cross-check that information with other sources, and cite sources in essays to show readers the reliability of those sources and to avoid plagiarism. The following research skills will help you to answer select multiple-choice questions and write responses to essay prompts on the Praxis Core Writing test.

Effective Researching Strategy

After receiving an assignment, a seasoned writer does not simply launch herself into a library and wait for inspiration to strike. Effective research is organized and methodical, even if there is not necessarily one right way to do it. Processes may vary, but some essential steps are fairly constant:

> *Step 1—Absorb the assignment.* Writers should familiarize themselves with their assignments carefully. One small detail may affect the whole in major ways. For example, an assignment for writing an essay on a piece of seventeenth century literature will go seriously wrong if the writer fails to notice that just any piece of literature will not do—it must be from the *seventeenth century*. Imagine putting a tremendous amount of work into writing an essay about a

book that was published last year only to find it fails to meet the requirements of the assignment!

Step 2—Choosing and using sources. After selecting a topic, the next step is to locate credible and relevant sources. You will learn more about how to do this in the next section, but it is important to first understand that one source is never enough when writing an essay. There's no way around the fact that effective research is a time-consuming process that involves reading many books and articles about the topic.

Step 3—Citing sources. The final step in performing research will also be covered more extensively later in this book. However, a writer should be aware that consulting sources is not enough. The writer must credit, or *cite*, those sources in his or her essay—so, before returning those books to the library or closing out that web page, he or she should write down all information needed for proper citation. That information will then be collected in a bibliography at the end of the essay.

Credible and Relevant Sources

As Internet access, personal computers, smart phones, and iPads become more and more common in our homes, performing research is becoming easier and easier. Writers no longer need expansive libraries on their bookshelves in order to be able to look up new information whenever they want to know it. All one needs to do is pop open a web browser and a literal world of information is there to read. However, that wealth of information available on the Internet that anyone who sets up a free blog page can post is not necessarily as reliable as those books that once occupied our shelves. More than ever, it is now important to carefully assess the credibility and reliability of the sources writers use for research.

There is so much to learn about any topic, but not everything is going to be **relevant** to a particular discussion of that topic. The Xia may have been China's first ruling dynasty, but that fact is not necessarily relevant to an informative essay on the establishment of the Republic of China in 1912. Information that strays off on tangents should be noted and cut from a strong essay. Irrelevant information is distracting and confusing and can cause readers to either lose interest in an essay or question its soundness.

Take a look at the following example:

Arguments against vegetarianism often begin with the basic assertion that cutting meat from one's diet is unhealthy, depriving the body of needed protein. While protein is indeed one of the most essential nutrients, fatty red meats may actually shorten life spans, according to a 2012 study conducted the same year as an extensive study of school health policies and practices.

This paragraph begins strongly with information relevant to the topic of refuting the idea that eating meat is healthier than vegetarianism. However, the final detail strays off topic by mentioning a study of school health policies and practices. What does this detail have to do with the topic of vegetarianism versus meat eating? Both topics relate to health, but other than that, their relationship is unclear, and quite likely, nonexistent. The paragraph would be more focused without this detail about a study of school health policies and practices.

Credibility refers to the trustworthiness of a given source. For example, Wikipedia has become one of the most frequently accessed websites on the Internet. Free and easily accessible, Wikipedia is an online encyclopedia covering every topic under the sun, from the most significant historical events to the most obscure movies. However, its prefix, *Wiki-*, refers to a website that *anyone* can write or revise. A person can add or change information on Wikipedia no matter how qualified or unqualified that person is. So, does Wikipedia seem like a credible source? Perhaps not; but the sources writers use to research the articles they post on Wikipedia might be reliable. If the source is a book written by a noted expert in a particular field or published by a university press, it is likely to be reliable. Similarly, websites with **domain names** ending in .gov (indicating a government website) and .edu (indicating the website of an educational institution) are more likely to be reliable than those ending with the more common .com, a domain that does not indicate a particular reliable institution.

You must also use your critical-thinking skills when assessing the credibility of a source. Information is not necessarily accurate just because it is published in a book printed by a university press or because it appears on a .gov website. While the truth is a constant, our understanding of the facts changes. For example, as recently as the mid-1990s, scientists believed all dinosaurs were covered in scaly skin like alligators are. However, discovery of dinosaur fossils with preserved feathers has since inspired a rethink of old images of the velociraptor and the sinosauropteryx. You should always look for the **date** identifying when the source was published. A more recent publication may be more credible than an older one.

Periodicals may also prove to be useful research sources. Newspapers such as *The New York Times* and magazines such as *National Geographic* are institutions and generally can be considered reliable. However, even major publications such as these make errors. Therefore, it is wise to **cross-check** all of the information in an essay to ensure that it is not limited to a single, possibly faulty, source. Information that appears in more than one source is likelier to be credible—however, even this is not a hard-and-fast rule.

Elements of Citation

Sources may always be questioned. Therefore, it is important for writers to always cite them carefully so readers can assess their credibility. **Citation** is also important because it gives credit to the writers who performed the original research. Without citation, readers may mistakenly believe that all of the research and ideas that went into an essay, article, or book originated with the writer of that essay, article, or book. Citation is particularly important when quoting a source. Quoting a source without citing its writer and original publication is a violation of copyright, and the authors and publishers of the original publication would be within their rights to pursue legal action in that event. So citation is important for ethical *and* legal reasons, as well as reasons of clarity.

There are several citation formats, the most common being MLA (Modern Language Association), APA (American Psychological Association), and *Chicago* (*The Chicago Manual of Style*). For the purposes of the Praxis Core Writing test, we will focus on the MLA citation format.

MLA CITATION STYLE

Text Type	Elements	Example
Citing books:		
Book	Author(s)/Editor(s). *Title of Book.* City of Publisher: Publisher, Date of Publication. Medium of publication.	Silverman, Kenneth. *Edgar A. Poe: Mournful and Never-ending Remembrance.* New York: HarperPerennial, 1991. Print.
ebook	Author(s)/Editor(s). *Title of Book.* City of Publisher: Publisher, Date of Publication. *Name of database.* Medium of publication. Date accessed.	Melville, Herman. *Moby Dick.* New York: Harper & Brothers, 1851. *Project Gutenberg.* Web. 10 Feb. 2015.
Journal	Author(s). "Title of Article." *Title of Periodical* volume number. Issue number (Year of publication): Page Numbers. Medium of publication.	Dafny, Leemore S., PhD, and Thomas H. Lee, PhD. "The Good Merger." *The New England Journal of Medicine* volume 372. Issue 10 (2015): 62–85. Print.
Magazine	Author(s). "Title of Article." *Title of Periodical* Date of Publication: Page Numbers.	Gladwell, Malcolm. "The Engineer's Lament." *The New Yorker* May 4, 2015: 46–55.
Newspapers	Author(s). "Title of Article." *Title of Newspaper* Date of Publication: Page Numbers. Medium of publication.	Steinhauer, Jennifer, and Jonathan Weisman. "Senate to Take Up Spy Bill as Parts of Patriot Act Expire." *The New York Times* June 1, 2015: A1–A3. Print.
Web Page	Author/editor. "Title of Page from Web Site." *Title of Web Site.* Publisher or sponsor of the site (use N.p. if not applicable), Date of publication. Medium of publication. Date accessed.	Robinson, Tasha. "Stephen King grapples with artistic ownership in *Finders Keepers.*" *The AV Club.* The Onion, June 1, 2015. Web. July 13, 2015.

When quoting a source word-for-word, **in-text citation** is necessary in addition to citation in a bibliography at the end of the essay. In-text citation is not nearly as extensive as standard citation. The key elements are the author's last name and the page on which the quote originally appeared.

The format will depend on whether the essay writer specifically mentioned the author of the source in her or his text.

In-text citation example 1

As Silverman said of Edgar Allan Poe, his "sense of deprivation gave his code of independence a begrudging, envious quality." (12)

In-text citation example 2

Poe's "sense of deprivation gave his code of independence a begrudging, envious quality." (Silverman 12)

If citing more than one work by a particular author or citing a work by an unknown author, the title of the source should be used in lieu of a name.

Example

"Insects are so called from a separation in the middle of their bodies, seemingly cut into two parts, and joined together by a small ligature, as we see in wasps and common flies" (*The History of Insects* 1).

Now see if you can spot an error in the following citation of a print book:

16. <u>Hitchcock, Susan Tyler</u>. <u>*Frankenstein: A Cultural*</u>
         a   b

    <u>*History*</u>. <u>New York: W.W. Norton & Company,</u>
                          c

    <u>Inc., 2007.</u> <u>No error.</u>
        d   e

16. d. The final element of this citation is missing the medium of the publication. It should read <u>2007. Print.</u>

Introducing the Essay

Essay tests can intimidate anyone—even prospective teachers. You know you will be asked to write an essay, but you don't know your topic beforehand. And you are under pressure: You have only 30 minutes to complete each essay. Even though this sounds nerve-racking, with preparation you will be ready to produce your best writing. The good news is that because the time limit is brief, your essay doesn't need to be long (about four to five paragraphs). Furthermore, because you are provided with a topic—and in the case of the source-based essay, two sources—you don't need to spend valuable time deciding what to write about. Also, you can be confident that you will be able to answer the question: All the topics, or writing prompts, on the Praxis Core Writing test are designed to be general, so that you do not need any specialized knowledge or experience to write about them.

Creative, innovative writing is not the goal of the Praxis essays. Instead, the essays aim to measure your ability to generate ideas and support them through details and evidence in clear, concise writing. They test how effectively and logically you organize your thoughts, and evaluate your ability to use correct grammar and appropriate word choice. Do not spend a lot of time trying to produce a masterpiece—simply express your views through precise, direct language.

To learn more about the criteria on which your essay will be judged, review the rubrics provided in the answer explanations found after each practice exam.

What to Expect

All the possible writing prompts in the Praxis Core Writing test present a statement and ask you to respond to it. Be ready to explain and back up your position with specific reasons and examples from your personal experience, observations, or reading. You do not need any background knowledge to respond to the prompt. **Do not write about a topic**

other than the one provided. To receive a score, you must write in English.

There are two kinds of essays on the Praxis Core Writing test. One will be argumentative. The other will be a source-based informative essay. Although the two essay types are different in several key ways, neither will require you to perform outside research or study particular topics before taking the test. You will be provided with all necessary research materials at test time.

The **argumentative essay** requires you to make an argument for or against a particular issue. To respond to the prompt, you will draw on your own personal experiences, observations, and readings. You will not have to perform additional readings to compose your response. Here are some examples of topics for argumentative essays you might find on the exam:

- We live in a culturally diverse society. In-depth study of different cultures should be mandatory for all students.
- Celebrities are just ordinary people with high-profile jobs. They don't have more responsibility than other adults to act as role models for children.
- Because of the prevalence of information technology in society, computer training should be required for all teachers, regardless of the subject the instructor will teach.
- Using a grade scale of A–F creates unnecessary competition and negative stress. Colleges and universities should replace the grade scale with a pass/fail report.

The **source-based essay** does not have to be as opinionated as the argumentative essay is. To complete this task, you will receive two sources that you will use to research and support your essay. Your ability to comprehend, integrate, and paraphrase these sources is of paramount importance. You are expected

to cite the sources when you quote or paraphrase them just as you would when writing any essay. See the previous section for proper citation formats.

- What do scientists predict will be the long-term effects of climate change, and what can be done to reduce the ill effects?
- President Barack Obama signed the Affordable Health Care Act into law on March 23, 2010, drawing a great deal of praise and a great deal of criticism. What are the main arguments in favor of the Affordable Health Care Act? What are the main arguments against it?
- As children become more comfortable using new technologies, they face new challenges in both their socialization and education. What do experts suggest about how new technologies affect children?
- In recent years, the physical dangers professional football players face have been receiving more attention in the press. What are these dangers, and how are they likely to affect the sport in the future?

Manage Your Time

You have 30 minutes to produce each clear, strong essay. Should you jump right into the writing or take time to plan your response? Even with a time limit, your ability to craft a well-organized, well-written essay improves if you take time to plan. Allow time for each step of the writing process: planning, writing, and proofreading. You can break down the 30 minutes for each essay this way:

5–10 minutes	Plan (choose your thesis, brainstorm, and organize).
15–20 minutes	Write.
5 minutes	Proofread (read for errors or adjust word choice).

Steps to a Strong Essay

The prewriting—or planning—process is essential to developing a clear, organized essay. Because of the time limit, you may be tempted to skip the prewriting stage. However, the 5 to 10 minutes that you spend planning will be worth it. Prewriting consists of some quick, basic steps: carefully reading and understanding the writing prompt, formulating a thesis, brainstorming for examples that will support your thesis, and drafting an outline or basic structure for your essay.

Step 1—Create a Clear Thesis

To begin, carefully read the statement presented in the writing prompt. Make sure that you fully understand it. For your source-based essay, your **thesis** will fill in the gaps of the prompt by giving a taste of the details to follow.

> **Sample prompt:** What do scientists predict will be the long-term effects of climate change, and what can be done to reduce the ill effects?
> **Sample thesis statement:** Scientists predict that climate change will continue to accelerate the sea level and intensify heat waves until the planet is uninhabitable if the world's governments do not form a unified front against global warming.

For your argumentative essay, you will have to decide what your position is: Do you agree or disagree with the statement? Consider to what extent you agree or disagree with the position: Are you in 100% agreement, or do you only partly agree with the statement? Your answer to these questions will make up the main idea or thesis of your essay. It will form the foundation of your essay and will determine what kind of support, or examples, you will provide.

A strong thesis for an argumentative essay does not merely repeat or rephrase the question or prompt, and it does not state how others might respond to it. Rather, it presents your point of view.

A thesis statement should

- answer the question given in the writing prompt.
- tell the reader what your subject is.
- inform the reader what you think and feel about the subject.
- use clear, active language.

Don't waste time making your thesis statement a masterpiece. You will be able to grab the reader's attention by clearly stating your purpose in simple words.

Consider the following prompt:

> Focusing on fashion and clothes can distract students from learning. School uniforms should be mandatory for all high-school students.
>
> *Discuss the extent to which you agree or disagree with this opinion. Support your views with specific reasons and examples from your own experience, observations, or reading.*

The following sentences are not thesis statements:

- Many private schools already require school uniforms.
- Some students prefer school uniforms, while others detest them.
- Why do schools use uniforms?

The following *are* thesis statements; they relate directly to the prompt:

- School uniforms discourage high-school students from learning responsibility and developing individuality.
- School uniforms are effective in creating a positive learning environment.

Remember that you can also impose some conditions on your answer. For example, if you disagree with mandatory school uniforms, you can still qualify your answer: "I disagree that students should be required to wear school uniforms, but I believe a dress code helps create an effective learning atmosphere."

Step 2—Researching and Brainstorming

Once you've established your thesis, there is another step before you begin to organize and write your essay. For your source-based essay, you will perform **research** by examining the provided sources. As you write your essay, you will return to the sources to select relevant information to support your thesis. If you quote the provided sources directly, you will need to cite them properly in order to avoid plagiarism. Plagiarism is the theft of all or part of a copyrighted work, and like most forms of theft, it is illegal. Quoting too much of a published work is also a violation of copyright, so be sure to quote sparingly. A good rule of thumb would be to quote no more than a total of 10% of the provided sources in your essay, and always be sure that your quote is relevant. Never use quotes merely to pad your essay.

You will also synthesize the information in both sources by cross-checking details. You might consider not using information in one source if the other source contradicts it. See this book's lesson on performing research on page 164 to learn more about selecting relevant details, citation, and cross-checking.

Since you will not receive any sources to support your argumentative essay, you will have to use a different method to prepare it. Once you have decided what your position will be, you will begin to **brainstorm**—think up ideas that support your thesis. Try to generate about three to five reasons that back up your main idea.

Brainstorming is a valuable prewriting process for argumentative essays in which you imagine or write down any ideas that come to mind. To brain-

storm effectively, do not judge your ideas initially—simply put them down on paper. If you are stuck for ideas, try these brainstorming strategies:

- Try the **freewriting** technique in which you write nonstop for two minutes. Keep your pen to paper and your hand moving. Doubtlessly, your ideas will emerge.
- List as many ideas as you can. Don't edit for grammar or structure; just write down whatever comes to mind.
- Now get selective. Choose three to five of your strongest ideas for your essay.

For example, here's how you might brainstorm supporting ideas for the writing prompt mentioned earlier:

Thesis: Mandatory school uniforms are not effective tools for creating a positive, learning environment.

Examples
Why?
Uniforms don't give students the opportunity to make choices.
Uniforms send a message to students that they cannot be trusted.
Students find distractions in class even when they are wearing uniforms.
Teenage years are a time of self-exploration.
Learning isn't only something you read in a book—it's about finding out who you are.
Students need to learn about making good choices.
Personal experience—In my parochial high school, kids wore uniforms.
Lack of trust—We couldn't be trusted to do even a simple thing like dressing ourselves.
Found other ways to rebel—smoking, wearing makeup, dyeing our hair to attract attention.

Distractions in class other than clothes —note writing, gossip, cell phones
Self-exploration—Clothes let teens try on different identities (sporty, punk, artistic).
Learning about good choices—Introduce a forum for students where they can talk about making choices? Encourage kids to talk about how they present themselves when they wear different clothes; talk about choices teens make that can be dangerous; talk about choices adults face.

Step 3—Outline Your Essay

To make sure that your source-based and argumentative essays are well developed and organized, draft an outline for each. An outline will help you put your ideas into a logical order and identify any gaps in your supporting details. Essays follow a basic three-part structure:

1. **Introduction:** State your thesis. Present your position to your readers.
2. **Body:** Provide specific support for your thesis.
3. **Conclusion:** Bring closure to your essay and restate your thesis.

Your Praxis Core essays should follow this basic structure, too. Because the essay is short, plan on writing about five paragraphs, listing one point on your outline for each paragraph. The body of your essays will be broken down into three supporting ideas:

1. Introduction
2. Body: support 1
3. Body: support 2
4. Body: support 3
5. Conclusion

Although you don't have to follow this model exactly, keep in mind that developing three supporting paragraphs is a good guide for both Praxis Core essays. By providing three supporting paragraphs, you will give enough support for your source-based thesis or to make a strong case for your argument.

Essay Structure

Where you put your introduction and conclusion is obvious. However, you need a pattern, or structure, to organize the ideas in the body of your essays. The four most common patterns are **chronological order**, **order of importance**, **comparison and contrast**, and **cause and effect**. The following chart lists each organizing principle's key characteristics and effective uses in writing:

ORGANIZATIONAL PATTERN	CHARACTERISTICS	EFFECTIVE USES
chronological order	uses time as organizing principle; describes events in the order in which they happened	historical texts, personal narratives, fiction
order of importance	arranges ideas by rank instead of time	persuasive essays, newspaper articles
comparison and contrast	places two or more items side by side to show similarities and differences	comparative essays
cause and effect	explains possible reasons why something took place	historical analysis, analysis of current events

BEST BET: ORDER OF IMPORTANCE

What is the most effective way to organize your Praxis Core essays when you don't have much time to consider the options? One logical and effective strategy is to organize your ideas by their importance, or rank. Using this pattern, you can arrange your ideas in one of two ways:

1. by increasing importance (Begin with your least important idea and build up to your most important idea.)

2. by decreasing importance (Start with your strongest idea and end with your least important idea.)

Either arrangement works. However, if you develop your essay by the principle of increasing importance, you save your strongest idea for last, creating a greater impact in your conclusion.

Now it's time to make a detailed outline based on the argumentative-essay writing prompt described earlier in the chapter. The outline organizes the supporting ideas by increasing importance. It includes reasons that support the thesis and examples that support each reason. Because this outline is so detailed, it offers a guide for almost every sentence in the body of the essay.

Introduction
Thesis: Mandatory school uniforms are not effective tools for creating a positive learning environment.
Reason 1: When students feel that they are not trusted, they "live down" to expectations.
Examples: Feel need to prove individuality through attention to makeup, hair; draw attention through risky behaviors like smoking; continue to find distractions like gossip, note passing, cell phones
Reason 2: School uniforms discourage self-discovery and individuality.
Examples: Can't try out looks that come with different identities (sporty, punk, artistic); fashion is harmless way to find out who you are

Reason 3: Students don't learn to make good choices.
Examples: Students aren't prepared for making decisions, simple (clothes, nutrition) or big (college, jobs, whether to engage in risky behaviors, friends, romantic relationships).

Conclusion:
Robbing students of choice discourages self-discovery and does not prepare students for making decisions. Allow students to make choices about their clothes, but also provide a class or forum for discussing how to make good choices, both big and small.

Target Your Audience

Effective writing pays close attention to its audience. Effective writers consider their readers: Who are they? What do they know about the subject? What preconceived notions do they have? What will hold their attention?

On the Praxis Core Writing test, you will be writing to a general audience, meaning that your readers are people with a variety of interests and backgrounds. Knowing your audience helps you make key writing decisions about your level of formality and detail. Your level of formality determines whether you will use slang, an informal tone, technical jargon, or formal language in your writing. A good guide for the Praxis Core Writing test is a balanced approach:

- Treat your readers with respect.
- Don't put off your readers with language that is too formal or pretentious.
- Don't try to use big, important-sounding words.
- Avoid slang (too informal) or jargon (technical or specialized language).
- Aim for a natural tone, without being too informal.

Your level of detail is also based on your audience. Because you are writing for a general audience and not for friends or family, your readers will not be familiar with your background or experiences. For example, if you are arguing against mandatory student uniforms, do not assume that your readers know whether your child's high school implemented such a rule. Give your readers adequate context by briefly describing your experience as it applies to your argument.

First Impression—The Introduction

Once you have completed your detailed outline, you are ready to write. Because you only have 15 to 20 minutes to write, you don't have time to perfect the wording of your introduction. Instead, use clear, direct language to introduce your reader to your thesis and focus. A good way to begin is to restate in your own words the quotation given in the prompt and then state your thesis. Here is an example using the prompt discussed earlier:

Although fashion and clothes can sometimes distract students, mandatory school uniforms are not the answer to creating a good learning environment.

Another useful technique for creating a strong introduction is to begin with your thesis and then give a summary of the evidence (supporting details) you will be presenting in the body of your essay. Here is an expanded version of the preceding thesis statement:

Although fashion and clothes can sometimes distract students, mandatory school uniforms are not the answer to creating a good learning environment. School uniforms can be a negative influence in that they send a message that students can't be trusted to make good choices. High school students need to explore different identities through the harmless means of fashion.

Notice how this introduction outlines the first two main points of the essay's body: how mandatory school uniforms (1) send a negative message about students' ability to make decisions and (2) discourage self-discovery.

Supporting Paragraphs—The Body of the Essay

Working from your detailed outline, begin composing the body of your essay (about three paragraphs long). Treat each of your paragraphs like a mini-essay, with its own thesis (a topic sentence that expresses the main idea of the paragraph) and supporting details (examples). Follow these guidelines for creating supporting paragraphs:

- **Avoid introducing several ideas within one paragraph.** By definition, a paragraph is a group of sentences about the *same* idea.
- **Use at least one detail** or example to back up each main supporting idea.
- **Aim for about three or four sentences in each paragraph.** Your essay will be short. If you write more sentences for each paragraph, you may run short on time and space. If you write fewer sentences, you may not develop your idea adequately.
- **Use transitions.** Key words and phrases can help guide readers through your essay. You can use

these common transitions to indicate the order of importance of your material: *first and foremost, most important, first, second, third, moreover, finally,* and *above all.* Do not use *firstly, secondly,* or *thirdly*—these forms are incorrect and awkward.

Active versus Passive Voice

For precise, direct writing, use the active voice. In English grammar, voice expresses a relationship between the verb and the subject of the sentence or its direct object. When you write in the active voice, the subject of the sentence causes, or is the source of, the action (verb). When you use the passive voice, the subject does not perform the action, but rather is acted on. Sentences in the passive voice are often wordier and more difficult to understand. Here are some examples of active versus passive voice:

Active: We suggest that you organize your ideas by importance.

Passive: It is suggested that you organize your ideas by importance. (Note that this sentence does not say *who* performed the action.)

Active: Her brother typed the letter.

Passive: The letter was typed by her *brother.* (Here the *doer* of the action is the direct object <u>brother</u>, not the subject of the sentence, *letter.*)

Sentence Variety

Strong essays will show your ability to manipulate sentence structure for effect. Sentence structure is an important element of style. If all of your sentences have the same pattern, your writing will be monotonous and dull:

School uniforms are negative. They don't boost students' confidence. They don't make students feel trustworthy. They don't let students explore different styles and personalities.

Although these sentences are simple and direct, they are unlikely to captivate a reader. Because they all have the same length and structure, they create a monotonous pattern. Here is the same paragraph, revised to show variety in sentence structure:

School uniforms are negative because they do not boost students' confidence or make them feel trustworthy. Fashion choices allow students to explore different styles and personalities.

Four sentences are reduced to two; the pronoun *they* is no longer repeated; and verb choices are active and varied. You can also create emphasis in your writing through sentence structure. The best place to put sentence elements that you want to emphasize is at the end. What comes last lingers longest in the reader's mind.

He is tall, dark, and handsome. (The emphasis is on *handsome.* If tall is the most important characteristic, then it should come last.)

You can also use a dash to set off a part of a sentence for emphasis:

He is tall, dark, handsome—and married.

The dash emphasizes the last element, heightening the sense of disappointment the writer is trying to convey.

Your Conclusion

The last paragraph of your essay should sum up your argument. Avoid introducing new ideas or topics. Instead, your concluding paragraph should restate your thesis, but in new words. Your conclusion should demonstrate that you covered your topic fully and should convince readers that they have learned something meaningful from your information or argument. Here's an example:

School uniforms might be the easy answer: They create conformity and minimize distractions in the classroom. However, in order to teach students how to make good choices when they face tough decisions, school administrators need to invest students with the responsibility to practice everyday choices—like deciding what they wear to school.

The Last Step—Proofread

On the timed essay test, you should take about five minutes to proofread—a time allowance that does not let you substantially revise or rewrite your piece. Much of what happens when you rewrite—like reorganizing your argument or making sure you present adequate support—must occur during the *prewriting* process, when you are outlining your essay. The goal of proofreading is to give your essay a final polish by checking your spelling, correcting grammatical errors, and, if needed, changing word order or word choice. To proofread, carefully read your essay, paying attention to anything that doesn't sound right. The following checklist outlines some basic grammatical problems to look out for as you proofread. (All these grammar trouble spots are discussed earlier in the chapter.) Keep in mind that you will apply the following proofreading criteria both to your essay and to **revision-in-context multiple-choice questions** on the Praxis Core Writing test, a sample of which is included at the end of this chapter.

- **Make sure nouns and verbs agree.** The subject of the sentence must match the verb in number. If the subject is singular, the verb is singular. If the subject is plural, the verb is plural.
- **Make sure pronouns and antecedents agree.** Pronouns and the nouns they represent (antecedents) must agree in number. If the antecedent is singular, the pronoun is singular; if the antecedent is plural, the pronoun is plural.
- **Check your modifiers.** Look out for modifiers that are easy to confuse, such as *good/well*, *bad/*

badly, and *fewer/less*. Remember: Adjectives modify nouns and pronouns; adverbs describe verbs, adjectives, or other adverbs.
- **Keep your verb tense consistent.** Switching tense within a sentence can change its meaning. Generally, a sentence or paragraph that begins in the present tense should continue in the present tense.
- **Review prepositional idioms.** If you have studied the list of prepositional idioms on page 159, you may be able to "hear" whether a preposition (*to, of, about, for, with, about, on*) sounds right with a particular phrase or verb.
- **Check your sentence structure.** Look for sentence fragments, run-on sentences, comma splices, and misplaced or dangling modifiers.

You should not just look for and revise errors and mechanics when proofreading. You should also think about other ways to improve your essays by revising your wording.

- **Revise words and phrases for effect.** Revive dull sentences with livelier wording and more dramatic punctuation.
- **Revise words and phrases to convey ideas precisely.** Check to see if you have overused pronouns or if your phrasing can be more precise for the sake of clarity and maintaining interest.
- **Revise to maintain consistency in style and tone.** Remember who your intended audience is and make sure you've written every part of your essays for that audience. If your language lapses into over-familiarity as your writing progresses, revise it to make it more formal.

Now you will use the skills covered in this review to answer the revision-in-context questions that follow this sample source-based essay.

Prompt: As children become more comfortable using new technologies, they face new challenges in both their socialization and education. What do experts suggest about how new technologies affect children?

(1) Recent technological developments has created a world in constant communication and in a constant state of socializing. (2) People no longer limit their socializing to face-to-face meetings and phone calls; they communicate by emailing, instant messaging, texting, and using social media websites such as Facebook. (3) Children have taken to these new methods of communication as readily as adults, which can be a source of alarm for parents. (4) Growing up is difficult enough without doing it on a public platform like the Internet, "cyber bullying" is a new and disturbing phenomenon that has turned every personal computer and cell phone into a playground on which kids pick on other kids. (5) According to a recent poll by the safety watchdog group Enough Is Enough, one in three kids who use social networking sites have suffered cyber bullying.

(6) There are also arguments in favor of allowing kids to use social networking sites. (7) It is a way for kids to learn to use technologies many will be expected to use in the increasingly tech-focused work force. (8) It also helps all of you moms and dads to monitor children's social interactions. (9) However, in an article titled "What age should my kids be before I let them use Instagram, Facebook, and other social media services?", the advocate website Common Sense Media.org recommends that parents restrict social media use until the age of 13 when kids develop "a better sense of what's appropriate to share online."

1. In context, which is the best revision of the underlined portion of sentence 1 (reproduced below)?

Recent <u>technological developments has created</u> a world in constant communication and in a constant state of socializing.

a. (As it is now)
b. technological development has created
c. technological developments has creating
d. technological developments have created
e. technological developments will create

2. Which is the best revision of sentence 4 (reproduced below)?

Growing up is difficult enough without doing it on a public platform like the Internet, "cyber bullying" is a new and disturbing phenomenon that has turned every personal computer and cell phone into a playground on which kids pick on other kids.

a. (As it is now)
b. Growing up is difficult enough without doing it on a public platform like the Internet—"cyber bullying" is a new and disturbing phenomenon that has turned every personal computer and cell phone into a playground on which kids pick on other kids.
c. Growing up is difficult enough without doing it on a public platform like the Internet: "cyber bullying" is a new and disturbing phenomenon that has turned every personal computer and cell phone into a playground on which kids pick on other kids.
d. Growing up is difficult enough without doing it on a public platform like the Internet.

6 ▶ PRAXIS® CORE ACADEMIC SKILLS FOR EDUCATORS: MATHEMATICS TEST REVIEW

CHAPTER SUMMARY

This review covers the math skills you need to know for the Praxis Core Mathematics test. First you will learn about the test, including question types, and then you will learn about number and quantity, algebra and functions, geometry, and statistics and probability.

The Praxis® Core Academic Skills for Educators: Mathematics test measures those mathematical skills and concepts necessary to master before you embark on a career in education. The exam asks you to answer 56 questions in 85 minutes. The majority of these questions are multiple-choice, where you are asked to select *one* correct answer out of five choices presented. In addition, there are two other question types: multiple-choice questions where you are asked to select one or *more* correct answer choices, and numeric entry questions, where there are no choices presented—you must generate an answer to the questions yourself by typing the correct number(s) into a box on the screen.

A NOTE ABOUT CALCULATORS

You may *not* bring any outside calculator when you take the Praxis Core Mathematics test. You will, however, have access to an on-screen calculator for the duration of the exam. The calculator provided is simple and four-function (+, −, ×, ÷), without the more advanced capabilities of a scientific calculator. All questions can be answered *without* the use of a calculator, so try to use it sparingly—ideally, only to check your work.

Many of the problems on the Praxis Core Math exam require the integration of multiple skills to achieve a solution. This test covers several types of questions, and several types of math. Before you start reviewing math concepts, you should familiarize yourself with the content of the test.

Number and Quantity

- **Order:** These questions require an understanding of order among integers, fractions, and decimals.
- **Equivalence:** These questions require an understanding that numbers can be represented in more than just one way.
- **Numeration and place value:** These questions require an understanding of how numbers are named, place value, and order of value.
- **Number properties:** These questions require an understanding of the properties of whole numbers.
- **Operation properties:** These questions require an understanding of the properties (commutative, associative, and distributive) of the basic operations (addition, subtraction, multiplication, and division).
- **Computation:** These questions require an ability to perform computations, change the result of a computation to fit the context of a problem, and recognize what is needed to solve a problem.
- **Estimation:** These questions require an ability to estimate and to determine the validity of an estimate.
- **Ratio, proportion, and percent:** These questions require an ability to solve problems involving ratio, proportion, and percent.
- **Numerical reasoning:** These questions require the ability to interpret statements that use logical connectives or quantifiers, to use reasoning to determine whether an argument is valid or invalid, and to identify a generalization or an assumption.
- **Exponents and Radicals:** These problems require you to use exponent rules to manipulate a quantity.

- **Units:** These problems require you to connect from one unit to another.

Algebra and Functions

- **Equations and inequalities:** These questions require an ability to solve simple equations and inequalities and to guess the result of changing aspects of a problem.
- **Algorithmic thinking:** These questions require an ability to understand an algorithmic view. In other words, you must follow procedure, understand different ways to solve a problem, identify or evaluate a procedure, and recognize patterns.
- **Patterns:** These questions require an ability to understand patterns in data, including variation.
- **Algebraic representations:** These questions require an ability to understand the relationship between verbal or symbolic expressions and graphical displays.
- **Functions:** These questions ask you to interpret functional relationships and build functions from given information.
- **Algebraic reasoning:** These questions require the ability to interpret statements that use logical connectives or quantifiers, to use reasoning to determine whether an argument is valid or invalid, and to identify a generalization or an assumption.

Geometry

- **Geometric properties:** These questions require an ability to use geometric properties and relationships in real-life applications.
- **The *xy*-coordinate plane:** These questions require you to use coordinate geometry to represent geometric concepts.
- **Geometric reasoning:** These questions require the ability to interpret statements that use logical connectives or quantifiers, to use reasoning to determine whether an argument is valid or invalid, and to identify a generalization or an assumption.

- **Measurement:** These questions require an ability to recognize the measurements needed to solve a problem. You must also be able to solve for area, volume, and length, including using formulas, estimation, rates, and comparisons.
- **Circles and right triangles:** These questions require you to understand and apply theorems about both shapes.

Statistics and Probability

- **Data interpretation:** These questions require an ability to read and interpret displays of information, including bar graphs, line graphs, pie charts, pictographs, tables, scatter plots, schedules, simple flowcharts, and diagrams. You must also have the ability to recognize relationships and understand statistics.
- **Data representation:** These questions require an understanding of the correspondence between data sets and their graphical displays.
- **Trends and inferences:** These questions require an ability to recognize, compare, contrast, and predict based on given information and an ability to make conclusions or inferences from given data.
- **Measures of center and spread:** These questions involve mean, median, mode, and range.
- **Probability:** These questions require an ability to evaluate numbers used to express simple probability and to figure the probability of a possible outcome.

Now that you understand the test specifications, let's review the skills in each of the four categories you will need to know to do well on the mathematics portion of the exam.

Number and Quantity

This section covers the basics of mathematical operations of whole numbers, integers, fractions, and decimals.

Numbers, Symbols, and Terminology

You should be familiar with the math terminology that the Praxis Core might use on test day. Here are some definitions you should know.

- **Counting numbers** (or natural numbers): 1, 2, 3, . . .
- **Whole numbers** include the counting numbers and zero: 0, 1, 2, 3, 4, 5, 6, . . .
- **Integers** include the whole numbers and their opposites. Remember, the opposite of zero is zero: . . . −3, −2, −1, 0, 1, 2, 3, . . .
- **Rational numbers** are all numbers that can be written as fractions, where the numerator and denominator are both integers, but the denominator is not zero. For example, $\frac{2}{3}$ is a rational number, as is $\frac{-6}{5}$. The decimal form of these numbers is either a terminating (ending) decimal, such as the decimal form of $\frac{3}{4}$ which is 0.75; or a repeating decimal, such as the decimal form of $\frac{1}{3}$, which is 0.3333333 . . .
- **Irrational numbers** are numbers that cannot be expressed as terminating or repeating decimals (i.e., nonrepeating, nonterminating decimals such as π, $\sqrt{2}$, $\sqrt{12}$).

The number line is a graphical representation of the order of numbers. As you move to the right, the value increases. As you move to the left, the value decreases.

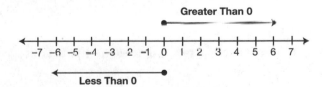

Comparison Symbols

The following table illustrates some comparison symbols.

=	is equal to	5 = 5
≠	is not equal to	4 ≠ 3
>	is greater than	5 > 3
≥	is greater than or equal to	$x \geq 5$ (x can be 5 or any number > 5)
<	is less than	4 < 6
≤	is less than or equal to	$x \leq 3$ (x can be 3 or any number < 3)

Symbols and Terminology of Addition and Subtraction

In addition, the numbers being added are called **addends**. The result is called a **sum**. The answer to a subtraction problem is called a **difference**. In the following example, 4 and 5 are addends and 9 is the sum:

$$4 + 5 = 9$$

Symbols of Multiplication

When two or more numbers are being multiplied, they are called **factors**. The result of multiplication is called the **product**. In the following example, 5 and 6 are factors and 30 is their product:

$$5 \times 6 = 30$$

There are several ways to represent multiplication in this mathematical statement.

- A dot between factors indicates multiplication:
  $5 \cdot 6 = 30$
- Parentheses around any one or more factors indicate multiplication:
  $(5)6 = 30, 5(6) = 30,$ and $(5)(6) = 30.$

- Multiplication is also indicated when a number is placed next to a variable:
  $5a = 30.$
  In this equation, 5 is being multiplied by a.

Symbols of Division

In division, the number being divided *by* is called the **divisor**. The number being divided *into* is called the **dividend**. The answer to a division problem is called the **quotient**.

There are a few different ways to represent division with symbols. In each of the following equivalent expressions, 3 is the divisor and 8 is the dividend:

$$8 \div 3, 8/3, \frac{8}{3}, \text{ and } 3\overline{)8}$$

Prime and Composite Numbers

A whole number greater than 1 is either prime or composite, but not both.

- A **prime** number is a number that has exactly two factors: 1 and itself.

  Examples
  2, 3, 5, 7, 11, 13, 17, 19, 23

- A **composite** number is a number that has more than two factors.

  Examples
  4, 6, 8, 9, 10, 12, 14, 15, 16

Every composite number can be written as a product of prime numbers; the product is called the **prime factorization** of the number. For instance, 90 $= 2 \times 3 \times 3 \times 5$. This product can be written more succinctly as $90 = 2 \times 3^2 \times 5$, where we have used an **exponent** on 3. This shorthand notation works for any natural number that occurs any number of times. If b and n are natural numbers, then $b^n = \underbrace{b \times \ldots \times b}_{n \text{ times}}$.

The following divisibility rules are useful when determining factors of a natural number:

NATURAL NUMBER	A NATURAL NUMBER n IS DIVISIBLE BY THE NUMBER IN THE LEFT COLUMN IF . . .
2	The number n ends in 0, 2, 4, 6, or 8.
3	The digit sum* of n is divisible by 3.
4	The last two numbers of n, taken as a number in and of itself, is divisible by 4.
5	The number n ends in 0 or 5.
6	The number n is divisible by both 2 and 3.
9	The digit sum of n is divisible by 9.
10	The number n ends in 0.

* The digit sum is the sum of all digits in the numeral n.

For instance, 1,245 is divisible by 3 because the digits sum $(1 + 2 + 4 + 5 = 12)$ is divisible by 3. It is also common to say "3 *divides* 1,245."

Integers

The set of integers is comprised of the natural numbers, their negatives, and 0. We write this as the set $\{. . . , -3, -2, -1, 0, 1, 2, 3, . . .\}$. Arithmetic involving integers is the same as for natural numbers, but we must be careful with negative signs. The following rules and terminology are useful when working with integers:

1. $-(-a) = a$, for any integer a
2. $a - (-b) = a + b$, for any integers a, b
3. An integer is *even* if it is a multiple of 2.
4. An integer is *odd* if it is not a multiple of 2.
5. Sums of positive integers are positive.
6. Sums of negative integers are negative.
7. A product of two negative integers is negative.
8. A product of one positive and one negative integer is negative.

Here are some specific examples.

Adding

Adding integers with the same sign results in a sum of the same sign:

(positive) + (positive) = positive   and
(negative) + (negative) = negative

When adding integers of different signs, follow this two-step process:

1. Subtract the positive values of the integers. Positive values are the values of the integers without any signs.
2. Keep the sign of the integer with the larger positive value.

Example
$-2 + 3 =$

1. Subtract the positive values of the integers: $3 - 2 = 1$.
2. The number 3 is the larger of the two positive values. Its sign in the original example was positive, so the sign of the answer is positive. The answer is positive 1.

Example
$8 + -11 =$

1. Subtract the positive values of the integers: $11 - 8 = 3$.
2. The number 11 is the larger of the two positive values. Its sign in the original example was negative, so the sign of the answer is negative. The answer is negative 3.

Subtracting

When subtracting integers, change the subtraction sign to addition and change the sign of the number being subtracted to its opposite. Then, follow the rules for addition.

Examples

$(+10) - (+12) = (+10) + (-12) = -2$

$(-5) - (-7) = (-5) + (+7) = +2$

$\frac{12}{-3} = -4$

$\frac{15}{3} = 5$

Multiplying and Dividing

A simple method for remembering the rules of multiplying and dividing is that if there is an even number of relative signs, the product quotient will be positive. If there is an odd number of negative signs, the answer will be negative.

Examples

$(10)(-12) = -120$

$-5 \times -7 = 35$

Fractions

A **fraction** is a quotient of two whole numbers, denoted by $\frac{a}{b}$, where $b \neq 0$. (Remember, you cannot divide by 0!) The top number is called the **numerator** and the bottom one is the **denominator**. Such a fraction is *simplified* or *in reduced form* if a and b do not share common factors. If $a \neq 0$, the **reciprocal** of $\frac{a}{b}$ can be computed by flipping the fraction over to get $\frac{b}{a}$.

The rules of arithmetic of fractions are collected here:

ARITHMETIC OPERATION	RULE (IN SYMBOLS)	INTERPRETATION
1. Sum/Difference (same denominator)	$\frac{a}{b} \pm \frac{c}{b} = \frac{a \pm c}{b}$	When fractions have the same denominator, just add/subtract the numerators.
2. Sum/Difference (different denominators)	$\frac{a}{b} \pm \frac{c}{d} = \frac{ad \pm cb}{bd}$	When fractions have different denominators, first get a common denominator. Apply it to the fractions and then add the numerators.
3. Multiply by -1	$-\frac{a}{b} = \frac{-a}{b} = \frac{a}{-b}$	When multiplying a fraction by -1, you can multiply either the numerator or denominator by -1, but NOT both.
4. Product	$\frac{a}{b} \cdot \frac{c}{d} = \frac{ac}{bd}$	When multiplying two fractions, you can simply multiply their numerators and their denominators.
5. Simplifying/Reducing	$\frac{a \cdot c}{b \cdot c} = \frac{a}{b}$	You can cancel like factors in the numerator and denominator of a fraction to reduce it to lowest terms.
6. Quotient	$\frac{a}{b} \div \frac{c}{d} = \frac{a}{b} \cdot \frac{d}{c} = \frac{ad}{bc}$	When dividing two fractions, convert to a multiplication problem.
	$\frac{\frac{a}{b}}{\frac{c}{d}}$ means $\frac{a}{b} \div \frac{c}{d}$	

When performing arithmetic operations involving fractions, simplifying all fractions *first* will lead to smaller numbers that are easier to work with.

The following are some common errors when working with fractions.

STATEMENT	INTERPRETATION	EXAMPLE
$\frac{a}{b} + \frac{c}{d} \neq \frac{a+c}{b+d}$	When adding fractions, you do not simply add the numerators and denominators. You must first get a common denominator.	$\underbrace{\frac{1}{2} + \frac{1}{2}}_{=1} \neq \underbrace{\frac{1+1}{2+2}}_{\frac{2}{4}=\frac{1}{2}}$
$\frac{a}{b+c} \neq \frac{a}{b} + \frac{a}{c}$	You cannot pull a fraction apart as a sum of two fractions when the sum occurs in the denominator.	$\underbrace{\frac{1}{2+2}}_{=\frac{1}{4}} \neq \underbrace{\frac{1}{2} + \frac{1}{2}}_{=1}$
$\frac{a}{a+b} \neq \frac{d}{d+b}$	You cannot cancel *terms* in the numerator and denominator. You can only cancel *factors*.	$\underbrace{\frac{4}{4+8}}_{=\frac{1}{3}} \neq \underbrace{\frac{\not{4}}{\not{4}+8}}_{=\frac{1}{8}}$

Comparing Fractions
Rules:

If $\frac{a}{b} = \frac{c}{d}$, then $ad = bc$

If $\frac{a}{b} < \frac{c}{d}$, then $ad < bc$

If $\frac{a}{b} > \frac{c}{d}$, then $ad > bc$

Sometimes it is necessary to compare the sizes of fractions. This is very simple when the fractions are familiar or when they have a common denominator.

Examples

$\frac{1}{2} < \frac{3}{4}$ and $\frac{11}{18} > \frac{5}{18}$

- If the fractions are not familiar and/or do not have a common denominator, there is a simple trick to remember. Multiply the numerator of the first fraction by the denominator of the second fraction. Write this answer under the first fraction. Then multiply the numerator of the second fraction by the denominator of the first one. Write this answer under the second fraction. Compare the two numbers. The larger number represents the larger fraction.

Examples
Which is larger: $\frac{7}{11}$ or $\frac{4}{9}$?

Cross multiply.
$7 \times 9 = 63$ $4 \times 11 = 44$

$63 > 44$; therefore,
$\frac{7}{11} > \frac{4}{9}$

Compare $\frac{6}{18}$ and $\frac{2}{6}$.

Cross multiply.
$6 \times 6 = 36$ $2 \times 18 = 36$

$36 = 36$; therefore,
$\frac{6}{18} = \frac{2}{6}$

Converting Decimals to Fractions
- To convert a nonrepeating decimal to a fraction, the digits of the decimal become the numerator of the fraction, and the denominator of the fraction is a power of 10 that contains that number of digits as zeros.

Example
Convert .125 to a fraction.
The decimal .125 means 125 *thousandths*, so it is 125 parts of 1,000. An easy way to do this is to make 125 the numerator, and since there are three digits in the number 125, the denominator is 1 with three zeros, or 1,000.

$.125 = \frac{125}{1,000}$

Then we just need to reduce the fraction.

$\frac{125}{1,000} = \frac{125 \div 125}{1,000 \div 125} = \frac{1}{8}$

- When converting a repeating decimal to a fraction, the digits of the repeating pattern of the decimal become the numerator of the fraction, and the denominator of the fraction is the same number of 9s as digits.

  Example

  Convert $.\overline{3}$ to a fraction.

  You may already recognize $.\overline{3}$ as $\frac{1}{3}$. The repeating pattern, in this case 3, becomes our numerator. There is one digit in the pattern, so 9 is our denominator.

  $$.\overline{3} = \frac{3}{9} = \frac{3 \div 3}{9 \div 3} = \frac{1}{3}$$

  Example

  Convert $.\overline{36}$ to a fraction.

  The repeating pattern, in this case 36, becomes our numerator. There are two digits in the pattern, so 99 is our denominator.

  $$.\overline{36} = \frac{36}{99} = \frac{36 \div 9}{99 \div 9} = \frac{4}{11}$$

Converting Fractions to Decimals

- To convert a fraction to a decimal, simply treat the fraction as a division problem.

  Example

  Convert $\frac{3}{4}$ to a decimal.

  $$4\overline{)3.00}^{.75}$$

  So, $\frac{3}{4}$ is equal to .75.

Converting Mixed Numbers to and from Improper Fractions

Rule:

$$a\frac{b}{c} = \frac{ac + b}{c}$$

- A mixed number is a number greater than 1 that is expressed as a whole number joined to a proper fraction. Examples of mixed numbers are $5\frac{3}{8}$ and $2\frac{1}{3}$. To convert from a mixed number to an improper fraction (a fraction where the numerator is greater than the denominator), multiply the whole number and the denominator, and then add the numerator. This becomes the new numerator. The new denominator is the same as the original in the fraction.

  Example

  Convert $5\frac{3}{8}$ to an improper fraction.

  Using the conversion formula,

  $$5\frac{3}{8} = \frac{5 \times 8 + 3}{8} = \frac{43}{8}.$$

  Example

  Convert $-4\frac{5}{6}$ to an improper fraction.

  Temporarily ignore the negative sign and perform the conversion:

  $$4\frac{5}{6} = \frac{4 \times 6 + 5}{6} = \frac{29}{6}.$$

  The final answer includes the negative sign:

  $$-\frac{29}{6}.$$

- To convert from an improper fraction to a mixed number, simply treat the fraction like a division problem and express the answer as a fraction rather than a decimal.

  Example

  Convert $\frac{23}{7}$ to a mixed number.

  Perform the division:

  $$23 \div 7 = 3\frac{2}{7}.$$

Decimals

The arithmetic of decimals resembles that of the natural numbers with the additional task of correctly positioning the decimal point.

1	2	6	8	.	3	4	5	7
T H O U S A N D S	H U N D R E D S	T E N S	O N E S	D E C I M A L POINT	T E N T H S	H U N D R E D T H S	T H O U S A N D T H S	T E N T H O U S A N D T H S

In expanded form, this number can also be expressed as:

$$1{,}268.3457 = (1 \times 1{,}000) + (2 \times 100) +$$
$$(6 \times 10) + (8 \times 1) + (3 \times .1) + (4 \times .01) +$$
$$(5 \times .001) + (7 \times .0001)$$

Comparing Decimals

Comparing decimals is actually quite simple. Just line up the decimal points and then fill in zeros at the ends of the numbers until each one has an equal number of digits.

Example

Compare .5 and .005.

Line up decimal points.   .5
    .005

Add zeros.   .500
    .005

Now, ignore the decimal point and consider, which is bigger: 500 or 5?

500 is definitely bigger than 5, so .5 is larger than .005.

The following are some rules of thumb to apply when working with decimals:

1. When *adding or subtracting decimals*, line up the decimal points and add or subtract as you would natural numbers, keeping the decimal point in the same position.
2. When *multiplying* decimals, multiply the numbers as you would natural numbers, and to determine the position of the decimal point, count the number of digits present after the decimal point in all numbers being multiplied and move that many steps from the right of the product and then insert the decimal point.

Converting Decimals to Fractions

- To convert a nonrepeating decimal to a fraction, the digits of the decimal become the numerator of the fraction, and the denominator of the fraction is a power of 10 that contains that number of digits as zeros.

Example

Convert .125 to a fraction.
The decimal .125 means 125 *thousandths*, so it is 125 parts of 1,000. An easy way to do this is to make 125 the numerator, and since there are three digits in the number 125, the denominator is 1 with three zeros, or 1,000.

$$.125 = \frac{125}{1{,}000}$$

Then we just need to reduce the fraction.

$$\frac{125}{1{,}000} = \frac{125 \div 125}{1{,}000 \div 125} = \frac{1}{8}$$

- When converting a repeating decimal to a fraction, the digits of the repeating pattern of the decimal become the numerator of the fraction, and the denominator of the fraction is the same number of 9s as digits.

Example

Convert $.\overline{3}$ to a fraction.

You may already recognize $.\overline{3}$ as $\frac{1}{3}$. The repeating pattern, in this case 3, becomes our numerator. There is one digit in the pattern, so 9 is our denominator.

$$.\overline{3} = \frac{3}{9} = \frac{3 \div 3}{9 \div 3} = \frac{1}{3}$$

Example

Convert $.\overline{36}$ to a fraction.

The repeating pattern, in this case 36, becomes our numerator. There are two digits in the pattern, so 99 is our denominator.

$$.\overline{36} = \frac{36}{99} = \frac{36 \div 9}{99 \div 9} = \frac{4}{11}$$

Converting Fractions to Decimals

- To convert a fraction to a decimal, simply treat the fraction as a division problem.

Example

Convert $\frac{3}{4}$ to a decimal.

$$4\overline{)3.00} \quad .75$$

So, $\frac{3}{4}$ is equal to .75.

All rational numbers can be converted into a decimal by dividing the numerator by the denominator. All such decimals will either terminate or repeat. Any decimal that neither repeats nor terminates is said to be **irrational**. Some common irrational numbers are $\sqrt{2}$, π, and e. A **real number** is any number that is either rational or irrational.

Percents

The word **percent** means per hundred. A percent is used to express the number of *parts* of a *whole*. For instance, 25 percent means "25 parts of 100," which can be expressed as the fraction $\frac{25}{100}$ or as the decimal 0.25. It is also denoted as 25%. All three

representations are equivalent. (Note that to go from decimal form to percent form, you simply move the decimal point two units to the right and affix the % sign; to convert in the opposite manner, move the decimal point two units to the left, insert a decimal point and drop the % sign.)

Here are some conversions you should be familiar with:

FRACTION	DECIMAL	PERCENTAGE
$\frac{1}{2}$	0.5	50%
$\frac{1}{4}$	0.25	25%
$\frac{1}{3}$	0.333 . . .	$33.\overline{3}\%$
$\frac{2}{3}$	0.666 . . .	$66.\overline{6}\%$
$\frac{1}{10}$	0.1	10%
$\frac{1}{8}$	0.125	12.5%
$\frac{1}{6}$	0.1666 . . .	$16.\overline{6}\%$
$\frac{1}{5}$	0.2	20%

The following are some common scenarios that arise when working with percents.

PROBLEM TYPE	METHOD USED TO SOLVE THE PROBLEM	EXAMPLE
What percent of x is y?	Divide x by y.	Q: What percent of 200 is 40? A: $\frac{40}{200} = \frac{1}{5} = 0.20 = 20\%$
Compute $x\%$ of y.	Convert $x\%$ to a decimal and multiply by y.	Q: Compute 43% of 6. A: 0.43(6) = 2.58
x is $y\%$ of what number z?	Convert $y\%$ to a decimal, multiply it by z, and set equal to x. Solve for z.	Q: 24 is 40% of what number z? A: Solve $0.40z = 24$ for z to get $z = 60$.

Properties of Real Numbers

The following properties apply *for all* real numbers a, b, and c:

PROPERTY NAME	RULE (IN SYMBOLS)	INTERPRETATION
1. Commutative	$a + b = b + a$ $a \cdot b = b \cdot a$	The order in which real numbers are added or multiplied is not relevant.
2. Associative	$(a + b) + c = a + (b + c)$ $(a \cdot b) \cdot c = a (b \cdot c)$	The manner in which terms of a sum or a product comprised of more than two terms are grouped is not relevant.
3. Distributive	$a \cdot (b + c) = a \cdot b + a \cdot c$	To multiply a sum by a real number, multiply each term of the sum by the number and add the results.
4. FOIL	$(a + b) \cdot (c + d) =$ $a \cdot c + a \cdot d + b \cdot c + b \cdot d$	This follows from using the distributive property twice. The acronym FOIL means "First, Outer, Inner, Last," and signifies all combinations of terms to be multiplied.
5. Zero Factor Property	If $a \cdot b = 0$, then either $a = 0$ or $b = 0$, or both.	If a product of real numbers is zero, then at least one of the factors must be zero.

Additive and Multiplicative Identities and Inverses

- The **additive identity** is the value that, when added to a number, does not change the number. For all the sets of numbers defined previously (counting numbers, integers, rational numbers, etc.), the additive identity is 0.

  Examples
  $5 + 0 = 5$
  $-3 + 0 = -3$

  Adding 0 does not change the values of 5 and −3, so 0 is the additive identity.

- The **additive inverse** of a number is the number that, when added to the number, gives you the additive identity.

  Example
  What is the additive inverse of −3?

This means, "What number can I add to −3 to give me the additive identity (0)?"
$-3 + \underline{\quad} = 0$
$-3 + 3 = 0$
The answer is 3.

- The **multiplicative identity** is the value that, when multiplied by a number, does not change the number. For all of the sets of numbers defined previously (counting numbers, integers, rational numbers, etc.) the multiplicative identity is 1.

  Examples
  $5 \times 1 = 5$
  $-3 \times 1 = -3$

  Multiplying by 1 does not change the values of 5 and −3, so 1 is the multiplicative identity.

- The **multiplicative inverse** of a number is the number that, when multiplied by the number, gives you the multiplicative identity.

Example

What is the multiplicative inverse of 5?

This means, "What number can I multiply 5 by to give me the multiplicative identity (1)?"

$5 \times \underline{\quad} = 1$

$5 \times \frac{1}{5} = 1$

The answer is $\frac{1}{5}$.

There is an easy way to find the multiplicative inverse of a number. It is the **reciprocal** of the number, which is obtained by reversing the numerator and denominator of a fraction. In the preceding example, the answer is the reciprocal of 5; 5 can be written as $\frac{5}{1}$, so the reciprocal is $\frac{1}{5}$.

Here are some numbers and their reciprocals:

4	$\frac{1}{4}$
$\frac{2}{3}$	$\frac{3}{2}$
$-\frac{6}{5}$	$-\frac{5}{6}$
$\frac{1}{6}$	6

Note: Reciprocals do not change sign.

Note: The additive inverse of a number is the opposite of the number; the multiplicative inverse is the reciprocal.

Order of Operations

Often, you need to simplify an arithmetic expression involving all types of numbers and operations. In order to do so, you must use the following rules that tell us the *order of operations*:

Step 1: Simplify all expressions contained within parentheses.

Step 2: Simplify all expressions involving exponents.

Step 3: Perform all multiplication and division as it arises from left to right.

Step 4: Perform all addition and subtraction as it arises from left to right.

If there are multiple groupings, apply the same steps *within* each grouping.

Example

$\frac{(5+3)^2}{4} + 27$

$= \frac{(8)^2}{4} + 27$

$= \frac{64}{4} + 27$

$= 16 + 27$

$= 43$

Absolute Value

The **real number line** is a convenient way of gauging the relative position of real numbers with respect to the 0. Notice that the integers 5 and −5 are both 5 units away from 0, even though they occur on either side of 0.

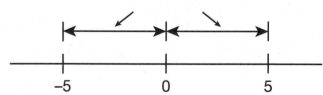

Both are 5 units from 0

For any real number a, we use the **absolute value** of a, denoted $|a|$, to measure the distance between a and 0. Since distance is a nonnegative quantity, we define this in two cases:

$$|a| = \begin{cases} a, & \text{if } a \geq 0 \\ -a, & \text{if } a < 0 \end{cases}$$

For instance, $|6| = 6$ and $|-6| = -(-6) = 6$. This definition works for integers, rational numbers, and irrational numbers alike. Often, we are interested in computing the *distance* between two real numbers p and q. This is interpreted as the length of the segment on the number line joining p and q, and is computed as $|p - q|$.

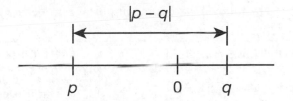

The following are some useful properties of absolute value.

PROPERTY (IN SYMBOLS)	PROPERTY (IN WORDS)
1. $|a| = b$ whenever $a = b$ or $a = -b$	The real numbers b and $-b$ are both $|b|$ units from the origin.
2. $|a \cdot b| = |a| \cdot |b|$	The absolute value of a product is the product of the absolute values.
3. $\left|\frac{a}{b}\right| = \left|\frac{a}{b}\right|$, whenever $b \neq 0$	The absolute value of a quotient is the quotient of the absolute values.
4. In general, $|a + b| \neq |a| + |b|$.	In general, the absolute value of a sum does not equal the sum of the absolute values.

Ordering of Real Numbers

Related to the notion of distance is **ordering**. On page 185, we discussed how to compare two fractions and two decimals, but in general, what does it mean for a real number p to be less than another real number q, written $p < q$? Pictorially, q would lie further to the right along the real number line than p, as shown here:

We also say that q is *greater than* p. For instance, $-1 < -\frac{3}{5}, 2 \leq 3.112, \pi \geq 3.11, 0 > -0.31$.

$p < q$ $\qquad$ $p < q$

p q 0 $\qquad$ p q

The following are some important properties involving inequalities of real numbers:

RULE (IN SYMBOLS)	RULE (IN WORDS)
1. If $0 < a < b$, then $\frac{1}{b} < \frac{1}{a}$.	If a and b are both positive and a is less than b, then the reverse inequality is true of the reciprocals of a and b.
2. If $a > 1$, then $a^2 > a$.	If a real number is greater than 1, then it is less than its square. (Said differently, squaring a number greater than 1 results in a larger number.)
3. If $0 < a < 1$, then $a^2 < a$.	If a real number is between 0 and 1, then it is greater than its square. (Said differently, squaring a number between 0 and 1 results in a smaller number.)
4. If $0 < a < b$, then $-b < -a < 0$.	If a and b are both positive and a is less than b, then the reverse inequality is true of the negatives of a and b.
5. If $a < b$ and $c < d$, then $a + c < b + d$.	You can add the left sides and right sides of inequalities involving the same sign, and the sums satisfy the same inequality.

Exponents and Exponent Rules

When b and n are natural numbers, we defined b^n (read as "b to the power n") to mean $\underbrace{b \times \ldots \times b}_{n \text{ times}}$. Here, b is called the **base** and n is the **exponent**. This definition can be extended in stages in such a way that exponents can be *any* real number. We won't go into those details here, but we *will* gather a group of properties that apply for all real number exponents. They are useful especially when solving various algebra problems, a task we undertake later in our review.

For the following, assume that the bases a and b are greater than 1, and that the exponents n and m are real numbers.

EXPONENT RULE (IN SYMBOLS)	INTERPRETATION
1. $a^0 = 1$	The result of raising any nonzero real number to the zero power is 1.
2. $a^{-n} = \frac{1}{a^n}$, $a^n = \frac{1}{a^{-n}}$	A term in the numerator that is raised to a negative exponent is equivalent to a term in the denominator with the same base, but positive exponent, and vice versa.
3. $a^n \cdot a^m = a^{n+m}$	When multiplying terms with the same base raised to powers, you add the powers.
4. $\frac{a^n}{a^m} = a^{n-m}$	When dividing terms with the same base raised to powers, you subtract the powers.
5. $(a^n)^m = a^{n \cdot m}$	When raising a term that is already raised to a power to another power, you multiply the powers.
6. $(a \cdot b)^n = a^n \cdot b^n$	When raising a product to a power, apply the power to each term and multiply the results.
7. $\left(\frac{a}{b}\right)^n = \frac{a^n}{b^n}$	When raising a quotient to a power, apply the power to each term and divide the results.
8. If $a = b$, then $a^n = b^n$, for any exponent n.	If two real numbers are equal, then their powers are also equal.
9. If $0 < a < b$, then $a^n < b^n$, for any positive exponent n.	If a is less than b, then you can raise both sides of the inequality to a positive power without having to reverse the sign.

It is very common to not only apply the exponent rules incorrectly, but also to mistakenly apply rules that do not even exist! The following are some common errors with examples that arise when working with exponents.

STATEMENT	INTERPRETATION	EXAMPLE
$(a + b)^n \neq a^n + b^n$	The power of a sum is not equal to the sum of the powers.	$(2 + 3)^3 \neq 2^3 + 3^3$
$a^n \cdot b^m \neq (a \cdot b)^{n + m}$	You cannot write the product of terms with different bases raised to different powers as a single product raised to a power.	$3^2 \cdot 5^3 \neq (3 \cdot 5)^{2 + 3}$
$\frac{a^n}{b^m} \neq (\frac{a}{b})^{n - m}$	You cannot write the quotient of terms with different bases raised to different powers as a single quotient raised to a power.	$\frac{3^2}{5^3} \neq (\frac{3}{5})^{2 - 3}$
$-a^2 \neq (-a)^2$	If the negative sign is *outside* the parentheses of a quantity being squared, then the square does not apply to it.	$(-5)^2 = (-5)(-5) = 25$ $-5^2 = (-1)(5)(5) = -25$

Examples

$5^{-1} = \frac{1}{5}$

$7^{-2} = (\frac{1}{7})^2 = \frac{1}{49}$

$(\frac{2}{3})^{-2} = (\frac{3}{2})^2 = \frac{9}{4}$

$2^2 \times 2^4 \times 2^6 = 2^{12}$

$a^2 \times a^3 \times a^5 = a^{10}$

$\frac{2^7}{2^3} = 2^4 \qquad \frac{a^9}{a^4} = a^5$

$(3^2)^7 = 3^{14} \qquad (g^4)3 = g^{12}$

A more complicated example is as follows:

$$\frac{3^{-2} \cdot 2^3}{3^2 \cdot 2^{-1}} = \frac{2^1 \cdot 2^3}{3^2 \cdot 3^2} \text{ (by Property 2)}$$

$$= \frac{2^{1 + 3}}{3^{2 + 2}} \text{ (by Property 3)}$$

$$= \frac{2^4}{3^4}$$

$$= \left(\frac{2}{3}\right)^4 \text{ (by Property 7)}$$

Radicals

You likely already know that $\sqrt{49} = 7$ and $\sqrt{81} = 9$, but why? The definition of a **square root** of a nonnegative real number a is another number b whose square is a, that is $b^2 = a$. In such case, we write $\sqrt{a} = b$. We call a the **radicand**. Note that $(-7)^2 = 49$ and $(-9)^2 = 81$, so -7 and -9 are also square roots of 49 and 81, respectively. When the square root symbol $\sqrt{}$ is used, it is understood to mean the **positive** (or *principal*) root. Square roots of negative numbers are not *real* numbers, but rather they are **imaginary**; meaning they involve i.

A **cube root** of a real number a is another number b whose cube is a, that is $b^3 = a$. In such case, we write $\sqrt[3]{a} = b$. For instance, $\sqrt[3]{64} = 4$ and $\sqrt[3]{-125} = -5$. General n^{th} roots can be defined in a similar way for any natural number n. We collectively refer to roots of any kind as **radicals**.

We can also describe radicals using fractional exponents. For instance, raising both sides the equation $b^2 = a$ to the $\frac{1}{2}$ power yields $\underbrace{(b^2)^{\frac{1}{2}}}_{= b} = \underbrace{a^{\frac{1}{2}}}_{= \sqrt{a}}$.

So, $\sqrt{a}$ can be expressed as $a^{\frac{1}{2}}$. Similarly, $\sqrt[3]{a} = a^{\frac{1}{3}}$ and more generally, $\sqrt[n]{a} = a^{\frac{1}{n}}$.

Here are some useful properties of exponents you should become familiar with for the Praxis®.

RADICAL RULE (IN SYMBOLS)	INTERPRETATION
1. $\left(\sqrt[n]{a}\right)^n = a$, for any natural number n. Specifically, $(\sqrt{a})^2 = a$.	Raising an nth root to the nth power gives back the original radicand.
2. $\sqrt{a^2} = |a|$	Since the square root symbol means the *principal* root, and a could technically be negative, we must take the absolute value of a to get $\sqrt{a^2}$.
3. $\sqrt{a \cdot b} = \sqrt{a} \cdot \sqrt{b}$, whenever $a \geq 0$ and $b \geq 0$.	Square root of a product is the product of the square roots. (This extends to all n^{th} roots and when n is odd, the restriction on the sign of a and b is dropped.)
4. $\sqrt{\frac{a}{b}} = \frac{\sqrt{a}}{\sqrt{b}}$, whenever $a \geq 0$ and $b > 0$.	Square root of a quotient is the quotient of the square roots. (This extends to all n^{th} roots and when n is odd, the restriction on the sign of a and b is dropped.)
5. $\frac{1}{\sqrt{a}} = \frac{1}{\sqrt{a}} \cdot \frac{\sqrt{a}}{\sqrt{a}} = \frac{\sqrt{a}}{a}$, whenever $a > 0$.	You can clear a square root from the denominator of a fraction by multiplying the top and bottom by it. (This is often called "multiplying by the *conjugate*" or "*rationalizing* the denominator.")
6. If $a = b$ and a and b are nonnegative, then $\sqrt{a} = \sqrt{b}$.	If two nonnegative real numbers are equal, then their square roots are also equal.
7. If $0 < a < b$, then $\sqrt{a} < \sqrt{b}$.	If a is less than b, then you can take the square root on both sides of the inequality without having to reverse the sign.

These properties can be used to simplify radicals. For instance:

$$\sqrt{48} = \sqrt{3 \cdot 16} = \sqrt{3} \cdot \sqrt{16} = \sqrt{3} \cdot 4 = 4\sqrt{3}$$

The following are some common errors with examples that arise when working with radicals.

STATEMENT	INTERPRETATION	EXAMPLE
$\sqrt{a + b} \neq \sqrt{a} + \sqrt{b}$	The square root of a sum is not the sum of the square roots. (This fact is true for all n^{th} roots.)	$\underset{=\sqrt{25}\,=\,5}{\sqrt{16 + 9}} \neq \sqrt{16} + \sqrt{9}$
$\sqrt{a^2 + b^2} \neq a + b$	This is a special case of the one above.	$\underset{=\sqrt{25}\,=\,5}{\sqrt{4^2 + 3^2}} \neq 4 + 3$

How do *you* add radical expressions? Well, it depends. If the terms of the sum have the same radical parts, we can just add the coefficients:

$$4\sqrt{3} + 8\sqrt{3} = (4 + 8)\sqrt{3} = 12\sqrt{3}$$

However, terms that have different radical parts cannot be combined. For instance:

$$3\sqrt{3} + 2\sqrt{7} - 9\sqrt{3} = (3 - 9)\sqrt{3} + 2\sqrt{7} = -6\sqrt{3} + 2\sqrt{7}$$

Example

Simplify $\frac{36\sqrt{5}}{18\sqrt{30}}$.

We must use the properties of radicals, together with how fractions are multiplied, to simplify this expression:

$$\frac{36\sqrt{5}}{18\sqrt{30}} = \frac{\cancel{18} \cdot 2\sqrt{5}}{18\sqrt{5 \cdot 6}} = \frac{2\cancel{\sqrt{5}}}{\cancel{\sqrt{5}} \cdot \sqrt{6}} = \frac{2}{\sqrt{6}}$$

Finally, we rationalize the denominator by multiplying the numerator and denominator by $\sqrt{6}$:

$$\underbrace{\frac{36\sqrt{5}}{18\sqrt{30}} = \frac{2}{\sqrt{6}}}_{\text{From above}} = \underbrace{\frac{2}{\sqrt{6}} \cdot \frac{\sqrt{6}}{\sqrt{6}}}_{\substack{\text{Rationalizing the} \\ \text{denominator}}} = \frac{2\sqrt{6}}{6} = \frac{\sqrt{6}}{3}$$

Estimation

Computations often arise in which either the numbers are so large that working with them directly is difficult or the expressions involve roots or irrational numbers that hinder precision. In these cases, we resort to approximation.

A common technique is to round large numbers to the nearest *thousand, ten thousand*, etc. Suppose you want to round a whole number to the nearest thousand, for instance. Look at the digit to the immediate right, which in this case is the hundreds place. If that digit is 5 or greater, increase the digit in the thousands place by one, and replace all digits to its right by zeros; if the digit is 4 or less, keep the thousands place as is and replace all digits to its right by zeros. For example, 343,783 rounded to the nearest thousand is 344,000, while 214,332,499 rounded to the nearest thousand is 214,332,000. The same technique works when rounding any real number expressed as a decimal to any place desired.

Estimating roots, such as $\sqrt{31}$ and $\sqrt[3]{4}$, can be tricky. Sometimes, providing a single estimate is not easily done, but providing a *range* of values is doable and useful. For instance, we cannot compute $\sqrt{31}$ directly very easily, but we can determine numbers whose square roots are easily computed on either side of 31, namely $25 < 31 < 36$. Then, we know that $\underbrace{\sqrt{25}}_{=5} < \sqrt{31} < \underbrace{\sqrt{36}}_{=6}$, so that $5 < \sqrt{31} < 6$. The same trick works for estimating cube roots, except in that case you want to find two numbers for which the *cube* root, not *square* root, is easily computed.

Other irrational numbers, such as π and e, enter into computations. Common approximations for these are $\pi \approx 3.14$ and $e \approx 2.718$.

Ratios and Proportions

A **ratio** is a comparison of one positive quantity x to another positive quantity y expressed as a fraction $\frac{x}{y}$, or sometimes using the notation $x{:}y$ (read "x to y"). It is often convenient to think of this in words as "for every x of one type, there are y of the second type." For example, if there are 2 girls to every 1 boy in a class, we say that the ratio of girls to boys is 2:1, or 2 to 1, and write the fraction $\frac{2}{1}$. Likewise, if there are 4 dogs for every 3 cats in a kennel, we say that the ratio of dogs to cats is 4:3, or 4 to 3, and write the fraction $\frac{4}{3}$.

The order in which a ratio is expressed is important because of the representation as a fraction. Consider the "dogs to cats" example in the above paragraph. We could alternatively describe the ratio as 3 cats for every 4 dogs, and say the ratio of cats to dogs is 3:4 and write the fraction $\frac{3}{4}$. This conveys the same information. However, since $\frac{3}{4} \neq \frac{4}{3}$, the two ratios are not *equal*. So, keep in mind that order matters when writing down a ratio $a{:}b$.

Ratios can often be simplified in the same manner fractions are. For instance, the ratio describing the scenario "there are 5 dead batteries for every 20 working batteries" is $\frac{5}{20}$, which is equivalent to $\frac{1}{4}$. This simplified fraction can be used to express the scenario equivalently as "there is 1 dead battery for every 4 batteries."

A **proportion** is an equation relating two ratios. In symbols, a proportion is expressed by setting two fractions equal to each other, say $\frac{a}{b} = \frac{c}{d}$. This is often read as "a is to b as c is to d." Proportions are often formulated when one ratio is known and one of the two quantities in an equivalent ratio is unknown. Proportions arise when solving many different types of problems, including changing units of measure and similar triangles. Let's look at a simple scenario.

Suppose it is known that there are 3 soccer balls for every 5 footballs in the storage locker room. If the last count was 40 footballs, how many soccer balls are in the storage room?

To solve this problem, let s denote the number of soccer balls in the storage room. We set up the proportion $\frac{3}{5\frac{3}{4}} = \frac{s}{40}$. To solve for s, we cross-multiply to get $3(40) = 5s$, or $120 = 5s$. Dividing both sides by 5 then yields $s = 24$. So, there are 24 soccer balls in the storage room.

Measurement and Unit Conversions

This section reviews the basics of measurement systems used in the United States (sometimes called *customary measurement*) and other countries, methods of performing mathematical operations with units of measurement, and the process of converting between different units.

The use of measurement enables a connection to be made between mathematics and the real world. To measure any object, assign a number and a unit of measure. For instance, when a fish is caught, it is often weighed in ounces and its length measured in inches.

Types of Measurements

The types of measurements used most frequently in the United States are listed here:

Units of Length
12 inches (in.) = 1 foot (ft.)
3 feet = 36 inches = 1 yard (yd.)
5,280 feet = 1,760 yards = 1 mile (mi.)

Units of Volume
8 ounces* (oz.) = 1 cup (c.)
2 cups = 16 ounces = 1 pint (pt.)
2 pints = 4 cups = 32 ounces = 1 quart (qt.)
4 quarts = 8 pints = 16 cups = 128 ounces = 1 gallon (gal.)

Units of Weight
16 ounces* (oz.) = 1 pound (lb.)
2,000 pounds = 1 ton (T.)

Units of Time
60 seconds (sec.) = 1 minute (min.)
60 minutes = 1 hour (hr.)
24 hours = 1 day
7 days = 1 week
52 weeks = 1 year (yr.)
12 months = 1 year
365 days = 1 year

*Notice that ounces are used to measure the dimensions of both volume and weight.

Converting Units

When performing mathematical operations, it may be necessary to convert units of measure in order to simplify a problem. Units of measure are converted by using either multiplication or division.

■ To convert from a larger unit into a smaller unit, *multiply* the given number of larger units by the number of smaller units in only one of the larger units:

(given number of the larger units) × (the number of smaller units per larger unit) = answer in smaller units

For example, to find the number of inches in 5 feet, multiply 5, the number of larger units, by 12, the number of inches in one foot:

5 feet = __?__ inches

5 feet × 12 (the number of inches in a single foot) = 60 inches: $5 \text{ ft.} \times \frac{12 \text{ in.}}{1 \text{ ft.}} = 60 \text{ in.}$ Therefore, there are 60 inches in five feet.

Example
Convert 3.5 tons to pounds.

3.5 tons = __?__ pounds
$3.5 \text{ tons} \times \frac{2,000 \text{ pounds}}{1 \text{ ton}} = 7,000 \text{ pounds}$
Therefore, there are 7,000 pounds in 3.5 tons.

- To change a smaller unit to a larger unit, *divide* the given number of smaller units by the number of smaller units in only one of the larger units:

$$\frac{\text{given number of smaller units}}{\text{the number of smaller units per larger unit}} = \text{answer in larger units}$$

For example, to find the number of pints in 64 ounces, divide 64, the number of smaller units, by 16, the number of ounces in one pint.

64 ounces = __?__ pints

$$\frac{64 \text{ ounces}}{16 \text{ ounces per pint}} = 4 \text{ pints}$$

Therefore, 64 ounces equals four pints.

Example

Convert 32 ounces to pounds.

32 ounces = __?__ pounds

$$\frac{32 \text{ ounces}}{16 \text{ ounces per pound}} = 2 \text{ pounds}$$

Therefore, 32 ounces equals two pounds.

Basic Operations with Measurement

You may need to add, subtract, multiply, and divide measurement quantities. The mathematical rules needed for each of these operations with measurement follow.

Addition with Measurements

To add measurements, follow these two steps:

1. Add like units.
2. Simplify the answer by converting smaller units into larger units when possible.

Example

Add 4 pounds 5 ounces to 20 ounces.

```
  4 lb.   5 oz.   Be sure to add ounces to ounces.
+        20 oz.
  4 lb. 25 oz.
```

Because 25 ounces is more than 16 ounces (1 pound), simplify by dividing by 16:

```
           1 lb.  r9 oz.
16 oz. ) 25 oz.
         −16 oz.
            9 oz.
```

Then add the 1 pound to the 4 pounds:

4 pounds 25 ounces = 4 pounds + 1 pound 9 ounces = 5 pounds 9 ounces

Subtraction with Measurements

1. Subtract like units if possible.
2. If not, regroup units to allow for subtraction.
3. Write the answer in simplest form.

Example

What is 6 pounds 2 ounces subtracted from 9 pounds 10 ounces?

```
  9 lb. 10 oz.    Subtract ounces from ounces.
− 6 lb.  2 oz.    Then subtract pounds from
  3 lb.  8 oz.    pounds.
```

Sometimes, it is necessary to regroup units when subtracting.

Example

Subtract 3 yards 2 feet from 5 yards 1 foot.

Because 2 feet cannot be taken from 1 foot, regroup 1 yard from the 5 yards and convert the 1 yard to 3 feet. Add 3 feet to 1 foot. Then subtract feet from feet and yards from yards:

```
  $\overset{4}{\cancel{5}}$ yd. $\overset{4}{\cancel{1}}$ ft.
− 3 yd. 2 ft.
  1 yd. 2 ft.
```

Therefore, 5 yards 1 foot − 3 yards 2 feet = 1 yard 2 feet.

Multiplication with Measurements

1. Multiply like units if units are involved.
2. Simplify the answer.

Example

Multiply 5 feet 7 inches by 3.

5 ft. 7 in.	Multiply 7 inches by 3, then multiply 5 feet by 3. Keep the units separate.
× 3	
15 ft. 21 in.	Because 12 inches = 1 foot, simplify 21 inches.

15 ft. 21 in. = 15 ft. + 1 ft. 9 in. = 16 ft. 9 in.

Example

Multiply 9 feet by 4 yards.

First, decide on a common unit: either change the 9 feet to yards, or change the 4 yards to feet. Both options are explained next:

Option 1:

To change yards to feet, multiply the number of feet in a yard (3) by the number of yards in this problem (4).

3 feet in a yard × 4 yards = 12 feet

Then multiply:

9 feet × 12 feet = 108 square feet.

(Note: feet × feet = square feet = ft.^{2})

Option 2:

To change feet to yards, divide the number of feet given (9) by the number of feet in a yard (3).

9 feet ÷ 3 feet in a yard = 3 yards

Then multiply:

3 yards × 4 yards = 12 square yards.

(Note: yards × yards = square yards = yd.^{2})

Division with Measurements

1. Divide into the larger units first.
2. Convert the remainder to the smaller unit.
3. Add the converted remainder to the existing smaller unit, if any.
4. Divide into smaller units.
5. Write the answer in simplest form.

Example

Divide 5 quarts 4 ounces by 4.

1. Divide into the larger unit:

$$\begin{array}{r} 1 \text{ qt. r1 qt.} \\ 4\overline{)5 \text{ qt.}} \\ \underline{-4 \text{ qt.}} \\ 1 \text{ qt.} \end{array}$$

2. Convert the remainder:

1 qt. = 32 oz.

3. Add remainder to original smaller unit:

32 oz. + 4 oz. = 36 oz.

4. Divide into smaller units:

36 oz. ÷ 4 = 9 oz.

5. Write the answer in simplest form:

1 qt. 9 oz.

Metric Measurements

The metric system is an international system of measurement also called the **decimal system**. Converting units in the metric system is much easier than converting units in the customary system of measurement. However, making conversions between the two systems is much more difficult. The basic units of the metric system are the meter, gram, and liter. Here is a general idea of how the two systems compare:

METRIC SYSTEM	CUSTOMARY SYSTEM
1 meter	A meter is a little more than a yard; it is equal to about 39 inches.
1 gram	A gram is a very small unit of weight; there are about 30 grams in one ounce.
1 liter	A liter is a little more than a quart.

Prefixes are attached to the basic metric units to indicate the amount of each unit. For example, the prefix deci means one-tenth ($\frac{1}{10}$); therefore, one deci-gram is one-tenth of a gram, and one decimeter is one-tenth of a meter. The following six prefixes can be used with every metric unit:

KILO	HECTO	DEKA	DECI	CENTI	MILLI
(k)	(h)	(dk)	(d)	(c)	(m)
1,000	100	10	$\frac{1}{10}$	$\frac{1}{100}$	$\frac{1}{1,000}$

Examples

- 1 hectometer = 1 hm = 100 meters
- 1 millimeter = 1 mm = $\frac{1}{1,000}$ meter = 0.001 meter
- 1 dekagram = 1 dkg = 10 grams
- 1 centiliter = 1 cL* = $\frac{1}{100}$ liter = 0.01 liter
- 1 kilogram = 1 kg = 1,000 grams
- 1 deciliter = 1 dL* = $\frac{1}{10}$ liter = 0.1 liter

*Notice that liter is abbreviated with a capital letter—*L*.

The following chart illustrates some common relationships used in the metric system:

LENGTH	WEIGHT	VOLUME
1 km = 1,000 m	1 kg = 1,000 g	1 kL = 1,000 L
1 m = 0.001 km	1 g = 0.001 kg	1 L = 0.001 kL
1 m = 100 cm	1 g = 100 cg	1 L = 100 cL
1 cm = 0.01 m	1 cg = 0.01 g	1 cL = 0.01 L
1 m = 1,000 mm	1 g = 1,000 mg	1 L = 1,000 mL
1 mm = 0.001 m	1 mg = 0.001 g	1 mL = 0.001 L

Conversions within the Metric System

An easy way to do conversions within the metric system is to move the decimal point either to the right or to the left, because the conversion factor is always ten or a power of ten. Remember, when changing from a large unit to a smaller unit, multiply. When changing from a small unit to a larger unit, divide.

Making Easy Conversions within the Metric System

When multiplying by a power of ten, move the decimal point to the right because the number becomes larger. When dividing by a power of ten, move the decimal point to the left because the number becomes smaller.

To change from a larger unit to a smaller unit, move the decimal point to the right.

$$\rightarrow$$

kilo hecto deka UNIT deci centi milli

$$\leftarrow$$

To change from a smaller unit to a larger unit, move the decimal point to the left.

Example

Change 520 grams to kilograms.

1. Be aware that changing grams to kilograms is going from small units to larger units and, thus, requires that the decimal point move to the left.
2. Beginning at the unit (for grams), note that the kilo heading is three places away. Therefore, the decimal point will move three places to the left.

k h dk unit d c m

3. Move the decimal point from the end of 520 to the left three places.
520
$\leftarrow$
.520
Place the decimal point before the 5: 0.520
The answer is 520 grams = 0.520 kilograms.

Example

Ron's supply truck can hold a total of 20,000 kilograms. If he exceeds that limit, he must buy stabilizers for the truck that cost $12.80 each. Each stabilizer can hold 100 additional kilograms. If he wants to pack 22,300,000 grams of supplies, how much money will he have to spend on the stabilizers?

1. First, change 22,300,000 grams to kilograms.

kg hg dkg g dg cg mg

2. Move the decimal point three places to the left: 22,300,000 g = 22,300.000 kg = 22,300 kg.
3. Subtract to find the amount over the limit: 22,300 kg − 20,000 kg = 2,300 kg.
4. Because each stabilizer holds 100 kilograms and the supplies exceed the weight limit of the truck by 2,300 kilograms, Ron must purchase 23 stabilizers:
2,300 kg ÷ 100 kg per stabilizer = 23 stabilizers.
5. Each stabilizer costs $12.80, so multiply $12.80 by 23:
$12.80 × 23 = $294.40.

Algebra and Functions

Algebra includes everything from dealing with expressions involving variables and solving different types of equations, to graphing functions and setting up and solving systems of linear equations and inequalities.

Algebraic Expressions

What makes algebra different from just basic work with number systems is the use of variables. A **variable** is an unknown quantity represented by a letter, like x, y, or z; a **constant** is just a real number whose value does not change. A **term** is a variable or constant, or products of powers thereof. An **algebraic**

expression is an arithmetic combination of terms, like $5x - 3yz$ or $2xy^3 - 5xz + 3$.

If two terms have the same "variable part," then they are called **like terms**. For instance, $43a^5$ and $-6a^5$ are like terms because both have a base of a with an exponent of 5. Even though the terms have different coefficients, they are still like terms. If two terms have different variable parts, then the two terms are NOT like terms. For example, $7zy$ and $7xy$ are unlike because they have different variable parts; $3m^3$ and $4m^6$ are also unlike even though the bases are powers of the same variable. The powers must be the same too!

Since variables represent real numbers, it makes sense that all of the rules (e.g., order of operations, exponent rules, etc.) and properties of arithmetic (e.g., commutative property, associative property, distributive property) should apply to algebraic expressions. To add (or subtract) like terms, we add (or subtract) the coefficients of the terms and keep the variable parts unchanged. For instance, $2x^4 + 4x^4 = 6x^4$. When multiplying or dividing terms, use the exponent rules just as when simplifying arithmetic expressions. This might require using the distributive property repeatedly. Remember the FOIL method when multiplying two binomials? This is actually the distributive property applied twice! For instance,

$$(x + y)(2x - 1) = \underbrace{x(2x) + x(-1)}_{\substack{\text{first application of} \\ \text{distributive property}}} + \underbrace{y(2x) + y(-1)}_{\substack{\text{first application of} \\ \text{distributive property}}} = 2x^2 - x + 2xy - y$$

This same process works for multiplying trinomials and polynomials with even more terms. You simply have more products to compute and more terms to combine.

Example

Simplify $5x^3y - \dfrac{2x^5y^3}{(xy)^2}$.

We use the exponent rules to simplify the quotient in this expression, and then add like terms:

$$5x^3y - \frac{2x^5y^3}{(xy)^2} = 5x^3y - \frac{2x^5y^3}{x^2y^2}$$
$$= 5x^3y = 2x^3y$$
$$= 3x^3y$$

When evaluating algebraic expressions for specific values of the variables, simply substitute the values in and simplify the arithmetic expression as you learned in the previous section.

Example

Evaluate the expression $-s^2(s + 2t)^2 + 3st$ when $s = -1$ and $t = -2$.

Substitute $s = -1$ and $t = -2$ into the expression and simplify using the order of operations:

$$
\begin{aligned}
-s^2(s + 2t)^2 + 3st &= -(-1)^2(-1 + 2(-2))^2 + 3(-1)(-2) \\
&= -(-1)(-5)^2 + 3(-1)(-2) \\
&= -1(25) + 3(-1)(-2) \\
&= -25 + 6 \\
&= -19
\end{aligned}
$$

Algebraic Fractions

Working with algebraic fractions is very similar to working with fractions in arithmetic. The difference is that algebraic fractions contain algebraic expressions in the numerator and/or denominator.

Example

A hotel currently has only one-fifth of its rooms available. If x represents the total number of rooms in the hotel, find an expression for the number of rooms that will be available if another tenth of the total rooms are reserved.

Because x represents the total number of rooms, $\frac{x}{5}$ (or $\frac{1}{5}x$) represents the number of available rooms. One-tenth of the total rooms in the hotel would be represented by the fraction $\frac{x}{10}$. To find the new number of available rooms, find the difference:

$$\frac{x}{5} - \frac{x}{10}.$$

Write $\frac{x}{5} - \frac{x}{10}$ as a single fraction.

Just like in arithmetic, the first step is to find the LCD of 5 and 10, which is 10. Then, change each fraction into an equivalent fraction that has 10 as the denominator.

$$\frac{x}{5} - \frac{x}{10} = \frac{x(2)}{5(2)} - \frac{x}{10}$$

$$= \frac{2x}{10} - \frac{x}{10}$$

$$= \frac{x}{10}$$

Therefore, $\frac{x}{10}$ rooms will be available after another tenth of the rooms are reserved.

Linear Equations and Inequalities

Linear equations are equations in which the unknown variable is raised to the first power, like $5x = 13$ and $4(x - 1) = 3$. The strategy used to solve linear equations involves simplifying various expressions by clearing fractions and using the order of operations, together with the distributive property of multiplication, to isolate the variable on one side of the equation. The basic rule to remember is *balancing* both sides of the equations. If you add or subtract a number from one side, you MUST do so to the other; if you divide or multiply one side by a number, you MUST do it to the other side as well.

Here are two basic examples:

EQUATION	DESCRIPTION OF PROCESS
$3x = -9$ $\frac{1}{3} \cdot 3x = \frac{1}{3} \cdot (-9)$ $x = -3$	The variable is already on one side by itself. Simply divide both sides by its coefficient, which is the same thing as multiplying both sides by the reciprocal of the coefficient.
$2x - 5 = 13$ $2x - 5 + 5 = 13 + 5$ $2x = 18$ $\frac{1}{2} \cdot 2x = \frac{1}{2} \cdot 18$ $x = 9$	This one involves one additional step. First, in order to isolate x on one side, you must add 5 to both sides. Once done, divide both sides by the reciprocal of the coefficient of x, which is 2.

Solving all linear equations basically boils down to solving equations of the previous type, although it can take a significant amount of simplification to do so, as in the following sample equation.

Example

Solve the equation

$$5\lfloor 2 - 3(1 - 2x) \rfloor = 3 - 2x.$$

The order of operations applies to solving linear equations—after all, the variable x represents a real number. We simplify the left side using distributivity multiple times. We then get the x terms on the left side and constants on the right, combine like terms and finally divide by the coefficient of x:

$$5[2 - 3(1 - 2x)] = 3 - 2x$$
$$5[2 - 3 + 6x] = 3 - 2x$$
$$5[-1 + 6x] = 3 - 2x$$
$$-5 + 30x = 3 - 2x$$
$$5 - 5 + 30x = 5 + 3 - 2x$$
$$30x = 8 - 2x$$
$$30x + 2x = 8 - 2x + 2x$$
$$32x = 8$$
$$\tfrac{1}{32} \cdot 32x = \tfrac{1}{32} \cdot 8$$
$$x = \tfrac{1}{4}$$

Sometimes, a linear equation will involve multiple letters and you will be asked to solve for one of them in terms of the others. The same exact procedure applies, though it might look strange. For instance,

you can solve the equation $ax + by = c$ for y simply by subtracting ax from both sides and then dividing both sides by b:

$$ax + by = c$$
$$by = c - ax$$
$$y = \tfrac{c - ax}{b}$$

The same basic strategy is also used to solve linear inequalities, with the one additional step—the inequality sign is switched whenever both sides of the inequality are multiplied by a negative real number. Another distinguishing factor of linear inequalities in contrast to linear equations is that the **solution set** of an inequality (that is, set of real numbers that satisfies the inequality) contains infinitely many values whereas a linear equation has *one* solution. The solution set is often pictured on a number line or represented using **interval notation**, as follows:

LINEAR INEQUALITY	INTERVAL NOTATION	PICTURE ON NUMBER LINE
$x > a$	(a, ∞)	
$x \geq a$	$[a, \infty)$	
$x < a$	$(-\infty, a)$	
$x \leq a$	$(-\infty, a)$	
$a \leq x \leq b$	$[a, b]$	
$a < x < b$	(a, b)	
$-\infty < x < \infty$	$(-\infty, \infty)$	

Solving Compound Inequalities

To solve an inequality that has the form $c < ax + b < d$, isolate the variable by performing the same operation on each part of the inequality.

Example

If $-10 < -5y - 5 < 15$, find y.

- Add five to each part of the inequality.

  $-10 + 5 < -5y - 5 + 5 < 15 + 5$

  $-5 < -5y < 20$

- Divide each term by -5, changing the direction of both inequality symbols:

  $\frac{-5}{-5} < \frac{5y}{-5} < \frac{20}{-5}$

  $1 > y > -4$

The solution consists of all real numbers less than 1 and greater than -4.

Word Problems

Translating Words into Numbers

The most important skill needed for solving word problems is the ability to translate words into mathematical operations. The following will be helpful in achieving this goal by providing common examples of English phrases and their mathematical equivalents.

Phrases meaning addition: *increased by*; *sum of*; *more than*; *exceeds by*.

Examples

A number increased by five: $x + 5$.

The sum of two numbers: $x + y$.

Ten more than a number: $x + 10$.

Phrases meaning subtraction: *decreased by*; *difference of*; *less/fewer than*; *diminished by*.

Examples

Ten less than a number: $x - 10$.

The difference of two numbers: $x - y$.

Phrases meaning multiplication: *times*; *times the sum/difference*; *product of*.

Examples

Three times a number: $3x$.

Twenty percent of 50: $20\% \times 50$.

Five times the sum of a number and three: $5(x + 3)$.

Phrases meaning equals: *is*; *result is*.

Examples

Fifteen is 14 plus 1: $15 = 14 + 1$.

Ten more than two times a number is 15: $2x + 10 = 15$.

Assigning Variables in Word Problems

It may be necessary to create and assign variables in a word problem. To do this, first identify any knowns and unknowns. The known may not be a specific numerical value, but the problem should indicate something about its value. Then, represent the desired unknown by a variable, like x.

Examples

Max has worked for three more years than Ricky.

Unknown: Ricky's work experience = x

Known: Max's experience is three more years = $x + 3$

Heidi made twice as many sales as Rebecca.

Unknown: number of sales Rebecca made = x

Known: number of sales Heidi made is twice Rebecca's amount = $2x$

There are six less than four times the number of pens than pencils.
Unknown: the number of pencils = x
Known: the number of pens = $4x - 6$

Todd has assembled five more than three times the number of cabinets that Andrew has.
Unknown: the number of cabinets Andrew has assembled = x
Known: the number of cabinets Todd has assembled is five more than three times the number Andrew has assembled = $3x + 5$

Percentage Problems

To solve percentage problems, determine what information has been given in the problem and fill this information into the following template:

_____ is _____% of _____

Then translate this information into a one-step equation and solve. In translating, remember that *is* translates to = and *of* translates to ×. Use a variable to represent the unknown quantity.

Examples

Finding a percentage of a given number:
In a new housing development there will be 50 houses. 40% of the houses must be completed in the first stage. How many houses are in the first stage?

1. Translate.
   _____ is 40% of 50.
   $x = 0.40 \times 50$.

2. Solve.
   $x = 0.40 \times 50$
   $x = 20$

20 is 40% of 50. There are 20 houses in the first stage.

Finding a number when a percentage is given:
40% of the cars on the lot have been sold. If 24 cars were sold, how many total cars were there on the lot originally?

1. Translate.
   24 is 40% of _____.
   $24 = 0.40 \times x$.

2. Solve.
   $\frac{24}{0.40} = \frac{0.40x}{0.40}$
   $60 = x$
   24 is 40% of 60. There were 60 total cars on the lot.

Finding what percentage one number is of another:
Matt has 75 employees. He is going to give 15 of them raises. What percent of the employees will receive raises?

1. Translate.
   15 is _____% of 75.
   $15 = x \times 75$.

2. Solve.
   $\frac{15}{75} = \frac{75x}{75}$
   $.20 = x$
   $20\% = x$
   15 is 20% of 75. Therefore, 20% of the employees will receive raises.

Problems Involving Ratios

Ratio problems are solved using the concept of multiples.

Example

A bag contains a total of 60 screws and nails. The ratio of the number of screws to nails is 7:8. How many of each kind are there in the bag?

From the problem, it is known that 7 and 8 share a multiple and that the sum of their product is 60. Whenever you see the word *ratio* in a problem, place an "x" next to each of the numbers in the ratio, and those are your unknowns.

Let $7x$ = the number of screws.

Let $8x$ = the number of nails.

Write and solve the following equation:

$$7x + 8x = 60$$

$$\frac{15x}{15} = \frac{60}{15}$$

$$x = 4$$

Therefore, there are $(7)(4) = 28$ screws and $(8)(4) = 32$ nails in the bag.

Check: $28 + 32 = 60$ screws, $\frac{28}{32} = \frac{7}{8}$.

Problems Involving Variation

Variation is a term referring to a constant ratio in the change of a quantity.

- Two quantities are said to vary **directly** if their ratios are constant. Both variables change in the same direction. In other words, two quantities vary directly if an increase in one causes an increase in the other. This is also true if a decrease in one causes a decrease in the other.

    Example

    If it takes 300 new employees a total of 58.5 hours to train, how many hours will it take to train 800 employees?

    Because each employee needs about the same amount of training, you know that these values vary directly. Therefore, you can set the problem up the following way:

    $$\frac{\text{employees}}{\text{hours}} \rightarrow \frac{300}{58.5} = \frac{800}{x}$$

    Cross multiply to solve:

    $$(800)(58.5) = 300x$$

    $$\frac{46,800}{300} = \frac{300x}{300}$$

    $$156 = x$$

Therefore, it would take 156 hours to train 800 employees.

- Two quantities are said to vary **inversely** if their products are constant. The variables change in opposite directions. This means that as one quantity increases, the other decreases, or as one decreases, the other increases.

    Example

    If two people can plant a field in six days, how many days will it take six people to plant the same field? (Assume each person is working at the same rate.)

    As the number of people planting increases, the number of days needed to plant decreases. Therefore, the relationship between the number of people and days varies inversely. Because the field remains constant, the two products can be set equal to each other.

    $$2 \text{ people} \times 6 \text{ days} = 6 \text{ people} \times x \text{ days}$$

    $$2 \times 6 = 6x$$

    $$\frac{12}{6} = \frac{6x}{6}$$

    $$2 = x$$

    Thus, it would take six people two days to plant the same field.

Rate Problems

There are three main types of rate problems likely to be encountered in the workplace: cost per unit, movement, and work output. **Rate** is defined as a comparison of two quantities with different units of measure.

$$\text{rate} = \frac{x \text{ units}}{y \text{ units}}$$

Examples

$$\frac{\text{dollars}}{\text{hour}}, \frac{\text{cost}}{\text{pound}}, \frac{\text{miles}}{\text{hour}}$$

Cost per Unit

Some problems will require the calculation of unit cost.

Example

If 100 square feet of tile costs $1,000, how much does 1 square foot cost?

$$\frac{\text{total cost}}{\text{\# of square feet}} \;=\; \frac{\$1,000}{100 \text{ ft.}^2}$$
$$= \$10 \text{ per square foot}$$

Movement

In working with movement problems, it is important to use the following formula:

$$(\text{rate})(\text{time}) = \text{distance}$$

Example

A courier traveling at 15 mph traveled from his base to a company in $\frac{1}{4}$ of an hour less than it took when the courier traveled at 12 mph. How far away was his drop-off?

First, write what is known and unknown.
Unknown: time for courier traveling 12 mph = x
Known: time for courier traveling 15 mph = $x - \frac{1}{4}$.
Then, use the formula (rate)(time) = distance to find expressions for the distance traveled at each rate:

12 mph for x hours = a distance of
$12x$ miles
15 mph for $x - \frac{1}{4}$ hours = a distance of
$15x - \frac{15}{4}$ miles

The distance traveled is the same; therefore, make the two expressions equal to each other:

$$
\begin{array}{rcl}
12x &=& 15x - 3.75 \\
-15x & & -15x \\
\hline
\frac{-3x}{-3} &=& \frac{-3.75}{-3} \\
x &=& 1.25
\end{array}
$$

Be careful: 1.25 is not the distance; it is the time. Now you must plug the time into the formula (rate)(time) = distance. Either rate can be used.

$$12x = \text{distance}$$
$$12(1.25) = \text{distance}$$
$$15 \text{ miles} = \text{distance}$$

Work Output

Work-output problems are word problems that deal with the rate of work. The following formula can be used when solving these problems:

$$(\text{rate of work})(\text{time worked}) = \text{job or part of job completed}$$

Example

Danette can wash and wax two cars in six hours, and Judy can wash and wax the same two cars in four hours. If Danette and Judy work together, how long will it take them to wash and wax one car?

Because Danette can wash and wax two cars in six hours, her rate of work is $\frac{2 \text{ cars}}{6 \text{ hours}}$, or one car every three hours. Judy's rate of work is $\frac{2 \text{ cars}}{4 \text{ hours}}$, or one car every two hours. To solve this problem, it is helpful to make a chart:

	(Rate)	(Time)	= Part of job completed
Danette	$(\frac{1}{3})$	(x)	$= \frac{1}{3}x$
Judy	$(\frac{1}{2})$	(x)	$= \frac{1}{2}x$

Because they are both working on only one car, you can set the equation equal to one:
Danette's part + Judy's part = 1 car:

$$\tfrac{1}{3}x + \tfrac{1}{2}x = 1$$

Solve by using 6 as the LCD for 3 and 2 and clearing the fractions by multiplying by the LCD:

$$6(\tfrac{1}{3}x) + 6(\tfrac{1}{2}x) = 6(1)$$
$$2x + 3x = 6$$
$$\tfrac{5x}{5} = \tfrac{6}{5}$$
$$x = 1\tfrac{1}{5}$$

Thus, it will take Judy and Danette $1\tfrac{1}{5}$ hours to wash and wax one car.

Systems of Linear Equations

A **system of equations** is a set of two or more equations that d simultaneously. Two methods for solving a system of equations are substitution and elimination.

Substitution

Substitution involves solving for one variable in terms of another and then substituting that expression into the second equation.

Example

Solve the system $\begin{cases} 2p + q = 11 \\ p + 2q = 13 \end{cases}$

- First, choose an equation and rewrite it, isolating one variable in terms of the other. It does not matter which variable you choose.
$2p + q = 11$ becomes $q = 11 - 2p$.

- Second, substitute $11 - 2p$ for q in the other equation and solve for p:
$p + 2(11 - 2p) = 13$
$p + 22 - 4p = 13$
$22 - 3p = 13$
$22 = 13 + 3p$
$9 = 3p$
$p = 3$

- Now, substitute this answer into either original equation for p to find q.
$2p + q = 11$
$2(3) + q = 11$
$6 + q = 11$
$q = 5$

- Thus, $p = 3$ and $q = 5$.

Elimination

The elimination method involves multiplying one or both equations by constants so that when the resulting equations are added, one variable is eliminated.

Example

Solve $\begin{cases} x - 9 = 2y \\ x - 3 = 5y \end{cases}$

- If you subtract the two equations, the "x" terms will be eliminated, leaving only one variable:
Subtract:
$x - 9 = 2y$
$\underline{-(x - 3) = -5y}$
$-6 = -3y$
$y = 2$

- Substitute 2 for y in one of the original equations and solve for x.
$x - 9 = 2y$
$x - 9 = 2(2)$
$x - 9 = 4$
$x - 9 + 9 = 4 + 9$
$x = 13$

- The answer to the system of equations is $y = 2$ and $x = 13$.

If the variables do not have the same or opposite coefficients, as in the preceding example, adding or subtracting will not eliminate a variable. In this situation, it is first necessary to multiply one or both of the equations by some constant or constants so that the coefficients of one of the variables are the same or opposite. There are many different ways you can choose to do this.

Example

Solve: $\begin{cases} 3x + y = 13 \\ x + 6y = -7 \end{cases}$

We need to multiply one or both of the equations by some constant that will give equal or opposite coefficients of one of the variables. One way to do this is to multiply every term in the second equation by -3.

$3x + y = 13$

$-3(x + 6y = -7) \rightarrow -3x - 18y = 21$

Now if you add the two equations, the "x" terms will be eliminated, leaving only one variable. Continue as in the preceding example.

$$3x + y = 13$$
$$-3x - 18y = 21$$
$$\frac{-17y}{-17} = \frac{34}{-17}$$
$$y = -2$$

- Substitute -2 for y in one of the original equations and solve for x.

$$3x + y = 13$$
$$3x + (-2) = 13$$
$$3x + (-2) + 2 = 13 + 2$$
$$3x = 15$$
$$x = 5$$

- The answer to the system of equations is $y = -2$ and $x = 5$.

The Coordinate Plane

Coordinate geometry is a form of geometrical operations in relation to a **coordinate plane**. A coordinate plane is a grid of square boxes divided into four quadrants by both a horizontal x-axis and a vertical y axis. These two axes intersect at one coordinate point, $(0,0)$, called the **origin**. A **coordinate point**, also called an **ordered pair**, is a specific point on the coordinate plane, with the first number representing the horizontal placement and the second number representing the vertical placement. Coordinate points are given in the form of (x,y).

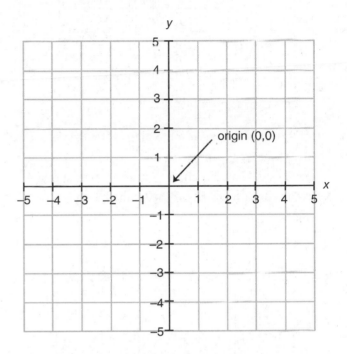

Graphing Ordered Pairs (Points)

- The x-coordinate is listed first in the ordered pair and tells you how many units to move to either the left or the right. If the x-coordinate is positive, move to the right. If the x-coordinate is negative, move to the left.
- The y-coordinate is listed second and tells you how many units to move up or down. If the y-coordinate is positive, move up. If the y-coordinate is negative, move down.

Example

Graph the following points: $(2,3)$, $(3,-2)$, $(-2,3)$, and $(-3,-2)$.

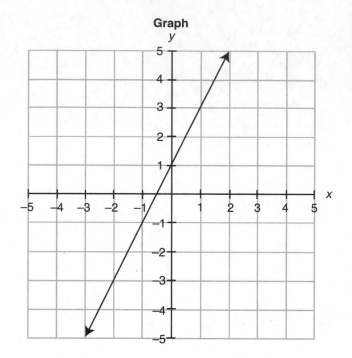

In Words
Javier has one more than two times the number of books Susanna has.

- Notice that the coordinate plane is broken up into four quadrants with one point plotted in each one. Here is a chart to indicate which quadrants contain which ordered pairs based on their signs:

Points	Sign of Coordinates	Quadrant
(2,3)	(+,+)	I
(−2,3)	(−,+)	II
(−3,−2)	(−,−)	III
(3,−2)	(+,−)	IV

Equation

$y = 2x + 1$

Functions

A function is a relationship between two variables x and y where for each value of x, there is *one and only one value of y*. Functions can be represented in four ways:

1. in words
2. a graph
3. an equation
4. a table or chart of values

Table

x	y
0	1
1	3
2	5
3	7
4	9

For example, the following four representations describe the same function.

A key part of the definition of a function is the assignment of each input to *exactly one* output. Consider the following examples:

x	y
5	2
3	−1
2	0
6	1
5	4

x	y
−2	5
−1	6
0	7
1	8
2	9

x	y
−2	3
−1	3
0	3
1	3
2	3

In this table, the
x-value of 5 has **two**
corresponding y-values,
2 and 4. Therefore,
it is **not** a function.

In this table, every
x-value
has **one** corresponding
y-value. This **is**
a function.

In this table, every
x-value
has **one** corresponding
y-value, even though
that value is 3
in every case.
This **is** a function.

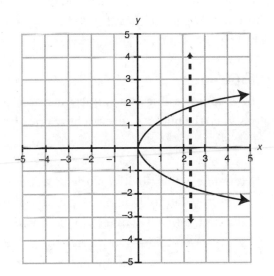

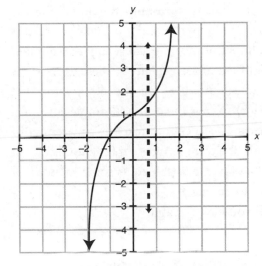

In this graph, there
is at least one vertical
line (the dotted line) that
can be drawn that intersects
the graph in more than one
place. Therefore, this is **not**
a function.

In this graph, there is no
vertical line that can be drawn
that intersects the graph
in more than one place.
This **is** a function.

Functions are generally described using algebraic expressions or graphs, and are denoted using letters, such as f or g. An expression of the form $y = f(x)$ is used to emphasize the input-output defining relationship of a function. Some examples of functions are $f(x) = 3x$, $g(x) = 2x^2 + 3x - 1$, and $h(x) = |x|$.

In order to evaluate a function, like $f(x)$, at a specific x-value, all you must do is substitute that value in for x and simplify the resulting arithmetic expression. For instance:

$$g(3) = 2(3)^2 + 3(3) - 1 = 18 + 9 - 1 = 10$$

The functions with which you will work are all **real-valued**, meaning that the input and output of the function are both real numbers. The **domain** of a function is the set of all possible x-values for which there corresponds an output, y. When an algebraic expression is used to define a function $y = f(x)$, the domain is thought about as the set of all values of x that can be substituted into the expression and yield a meaningful output. For example, the domain of the functions $f(x) = 3x$, $g(x) = 2x^2 + 1$ and $h(x) = |x|$ is the set of all real numbers because *any* real number that is substituted in for x in any of these expressions will yield a real number. On the other hand, the domain of $j(x) = \sqrt{x}$ is the set of all nonnegative real numbers because you cannot take the square root of a negative number. The **range** of a function is the set of all possible y-values attained at some member of the domain. Generally, this is more difficult to determine unless you have a graph.

Example

For $f(x) = \frac{2x}{2x-1} - \frac{x}{x^2+1}$, compute $f(-1)$, if possible.

Everywhere you see an x, substitute -1 and then simplify the resulting arithmetic expression:

$$f(-1) = \frac{2(-1)}{2(-1)-1} - \frac{(-1)}{(-1)^2+1} = \frac{-2}{3} - \frac{-1}{2} = \frac{2}{3} + \frac{1}{2} = \frac{7}{6}$$

Based on our experience adding, subtracting, multiplying, and dividing real numbers, we can define arithmetic operations on *functions*. Let f and g be functions. The sum function $(f + g)(x)$ is defined to be $f(x) + g(x)$. Likewise, the difference function $(f - g)(x)$ is defined to be $f(x) - g(x)$, and the product function $(f \cdot g)(x)$ is defined to be $f(x) \cdot g(x)$. The domains of each of these new functions contain only those x-values for which both $f(x)$ and $g(x)$ are defined. If either one is *not* defined at a particular x, then these arithmetic combinations are not defined at that value. The quotient function $(\frac{f}{g})(x)$ is defined to be $\frac{f(x)}{g(x)}$. Its domain contains only those x-values for which both $f(x)$ *and* $g(x)$ are defined AND for which $g(x)$ is not equal to zero (otherwise, you would be dividing by zero). Arithmetic combinations of more than two functions can be formed in the same way.

Graphing Linear Functions

A **linear function** is a function defined by an equation of the form $f(x) = mx + b$, where m and b are real numbers. You study these functions in disguise when studying lines and linear equations.

Slope

The **slope** of a line is a numerical value indicating how steep the line is. A line can have one of four types of slope:

1. A line with a **positive slope** increases from the bottom left to the upper right on a graph.
2. A line with a **negative slope** decreases from the upper left to the bottom right on a graph.
3. A horizontal line is said to have a **zero slope**.
4. A vertical line is said to have **no slope** (undefined).

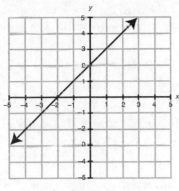

Positive slope

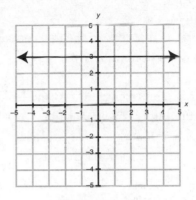

Zero slope

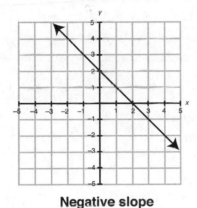

Negative slope

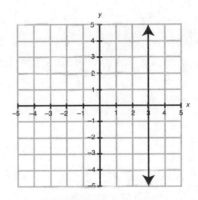

Undefined (no) slope

The slope of a line can be found if you know the coordinates of any two points that lie on the line. It does not matter which two points you use. Slope is found by writing the change in the y-coordinates of any two points on the line over the change in the corresponding x-coordinates. (This is also known as the *rise* over the *run*.)

The formula for the slope of a line containing points (x_1, y_1) and (x_2, y_2):
$$m = \frac{y_2 - y_1}{x_2 - x_1}.$$

Example

Determine the slope of the line containing points $A(-3,5)$ and $B(1,-4)$.

Let (x_1, y_1) represent point A, and let (x_2, y_2) represent point B. This means that $x_1 = -3$, $y_1 = 5$, $x_2 = 1$, and $y_2 = -4$. Substituting these values into the formula gives us:

$$m = \frac{y_2 - y_1}{x_2 - x_1}$$

$$m = \frac{-4 - 5}{1 - (-3)}$$

$$m = \frac{-9}{4}$$

Example

Determine the slope of the line graphed below.

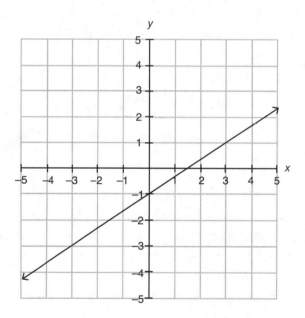

Two points that can be easily determined on the graph are $(3,1)$ and $(0,-1)$. Let $(3,1) = (x_1, y_1)$, and let $(0,-1) = (x_2, y_2)$. This means that $x_1 = 3$, $y_1 = 1$, $x_2 = 0$, and $y_2 = -1$. Substituting these values into the formula gives us:

$$m = \frac{-1 - 1}{0 - 3}$$

$$m = \frac{-2}{-3} = \frac{2}{3}$$

Note: If you know the slope and at least one point on a line, you can find the coordinates of other points on the line. Simply move the required number of units determined by the slope. For

example, from $(8,9)$, given the slope $\frac{7}{5}$, move up seven units and to the right five units. Thus, another point on the line is $(13,16)$.

Determining the Equation of a Line

The equation of a line is given by $y = mx + b$, where:

- x and y are variables such that every coordinate pair (x,y) is on the line
- m is the slope of the line
- b is the **y-intercept**, or the y-value at which the line intersects (or intercepts) the y-axis

In order to determine the equation of a line from a graph, determine the slope and y-intercept and substitute them in the appropriate places in the general form of the equation.

Example

Determine the equation of the line graphed below:

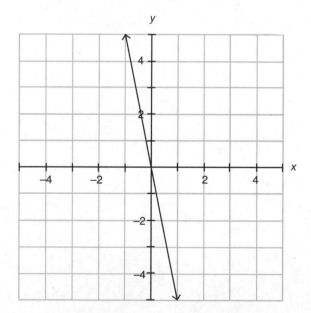

In order to determine the slope of the line, choose two points that can be easily determined on the graph. Two such points are $(-1,5)$ and $(1,-5)$. Let $(-1,5) = (x_1, y_1)$, and let $(1,-5) = (x_2, y_2)$. This means that $x_1 = -1$, $y_1 = 5$, $x_2 = 1$, and $y_2 = -5$. Substituting these values into the formula gives us:

$$m = \frac{-5-5}{1-(-1)} = \frac{-10}{2} = -5.$$

Looking at the graph, we can see that the line crosses the y-axis at the point $(0,0)$. The y-coordinate of this point is 0, which is the y-intercept.

Substituting these values into the general formula gives us $y = -5x + 0$, or just $y = -5x$.

Example

Determine the equation of the line graphed below.

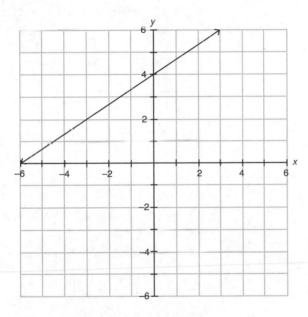

Two points that can be easily determined on the graph are $(-3,2)$ and $(3,6)$. Let $(-3,2) = (x_1, y_1)$, and let $(3,6) = (x_2, y_2)$. Substituting these values into the formula gives us:

$$m = \frac{6-2}{3-(-3)} = \frac{4}{6} = \frac{2}{3}.$$

We can see from the graph that the line crosses the y-axis at the point $(0,4)$. This means the y-intercept is 4.

Substituting these values into the general formula gives us $y = \frac{2}{3}x + 4$.

Angles
Naming Angles

An angle is a figure composed of two rays or line segments joined at a common endpoint called the **vertex** of the angle. Angles are usually named by three capital letters, where the first and last letter are points on the end of the rays, and the middle letter is the vertex.

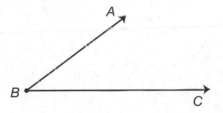

This angle can be named either $\angle ABC$ or $\angle CBA$, but because the vertex of the angle is point B, letter B must be in the middle.

We can sometimes name an angle by its vertex, as long as there is no ambiguity in the diagram. For example, in the preceding angle, we may call the angle $\angle B$ because there is only one angle in the diagram that has B as its vertex.

But in the following diagram, there are a number of angles that have point B as their vertex, so we must name each angle in the diagram with three letters.

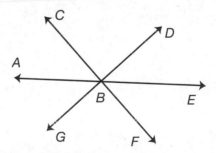

Other Common Functions

When you have a graph of a function, you can determine if an x-value belongs to the domain of f by simply determining if an ordered pair with that x-value belongs to the graph of f.

The following are the graphs of some of the most common functions you will encounter.

FUNCTION	TYPICAL GRAPHS
Linear Functions $f(x) = mx + b$	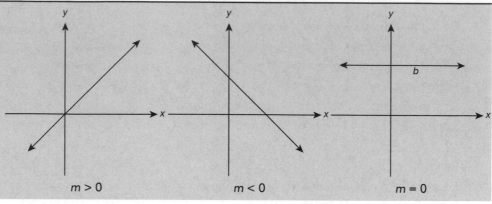
Quadratic Functions $f(x) = a(x - h)^2 + k$	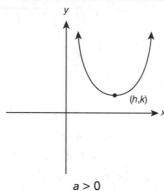 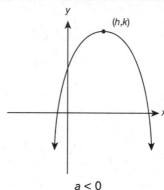
Cubic Function $f(x) = x^3$	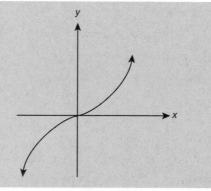
Square Root Function $f(x) = \sqrt{x}$	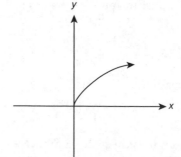

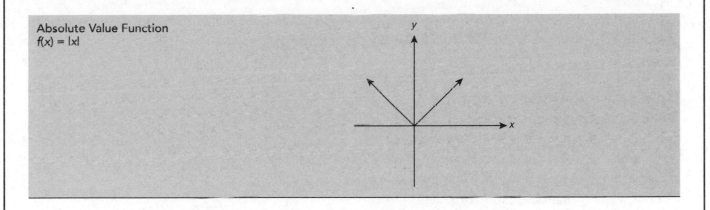

Absolute Value Function
$f(x) = |x|$

All of these functions can be moved about the coordinate plane using horizontal and vertical translations and reflections, defined as follows. Here, let h and k be positive real numbers.

NEW FUNCTION	VERBAL DESCRIPTION OF HOW TO GRAPH THIS FUNCTION BY TRANSLATION OR REFLECTING THE GRAPH OF $y = f(x)$
$F(x) = f(x) + k$	Translate the graph of $y = f(x)$ k units vertically upward.
$F(x) = f(x) - k$	Translate the graph of $y = f(x)$ k units vertically downward.
$F(x) = f(x - k)$	Translate the graph of $y = f(x)$ k units to the right.
$F(x) = f(x + k)$	Translate the graph of $y = f(x)$ k units to the left.
$F(x) = -f(x)$	Reflect the graph of $y = f(x)$ over the x-axis.

Of course, you can perform multiple translations and reflections to the same function to move it up or down, left or right, and flip or not flip.

The following are among the many features of the graphs of functions of the general form $y = f(x)$ that have important utility in application problems.

1. The *maximum of f* is the largest y-value in the range of f.
2. The *minimum of f* is the smallest y-value in the range of f.
3. f is *increasing* on an interval if its graph rises from left to right as you progress through the interval from left to right.
4. f is *decreasing* if its graph falls from left to right as you progress through the interval from left to right.

5. An *x-intercept of f* is a point of the form $(x,0)$. These are found solving $f(x) = 0$.
6. A *y-intercept of f* is the point of the form $(0,f(0))$.

Geometry

Geometry is the study of shapes and the relationships among them. This section familiarizes you with the properties of angles, lines, polygons, triangles, and circles, as well as with the formulas for area, volume, and perimeter.

Points, Segments, Lines, and Angles

You have encountered the terms *point*, *line*, *line segment*, *ray*, and *angle* throughout your elementary school and high school education. Let's review some of the more specialized terminology that you may have forgotten.

Lines, Line Segments, and Rays

A **line** is a straight geometric object that goes on forever in both directions. It is infinite in length and is represented by a straight line with an arrowheads affixed at both ends. Lines can be labeled with one letter (usually in italics) or with two capital letters near the arrows. A **line segment** is a portion of a line with two endpoints and a definitive length. Line segments are named by their endpoints. **Rays** have an endpoint and continue straight in one direction. Rays are named by their endpoint and one point on the ray.

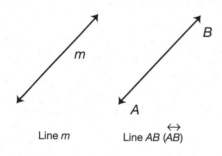

Line *m*   Line *AB* ($\overleftrightarrow{AB}$)

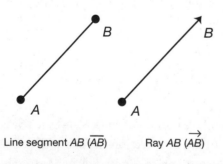

Line segment *AB* ($\overline{AB}$)   Ray *AB* ($\overrightarrow{AB}$)

Parallel and Perpendicular Lines

Parallel lines (or line segments) are a pair of lines that, if extended, would never intersect or meet. The symbol || is used to denote that two lines are parallel. **Perpendicular lines** (or line segments) are lines that

intersect to form right angles, and are denoted with the symbol ⊥.

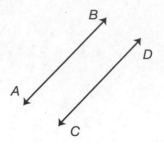

Parallel Lines *AB* and *CD*

$$\overleftrightarrow{AB} \parallel \overleftrightarrow{CD}$$

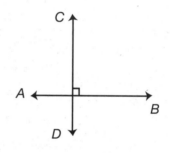

Perpendicular Lines *AB* and *CD*

$$\overleftrightarrow{AB} \perp \overleftrightarrow{CD}$$

Angles
Naming Angles

An angle is a figure composed of two rays or line segments joined at a common endpoint called the **vertex** of the angle. Angles are usually named by three capital letters, where the first and last letter are points on the end of the rays, and the middle letter is the vertex.

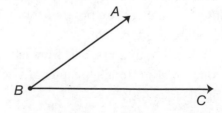

This angle can be named either $\angle ABC$ or $\angle CBA$, but because the vertex of the angle is point B, letter B must be in the middle.

We can sometimes name an angle by its vertex, as long as there is no ambiguity in the diagram. For example, in the preceding angle, we may call the angle $\angle B$ because there is only one angle in the diagram that has B as its vertex.

But in the following diagram, there are a number of angles that have point B as their vertex, so we must name each angle in the diagram with three letters.

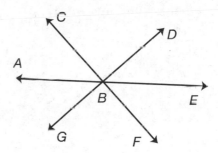

Angles are classified according to their "size" or **measure**, which is provided using the units' *degrees*. The notation $m(\angle A)$ is used to denote the measure of angle A. The following is some basic angle terminology with illustrations:

TERM	DEFINITION
Acute Angle	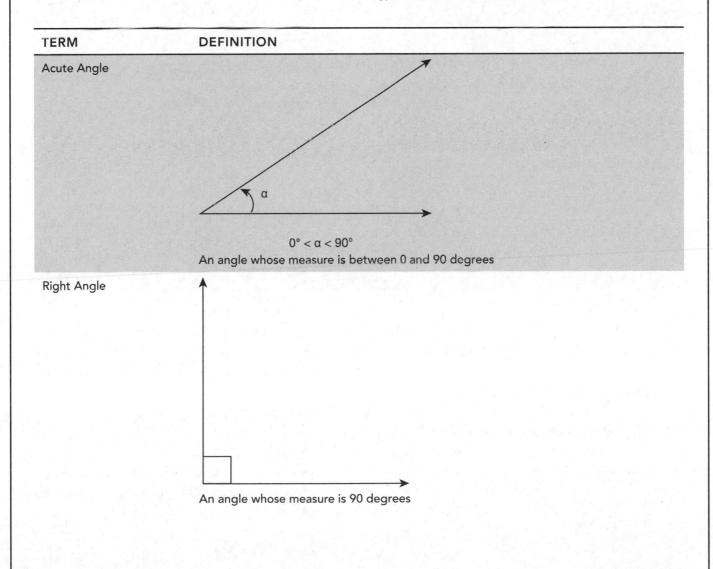

$0° < \alpha < 90°$
An angle whose measure is between 0 and 90 degrees

Right Angle

An angle whose measure is 90 degrees

Obtuse Angle

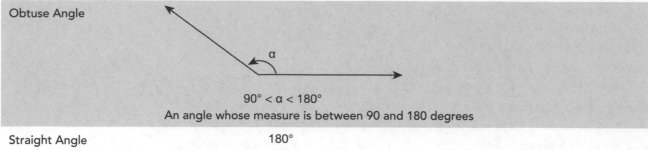

$90° < α < 180°$
An angle whose measure is between 90 and 180 degrees

Straight Angle $180°$

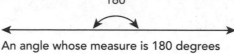

An angle whose measure is 180 degrees

Complementary Angles

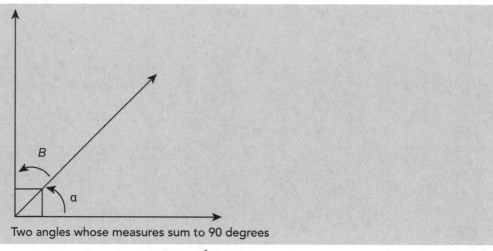

Two angles whose measures sum to 90 degrees

Supplementary Angles

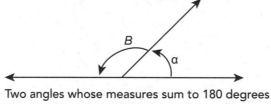

Two angles whose measures sum to 180 degrees

Congruent Angles   Two angles that have the same measure

Example

Two complementary angles have measures $2x°$ and $3x + 20°$. What are the measures of the angles?

Because the angles are complementary, the sum of their measures is 90°. We can set up an equation to let us solve for x:

$$2x + 3x + 20 = 90$$
$$5x + 20 = 90$$
$$5x = 70$$
$$x = 14$$

Substituting $x = 14$ into the measures of the two angles, we get $2(14) = 28°$ and $3(14) + 20 = 62°$. We can check our answers by observing that $28 + 62 = 90$, so the angles are indeed complementary.

Example

One angle is 40 more than 6 times the measure of its supplement. What are the measures of the angles?

Let $x =$ one angle.

Let $6x + 40$ = its supplement.

Because the angles are supplementary, the sum of their measures is 180°. We can set up an equation to let us solve for x:

$$x + 6x + 40 = 180$$
$$7x + 40 = 180$$
$$7x = 140$$
$$x = 20$$

Substituting $x = 20$ into the measures of the two angles, we see that one of the angles is 20°, and its supplement is $6(20) + 40 = 160°$. We can check our answers by observing that $20 + 160 = 180$, proving that the angles are supplementary.

Other pairs of angles are important as well. Consider the following diagram:

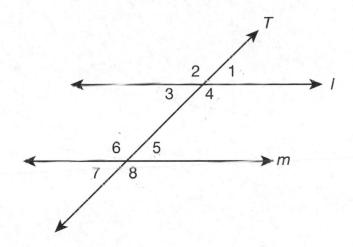

TERM	EXAMPLES FROM DIAGRAM
Vertical Angles	∠1 and ∠3, ∠6 and ∠8
Adjacent Angles	∠1 and ∠4, ∠7 and ∠8
Corresponding Angles	∠1 and ∠5, ∠3 and ∠7
Alternate Interior Angles	∠4 and ∠6, ∠3 and ∠5

Any two adjacent angles formed when two lines intersect form a linear pair; therefore, they are supplementary. In this diagram, ∠1 and ∠2, ∠2 and ∠3, ∠3 and ∠4, and ∠4 and ∠1 are all examples of linear pairs.

Also, the angles that are opposite each other are called **vertical angles**. Vertical angles are angles that share a vertex and whose sides are two pairs of opposite rays. Vertical angles are congruent. In this diagram, ∠1 and ∠3 are vertical angles, so ∠1 ≅ ∠3; ∠2 and ∠4 are congruent vertical angles as well.

Example

Determine the value of y in the following diagram:

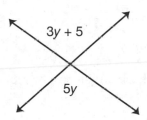

The angles marked $3y + 5$ and $5y$ are vertical angles, so they are congruent and their measures are equal. We can set up and solve the following equation for y:

$$3y + 5 = 5y$$
$$5 = 2y$$
$$2.5 = y$$

Replacing each instance of y with the value 2.5 gives us $3(2.5) + 5 = 12.5$ and $5(2.5) = 12.5$. This proves that the two vertical angles are congruent, with each measuring 12.5°.

Example

In the following diagram, line *l* is parallel to line *m*. Determine the value of *x*.

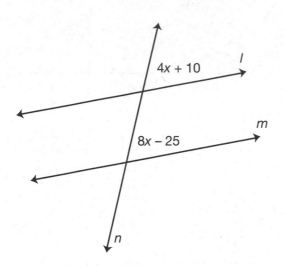

The two labeled angles are **corresponding** angle pairs because they are located on top of the parallel lines and on the same side of the transversal (same relative location). This means that they are congruent, and we can determine the value of *x* by solving the equation:

$$4x + 10 = 8x - 25$$
$$10 = 4x - 25$$
$$35 = 4x$$
$$8.75 = x$$

We can check our answer by replacing the value 8.75 for *x* in the expressions $4x + 10$ and $8x - 25$:

$$4(8.75) + 10 = 8(8.75) - 25$$
$$45 = 45$$

Distance and Midpoint Formulas

Two points with the same *y*-coordinate lie on the same horizontal line, and two points with the same *x*-coordinate lie on the same vertical line. The distance between a horizontal or vertical segment can be found by taking the absolute value of the difference of the two points.

Example

Find the lengths of line segments $\overline{AB}$ and $\overline{BC}$.

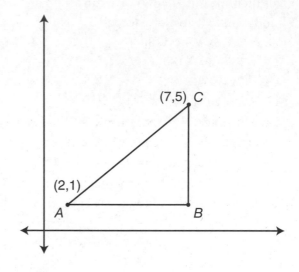

$$|2 - 7| = 5 = \overline{AB}$$
$$|1 - 5| = 4 = \overline{BC}$$

Distance Formula

The distance between any two points is given by the formula $d = \sqrt{(x_2 - x_1)^2 + (y_2 - y_1)^2}$, where (x_1, y_1) represents the coordinates of one point and (x_2, y_2) is the other. The subscripts are used to differentiate between the two different coordinate pairs.

Example

Find the distance between points $A(-3, 5)$ and $B(1, -4)$.

Let (x_1, y_1) represent point *A*, and let (x_2, y_2) represent point *B*. This means that $x_1 = -3$, $y_1 = 5$, $x_2 = 1$, and $y_2 = -4$. Substituting these values into the formula gives us:

$$d = \sqrt{(x_2 - x_1)^2 + (y_2 - y_1)^2}$$
$$d = \sqrt{(-3 - 1)^2 + (5 - (-4))^2}$$
$$d = \sqrt{(-4)^2 + (9)^2}$$
$$d = \sqrt{16 + 81}$$
$$d = \sqrt{97}$$

Midpoint

The **midpoint** of a line segment is the point located at an equal distance from each endpoint. This point is in the exact center of the line segment, and is said to be **equidistant** from the segment's endpoints.

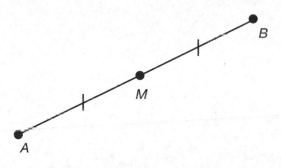

M is the midpoint of $\overline{AB}$

In coordinate geometry, the formula for finding the coordinates of the midpoint of a line segment whose endpoints are (x_1, y_1) and (x_2, y_2) is given by $M = (\frac{x_1 + x_2}{2}, \frac{y_1 + y_2}{2})$.

Example

Determine the midpoint of the line segment $\overline{AB}$ with $A(-3, 5)$ and $B(1, -4)$.

Let (x_1, y_1) represent point A, and let (x_2, y_2) represent point B. This means that $x_1 = -3$, $y_1 = 5$, $x_2 = 1$, and $y_2 = -4$. Substituting these values into the formula gives us:

$$M = (\frac{-3+1}{2}, \frac{5+(-4)}{2})$$

$$M = (\frac{-2}{2}, \frac{1}{2})$$

$$M = (-1, \frac{1}{2})$$

Note: There is no such thing as the midpoint of a line, as lines are infinite in length.

Triangles

Triangles arise when solving many different types of applied problems. They are classified using their angles and sides, as follows:

TYPE	DEFINING CHARACTERISTIC	ILLUSTRATION
Acute	All three angles are acute.	β α Θ
Right	One of the angles is a right angle. (The other two, therefore, must be acute.)	β α

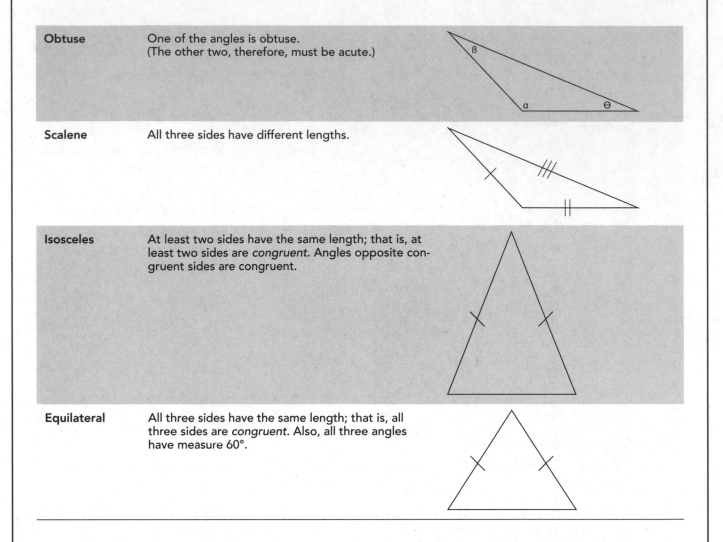

Obtuse	One of the angles is obtuse. (The other two, therefore, must be acute.)	
Scalene	All three sides have different lengths.	
Isosceles	At least two sides have the same length; that is, at least two sides are *congruent*. Angles opposite congruent sides are congruent.	
Equilateral	All three sides have the same length; that is, all three sides are *congruent*. Also, all three angles have measure 60°.	

Two important rules that all triangles obey are the **Triangle Sum Rule** and **Triangle Inequality**. The Triangle Sum Rule says that the sum of the measures of the three angles in any triangle must be 180°, and the Triangle Inequality says that the sum of the lengths of any two sides of a triangle must be strictly larger than the length of the third side. It is impossible to construct a triangle that does not satisfy *both* of these conditions.

Exterior Angles

An **exterior angle** can be formed by extending a side from any of the three vertices of a triangle. Here are some rules for working with exterior angles:

- An exterior angle and an interior angle that share the same vertex are supplementary. In other words, exterior angles and interior angles form straight lines with each other.
- An exterior angle is equal to the sum of the non-adjacent interior angles.
- The sum of the exterior angles of a triangle equals 360°.

Example

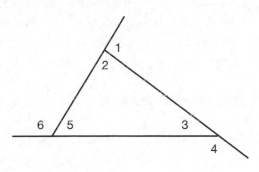

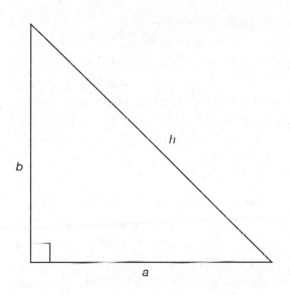

$\angle 1 + \angle 2 = 180°$ $\angle 1 = \angle 3 + \angle 5$

$\angle 3 + \angle 4 = 180°$ $\angle 4 = \angle 2 + \angle 5$

$\angle 5 + \angle 6 = 180°$ $\angle 6 = \angle 3 + \angle 2$

$\angle 1 + \angle 4 + \angle 6 = 360°$

Pythagorean Theorem

The sides of right triangles are particularly interesting because their lengths are related by the **Pythagorean theorem.**

For the right triangle shown here, the sides with lengths *a* and *b* are called *legs* and the side opposite the right angle is the **hypotenuse**; the hypotenuse is the longest side of a right triangle. The Pythagorean theorem says that $a^2 + b^2 = c^2$. This ONLY works for right triangles!

There are two triangles whose angles are such that we can represent the lengths of all sides using nice relationships; they are called 30 – 60 – 90 and 45 – 45 – 90 triangles, where the numbers are the angle measures. Below are the lengths of the sides of such triangles:

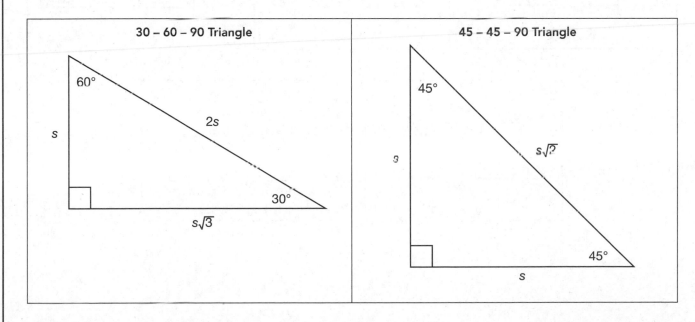

Congruent Triangles

Triangles are said to be congruent (indicated by the symbol ≅) when they have exactly the same size and shape. Two triangles are congruent if their corresponding parts (their angles and sides) are congruent.

There are a number of ways to prove that two triangles are congruent:

Side-Side-Side (SSS): If the three sides of one triangle are congruent to the three corresponding sides of another triangle, the triangles are congruent.

Side-Angle-Side (SAS): If two sides and the included angle of one triangle are congruent to the corresponding two sides and included angle of another triangle, the triangles are congruent.

Angle-Side-Angle (ASA): If two angles and the included side of one triangle are congruent to the corresponding two angles and included side of another triangle, the triangles are congruent.

Used less often but also valid:

Angle-Angle-Side (AAS): If two angles and the non-included side of one triangle are congruent to the corresponding two angles and non-included side of another triangle, the triangles are congruent.

Hypotenuse-Leg (Hy-Leg): If the hypotenuse and a leg of one right triangle are congruent to the hypotenuse and a leg of another right triangle, the triangles are congruent.

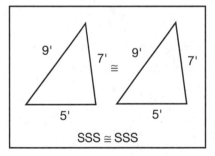

SSS ≅ SSS

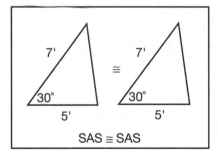

SAS ≅ SAS

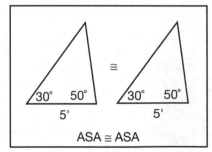

ASA ≅ ASA

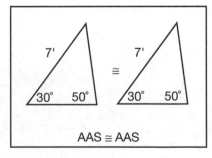

AAS ≅ AAS

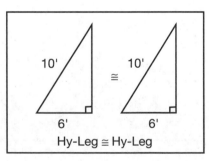

Hy-Leg ≅ Hy-Leg

Example

Determine whether these two triangles are congruent.

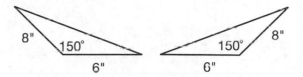

Although the triangles are not oriented the same, there are two congruent corresponding sides, and the angle between them (150°) is congruent. Therefore, the triangles are congruent by the SAS postulate.

Similar Triangles

Even if two triangles $\triangle ABC$ and $\triangle DEF$ are not congruent, they can still be proportional to each other in the sense that the ratios of the three pairs of corresponding sides are the same; that is, $\frac{AB}{DE} = \frac{BC}{EF} = \frac{AC}{DF} = k$, where k is a positive number. In such case, we say $\triangle ABC$ and $\triangle DEF$ are **similar**. Note that if two triangles are congruent, then this common ratio is $k = 1$.

It turns out that corresponding angles in two similar triangles must be congruent. A common method for showing two triangles are similar is to show they share two pairs of congruent angles.

Example

Consider the following diagram, where it is assumed that AB is parallel to CD.

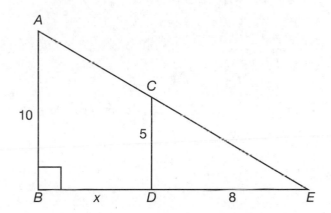

What is the value of x?

Since AB is parallel to CD, we know that $\angle A$ is congruent to $\angle C$ since they are corresponding angles. For the same reason, we know that $\angle B$ and $\angle D$ are both right angles. Therefore, $\triangle ABE$ is similar to $\triangle CDE$. As such, corresponding sides are in the same proportion. Applying this yields the equation $\frac{AB}{CD} = \frac{BE}{DE}$, which is equivalent to $\frac{10}{5} = \frac{x+8}{8}$. To solve for x, we cross multiply to get $80 = 5x + 40$, so that $5x = 40$ and $x = 8$.

Quadrilaterals and Polygons

Quadrilaterals are figures in the plane with four sides, each of which is a line segment. There are several common quadrilaterals (e.g., square, rectangle, parallelogram, etc.) that arise in solving practical problems. They are defined and illustrated in the following table.

QUADRILATERAL	DEFINING CHARACTERISTICS	ILLUSTRATION
Parallelogram	Two pairs of parallel sides	$\overline{AB}$ parallel to $\overline{DC}$ $\overline{AD}$ parallel to $\overline{BC}$
Rectangle	Two pairs of parallel sides and a right angle	$\overline{AB}$ parallel to $\overline{DC}$ $\overline{AD}$ parallel to $\overline{BC}$
Rhombus	Two pairs of parallel sides and all four sides are congruent	$\overline{AB}$ parallel to $\overline{DC}$ $\overline{AD}$ parallel to $\overline{BC}$
Square	Two pairs of parallel sides, all four sides congruent, and a right angle	$\overline{AB}$ parallel to $\overline{DC}$ $\overline{AD}$ parallel to $\overline{BC}$

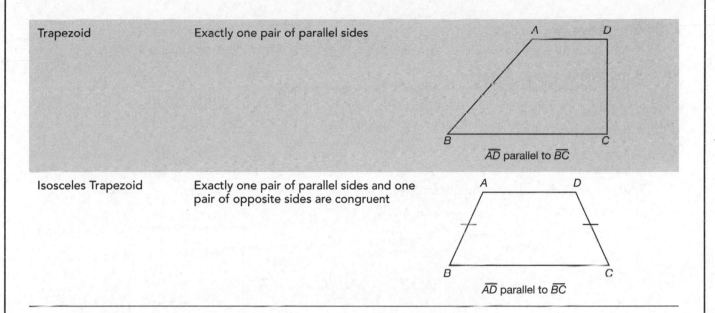

| Trapezoid | Exactly one pair of parallel sides | |
| Isosceles Trapezoid | Exactly one pair of parallel sides and one pair of opposite sides are congruent | |

$\overline{AD}$ parallel to $\overline{BC}$

$\overline{AD}$ parallel to $\overline{BC}$

The following properties hold for these quadrilaterals:

- Consecutive angles of a parallelogram are supplementary.
- Diagonals of a parallelogram bisect each other.
- Diagonals of a rhombus are perpendicular.
- Diagonals of a rectangle are congruent.
- Diagonals of a square are perpendicular and congruent.

Example
In parallelogram $ABCD$, the diagonal $\overline{AC} = 5x + 10$, and the diagonal $\overline{BD} = 9x$. Determine the value of x.

Because the diagonals of a parallelogram are congruent, the lengths are equal. We can then set up and solve the equation $5x + 10 = 9x$ to determine the value of x.

$5x + 10 = 9x$ Subtract $5x$ from both sides of the equation.

$10 = 4x$ Divide 4 from both sides of the equation.

$2.5 = x$

Two quadrilaterals of the same type are **congruent** if their corresponding sides are all congruent, and they are called **similar** if the four ratios of their corresponding sides are equal.

A **polygon** is a figure in the plane that has *several* sides, all of which are line segments. The naming convention is linked to the number of sides. For instance, a **pentagon** is a polygon with 5 sides, a **hexagon** is one with 6 sides, an **octagon** has 8 sides, etc. An *n*-gon is a polygon with *n* sides.

Terms Related to Polygons
- **Vertices** are the corner points of a polygon. The vertices in the polygon above are A, B, C, D, E, and F, and they are always labeled with capital letters.
- A **regular polygon** has congruent sides and congruent angles.
- An **equiangular polygon** has congruent angles.

Interior Angles

To find the sum of the interior angles of any polygon, use this formula:

$S = (x - 2)180°$, where x = the number of sides of the polygon.

Example

Find the sum of the interior angles in this polygon:

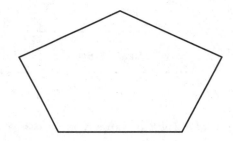

The polygon is a pentagon and has five sides, so substitute 5 for x in the formula:

$$S = (5 - 2) \times 180°$$
$$S = 3 \times 180°$$
$$S = 540°$$

Exterior Angles

Similar to the exterior angles of a triangle, the sum of the exterior angles of any polygon equals 360 degrees.

Similar Polygons

If two polygons are similar, their corresponding angles are congruent, and the ratios of the corresponding sides are in proportion.

Example

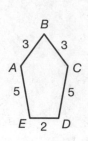
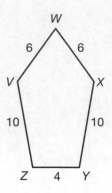

$$\angle A = \angle V = 140°$$
$$\angle B = \angle W = 60°$$
$$\angle C = \angle X = 140°$$
$$\angle D = \angle Y = 100°$$
$$\angle E = \angle Z = 100°$$

$$\frac{AB}{VW} = \frac{BC}{WX} = \frac{CD}{XY} = \frac{DE}{YZ} = \frac{EA}{ZV}$$

$$\frac{3}{6} = \frac{3}{6} = \frac{5}{10} = \frac{5}{10} = \frac{2}{4}$$

These two polygons are similar because their angles are congruent and the ratios of their corresponding sides are in proportion.

Circles

The set of all points in the plane that are a given distance r from a fixed point P is a **circle**. The following is basic terminology involving circles.

TERM	DEFINITION	ILLUSTRATION
Center	The point P equidistant from all points on the circle	
Radius	The common distance r of which points on the circle are from the center	
Chord	A line segment joining two points on the circle	
Diameter	A chord that passes through the center of the circle (Its length is twice the radius.)	
Tangent	A line or line segment outside the circle that intersects it in only one point	

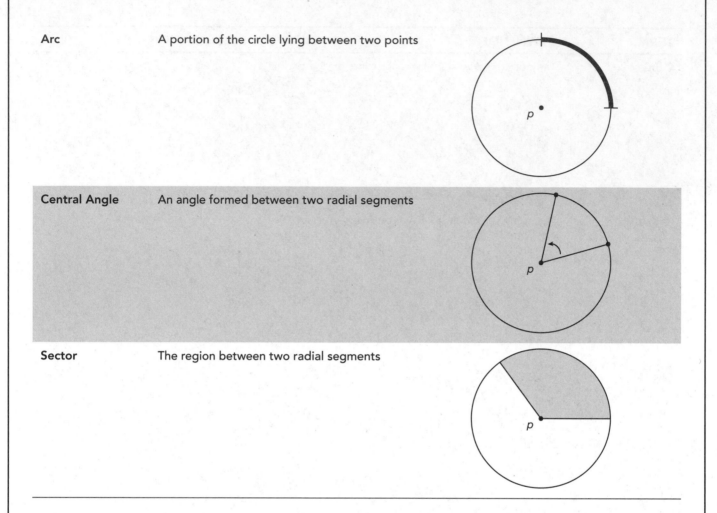

Arc	A portion of the circle lying between two points
Central Angle	An angle formed between two radial segments
Sector	The region between two radial segments

Perimeter

The **perimeter** of a region in the plane is the "distance around." The standard units of measure of length are *inches*, *feet*, *yards*, etc.; the metric system is also commonly used (e.g., *centimeters*, *meters*, etc.).

In the absence of actual units (like inches, feet, centimeters, etc.), we affix the phrase **units** to the end of a length measurement. The following are some standard perimeter formulas:

REGION	ILLUSTRATION	PERIMETER FORMULA
Square		$P = 4s$
Rectangle		$P = 2l + 2w$
Circle		Also called the *circumference*. Since the diameter d is $2r$, we have two expressions for this formula: $P = 2\pi r = \pi d$.
Arc of a Circle		$P = \left(\dfrac{\theta}{180°}\right) \cdot \pi$

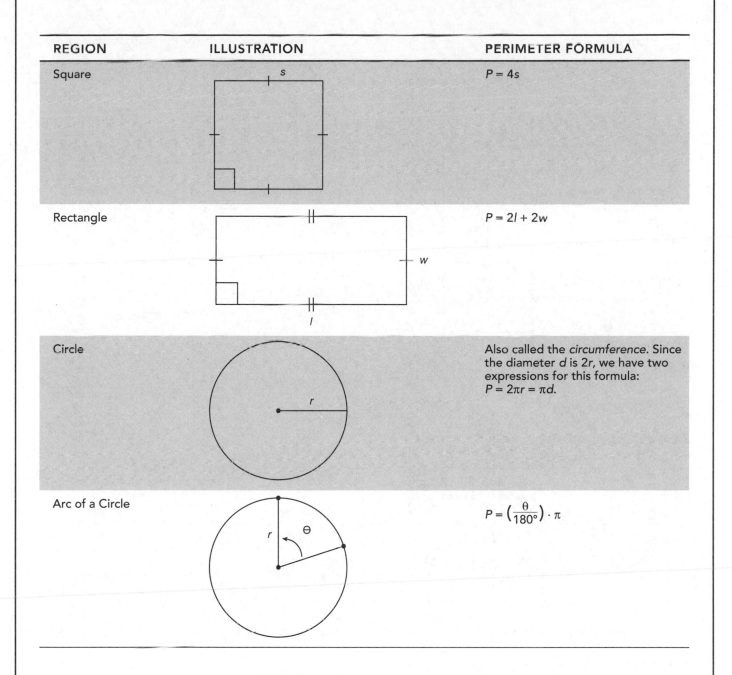

If two regions are congruent, then they have the same perimeter. The calculation of the perimeters of triangles, parallelograms, trapezoids, etc., unless we are given all of the measurements, usually requires that we measure the length of a diagonal (or hypotenuse of a triangle). This, in turn, requires the Pythagorean theorem.

Example

Determine the perimeter, rounded to the nearest tenth, of the following polygonal region:

The idea is to divide the polygonal curve into distinct line segments, as the following shows:

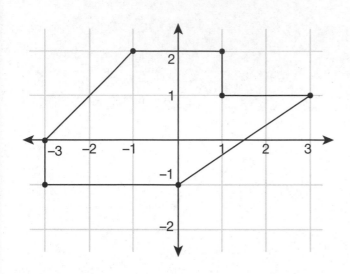

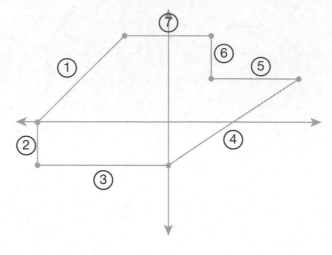

Now, find the lengths of each segment separately:

Length of **(1)**	Use distance formula with points (–1,2) and (–3,0): $\sqrt{(-1-(-3))^2 + (2-0)^2} = \sqrt{8}$	Length of **(4)**	Use distance formula with points (0,–1) and (3,1): $\sqrt{(0-3)^2 + (-1-1)^2} = \sqrt{13}$
Length of **(2)**	$0 - (-1) = 1$	Length of **(5)**	$3 - 1 = 2$
Length of **(3)**	$0 - (-3) = 3$	Length of **(6)**	$2 - 1 = 1$
		Length of **(7)**	$1 - (-1) = 2$

So, the perimeter of this region is the sum of the lengths of these seven segments, which is $9 + \sqrt{8} + \sqrt{13} \approx 15.4$ units.

Area

The **area** of a region in the plane is the number of <u>unit squares</u> needed to cover it. The standard units of measure of area are *square inches, square feet, square yards,* etc.; the metric system is also commonly used (e.g., *square centimeters, square meters,* etc.). In the absence of actual units (like inches, feet, centimeters, etc.), we affix the phrase *square units* (or equivalently, *units²*) to the end of an area measurement.

The following are some standard area formulas:

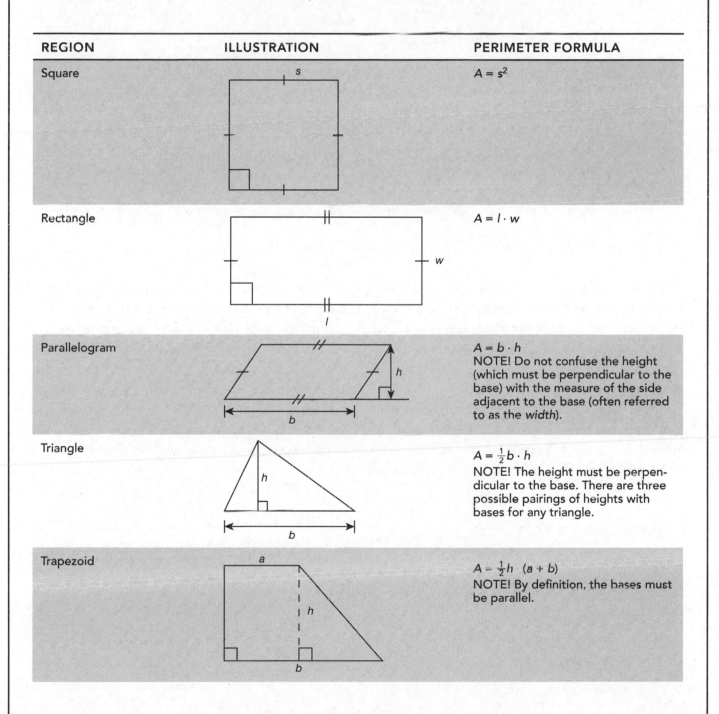

REGION	ILLUSTRATION	PERIMETER FORMULA
Square		$A = s^2$
Rectangle		$A = l \cdot w$
Parallelogram		$A = b \cdot h$ NOTE! Do not confuse the height (which must be perpendicular to the base) with the measure of the side adjacent to the base (often referred to as the *width*).
Triangle		$A = \frac{1}{2}b \cdot h$ NOTE! The height must be perpendicular to the base. There are three possible pairings of heights with bases for any triangle.
Trapezoid		$A = \frac{1}{2}h \ (a + b)$ NOTE! By definition, the bases must be parallel.

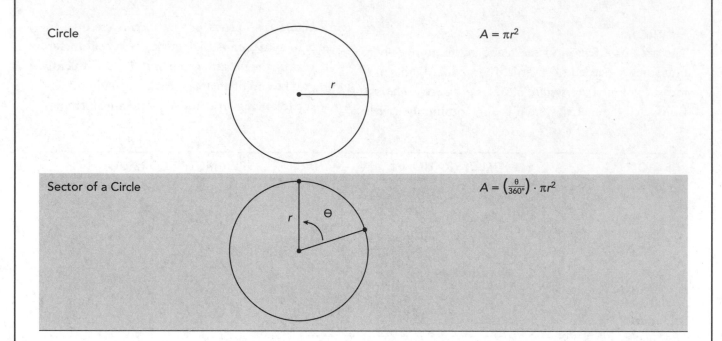

Circle $\qquad$ $A = \pi r^2$

Sector of a Circle $\qquad$ $A = \left(\frac{\theta}{360°}\right) \cdot \pi r^2$

Sometimes, figures are drawn in the coordinate plane. Using the previously shown property, we can chop them into distinct pieces for which there is a known area formula, and sum the areas of these pieces.

Surface Area

If a solid is cut up and flattened out so that it can be visualized as a bunch of recognizable figures whose areas can be computed easily, the sum of those areas is the *surface area* of the solid. Since it is a measure of area, the standard units of measure are *square inches*, *square feet*, *square yards*, etc.; the metric system is also commonly used (e.g., *square centimeters*, *square meters*, etc.). In the absence of actual units (like inches, feet, centimeters, etc.), we affix the phrase *square units* (or equivalently, *units²*) to the end of an area measurement.

The following are formulas for the surface area of some common three-dimensional figures:

SOLID	ILLUSTRATION	SURFACE AREA FORMULA
Cube		$SA = 6s^2$
Rectangular Prism		$SA = 2(lw + lh + wh)$
Circular Cylinder		$SA = 2\pi r^2 + 2\pi rh$
Circular Cone		$SA = \pi r^2 + \pi r\sqrt{r^2 + h^2}$

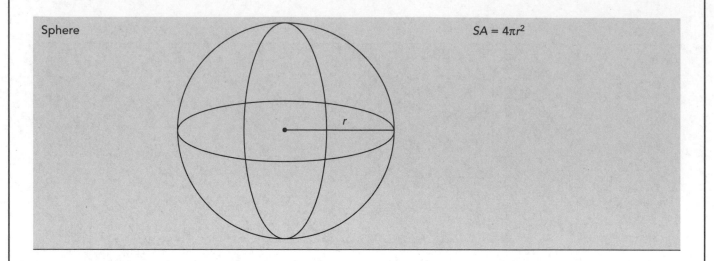

Sphere

$$SA = 4\pi r^2$$

Example

Dan wishes to apply sealant to the four walls and ceiling of the work shed. The ceiling has dimensions of 8 feet by 12 feet and the height of the shed is 9 feet. If each can of sealant is used to seal 200 square feet of wall, how many cans must be purchased?

First, we must determine the total surface area to be sealed. The shed is in the shape of a rectangular prism, whose surface area formula is given above. We must account for four walls and a ceiling, but NOT the floor. So, the surface area is:

$$\underbrace{(8 \cdot 12)}_{\text{Ceiling}} + \underbrace{2(8 \cdot 9) + 2(12 \cdot 9)}_{\text{Walls}} = 456 \text{ square feet.}$$

Since each can coats 200 square feet, Dan must purchase three cans of sealant.

Volume

The **volume** of a solid in space is the number of <u>unit cubes</u> needed to fill it. The standard units of measure of volume are *cubic inches, cubic feet, cubic yards*, etc.; the metric system is also commonly used (e.g., *cubic centimeters, cubic meters*, etc.). In the absence of actual units (like inches, feet, centimeters, etc.), we affix the phrase *cubic units* (or equivalently, *units*[3]) to the end of a volume measurement.

The following are formulas for the volume of some common solids:

SOLID	ILLUSTRATION	VOLUME FORMULA
Cube		$V = s^3$
Rectangular Prism		$V = lwh$
Circular Cylinder		$V = \pi r^2 h$
Circular Cone		$V = \frac{1}{3}\pi r^2 h$

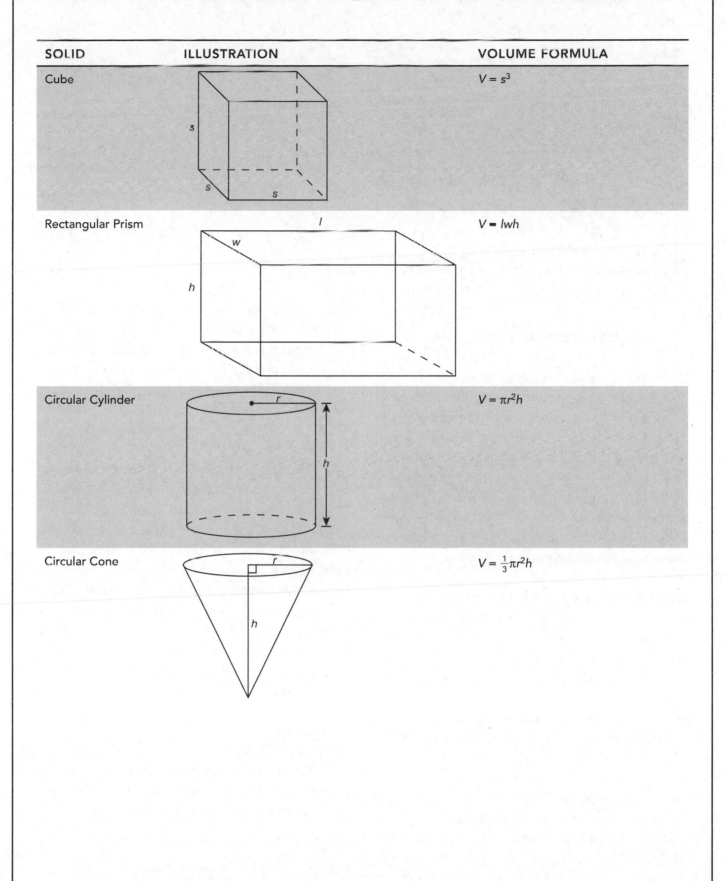

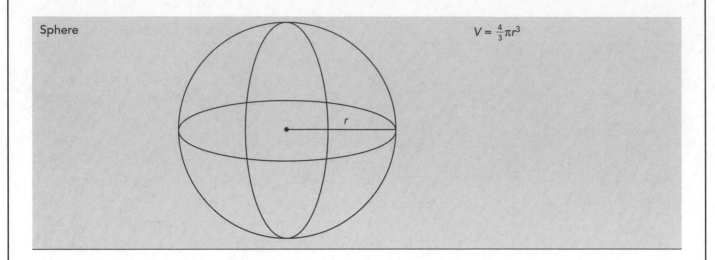

Sphere $\qquad$ $V = \frac{4}{3}\pi r^3$

Statistics and Probability

Statistics is a collection of procedures and principles used for gathering data and analyzing information which aid in making decisions and inferences when faced with uncertainty. Suppose you have a data— like the number of text messages people send daily, weights of cats at a pet store, etc. Each measurement in the data set originates from a distinct source (e.g., patient, plant, household, voter, rat, . . .) called a **unit**. The complete collection of units about which information is sought is called the **population**.

Data Collection and Sampling

Given a population, we often want to understand the responses of its members to some question. A **variable** is simply a characteristic of the population of units that we are interested in. The **data** are the observed values of a variable. There are two main types of variables: qualitative and quantitative. A **qualitative variable** is one whose values are categories (e.g., gender, hair color, demographic information). There is not a unique numerical ordering of the outputs. A **quantitative variable** is one whose values are numerical quantities (e.g., height, temperature, number of heads obtained in 3 flips of a coin).

It is rarely possible to collect data for each unit in a population due to limited resources and/or the inability to actually make infinitely many scientific measurements. As such, a representative subset of the population of units, called a **sample**, is chosen for which you will attempt to gather information for the variable of interest.

The sample should be reasonably large. For instance, if the population of your study is the entire U.S. population, you wouldn't want to choose your sample to consist of merely 5 people from Ohio. Also, the sample should be devoid of **bias**. A study is said to be **biased** if it systematically favors certain outcomes. For instance, suppose that you were investigating a question in which females would likely respond differently than males and that your population is equally split between males and females. In such case, a sample consisting of 95% females could potentially yield biased results.

Probability

Any process that involves uncertainty or chance (e.g., predicting the stock market or weather, guessing the percentage of votes a candidate will receive, or simply flipping a coin) falls within the realm of probability.

An **outcome** is the result of a single trial of a probability experiment. The collection of all outcomes is the *sample space*, which is written as a set. For instance, if you roll a typical six-sided die and record the number of the face on which it comes to rest, the outcomes are the labels on the faces, namely $S = \{1, 2, 3, 4, 5, 6\}$. An **event** is a subset of the sample space and is usually described using one or more conditions. For instance, the event that "the die lands on an even number" is the subset $E = \{2, 4, 6\}$. Suppose E and F represent events of some probability experiment. Some common events formed using them are as follows:

EVENT	DESCRIPTION IN WORDS
Complement of E	All outcomes NOT in E
E or F	All outcomes in E or in F or in both
E and F	All outcomes in common to E and F

Two events are **mutually exclusive** if they do not share any outcomes.

You are undoubtedly familiar with the notion of chance, be it in the form of percent chance of rain today, likelihood that a professional basketball player will make a 3-point shot, etc. Using the new terminology, the **probability** of an event A is denoted by $P(A)$ and is a number between 0 and 1, inclusive, that is in some sense a percent chance of event A occurring. But, how do we actually compute such a quantity? The answer can be rather complicated, but for most of the experiments you will encounter, each outcome in the sample space is *equally likely*. So, if the sample space contains N outcomes, then the probability of any *one* of them occurring is $\frac{1}{N}$. This can be extended to events in the sense that if A contains k elements, then

$$P(A) = \frac{\text{Number of outcomes in } A}{\text{Number of possible outcomes}} = \frac{k}{N}.$$

For instance, in the above dice experiment, since the event "the die lands on an even number" is the subset $E = \{2, 4, 6\}$, and all outcomes are equally likely, $P(E) = \frac{3}{6} = \frac{1}{2}$. So, there's a 50% chance of the die landing on an even number, which is intuitive!

Sometimes, data from an experiment (like a survey) is of the form of **frequencies**. For instance, you ask a question of 120 people, all randomly chosen, and there is one of 5 responses possible. You tabulate the number of responses (that is, the *frequencies*) for each choice and divide that number by 120 (the total number of responses). This **relative frequency** can be used to make an educated guess about how *the entire population from which the respondents were chosen* would answer this question.

Computing the probability of a **compound event**, like A or B, can be a bit tricky because there can be outcomes common to both A and B, and we don't want to count them twice! This is where the following addition formula is useful:

$$P(A \text{ or } B) = P(A) + P(B) - P(A \text{ and } B)$$

When A and B are mutually exclusive, $P(A \text{ and } B) = 0$ and so this formula simplifies.

Example

Suppose you select a card at random from a standard 52-card deck. What is the probability that the card you pull is a queen or a spade?

Let A be the event "card is a queen" and B be the event "card is a spade." Since there are 4 queens in a standard deck, $P(A) = \frac{4}{52} = \frac{1}{13}$, and since there are 13 spades in a standard deck, $P(B) = \frac{13}{52} = \frac{1}{4}$. Finally, there is ONE queen of spades. So, $P(A \text{ and } B) = \frac{1}{52}$. Using the addition formula then gives:

$$P(A \text{ or } B) = P(A) + P(B) - P(A \text{ and } B) = \frac{1}{13} + \frac{1}{4} - \frac{1}{52} = \frac{16}{52} = \frac{4}{13}$$

Measures of Central Tendency and Variability

When dealing with a numerical data set, we are interested in finding where the middle (and potentially the bulk) of where the data values lie. There are three ways to define such a *measure of center*: mean, median, and mode.

The **mean** of a data set is the most familiar—it is just the usual arithmetic average of the data values. Just add them up and divide by the number of values you added. Even if zero is among the values you included in the sum, you MUST include that value in the total count by which you divide; otherwise, you *haven't* accounted for its effect on the average. If there are no "extreme values" in the data set, then this gives a good idea about the average value of the data set. But, in a data set like {10, 10, 10, 10, 110}, in some sense the "average value" is 10 since 4 of the 5 values are 10, but the arithmetic average, or mean, is actually 30, which is not a good descriptor of the center of this data set! For such a situation, we need a different way of computing "average" or center. Data sets for which the mean is an appropriate measure of center have **symmetric histograms**, meaning that the picture is more or less bell-shaped with the peak at or near the mean, as shown in the following:

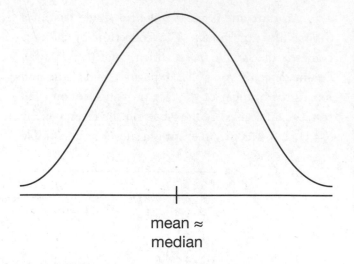

mean ≈
median

The **median** is another way of computing the center of a data set that is immune to such effects of extreme values. To compute it, arrange the values in the data set in numerical order, from smallest to largest. If there is an odd number of data values, then the median is the data value smack dab in the middle of the set. For instance, if there are 21 data values arranged in numerical order, the median is the value in the 11th position (obtained by dividing 21 by 2 and adding 1 to the whole part). If, on the other hand, there is an even number of data values, then the median is the arithmetic average of the "middle two" values. For instance, if there are 20 data values arranged in numerical order, then median is the average of the values in the 10th and 11th positions. By definition, literally half of the data values lie to the left of the median and half lie to its right. Data sets for which the median is an appropriate measure of center have **skewed histograms**, meaning that the picture meaning has a peak to the left or right with a large tail to the other side; the median is positioned near the peak, but the mean is pulled toward the tail, as shown below:

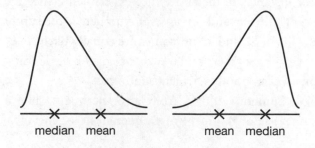

median mean   mean median

The mean and median are only defined for data sets of numerical values. If the data was **qualitative** in nature (e.g., favorite sport, ice cream flavor preference, etc.), then they cannot be used to talk about "average value." That's where the **mode** comes into play. The mode of a data set is the value(s) that occur most frequently; it is defined for all data sets, but has limited utility if there is a large variety of data values that occur or are possible. For instance, the mode of the data set {vanilla, vanilla, chocolate, vanilla, strawberry, butter pecan} is vanilla, while the modes of the data set {3, 5, 5, 3, 6, 7, 5, 3} are 3 and 5. If all values of a data set occur the same number of times, then we say there is no mode.

Measures of center provide half the story. They give us an idea of where the balance point of the data set is, but they do not give us any indication of how the data is *spread out*. For instance, the following two data sets both have a mean of 10, but they are VERY different:

$$\{10, 10, 10, 10, 10, 10\} \text{ and } \{5, 5, 5, 15, 15, 15\}$$

There are two commonly used **measures of variability**: standard deviation, and interquartile range. Which one is used depends on which measure of center—mean or the median—is being used.

The standard deviation, s, is based on the mean, so it is generally used with data sets whose center is best described by the mean. It is a measure of the **typical distance** that data values are from the mean. The formula for the standard deviation for a data set containing n data values is as follows:

$$s = \sqrt{\frac{\Sigma(x - \text{mean})^2}{n - 1}}$$

Here, x represents the data values. In words, you subtract the mean from each data value, square those differences, add them up, divide the sum by $n - 1$, and take the square root of the whole quantity. You will likely not need to compute this by hand, but you should know that the larger the s value, the more

spread out the data. In the extreme case that $s = 0$, all data values would be identical (as in the data set {10, 10, 10, 10, 10}), and hence each one would equal the mean. Any value that is more than two standard deviations from the mean is called an **outlier**, or unusual value.

The **interquartile range**, IQR, is used with data sets whose center is best described by the median. This measures the spread of the middle 50% of the data set. In order to compute the IQR, we must determine the **quartiles**, or data values in the 25th, 50th and 75th positions in the data set once it has been arranged in numerically increasing order. The 50th quartile is just the median, so we already have that. To find the 25th quartile, divide the number of values in the data set by 4. The resulting number is the position of the 25th quartile; to get the value, locate the data value whose position is the *whole* portion of this quotient. If the decimal portion is between 0 and 0.35, use that as the position; if it is between 0.35 and 0.65, average that data value and the next one to get the quartile; and if the decimal portion is larger than 0.65, use the value in the next position as the quartile. The value you get is denoted Q_1 and 25% of the data set lies below it. The third quartile, denoted by Q_3, is computed in a similar manner; 75% of the data set lies below it. The IQR is defined to be $Q_3 - Q_1$. This tells you that the middle 50% of the data set varies by about $Q_3 - Q_1$ *units*.

Visualizing Data

Data analysis involves reading graphs, tables, and other graphical representations. You should be able to do the following:

- read and understand scatter plots, graphs, tables, diagrams, charts, figures, and so on
- interpret graphs, tables, diagrams, charts, figures, and so on
- compare and interpret information presented in graphs, tables, diagrams, charts, figures, and so on

- draw conclusions about the information provided
- make predictions about the data

It is important to read tables, charts, and graphs very carefully. Read all the information presented, paying special attention to headings and units of measure. This section covers tables and graphs. The most common types of graphs are scatter plots, bar graphs, and pie graphs. What follows is an explanation of each, with examples for practice.

Tables

All tables are composed of **rows** (horizontal) and **columns** (vertical). Entries in a single row of a table usually have something in common, and so do entries in a single column. Look at the following table that shows how many cars, both new and used, were sold during particular months.

MONTH	NEW CARS	USED CARS
June	125	65
July	155	80
August	190	100
September	220	115
October	265	140

Tables are very concise ways to convey important information without wasting time and space. Just imagine how many lines of text would be needed to convey the same information. With the table, however, it is easy to refer to a given month and quickly know how many total cars were sold. It would also be easy to compare month to month. In fact, practice by comparing the total sales of July with that of October.

In order to do this, first find out how many cars were sold in each month. There were 235 cars sold in July (155 + 80 = 235) and 405 cars sold in October (265 + 140 = 405). With a little bit of quick arithmetic it can quickly be determined that 170 more cars were sold during October than during July (405 − 235 = 170).

Bar Graphs

Bar graphs are often used to indicate an amount or level of occurrence of a phenomenon for different categories. Consider the following bar graph. It illustrates the number of employees who were absent due to illness during a particular week in two different age groups.

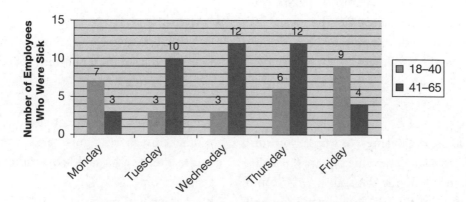

In this bar graph, the categories are the days of the week, and the frequency represents the number of employees who were sick. It can be immediately seen that younger employees were sick before and after the weekend. There is also an inconsistent trend for the younger employees, with data ranging all over the place. During midweek, the older crowd tends to stay home more often.

How many people on average were sick in the 41–65 age group? To find the average, you first must determine how many illnesses occurred each week in the particular age group. There were 41 illnesses in total for a five-day period ($3 + 10 + 12 + 12 + 4 = 41$). To calculate the average, just divide the total illnesses by the number of days for a total of 8.2 illnesses ($\frac{41}{5} = 8.2$) or, more realistically, 8 absences per day.

Pie Charts and Circle Graphs

Pie charts and **circle graphs** are often used to show what percent of a total is taken up by different components of that whole. This type of graph is representative of a whole and is usually divided into percentages. Each section of the chart represents a portion of the whole, and all these sections added together will equal 100% of the whole. The following chart shows the three styles of model homes in a new development and what percentage of each there is.

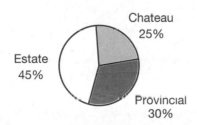

Models of Homes

The chart shows the different models of homes. The categories add up to 100% ($25 + 30 + 45 = 100$). To find the percentage of Estate homes, you can look at the pie chart and see that 45% of the homes are done in the Estate model.

Broken Line Graphs

Broken line graphs illustrate a measurable change over time. If a line is slanted up, it represents an increase, whereas a line sloping down represents a decrease. A flat line indicates no change.

In the following broken line graph, the number of delinquent payments is charted for the first quarter of the year. Each week the number of delinquent customers is summed and recorded.

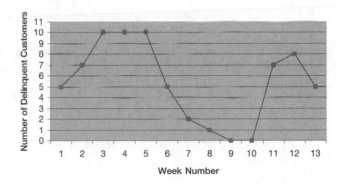

There is an increase in delinquency for the first two weeks, and then the level is maintained for an additional two weeks. There is a steep decrease after week 5 (initially) until the ninth week, where it levels off again, but this time at 0. The 11th week shows a radical increase followed by a little jump up at week 12, and then a decrease to week 13. It is also interesting to see that the first and last weeks have identical values.

Box Plots

A **box plot** is a way to visualize a data set using five summary statistics: minimum value, first quartile, median, third quartile, and maximum value. The graph consists of two points corresponding to the smallest and largest values in the data set, and three vertical line segments corresponding to the quartiles and median. A box is constructed with the quartiles as two parallel sides, and line segments are drawn from these two sides to the minimum and maximum values. For instance, consider the following example:

Given Data Set: 2, 3, 3, 3, 4, 4, 5, 4, 4, 6, 6, 7, 7, 8, 11
Ordered Data Set: 2, 3, 3, 3, 4, 4, 4, 4, 5, 6, 6, 7, 7, 8, 11

Summary Statistics:
Minimum = 2
Q_1 = 3
Median = 4
Q_3 = 6
Maximum = 11

Outliers can be detected using the IQR. Here, IQR = $6 - 3 = 3$. A general rule of thumb is the following:

An outlier is a value in the data set that is less than $Q_1 - 1.5 * IQR$ or larger than $Q_3 + 1.5 * IQR$.

For the above example, any value less than $3 - 1.5(3) = -1.5$ or greater than $6 + 1.5(3) = 10.5$ is an outlier; so, 11 is an outlier.

Box plots are also useful when trying to compare two data sets on the same variable.

Linear Relationships

Often, we are interested in visualizing the relationship between two variables, X and Y. A *scatterplot* is a way of representing this relationship by plotting ordered pairs (x,y) on a coordinate plane.

For instance, a study investigates the question, "Is the value of an education worth its cost?" Education costs are continually on the rise, and costs of education include tuition, books, and living expenses. One-hundred-fifty 30-year-old men and women were asked how many years of formal education he or she had completed and his or her income for the previ-

ous 12 months. The following scatterplot describes the relationship between years of education and income.

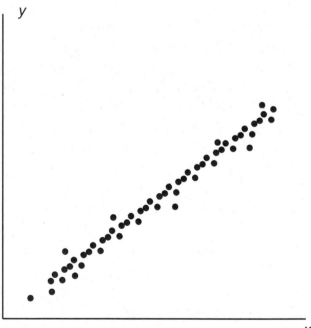

From this scatterplot, we can infer that the more years of education a person has, the higher their salary. This trend can be described even more precisely by fitting a "best fit line" (called a **regression line**) to the scatterplot. Once the equation of the line was known, you could actually predict the salary based on the number of years of education.

We call the relationship between X and Y linear, if the trend between X and Y is reasonably described by a line. If there is another curve (e.g., parabola, exponential curve, etc.) that more reasonably describes the relationship, we call it **nonlinear**.

Generally, the more tightly packed the points are in a scatterplot, the stronger the relationship. If the data points rise from left to right, we say the relationship is *positive*, while if they fall from left to right, we say the trend is *negative*.

We give some basic scenarios below:

RELATIONSHIP BETWEEN X AND Y	TYPICAL SCATTERPLOT
Strong positive linear relationship	
Strong negative linear relationship	

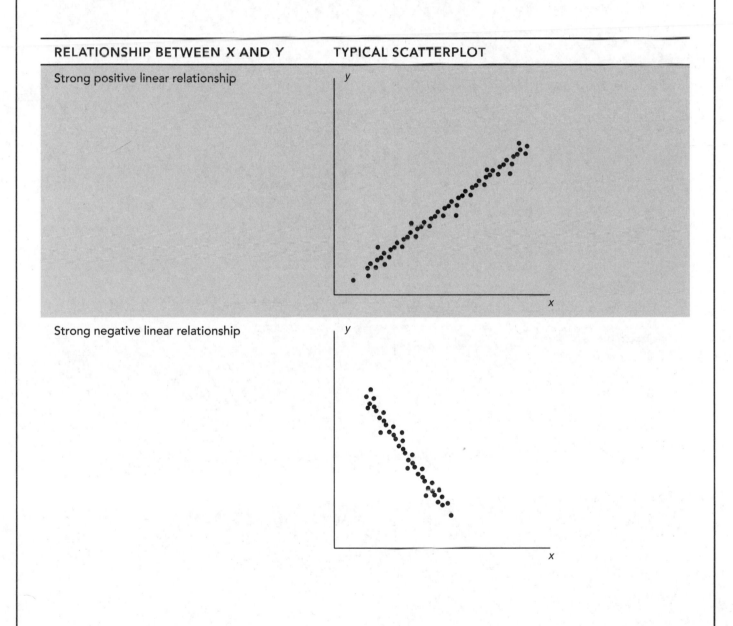

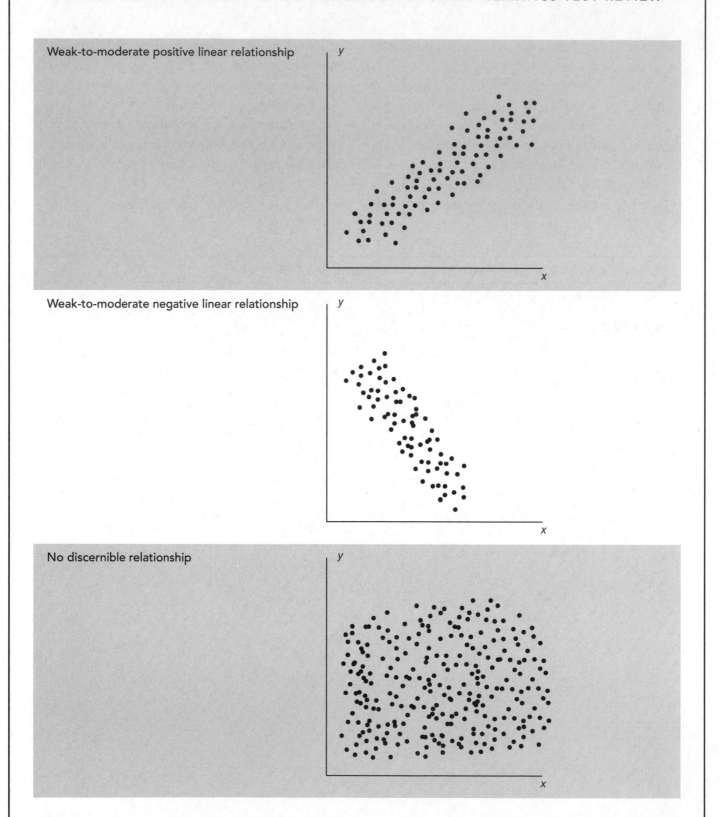

Weak-to-moderate positive linear relationship

Weak-to-moderate negative linear relationship

No discernible relationship

Strong nonlinear relationship

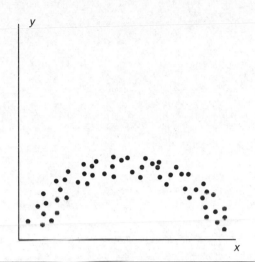

Now that you have reviewed all of the major concepts that are tested on the Praxis Core Mathematics Exam, try completing the practice exams. Good luck!

7 ▶ PRAXIS® CORE ACADEMIC SKILLS FOR EDUCATORS: PRACTICE TEST 1

CHAPTER SUMMARY

Here is a full-length test for each Praxis® Core Academic Skills for Educators test: Reading, Writing, and Mathematics. Now that you have completed the review chapters, take these tests to see how much your score has improved.

Like Chapter 3, this chapter contains three full-length tests that mirror the Reading, Writing, and Mathematics Core tests. Although the actual exam you will take is computer-based, the question types for each exam are replicated here for you in the book.

This time, as you take these practice tests, you should simulate the actual test-taking experience as closely as you can. Find a quiet place to work where you won't be disturbed. Follow the time constraints noted at the beginning of each test.

After you finish taking your tests, review the answer explanations. (Each individual test is followed by its own answer explanations.) See **A Note on Scoring** on page 407 to find information on how to score your exam. Good luck!

Praxis® Core Academic Skills for Educators: Reading Practice Test 1

Time: 40 Minutes

Use the following passage to answer questions 1 through 4.

It is generally allowed that Guyana and Brazil, to the north and south of the Pará district, form two distinct provinces, as regards their animal and vegetable inhabitants. This means that the
5   two regions have a very large number of forms peculiar to themselves, and which are supposed not to have been derived from other quarters during modern geological times. Each may be considered as a center of distribution in the lat-
10   est process of dissemination of species over the surface of tropical America. Pará lies midway between the two centers, each of which has a nucleus of elevated tableland, while the inter-mediate river valley forms a wide extent of low-
15   lying country. It is, therefore, interesting to ascertain from which the latter received its pop-ulation, or whether it contains so large a num-ber of endemic species as would warrant the conclusion that it is itself an independent prov-
20   ince. To assist in deciding such questions as these, we must compare closely the species found in the district with those of the other contiguous regions, and endeavor to ascertain whether they are identical, or only slightly
25   modified, or whether they are highly peculiar.

1. Which sentence best summarizes the main point of the passage?
   a. The fauna and flora of Pará are distinct from both the flora and fauna of Guyana and the fauna and flora of Brazil.
   b. Pará supports a very large number of ecologically distinct habitats.
   c. Ecological considerations override all others with respect to Pará.
   d. It has not yet been determined whether Pará is an ecologically distinct district.
   e. The government of Pará has historically not been supportive of biological expeditions.

2. Each of the following conclusions can be made from the passage EXCEPT
   a. both Guyana and Brazil are ecologically distinct provinces in South America.
   b. both Guyana and Brazil are centers of distribution for the dissemination of species into Pará.
   c. Pará consists of a nucleus of elevated tableland and a low-lying river valley.
   d. the Pará district can be found to the north of Brazil.
   e. Guyana, Brazil, and the Pará district can all be considered part of tropical America.

3. It can be inferred from this passage that the main criterion for declaring any given area a distinct province in terms of its flora and fauna is
   a. the particulars of the district's geographical features, including its isolation or lack thereof.
   b. the number of peculiar species endemic to the district.
   c. the district's proximity to natural populations of endemic species.
   d. the number of identical species inhabiting contiguous regions.
   e. the diversity of species within geographical boundaries.

4. The author describes the terrain in and around Pará to
   a. indicate that the terrain cannot help explain the origin of its animal and plant life.
   b. prove its animal life originated in Guyana and its plant life originated in Brazil.
   c. show that there is little to distinguish the terrain of Guyana from that of Brazil.
   d. explain where the animal and plant life in Pará originated.
   e. make a broad comment about how animals can traverse the Earth's most difficult terrains.

Use the following passage pair to answer questions 5 through 8.

Passage 1
Many studies make it clear that sleep deprivation is dangerous. Sleep-deprived people who are tested by using a driving simulator or by performing a hand-eye coordination task per-
5   form as badly as or worse than those who are intoxicated. Sleep deprivation also magnifies alcohol's effects on the body, so a fatigued person who drinks will become much more impaired than someone who is well rested.
10   Since drowsiness is the brain's last step before falling asleep, driving while drowsy can—and often does—lead to disaster. Caffeine and other stimulants cannot overcome the effects of severe sleep deprivation.

Passage 2
I used to have terrible trouble sleeping—or more accurately—staying asleep. The cause was not psychological but physical. I would wake up in the middle of the night with severe lower back pains and be unable to fall back to sleep for as much as four hours. I initially thought the cause of this pain was my daytime activities.

Perhaps I was exercising improperly or I was lugging around too much weight in my back-pack during my morning and evening com-mutes. Ultimately, I realized the problem was my mattress. The pillow-top mattress on my bed seemed so comfortable in the showroom, but it does not provide uniform body support. Not long after purchasing a new, medium-firm mattress, I enjoyed my first night of uninter-rupted sleep in years.

5. For which of the following situations would information in both Passage 1 and Passage 2 be useful?
   a. improving one's health
   b. selecting the best mattress
   c. understanding the effects of caffeine
   d. writing an essay on hand-eye coordination
   e. evaluating the effectiveness of sleeping pills

6. Which of the following statements best describes the relationship between the two passages?
   a. Passage 1 describes a cause and Passage 2 describes an effect.
   b. Passage 1 describes the first step in a process, and Passage 2 describes the next step.
   c. Passage 1 describes a problem, and Passage 2 describes a possible solution.
   d. Passage 1 describes a general principle, and Passage 2 describes a specific detail.
   e. Passage 1 describes a condition, and Passage 2 contrasts it by describing the opposite condition.

7. The author of Passage 2 explains that he thought his daytime activities caused his back pains to
   a. imply that his conclusions may not be entirely reliable.
   b. indicate that understanding the cause of back pains can be difficult.
   c. explain all the possible causes of back pains.
   d. prove that the source of back pains can never be explained definitively.
   e. show that he was putting too much strain on his back during the daytime.

8. In Passage 1, the term *impaired* most nearly means
   a. sentient.
   b. apprehensive.
   c. disturbed.
   d. blemished.
   e. hampered.

Use the following passage to answer questions 9 through 12.

From *History of the Revolt of the Netherlands* by Friedrich von Schiller

Necessity is the first lawgiver; all the wants that had to be met by this constitution were originally of a commercial nature. Thus, the whole constitution was founded on commerce, and
5   the laws of the nation were adapted to its pur-
suits. The last clause, which excluded foreigners from all offices of trust, was a natural consequence of the preceding articles. So compli-
cated and artificial a relation between the
10 sovereign and his people, which in many prov-
inces was further modified according to the peculiar wants of each, and frequently of some

single city, required for its maintenance the liveliest zeal for the liberties of the country,
15 combined with an intimate acquaintance with them. From a foreigner, neither could well be expected. This law, besides, was enforced recip-
rocally in each particular province; so that in Brabant no Fleming, and in Zealand no Hol-
20 lander could hold office; and it continued in force even after all these provinces were united under one government.

Above all others, Brabant enjoyed the highest degree of freedom. Its privileges were
25 esteemed so valuable that many mothers from the adjacent provinces removed thither about the time of their accouchement, in order to entitle their children to participate, by birth, in all the immunities of that favored country; just
30 as, says Strada, one improves the plants of a rude climate by removing them to the soil of a milder.

9. The author of this passage would most likely agree with which of the following assumptions?
   a. Foreigners are generally not to be trusted.
   b. Crossing borders to give birth is morally suspect.
   c. Laws, as a rule, develop in response to a need for laws.
   d. Unification is a natural tendency for smaller provinces.
   e. No person should be immune to legal restrictions.

10. Which statement, if true, would most weaken the position that foreigners are not able to hold a position of trust?

a. People are able to study the laws of other countries through comprehensive programs designed to immerse them in the intricacies of the laws.

b. Even many years after living in a foreign land, politicians have generally shown favoritism toward their native land.

c. Research shows that the age of a candidate holding an office of trust has a greater influence than his or her country of origin on his or her ability to succeed.

d. The level of distrust a population feels for a foreign-born leader or politician can rarely be eradicated.

e. Many successful nations, such as the United States, were built on a population that mostly originated from other locations.

11. This passage can best be summarized as a

a. defense of a thesis that increased freedom leads to more vigorous commerce.

b. reconciliation of opposing views of constitutional development.

c. contrast and comparison of vagaries of preunification provincial law.

d. review of similarities and contrasts among preunification provincial laws.

e. polemic advocating the desirability of legal reciprocity among neighboring provinces.

12. Which justification does the text provide as support for the exclusion of foreigners from all offices of trust?

a. The laws were extremely complex, necessitating extensive familiarity with their nuances.

b. Stringent enforcement of the laws would be impossible.

c. Mutual distrust prevailed at this time among the various provinces.

d. The election of foreigners to offices of trust would necessitate an unnatural unification.

e. Opening up positions to foreigners that were previously limited to citizens could take away local job opportunities.

Use the following passage to answer questions 13 through 16.

From *Great Astronomers* by Robert S. Ball

The night and the day are not generally equal. There is, however, one occasion in spring, and another in autumn about half a year later, on which the day and the night are each twelve
5   hours at all places on Earth. When the night and day are equal, the point which the Sun occupies on the heavens is termed the equinox; an equinox occurs in March and then again in September. In any investigation of the celestial
10   movements, the positions of these two equinoxes on the heavens are of primary importance. The discovery of this remarkable celestial movement known as the precession of the equinoxes is attributed to the mastermind
15   Hipparchus. The inquiry that led to his discovery involved a most profound investigation, especially when it is remembered that in the days of Hipparchus, the means of observation of the heavenly bodies were only of the crudest

20   description. We can but look with astonishment
on the genius of the man who, in spite of such
difficulties, was able to detect such a phenomenon as the precession, and to exhibit its actual
magnitude. The ingenuity of Hipparchus

25   enabled him to determine the positions of each
of the two equinoxes relative to the stars that lie
in its immediate vicinity. After examination of
the celestial places of these points at different
periods, he was led to the conclusion that each

30   equinox was moving relatively to the stars,
though that movement was so slow that 25,000
years would necessarily elapse before a complete circuit of the heavens was accomplished.
It can be said of his discovery that this was the

35   first instance in the history of science in which
we find that combination of accurate observation with skillful interpretation, of which, in
the subsequent development of astronomy, we
have so many splendid examples.

13. It can be inferred from the passage that the way
in which Hipparchus contributed most importantly to science was which of the following?
  a. He was the first to observe the heavens.
  b. He was first to perceive the equinoxes.
  c. He was the first to combine observation with
    skillful interpretation.
  d. He worked primarily with crude
    instruments of observation.
  e. He was the first to realize that the Earth
    rotates with a tilted axis around the Sun.

14. According to the passage, which is NOT a true
statement about the earth's equinoxes?
  a. Day and night are equivalent in length on
    the equinoxes.
  b. The equinoxes fall on the same day for both
    the northern and southern hemispheres.
  c. It takes 25,000 years for a complete
    precession to occur.
  d. The distance from the Earth to the Sun is the
    same on the equinoxes.
  e. One equinox follows about six months after
    another.

15. Which best describes the general organization
of the passage?
  a. Two opposing scientific theories are
    introduced, and then those theories are
    dissected.
  b. The problem of balanced sunlight is
    presented, and then the solution is
    determined.
  c. An inequality is established, and then the
    causes of the inequality are investigated.
  d. A scientific breakthrough is portrayed, and
    then the resulting effects are illustrated.
  e. A natural phenomenon is described, and
    then its definition and discovery are detailed.

16. In the context of the text, the word *immediate*
in line 27 could be replaced with which of the
following words to have the LEAST impact on
what the sentence means?
  a. swift
  b. neighboring
  c. firsthand
  d. current
  e. remote

Use the following passage to answer questions 17 through 19.

The information on a standard compact disc (CD) is contained in a single spiral track of pits, starting at the inside of the disk and circling its way to the outside. This information is read by
5 shining light from a 780 nm wavelength semi-conductor laser. Information is read as the laser moves over the bumps (where no light will be reflected) and the areas that have no bumps, also known as land (where the laser light will be
10 reflected off the aluminum). The changes in reflectivity are interpreted by a part of the com pact disc player known as the detector. It is the job of the detector to convert the information collected by the laser into the music that was
15 originally recorded onto the disk.

LASER DISC MEDIA			
MEDIA	THICKNESS	LASER WAVELENGTH	INFORMATION CAPACITY
CD	1.2 mm	780 nm	700 MB
DVD	0.6 mm	650 nm	4.7 GB
Blu-ray Disc	1.1 mm	405 nm	25 GB

17. According to the table, if a disc's capacity depends on the size of the laser's wavelength, and 1 gigabyte (GB) equals 1,000 megabytes (MB), then
   a. the longer the wavelength, the smaller the capacity.
   b. the shorter the wavelength, the smaller the capacity.
   c. the longer the wavelength, the larger the capacity.
   d. the shorter the wavelength, the larger the capacity.
   e. the wavelength and the capacity are unrelated.

18. Which information is included in both the passage and the table?
   a. The length of the laser that reads a CD.
   b. How a laser reads a CD.
   c. A comparison between the DVD and the CD.
   d. The capacity of a CD.
   e. The length of the laser that reads a DVD.

19. Based on the information in the passage, what would most likely happen if the detector on a CD player malfunctioned?
   a. The spiral track would not be read properly.
   b. The pits and land would look like one unit.
   c. The changes in reflectivity would be absorbed back into the laser.
   d. The music would play backward.
   e. The information read by the laser would not be converted into music.

Use the following passage to answer questions 20 and 21.

Astronauts expose themselves to a wide range of dangers and hardships as a result of their pro-fession. Space travel is itself, of course, a risky endeavor. But one of the most imperceptible
5 sources of distress for astronauts is the constant exposure to microgravity, a gravitational force in space that is one millionth as strong as the force on Earth. In prolonged space flight, aside from the obvious hazards of meteors, rocky

10 debris, and radiation, astronauts have to deal
with muscle atrophy brought on by weightlessness caused by this microgravity. To try to
counteract this deleterious effect, astronauts
engage in a daily exercise regimen while in
15 space. Effective workouts while in space include
riding a stationary bike, treadmill running
while harnessed, and working against a resistive
force, such as a bungee cord. When they return
to Earth, astronauts face a protracted period of
20 weight training to rebuild their strength.

20. Which sentence in the passage best presents
readers with a major point rather than a minor
point of the passage?
a. "Astronauts expose . . . profession."
b. "Space travel . . . endeavor."
c. "But one . . . Earth."
d. "To try . . . space."
e. "Effective workouts . . . cord."

21. As it appears in the passage, the word *atrophy*
(line 11) most closely means
a. pain.
b. deterioration.
c. weakening.
d. cramping.
e. augmentation.

*Use the following passage to answer questions 22
through 24.*

From *The Special Theory of Relativity*
by Albert Einstein

Geometry sets out from certain conceptions
such as "plane," "point," and "straight line," with
which we are able to associate definite ideas,
and from certain simple propositions (axioms)

5 which, in virtue of these ideas, we are inclined
to accept as "true." Then, on the basis of a logical process, the justification of which we feel
ourselves compelled to admit, all remaining
propositions are shown to follow from those
10 axioms, i.e., they are proven. A proposition is
then correct ("true") when it has been derived
in the recognized manner from the axioms. The
question of "truth" of the individual geometrical propositions is thus reduced to one of the
15 "truth" of the axioms. Now it has long been
known that the last question is not only unanswerable by the methods of geometry, but that
it is in itself entirely without meaning. We cannot ask whether it is true that only one straight
20 line goes through two points. We can only say
that Euclidean geometry deals with things
called "straight lines," to each of which is
ascribed the property of being uniquely determined by two points situated on it.

22. The author's assertion in line 18 that *it is in
itself entirely without meaning* refers to
a. geometrical propositions.
b. the nature of straight lines.
c. the truth of the axioms of geometry.
d. the methods of geometry.
e. any question of the truth of geometry.

23. It can be inferred from the passage that the
truth of a geometrical proposition depends on
which of the following?
a. the concept of straight lines
b. the validity of Euclidean geometry
c. the logical connection of the ideas of
geometry
d. our inclination to accept it as true
e. the truth of the axioms

24. In this passage, the author is chiefly concerned with which of the following topics?
a. a definition of geometric axioms
b. the truth, or lack thereof, of geometrical propositions
c. the logical process of defining straight lines
d. the ability to use geometrical propositions to draw conclusions
e. the precise conceptions of objects such as planes or points.

Use the following passage to answer questions 25 through 30.

For reasons scientists haven't yet fully understood but that may be related to warming water
temperatures or overfishing, jellyfish populations are swelling across the planet's oceans. For
5   swimmers and recreational divers, this is bad
news, as jellyfish are not only a nuisance but
also a potential danger. Unfortunately, jellyfish
offer almost no nutritional value and serve little
function in the seas—meaning that their
10 unpleasant population growth may be difficult
to curtail. However, one animal that can help is
the ocean sunfish. One of the most unusual-
looking creatures found in the oceans, the
mammoth and oddly-shaped ocean sunfish is
15 the heaviest bony fish ever discovered. This
giant fish averages more than a ton in weight,
and its diet consists almost entirely of jellyfish.
Because jellyfish contain so few nutrients, the
sunfish must eat the jellyfish in large quantities.
20 Though sunfish are a delicacy in some countries, such as Japan, the world would be better
served to adopt the European Union's ban on
the sales of all sunfish.

25. Which animal is most similar to the sunfish, in that its diet is beneficial to human beings?
a. spiders, whose diet includes mosquitoes and other insects
b. tuna, whose diet includes squid and shellfish
c. rhinoceros, whose diet includes grass and fruits
d. grizzly bears, whose diet includes fish
e. ticks, whose diet includes mammalian blood

26. Which description of a sunfish best represents a statement of opinion rather than a fact?
a. It is the largest bony fish.
b. It eats primarily jellyfish.
c. It has an unusual appearance.
d. Its sale is banned in Europe.
e. It is eaten by people.

27. Which organization best describes how the passage is structured?
a. Two ocean creatures are compared and contrasted.
b. The main idea is presented, and then supporting ideas provide support.
c. A fascinating sea creature is defined, and then its attributes are detailed.
d. The dietary constraints of one creature are listed, and then a solution is given.
e. A distressing trend is described, and then a potential solution is provided.

28. In the context of the passage, the word *curtail* (line 11) most nearly means
a. reverse.
b. increase.
c. withstand.
d. curb.
e. liberate.

29. Which key word from the passage helps transition the passage from the negative characteristics of jellyfish to the positive attributes of ocean sunfish?
   a. unfortunately
   b. difficult
   c. however
   d. entirely
   e. though

30. Which statement best describes the author's attitude toward the ocean sunfish?
   a. It is not necessarily the largest creature in the ocean.
   b. Its population change remains a mystery to scientists.
   c. It should expand its diet to other non-jellyfish creatures to better adapt.
   d. It should be protected to help limit the escalation of jellyfish populations.
   e. It does not serve a valuable or important purpose in the oceans.

Use the following passage pair to answer questions 31 through 35.

Passage 1
The demotion of Pluto's status in our solar system from planet to dwarf planet in 2006 was an upsetting development for many fans. After all, Pluto is shaped like the other planets—and
5 Pluto even has its own moon! However, the recent discovery of additional celestial bodies similar to Pluto's shape and size forced scientists to agree on the definition of a planet; planets must now be round, orbit the sun, and
10 dominate the neighborhood along their orbit through their gravitational pull.

Passage 2
A dwarf planet has the mass of a standard planet, but it does not orbit the sun. The term came into use in 2006 as part of a recategorization of our Sun's natural satellites. It became a household word when Pluto—formerly categorized as one of our solar system's nine planets—became a dwarf planet officially. Surely, it is the best-known dwarf planet, yet it is only one of four in our solar system. Closer to Earth than Pluto is Ceres, which was also formerly classified as a planet. Further out are Haumea, Makemake, and Eris. Eris is informally known as "the tenth planet."

31. Which of the following best describes the relationship between Passage 1 and Passage 2?
   a. Passage 1 introduces an idea and Passage 2 expands upon it.
   b. Passage 1 makes an argument and Passage 2 contradicts it.
   c. Passage 1 introduces a difficult concept and Passage 2 explains it.
   d. Passage 1 states facts and Passage 2 states opinions.
   e. Passage 1 makes a claim and Passage 2 supports that claim.

32. Which of the following phrases from Passage 2 is an example of figurative language?
   a. standard planet
   b. household word
   c. best-known
   d. formerly classified
   e. the tenth planet

33. In what way is the attitude of the author of Passage 1 different from that of the author of Passage 2?

    a. The author of Passage 1 is more serious than the author of Passage 2.

    b. The author of Passage 1 is more skeptical than the author of Passage 2.

    c. The author of Passage 1 is more cynical than the author of Passage 2.

    d. The author of Passage 1 is more technical than the author of Passage 2.

    e. The author of Passage 1 is more playful than the author of Passage 2.

34. Which statement, if true, would best help to explain why Pluto lost its official designation as a planet?

    a. Its size was significantly smaller than any other designated planet.

    b. Its general orbit contains a greater amount of debris in its path than the other planets.

    c. Its moon was discovered to be merely an asteroid that was captured by Pluto's gravity.

    d. Its orbit around the sun had a greater elliptical shape than the orbits of the other planets.

    e. Its mass is responsible for hydrostatic equilibrium, creating a nearly round shape.

Use the following passage to answer questions 35 through 37.

Jessie Street is sometimes called the Australian Eleanor Roosevelt. Like Roosevelt, Street lived a life of privilege, while at the same time devoting her efforts to working for the rights of the dis-
5 enfranchised, including workers, women, refugees, and Aborigines. In addition, she gained international fame when she was the only woman on the Australian delegation to the conference that founded the United Nations—just
10 as Eleanor Roosevelt was for the United States.

JESSIE STREET TIMELINE	
DATE	EVENT
April 18, 1889	Born
June 17, 1911	Joins suffragettes to fight for women's right to vote
February 10, 1916	Marries Kenneth Whistler Street
December 18, 1929	Establishes the United Associations of Women
March 12, 1932	Proposes the General Social Insurance Scheme
April 1945	Appointed to Australia's delegation to found the United Nations
November 1945	Helps found the Women's International Democratic Federation
February 1947	Becomes the deputy chair of the Status of Women Commission
March 14, 1967	Publishes her autobiography, *Truth or Repose*
July 2, 1970	Dies

35. Based on information in the passage and the chart, when did Jessie Street gain international fame?
- **a.** April 1889
- **b.** June 1911
- **c.** December 1929
- **d.** April 1945
- **e.** March 1967

36. Which of the following can only be learned by reading the chart?
- **a.** Jessie Street worked for women's rights.
- **b.** Jessie Street was interested in the plight of Aborigines.
- **c.** Jessie Street lived a life of privilege.
- **d.** Jessie Street was very similar to Eleanor Roosevelt.
- **e.** Jessie Street wrote an autobiography.

37. Which of the following inferences may be drawn from the information presented in the passage?
- **a.** Eleanor Roosevelt and Jessie Street worked together to include women in the United Nations Charter.
- **b.** Usually, people who live lives of privilege do not spend much time participating in political activities.
- **c.** Discrimination in Australia is much worse than it ever was in the United States.
- **d.** At the time of the formation of the United Nations, few women were involved in international affairs.
- **e.** The United Nations has been ineffective in helping the disenfranchised all over the world.

Use the following passage to answer questions 38 through 41.

Mental and physical health professionals may consider referring clients and patients to a music therapist for a number of reasons. It seems a particularly good choice for the social
5 worker who is coordinating a client's case. Music therapists use music to establish a relationship with the patient and to improve the patient's health, using highly structured musical interactions. Patients and therapists may sing,
10 play instruments, compose music, dance, or simply listen to music.

The course of training for music therapists is comprehensive. In addition to their formal musical and therapy training, music
15 therapists are taught to discern what kinds of interventions will be most beneficial for each individual patient. Because each patient is different and has different goals, the music therapist must be able to understand the patient's
20 situation and choose the music and activities that will do the most toward helping the patient achieve his or her goals. The referring social worker can help this process by clearly articulating each client's history.
25 Although patients may develop their musical skills, that is not the main goal of music therapy. Any client who needs particular work on communication or on academic, emotional, and social skills, and who would benefit
30 from music therapy, is an excellent candidate for music therapy.

38. Which of the following would be the most appropriate title for this passage?

  a. "The Use of Music in the Treatment of Autism"

  b. "How to Use Music to Combat Depression"

  c. "Music Therapy: A Role in Social Work?"

  d. "Training for a Career in Music Therapy"

  e. "The Social Worker as Music Therapist"

39. Which of the following inferences can be drawn from the passage?

  a. Music therapy can succeed where traditional therapies have failed.

  b. Music therapy is a relatively new field.

  c. Music therapy is particularly beneficial for young children.

  d. Music therapy probably will not work well for psychotic people.

  e. Music therapy is appropriate in only a limited number of circumstances.

40. Which of the following best organizes the main topics addressed in this passage?

  a. I. the role of music therapy in social work
     II. locating a music therapist
     III. how to complete a music therapist referral

  b. I. using music in therapy
     II. a typical music therapy intervention
     III. when to prescribe music therapy for sociopaths

  c. I. music therapy and social work
     II. training for music therapists
     III. skills addressed by music therapy

  d. I. how to choose a music therapist
     II. when to refer to a music therapist
     III. who benefits the most from music therapy

  e. I. music therapy as a cost-effective treatment
     II. curriculum of a music therapy program
     III. music therapy and physical illness

41. Which of the following lines from the passage contains an error in logic?

  a. Mental and physical health professionals may consider referring clients and patients to a music therapist for a number of reasons.

  b. Music therapists use music to establish a relationship with the patient and to improve the patient's health, using highly structured musical interactions.

  c. The course of training for music therapists is comprehensive.

  d. Because each patient is different and has different goals, the music therapist must be able to understand the patient's situation and choose the music and activities that will do the most toward helping the patient achieve his or her goals.

  e. Any client who needs particular work on communication or on academic, emotional, and social skills, and who would benefit from music therapy, is an excellent candidate for music therapy.

Use the following passage to answer question 42.

According to a recent poll, the number of students in the high school environmental club has increased by 40% over the past three years. This increase is the reason why more students
5 have begun recycling their paper and cans during this period.

42. Which of the following, if true, most significantly weakens the preceding argument?

    a. The school installed recycling bins in all classrooms five years ago.

    b. Most students join the environmental club in order to add one more activity to their college applications.

    c. Not all students participated in the poll.

    d. Two years ago, the school began giving detention to any student caught throwing recyclable materials in the regular trash.

    e. The environmental club has begun hanging up more posters about recycling.

Use the following passage to answer questions 43 through 45.

    Businesses today routinely keep track of large amounts of both financial and nonfinancial information. Sales departments keep track of current and potential customers; marketing
5   departments keep track of product details and regional demographics; accounting departments keep track of financial data and issue reports. To be useful, all this data must be organized into a meaningful and useful system.
10   Such a system is called a *management information system*, abbreviated MIS. The financial hub of the MIS is accounting.

43. This passage is most likely taken from

    a. a newspaper column.

    b. an essay about modern business.

    c. a legal brief.

    d. a business textbook.

    e. a business machine catalog.

44. According to the information in the passage, which of the following is least likely to be a function of accounting?

    a. helping businesspeople make sound judgments

    b. producing reports of many different kinds of transactions

    c. assisting with the marketing of products

    d. assisting companies in important planning activities

    e. providing information to potential investors

45. According to the information in the passage, all of the following would be included in a company's MIS EXCEPT

    a. potential customers.

    b. financial data.

    c. regional demographics.

    d. employee birthdates.

    e. product details.

Use the following passage to answer question 46.

    The salesperson of the month at Smith's Used Cars sold 26 cars in February. Diana sold 22 cars in February.

46. Based only on the information provided, which of the following must be true?

    a. Diana is not salesperson of the month at Smith's Used Cars.

    b. The salesperson of the month is the person who sold the most cars that month.

    c. Diana does not work at Smith's Used Cars.

    d. The salesperson of the month made more money in February than Diana did.

    e. The salesperson of the month is better at selling cars than Diana is.

Use the following passage to answer question 47.

    Thomas Nast (1840–1902), the preeminent political cartoonist of the second half of the nineteenth century, demonstrated the power of his medium when he used his art to end the
5   corrupt Boss Tweed Ring in New York City. His images, first drawn for *Harper's Weekly*, are still

in currency today: Nast created the tiger as the symbol of Tammany Hall, the elephant for the Republican Party, and the donkey for the
10 Democratic Party.

47. The author cites Thomas Nast's depiction of an elephant for the Republican Party as an example of
  a. an image that is no longer recognized by the public.
  b. the saying, "the pen is mightier than the sword."
  c. art contributing to political reform.
  d. a graphic image that became an enduring symbol.
  e. the ephemeral nature of political cartooning.

Use the following passage to answer questions 48 and 49.

Typically people think of genius, whether it manifests in Mozart's composing symphonies at age five or Einstein's discovery of relativity, as having a quality not just of the supernatural,
5 but also of the eccentric. People see genius as a "good" abnormality; moreover, they think of genius as a completely unpredictable abnormality. Until recently, psychologists regarded the quirks of genius as too erratic to describe
10 intelligibly; however, Anna Findley's ground-breaking study uncovers predictable patterns in the biographies of geniuses. These patterns do not dispel the common belief that there is a kind of supernatural intervention in the lives of
15 unusually talented men and women, however, even though they occur with regularity. For example, Findley shows that all geniuses experi-ence three intensely productive periods in their lives, one of which always occurs shortly before
20 their deaths; this is true whether the genius lives to 19 or 90.

48. Which of the following would be the best title for this passage?
  a. "Understanding Mozarts and Einsteins"
  b. "Predicting the Life of a Genius"
  c. "The Uncanny Patterns in the Lives of Geniuses"
  d. "Pattern and Disorder in the Lives of Geniuses"
  e. "Supernatural Intervention in the Life of the Genius"

49. Given the information in the passage, which of the following statements is true?
  a. Anna Findley is a biographer.
  b. All geniuses are eccentric and unpredictable.
  c. A genius has three prolific periods in his or her life.
  d. Mozart discovered relativity.
  e. Geniuses experience three fallow periods in their lives.

Use the following passage to answer question 50.

Sushi, the thousand-year-old Japanese delicacy, was once thought of in this country as <u>unpalatable</u> and too exotic. But tastes have changed, for a number of reasons.

50. In the passage, *unpalatable* most nearly means
  a. not visually appealing.
  b. not tasting good.
  c. bad smelling.
  d. too expensive.
  e. rough to the touch.

Use the following passage to answer questions 51 through 54.

The Caribbean island of Saint Martin is a favorite vacation spot, one that is popular with tourists from various countries. The French and Dutch settled on the island in the 1600s. Today,
5 the island is divided between the two. The French capital is Marigot; the Dutch capital is Philipsburg.

Tourists on vacation soon discovered that Saint Martin has an intriguing history. Twelve
10 hundred years ago, the Arawak Indians inhabited all the islands of the West Indies, and were a peaceful people living under the guidance of their chiefs. In the 1300s, three hundred years after the Arawaks first arrived on Saint Martin,
15 they were defeated and forced to abandon the island by a more hostile tribe of Indians that originated in South America. This new tribe was called the Carib. The Caribbean Sea was named after them. Unlike the Arawaks, they
20 had no permanent chiefs or leaders, except in times of strife. They were also extremely warlike. Worse, they were cannibalistic, eating the enemy warriors they captured. In fact, the very word *cannibal* comes from the Spanish name
25 for the Carib Indians. The Spanish arrived in the fifteenth century and, unfortunately, they carried diseases to which the Indians had no immunity. Many Indians succumbed to common European illnesses. Others died from the
30 hard labor forced upon them.

51. According to the passage, all the following are true about the Carib Indians EXCEPT
 a. a sea was named after them.
 b. they were peaceful fishermen, hunters, and farmers.
 c. they ate human flesh.
 d. they settled after defeating the Arawak Indians.
 e. during times of war, they had temporary leaders.

52. According to the passage, the Carib Indians were finally defeated by
 a. sickness and forced labor.
 b. the more aggressive Arawak tribe.
 c. the Dutch West India Company.
 d. the French explorers.
 e. a cannibalistic tribe.

53. One can infer from the passage that the word *strife* (line 21) means
 a. cannibalistic.
 b. war.
 c. labor.
 d. chief.
 e. Carib.

54. According to the article, present-day Saint Martin
 a. belongs to the Spanish.
 b. is independent.
 c. belongs to the Carib.
 d. is part of the U.S. Virgin Islands.
 e. is shared by the French and the Dutch.

Use the following passage to answer questions 55 and 56.

Although protected by the Australian government, the Great Barrier Reef faces environmental threats. Crown-of-thorns starfish feed on coral and can destroy large portions of reef.
5   Pollution and rising water temperatures also threaten the delicate coral. But the most preventable hazard to the reef is tourists. Tourists have contributed to the destruction of the reef ecosystem by breaking off and removing pieces
10   of coral to bring home as souvenirs. The government hopes that by informing tourists of the dangers of this seemingly harmless activity they will quash this creeping menace to the fragile reef.

55. Which key word from the passage helps the transition from the natural threats the Great Barrier Reef faces to the human-caused threats it faces?
   a. Although
   b. also
   c. But
   d. and
   e. creeping

56. The primary purpose of this passage is to
   a. inform the reader that coral reefs are a threatened, yet broadly functioning, ecosystem.
   b. alert the reader to a premier vacation destination in the tropics.
   c. explain in detail how the Great Barrier Reef is constructed.
   d. recommend that tourists stop stealing coral off the Great Barrier Reef.
   e. dispel the argument that coral is a plant, not an animal.

Praxis® Core Academic Skills for Educators: Reading Practice Test 1 Answers and Explanations

1. d. The author's main point in this passage is to set forth the need to investigate the ecological status of Pará and the means by which the investigation should proceed. The flora and fauna of Guyana are distinct from the flora and fauna of Brazil. However, the fauna and flora of Pará are not necessarily distinct; the passage even asks whether the species in the Pará district are identical, modified, or peculiar to the species of the other regions. Therefore, choice **a** is incorrect. The passage states that Guyana and Brazil support a very large number of ecologically distinct habitats, but it does not make this claim definitively about Pará, making choice **b** incorrect. The focus of the passage is not about the overriding importance of Pará's ecological considerations, and there is no support in the passage to make the claim that Pará's government has not been supportive of expeditions; therefore, choices **c** and **e** are incorrect.

2. c. The physical description in this answer choice is not correct for Para, though it is correct for both Guyana and Brazil. The first sentence of the passage describes both Guyana and Brazil as ecologically distinct provinces. Because this is a true statement, choice **a** cannot be correct. The passage says that both Guyana and Brazil are centers of distribution for the dissemination of species into Pará, so choice **b** is not correct. It can be concluded from the passage that Para lies between Guyana and Brazil, with Brazil to the south. Therefore, choice **d** is not correct. Both Guyana and Brazil are listed as a center of distribution in the latest process of dissemination of species over the surface of tropical America. Pará lies in between them, so it would also belong to tropical America; this means choice **e** is incorrect as well.

3. b. The author suggests evaluating Pará to see whether it "contains so large a number of endemic species as would warrant the conclusion that it is itself an independent province." The species in an area determine whether it is a distinct province, not the area's geographical features, so choice **a** is incorrect. The passage does not indicate that it is a district's proximity that determines whether it is distinct, so choice **c** is incorrect. It is not the number of *identical* species that determines whether a province is distinct, so choice **d** is incorrect. The species that are endemic to the district determine whether the province is distinct, so choice **e** is incorrect.

4. a. The description indicates that both Guyana and Brazil have similar terrains on the edges of Pará, so other considerations must be made to figure out where its diverse animal and plant life originated, such as comparing these species with those found in other regions. Because that terrain cannot explain where Pará's animal and plant life originated, choices **b** and **d** do not make sense. The author only describes the terrain of Guyana and Brazil on the very edges of Pará, so there is not enough information about these countries' terrains to draw the conclusion in choice **c**. Choice **e** draws a conclusion that the information in the passage does not support.

5. a. A good night of rest is essential to good health, and both of these passages suggest ways to achieve better rest. Passage 1 suggests drinking less alcohol and Passage 2 suggests sleeping on a mattress that provides uniform body support. Choice **b** is too specific; only Passage 2 refers to mattress selection, so this choice does not make use of information in both passages. Only Passage 1 refers to caffeine, and it only explains that caffeine does not help one to stay awake; it does not explain the effects of caffeine (choice **c**). Only Passage 1 refers to hand-eye coordination, and the passage does not provide very much information about it, so the passage would not be a very good source for an essay on hand-eye coordination (choice **d**). Neither passage mentions sleeping pills (choice **e**).

6. c. Passage 1 describes the problem of sleep deprivation, and for those suffering sleep deprivation because they sleep on an inadequate mattress, Passage 2 provides a possible solution to that problem. Passage 1 neither describes a cause (choice **a**) nor a first step in a process (choice **b**) nor a general principle (choice **d**). Although Passage 1 does describe the condition of sleep deprivation, Passage 2 does not contrast it by describing the opposite condition (choice **e**); the conditions in both passages are very similar.

7. b. If understanding the cause of back pains was not difficult, the author would have known his mattress was causing his pains right away. This information helps the reader understand that back pains can have a number of causes, and figuring out the exact cause might not be easy. Making a wrong guess is not enough to prove that someone's ultimate findings should be questioned, so **a** is not the best answer choice. The author's daytime activities only explain a couple of possible causes of back pains, so choice **c** is too extreme. The author's back pains reduce dramatically, so that he can enjoy his "first night of uninterrupted sleep in years" after getting a new mattress, which indicates that the source of back pains can be explained definitively and contradicts choice **d**. Since the author's daytime activities were not the cause of his back pains, choice **e** does not make sense.

8. e. The passage claims that lack of sleep *magnifies alcohol's effects on the body*, implying that it *hampers* a person's ability to function. The other choices (**a**, **b**, **c**, and **d**) aren't accurate definitions of *impaired*.

9. c. The assertion that laws develop in response to a need for laws is contained in the first sentence of the passage and further supported in the second sentence. Choice **a** is incorrect; while the author explicitly argues that foreigners should not hold a position of offices of trust, the reason is not simply because they are "not to be trusted." The author provides the example of children being born in a different province "to entitle their children to participate," but he gives no clear indication as to whether such a practice is or is not morally suspect, so choice **b** is incorrect. The author gives no indication that unification is a natural tendency for smaller provinces, making choice **d** incorrect. The statement in choice **e** may seem like something the author might agree with, given that the author supports foreigners' exclusion from holding offices of trust. However, it is a leap to assume that he would necessarily agree that just because foreigners should not hold an office of trust, no person should be immune to legal restrictions. It is beyond the scope of the passage.

10. a. One reason the author provides as to why foreigners cannot hold offices of trust is because they cannot be as familiar with the laws as natural-born citizens. However, a program such as the one described in this choice might eliminate this unfamiliarity, thus weakening the author's argument. Choices **b** and **d** are incorrect because either would *strengthen* the author's position; they would provide further evidence that foreigners should not hold offices of trust. The fact in choice **c** might weaken the author's argument slightly—by suggesting that age is an even greater factor in a person's ability to hold an office of trust—but it does not say that being born abroad is not still a factor. A better choice more significantly weakens the argument. The overly general statement in choice **e** does not address the specific issues that the author raises in regard to a foreigner's ability to hold an office of trust. While this point may help weaken the argument somewhat, there is a more specific statement that weakens the argument more significantly.

11. d. The author discusses the laws of pre-unified European provinces, specifically pointing out similarities and differences, such as that certain laws were enforced in each province but that other provinces were so free that mothers moved there before giving birth to earn the immunities of that land. The passage does not defend the argument that increased freedom leads to increased commerce, so choice **a** is incorrect. Choice **b** is incorrect: This passage discusses the origins of provincial law in pre-unified Europe, but the only mention of a constitution is to suggest that it was founded on commerce. Choice **c** is incorrect. To know that this choice is incorrect requires you to know the meaning of the word *vagaries*, which connotes capriciousness and does not apply to the author's discussion of legal development in the provinces. Choice **e** is incorrect; the reciprocity amounts in neighboring provinces is mentioned in this passage in regard to the rights of foreigners holding office. However, this specific attribute of the law—or the advocacy of its desirability—is *not* the main point of the passage.

12. a. The first three sentences set up and support the discussion of the exclusion of foreigners from office. In that section of the passage, it is mentioned that a foreigner could not be expected to be acquainted with these unnecessarily complicated laws, meaning that choice **a** is correct. The end of the first paragraph refers to the reciprocity of the laws across provinces, suggesting that the laws would need to be enforced. But that did not say that enforcement would be *impossible*, making choice **b** incorrect. Even though foreigners were excluded from holding office, the passage does not provide *distrust*, choice **c**, as a cause of the exclusion. Neither a necessary unification nor a potential job loss is given as support for the main idea, so choices **d** and **e** are both incorrect.

13. c. This passage discusses Hipparchus's discovery of the equinoxes. The final sentence in the passage sums up the importance in terms of the discovery's contribution to science, saying that it was the "first instance in the history of science" in which observation was combined with such skillful interpretation. Hipparchus observed the heavens as part of his investigation, but the passage does not suggest that he was the *first* to do this, making choice **a** incorrect. The statement in choice **b** is not supported by the passage; Hipparchus may have discovered the equinoxes and determined the magnitude of its precession, but he was not the first to perceive them. The passage states that Hipparchus used crude instruments, but this statement is not given to describe his most important contribution to the sciences, so choice **d** is incorrect. The statement in choice **e** is not a contribution made by Hipparchus, at least not as mentioned in the given passage. The Earth's tilt may cause the seasons, but that is not mentioned in the passage, nor is Hipparchus given the credit for the contribution.

14. d. The passage makes no statement about the distance from the Sun to the Earth on the equinoxes, so there is no support for the statement in choice **d**. The passage begins with the statement that day and night are not generally equal. However, it then states that the day and night *are* equal on the equinoxes, making choice **a** incorrect. By suggesting that this occurs "at all places on Earth," the passage indicates that the equinoxes fall on the same day for both hemispheres. While the spring equinox occurs in the northern hemisphere in March and the southern hemisphere in September, the two general equinoxes both share the same day on Earth. Therefore, choice **b** is also incorrect. Hipparchus discovered that the equinox was moving relatively to the stars, but that it would take 25,000 years to complete a precession, making choice **c** incorrect. Because the equinoxes are separated by "half a year" in the passage, choice **e** must be incorrect as well.

15. e. The passage begins with a description of the phenomenon of the equinoxes, then the passage goes on to define the term *equinox* and explain its discovery by Hipparchus. The passage does not begin with an introduction of opposing scientific theories or a problem, so choices **a** and **b** are incorrect. Likewise, the passage does not begin with a scientific breakthrough, so choice **d** cannot be correct. Choice **c** mentions an inequality, which could describe the unequal day and night, but it is not the inequality but the equality— the equivalent day and night on the equinoxes—that the passage focuses on, making choice **c** incorrect.

16. b. The word *immediate* in the sentence is being used to describe the nearby stars that are adjacent to the area of the equinoxes. The words in choices **a**, **c**, and **d** could each be used to replace the word *immediate* in different sentences, but they would impact the meaning of the sentence from this passage. Therefore, each is incorrect. *Remote*, choice **e**, nearly means the opposite of the word *immediate* as it appears in this passage, so it is not correct either.

17. d. According to the table, the Blu-ray disc is the disc that uses the laser with the shortest wavelength (405 nm), and it also has the largest capacity (25 GB), therefore it is reasonable to conclude that the shorter the wavelength, the larger the capacity. Choice **e** contradicts the question.

18. a. The length of the laser that reads a CD (780 nm) is the only information included in both the passage and the table. There is no mention of the DVD in the passage, so choices **c** and **e** do not make sense. How a laser reads a CD is only discussed in the passage (choice **b**), and a CD's capacity (choice **d**) is only included in the chart.

19. e. The last sentence in the passage states that the detector's function is to convert the information collected by the laser into music, which wouldn't happen if the detector malfunctioned. The other choices (**a**, **b**, **c**, and **d**) aren't the most accurate or likely occurrences of a detector malfunction.

20. c. The main point of the passage is the effect of microgravity on astronauts. This third sentence of the passage both introduces microgravity to the reader and describes it as an imperceptible source of distress for astronauts. The initial sentence of the passage, choice **a**, makes a general claim about the difficulties of life as an astronaut. However, the passage is not merely about these difficulties, but it is specifically about one particular danger: microgravity and its effects. The fact that space travel is a risky endeavor, choice **b**, is not the main point of the passage. This sentence serves to point out the obvious, but it is the following sentence—which serves to contrast this apparent fact—that better sums up the main point of the passage. The main point of the passage is not the astronauts' attempts to counteract the negative effects of microgravity or a list of astronauts' workouts, so choices **d** and **e** are incorrect.

21. b. Atrophy represents *deterioration*, frequently in response to underuse. When in space, muscles adapt to the lack of gravity and lose their strength through deterioration. There is no indication in the passage that atrophied muscles cause the astronauts any amount of pain, so choice **a** is incorrect. Although a muscle that atrophies may be weakened, the primary meaning of the phrase *to atrophy* is *to waste away* or *deteriorate*, making choice **c** incorrect. The passage does not suggest that astronauts' muscles cramp during space flight, so choice **d** is not correct. An augmentation means an increase or an expansion. This is the opposite effect that microgravity has on astronauts' muscles, so choice **e** is not correct either.

22. c. To answer this question, you have to find the antecedent of *it*. First, you discover that *it* refers to *the last question*. Then you must trace back to realize that *the last question* itself refers to *the "truth" of the axioms* in the previous sentence. By determining how the parts of the text relate to one another, you can determine the meaning of the assertion. Choice **a** is incorrect; the *it* in this line does not refer to geometrical propositions. While the question of the "truth" of the individual geometrical propositions is thus reduced to one of the "truth" of the axioms, it is therefore the *truths* that are being referred to as without meaning, not the propositions themselves. The passage does not delve into the nature of straight lines until after the line referred to in this question, so choice **b** is not correct. Choice **d** is incorrect; the passage states that *the last question is not only unanswerable by the methods of geometry*, meaning that the *it* is referring to the *last question* and not the subject of the prepositional phrase that follows: *by the methods of geometry*. Choice **e** is a bit tricky, but it can help to identify the subject. The *it* from this line refers to *the last question*, which can be traced back to mean the *"truth" of the axioms* in the previous sentence. It is not, therefore, the *questions* of the truth, but the truth itself.

23. e. Lines 12 through 15 contain the statement that argues that the truth of the propositions depends on the truth of the axioms, making choice **e** correct. The concept of straight lines is not addressed until late in the passage, and it is not introduced as the basis for the truth of geometrical propositions, so **a** is not correct. It is the truth of the axioms, not the validity of Euclidean geometry or a connection of geometric ideas, choices **b** and **c**, that plays the role of determining the truth of a geometrical proposition. Choice **d** is incorrect; there is no indication that suggests that it is merely our inclination to accept the truth that determines whether a geometrical proposition is indeed true.

24. b. The author repeatedly refers to *truth* in relation to geometrical propositions. See, for example, lines 12 through 15. The author (Albert Einstein) is laying the groundwork for an argument that the principles of geometry are only *apparently* true. Choices **a** and **c** are incorrect. While the author presents a definition for axioms and straight lines, they are not the topic, which presents his chief concern. While geometrical propositions are a key aspect of the passage and the subject of the author's chief concern, it is not the ability to use them to draw conclusions, which is his primary focus, so choice **d** is incorrect. The author introduces planes and points as a starting point to show how geometry is built on certain conceptions. However, these conceptions are not the author's primary concern, so choice **e** is not the best answer.

25. a. The ocean sunfish eats jellyfish, which is beneficial to human beings. The spider's diet of mosquitoes is likewise beneficial to human beings, making choice **a** correct. The diet of tuna or grizzly bears may be similar to that of sunfish because both eat sea creatures, but that's not what the question asked about; it asked about similar diets that are beneficial to human beings, so choices **b** and **d** cannot be correct. The diet of a rhinoceros or a tick is neither similar to the sunfish nor beneficial to human beings, so choices **c** and **e** cannot be correct.

26. c. A statement of opinion is a statement that cannot be proven with facts; it cannot be proven that a fish has an unusual appearance because *unusual* is not a clearly defined term. On the other hand, it *can* be proven that the sunfish is the largest bony fish, choice **a**. Its diet of jellyfish, choice **b**, can likewise be verified and is therefore not an opinion. The fact that the sunfish is banned in Europe and is eaten as a delicacy by some people is mentioned in the final sentence of the passage; both statements are facts and not opinions, so choices **d** and **e** are not correct.

27. e. The beginning of the passage mentions the rapidly expanding population of jellyfish and the problems that the jellyfish present. The second half of the passage describes a specific type of fish that eats jellyfish in large quantities, thus acting as a potential solution for overpopulation; this describes the statement in choice **e** perfectly. While two creatures are described in the passage, the passage is not entirely about the comparison and contrast of them, making choice **a** incorrect. The main idea does not actually appear in the passage until the final sentence, so choice **b** cannot be correct. The passage does not begin with the definition of a fascinating sea creature or its dietary constraints, so choices **c** and **d** are not correct.

28. d. The word *curtail* in the passage is describing the difficulty of limiting the population growth of jellyfish. *Curtail*, therefore, must have a similar meaning as "limit," such as *curb*, choice **d**. If a growth were curtailed, it may not reverse completely, so choice **a** is not the closest meaning of *curtail* in this context. Choice **c**, *withstand*, does not refer to the potential for the population growth to continue unabated, so it is not correct. Both *increase* and *liberate*, choices **b** and **e**, mean the opposite of *curtail*, so they are not correct.

29. c. The beginning of the passage includes a negative description of jellyfish. The key word *however* suggests a change in direction within the passage as the positive attributes of the sunfish are introduced. The words *unfortunately*, *difficult*, and *entirely* do not help provide a transition from one direction to an opposite direction within the passage, making choices **a**, **b**, and **d** incorrect. The word *though* in choice **e** does provide a transition at the end of the passage, but it does not help transition from content about jellyfish to that of sunfish.

30. d. The author makes the case throughout the passage that unpleasant jellyfish are increasing in numbers, but the sunfish may be able to curtail their population growth. Therefore, the author would most likely agree that sunfish should be protected, choice **d**. There is no evidence in the passage that suggests the author's attitude is that the sunfish is not the largest creature in the ocean, choice **a**, even if that were true. Similarly, there is no proof to support the statement in choice **c**. The statements in choices **b** and **e** are in regard to jellyfish and not the ocean sunfish, so those choices cannot be correct.

31. a. Passage 1 introduces the ideas of dwarf planets and Pluto's status as a dwarf planet; Passage 2 expands upon those ideas by discussing other, less well-known dwarf planets. Neither passage makes an argument (choice **b**); both accept the idea of dwarf planets and Pluto's status as one. Passage 2 does not explain anything about dwarf planets that has not already been described in Passage 1, so choice **c** is incorrect. Both passages focus on facts without indulging in opinions, so choice **d** does not make sense. Passage 1 makes a claim that Pluto is a dwarf planet, but it also supports that claim with its own details; the details in Passage 2 are not needed to support Passage 1, so choice **e** is not the best answer choice.

32. d. The phrase "household word" is an idiom meaning a familiar name or phrase. Choices **a**, **b**, and **c** are not examples of figurative language. You may have been confused by choice **e** because it is a nickname, but a nickname is not a form of figurative language.

33. e. The author of Passage 1's playful attitude is evident in his description of Pluto's changed status as a "demotion" (planets cannot be demoted; only people can), his reference to the planet's "fans," and his exclamation that "Pluto even has its own moon!" There are no such playful touches in Passage 2. The first author's playfulness contradicts the idea that he is more serious than the author of Passage 2, so choice **a** is incorrect. The author of Passage 1 is nether skeptical (choice **b**) nor cynical (choice **c**). One cannot have a technical (choice **d**) attitude.

34. b. The final stipulation of a planet's attributes, according to the new definition of a planet, is that it must dominate the neighborhood along its orbit through its gravitational pull. The statement in choice **b**, referring to the debris in its path, suggests that Pluto does *not* dominate its neighborhood in the same way that the other planets do. It is true that Pluto is much smaller than the other planets, choice **a**, but the size of an object is not listed among the new criteria for a planet. Pluto had always been much smaller than any other planet. Passage 1 mentions that Pluto has a moon as evidence for its status as a planet. However, the absence or presence of a moon is not cited as justification for the classification of a planet, making choice **c** incorrect. According to the new definition of a planet, a planet must orbit the sun. But neither passage mentions the specific orbit of the sun—or its shape—so the statement in choice **d** cannot be concluded as a possible explanation. The statement in choice **e** describes why Pluto is round, as are the eight planets in our solar system. This actually meets the first definition of a planet and would therefore *not* be a reason why Pluto lost its status as an official planet.

35. d. According to the passage, Jessie Street "gained international fame when she was the only woman on the Australian delegation to the conference that founded the United Nations." The chart indicates this happened in April 1945. Choice **a** is very unlikely because few people gain international fame on the day they are born.

36. e. Only the chart mentions Jessie Street's autobiography, *Truth or Repose*. The fact that she worked to secure women's rights (choice **a**) is mentioned in both the passage and the chart. The information in choices **b**, **c**, and **d** is only mentioned in the passage.

37. d. Because the author mentions that two women attending an international conference is an accomplishment (for which at least one gained international fame), the reader can surmise that it was a rare occurrence. Choices **b**, **c**, and **e** are far beyond the scope of Passage 1; choice **a** might be true, but would require information not contained in the passage.

38. c. This passage provides information to social workers about music therapy, and makes the claim that it can have a positive role, which the title in choice **c** indicates. Choice **e** is incorrect because the first sentence speaks of mental and physical health professionals referring their clients and patients to music therapists, not actually serving as music therapists. Choice **d** is possible, but does not summarize the passage as well as choice **c**. Choices **a** and **b** refer to topics not covered in the passage.

39. a. Based on the information provided in the passage, particularly in the last sentence, choice **a** is the best inference. The other choices (choices **b**, **c**, **d**, and **e**) are beyond the scope of the passage.

40. c. Choice **c** provides the best outline of the passage. The other choices (**a**, **b**, **d**, and **e**) all contain points that are not covered by the passage.

41. e. The sentence in choice **e** makes the error of circular reasoning by stating that a client "who would benefit from music therapy . . . is an excellent candidate for music therapy." Circular reasoning is when someone makes a claim that is the same as its own conclusion. The statements in the other answer choices are perfectly logical.

42. d. If students have a strong motivation to recycle other than membership in the environmental club (i.e., detention), then this weakens the author's assertion that recycling has gone up because of increased membership in the club. Choice **a** is incorrect because it refers to a change made prior to the increase in the number of students recycling. Choice **b** is wrong because the students' motivation for joining the club is unrelated to whether they recycle. Choice **c** is incorrect because not all students need to participate in order for the poll to be valid. Choice **e** is incorrect because it would strengthen the author's argument, not weaken it.

43. d. The passage contains objective language and straightforward information about accounting, such as one might find in a business textbook. While the information could theoretically appear in any of the other answer choices (**a**, **b**, **c**, and **e**), a business textbook is the most likely spot.

44. c. The second sentence of the passage speaks of a marketing department separate from the accounting department, so it is least likely that assisting with the marketing of products would be a function of accounting. The other choices (**a**, **b**, **d**, and **e**) are much more likely to be handled by the accounting department.

45. d. All the other choices (**a**, **b**, **c**, and **e**) are listed in the passage; employee birthdates (choice **d**) would not be included.

46. a. While all the other choices (**b**, **c**, **d**, and **e**) may be true, the fact that Diana sold 22 cars in February and the salesperson of the month sold 26 means that they are not the same person. None of the other choices can be proven based only on the information given.

47. d. The author cites Thomas Nast's symbols for Tammany Hall and the Democratic and Republican Parties as examples of images that have entered the public consciousness and are "still in currency today"; thus they are enduring. Choices **a** and **c** are inaccurate, and choices **b** and **e** are unrelated to Nast's depiction.

48. c. This title expresses the main point of the passage—that while there are predictable patterns in the life of a genius, the pattern increases the sense of something supernatural touching his or her life. Choices **a** and **b** are too general. Choice **d** is inaccurate because the passage does not talk about disorder in the life of a genius. Choice **e** covers only one of the two main ideas in the passage.

49. c. Based on the information provided in the passage, it's true that a genius has three prolific periods in his or her life. All the other statements (choices **a**, **b**, **d**, and **e**) are not supported by information provided in the passage.

50. b. *Unpalatable* may be defined as not agreeable to taste (from the Latin *palatum*, which refers to the roof of the mouth). The other choices (**a**, **c**, **d**, and **e**) aren't accurate definitions of the word.

51. b. The Carib were not in any way described as peaceful, but rather as hostile people. All the other choices (**a**, **c**, **d**, and **e**) are accurate descriptions of the Caribs and are explicitly mentioned in the passage.

52. a. The last two lines of the passage explicitly state that the Caribs were defeated by sickness and the ravages of forced labor. Choice **b** is incorrect because the Arawaks were defeated by the Carib. Neither the Dutch (choice **c**) nor the French (choice **d**), nor another cannibalistic tribe (choice **e**), was mentioned in the role of conquerors.

53. b. *Strife* means war, which can be inferred by the information provided in the passage. Choice **a** is mentioned as a characteristic that the Carib exhibit toward their enemies in times of strife; it is not the meaning of *strife*. Choices **c** and **e** are not mentioned in conjunction with being warlike or with strife. Choice **d** makes no sense because the times of strife occurred when the tribe allowed a chief to be chosen.

54. e. Present-day Saint Martin belongs to the French and the Dutch. Choices **b** and **d** have no support in the passage. Choices **a** and **c** are incorrect. The Spanish are mentioned in the passage only in conjunction with the Carib Indians.

55. c. The sentence that introduces the idea of human-caused threats to the Great Barrier Reef is, "But the most preventable hazard to the reef is tourists." *But* is the transitional word that begins this sentence. *Although* (choice **a**), *also* (choice **b**), and *and* (choice **d**) can all be used as transitional words, but they are not used to transition from the natural threats the Great Barrier Reef faces to the human-caused threats it faces in this passage. You may have been confused by choice **e** since *creeping* seems like a threatening word. However, *creeping* cannot function as a transitional word.

56. a. This statement encapsulates the primary purpose of the entire passage, not just a part of it. Choices **c** and **e** are too specific to be correct. Choices **b** and **d** are not supported by the passage.

Praxis® Core Academic Skills for Educators: Writing Practice Test 1

Part I: Multiple-Choice
Time: 40 Minutes

Directions: Choose the letter for the underlined portion that contains a grammatical error. If there is no error in the sentence, choose e.

1. Even as the music industry pushes <u>further into</u>
   <u>a</u>   <u>b</u>
   the realm of the digital world, <u>there are</u> still a
                                    <u>c</u>
   large number of people who collect vinyl
   records and old-style <u>amplifiers and</u> speakers.
                          <u>d</u>
   <u>No error</u>
   <u>e</u>

2. <u>Today's</u> ski jackets are made with synthetic
   <u>a</u>
   fabrics <u>that are</u> very light <u>but yet</u> provide
           <u>b</u>   <u>c</u>
   exceptional <u>warmth and</u> comfort. <u>No error</u>
               <u>d</u>   <u>e</u>

3. After the <u>director and assistant</u> director both
             <u>a</u>
   resigned, <u>we</u> could only guess <u>who would be</u>
             <u>b</u>   <u>c</u>
   hired to take <u>their</u> positions. <u>No error</u>
                 <u>d</u>   <u>e</u>

4. In <u>Homers</u> <u>painting,</u> a man in a storm at sea
      <u>a</u>   <u>b</u>
   is <u>realistically</u> portrayed. <u>No error</u>
   <u>c</u> <u>d</u>   <u>e</u>

5. My favorite <u>part, though,</u> <u>is</u> the vegetable chips
                <u>a</u>   <u>b</u>
   my <u>mom</u> buys from the health food <u>store they</u>
      <u>c</u>   <u>d</u>
   are delicious. <u>No error</u>
                  <u>e</u>

6. *Kwanzaa,* a <u>S</u>wahili word meaning
                 <u>a</u>
   <u>a harvest's first fruits,</u> is a nonreligious holiday
   <u>b</u>
   <u>that honors</u> African-American <u>heritage and</u>
   <u>c</u>   <u>d</u>
   culture. <u>No error</u>
            <u>e</u>

7. The record time for solving a Rubik's cube
   <u>is</u> held by a <u>14-year-old</u> male named Feliks
   <u>a</u>   <u>b</u>
   Zemdegs, who <u>affectively</u> completed the puzzle
                <u>c</u>
   in 6.77 seconds on <u>November 13, 2010.</u> <u>No error</u>
                      <u>d</u>   <u>e</u>

8. There are many types of extreme sports, <u>such like</u>
                                            <u>a</u>
   slacklining, a sport of <u>daredevil</u> proportions
                          <u>b</u>
   <u>in which</u> athletes walk and tumble across nylon
   <u>c</u>
   webbing that has been stretched across <u>a cavern</u>
                                          <u>d</u>
   and anchored on each end. <u>No error</u>
                             <u>e</u>

9. Either the <u>physicians or</u> the hospital
                <u>a</u>
   administrator <u>are</u> going to have to make a
                 <u>b</u>
   decision to <u>ensure</u> the <u>fair</u> treatment of
               <u>c</u>   <u>d</u>
   patients. <u>No error</u>
             <u>e</u>

10. Because they <u>close</u> resemble each <u>other, many</u>
                  <u>a</u>   <u>b</u>
    people think that Sara and Heather <u>are</u>
                                        <u>c</u>
    identical twins <u>instead of</u> fraternal. <u>No error</u>
                    <u>d</u>   <u>e</u>

11. The Department of State <u>has</u> foreign policy
_a

<u>responsibilities</u> that include the promotion of
_b

peace, <u>must protect</u> U.S. citizens abroad, <u>and</u>
_c _d

the assistance of U.S. businesses in the foreign

marketplace. <u>No error</u>
_e

12. Contestants in the Scripps <u>national spelling bee</u>
_a

watched <u>eighth-grader</u> Sukanya Roy from
_b

Pennsylvania win the spelling <u>bee's</u> coveted
_c

trophy and $40,000 in <u>college scholarship funds.</u>
_d

<u>No error</u>
_e

13. Here <u>are</u> one of the three <u>scarves</u> you <u>left</u> at
_a _b _c

my house <u>yesterday</u> morning. <u>No error</u>
_d _e

14. I think I will do <u>good</u> on my final exam
_a

because I am <u>confident</u> that I am <u>well prepared,</u>
_b _c

rested, and relaxed <u>going into</u> the classroom.
_d

<u>No error</u>
_e

15. I thought <u>Johan's</u> dish of gumbo was
_a

<u>more spicier</u> than <u>Harold's,</u> but the <u>judges</u>
_b _c _d

disagreed. <u>No error</u>
_e

16. Last <u>Thursday,</u> as the <u>president of the university</u>
_a _b

addressed the <u>student body,</u> she made an
_c

<u>illusion to</u> the construction of a new stadium
_d

for the football team. <u>No error</u>
_e

Directions: Choose the best replacement for the underlined portion of the sentence. If no revision is necessary, choose **a**, which always repeats the original phrasing.

17. The <u>principle objective of the documentary is to show you how global warming will effect</u> climates around the world.
  a. principle objective of the documentary is to show you how global warming will effect
  b. principle objective of the documentary is to show you how global warming will affect
  c. principal objective of the documentary is to show you how global warming will affect
  d. principal objective of the documentary is to show you how global warming will effect
  e. principle objective of the documentary is to show you how global warming will have effected

18. <u>This was the third of the three assignments the professor gave during this the month of October.</u>
  a. This was the third of the three assignments the professor gave during this the month of October.
  b. Of the three assignments the professor gave during October, this was the third one.
  c. Thus far during the month of October, the professor had given three assignments and this was the third.
  d. This third assignment of the professor's given during the month of October was one of three assignments.
  e. This was the third assignment the professor had given during the month of October.

19. I don't have no math homework this weekend, but I have to work on my paper for social studies.
   a. I don't have no math homework this weekend, but I have to work on my paper for social studies.
   b. I dont have any math homework this weekend, but I have to work on my paper for social studies
   c. I don't have any math homework this weekend, but I have to work on my paper for social studies.
   d. I don't have any math homework this weekend, but I have too work on my paper for social studies.
   e. I don't have any math homework this weekend, but I has to work on my paper for social studies.

20. Built in Boston, the *U.S.S. Constitution* was given the nickname "Old Ironsides" because her thick oak planks had deflected many deadly cannonballs in battle.
   a. Built in Boston, the *U.S.S. Constitution* was given the nickname "Old Ironsides" because her thick oak planks had deflected
   b. Built in Boston, the *U.S.S. Constitution* was given the nickname "Old Ironsides" because her thick oak planks deflect
   c. The *U.S.S. Constitution*, being built in Boston, is nicknamed "Old Ironsides" because her thick oak planks had deflected
   d. Built in Boston, the *U.S.S. Constitution* will be given the nickname "Old Ironsides" because her thick oak planks had deflected
   e. The *U.S.S. Constitution*, to be built in Boston, was given the nickname "Old Ironsides" because her thick oak planks had deflected

21. Any passenger who is getting off at the next stop should move to the front.
   a. passenger who is getting off at the next stop
   b. passenger, who is getting off at the next stop
   c. passenger who is getting off at the next stop,
   d. passenger, who is getting off at the next stop,
   e. passenger, whom is getting off at the next stop,

22. The Gulf Stream is a warm current on the Atlantic's surface, it originates in the Gulf of Mexico and flows northeast.
   a. Atlantic's surface, it originates
   b. Atlantics' surface; it originates
   c. Atlantic's surface. Originating
   d. Atlantics' surface, and originating
   e. Atlantic's surface; it originates

23. My sister is mowing the lawn; my cousins and I is washing the windows.
   a. mowing the lawn; my cousins and I is washing the windows.
   b. mowing the lawn; my cousins and I are washing the windows.
   c. mowing the lawn, my cousins and I are washing the windows.
   d. mowing the lawn: my cousins and I are washing the windows.
   e. mowing the lawn my cousins and I are washing the windows.

24. Thomas has various study strategies: he <u>takes notes, an outline, and answering practice questions.</u>

   a. takes notes, an outline, and answering practice questions.

   b. took notes, outlining, and practicing questions.

   c. takes notes, makes outlines, and answers practice questions.

   d. taking notes, outlines and practiced questions.

   e. took notes, making outlines, and answer practice questions.

25. <u>Prometheus and epimetheus, his brother, created life on earth, Epimetheus began with animals.</u>

   a. Prometheus and epimetheus, his brother, created life on earth, Epimetheus began with animals.

   b. Prometheus and Epimetheus, his brother, created life on earth; Epimetheus began with animals.

   c. Prometheus and epimetheus his brother, created life on earth, Epimetheus began with animals.

   d. Prometheus and Epimetheus: his brother created life on earth; Epimetheus began with animals.

   e. Prometheus and Epimetheus, his brother, created life on earth Epimetheus began with animals.

26. We loved our trip to the top of the <u>Empire State Building where you could see</u> the Statue of Liberty, all of New York's bridges, and the tiny people on the streets below.

   a. Empire State Building where you could see

   b. Empire State Building; you could see

   c. Empire State Building; where we saw

   d. Empire State Building; we saw

   e. Empire State Building in that you saw

27. When my father was <u>young, him chopped</u> firewood with axes.

   a. When my father was young, him chopped firewood with axes.

   b. When my father was young, he chopped firewood with axes.

   c. When my father was young, his chopped firewood with axes.

   d. When my father was young, they chopped firewood with axes.

   e. When my father was young, it chopped firewood with axes.

28. <u>I have, an author of thrilling books for children, always admired Virginia Hamilton.</u>

   a. I have always, an author of thrilling books for children, admired Virginia Hamilton.

   b. I have, an author, always admired Virginia Hamilton, of thrilling books for children.

   c. I have always admired Virginia, an author of thrilling books for children, Hamilton.

   d. I have always admired Virginia Hamilton an author of thrilling books for children.

   e. I have always admired Virginia Hamilton, an author of thrilling books for children.

29. Which of the following pieces of information would be *least* relevant in an essay about the causes of World War II?

   a. The causes of World War II have been the topic of many books.

   b. World War II officially began when Germany invaded Poland.

   c. World War II began on September 1, 1939.

   d. The treaty that ended World War I caused unrest that led to World War II.

   e. World War II finally ended on September 2, 1945.

30. Which of the following pieces of information would be *least* relevant in an essay about the silent film era?
a. Buster Keaton, Lillian Gish, and Charlie Chaplin were some of the biggest stars of the silent film era.
b. The silent film era saw the rise of all the most important film genres, including drama, historical epic, comedy, horror, and science fiction.
c. Released in 1927, *The Jazz Singer* was the first film to include spoken dialogue.
d. Title cards with printed words conveyed dialogue and narration in silent films.
e. Many contemporary films include long stretches of silent footage.

Directions: *Choose the letter for the underlined portion of the citations that contains an error. If there is no error in the citation, choose e.*

31. ebook citation:
Brueton, Diana. <u>Many Moons: The Myth and Magic, Fact and Fantasy Of Our Nearest Heavenly Body</u>. New York: <u>Prentice Hall Press</u>, 1991.
      a   b
<u>*Google Books*</u>. Web. <u>July 17, 2015.</u> <u>No error.</u>
  c   d   e

32. Magazine citation:
<u>Bhob, Stewart.</u> <u>"Who Was William M. Gaines?"</u>
    a   b
<u>*Comics Buyers Guide*</u>. <u>February 28, 1997.</u>
           c   d
<u>No error.</u>
  e

Use the following passage to answer questions 33 through 36.

(1) According to the U.S. Centers for Disease Control (CDC), almost 50% of American teens are not vigorously active on a regular basis, contributing to a trend of sluggishness among Americans of all ages. (2) Adolescent female students are particularly inactive: 29% are inactive compared with 15% of male students. (3) Unfortunately, the sedentary habits of young "couch potatoes" often continues into adulthood. (4) According to both the CDC and the Surgeon General's 1996 Report on Physical Activity and Health, Americans become increasingly less active with each year of age. (5) Inactivity can be a serious health risk factor, setting the stage for obesity and associated chronic illnesses like heart disease or diabetes. (6) Exercise sets the stage for building bone, muscle, and joints, controlling weight, and preventing the development of high blood pressure.

(7) Some studies suggest that physical activity may have other benefits for you. (8) One CDC study found that high school students who take part in team sports or are physically active outside of school are less likely to engage in risky behaviors, like using drugs or smoking. (9) Physical activity does not need to be strenuous to be beneficial. (10) The CDC recommends moderate, daily physical activity for people of all ages, such as brisk walking for 30 minutes or 15-to-20 minutes of more intense exercise. (11) A survey conducted by the National Association for Sport and Physical Education questioned teens about their attitudes toward exercise and what it would take to get them moving. (12) Teens chose friends (56%) as their most likely motivators for becoming more active, followed by parents (18%), and professional athletes (11%).

33. Which conclusion does the writer support with evidence from multiple resources?

   a. Americans become increasingly less active with each year of age.

   b. Exercise sets the stage for building bone, muscle, and joints, controlling weight, and preventing the development of high blood pressure.

   c. Physical activity does not need to be strenuous to be beneficial.

   d. Inactivity can be a serious health risk factor, setting the stage for obesity and associated chronic illnesses like heart disease or diabetes.

   e. "Couch potatoes" are people who spend most of their time watching television and eating unhealthy snacks.

34. In context, which revision to sentence 3 (sentence 3 follows) is most needed?

     Unfortunately, the sedentary habits of young "couch potatoes" often continues into adulthood.

   a. (As it is now)

   b. Unfortunately, the sedentary habits of young "couch potatoes" often continuing into adulthood.

   c. Unfortunately, the sedentary habits of young "couch potatoes" often continue into adulthood.

   d. Unfortunately, the sedentary habit of young "couch potatoes" often continues into adulthood.

   e. The sedentary habits of young "couch potatoes" often continues into adulthood.

35. In context, which revision to sentences 5 and 6 (sentences 5 and 6 follow) is most needed?

     Inactivity can be a serious health risk factor, setting the stage for obesity and associated chronic illnesses like heart disease or diabetes. Exercise sets the stage for building bone, muscle, and joints, controlling weight, and preventing the development of high blood pressure.

   a. (As it is now)

   b. Inactivity can be a serious health risk factor, setting the stage for obesity and associated chronic illnesses like heart disease or diabetes. Building bone, muscle, and joints, controlling weight, and preventing the development of high blood pressure.

   c. Inactivity can be a serious health risk factor, setting the stage for obesity and associated chronic illnesses like heart disease or diabetes. Exercise sets the stages for building bone, muscle, and joints, controlling weight, and preventing the development of high blood pressure.

   d. Inactivity can be a serious health risk factor, setting the stage for obesity and associated chronic illnesses like heart disease or diabetes. Exercise sets the stage for building bone, muscle, and joints, and preventing the development of high blood pressure.

   e. Inactivity can be a serious health risk factor, setting the stage for obesity and associated chronic illnesses like heart disease or diabetes. The benefits of exercise include building bone, muscle, and joints, controlling weight, and preventing the development of high blood pressure.

36. In context, which revision to sentence 7 (sentence 7 follows) is most needed?

    Some studies suggest that physical activity may have other benefits for you.

  a. Change "studies" to "study."

  b. Replace "for you" with "as well."

  c. Replace "suggest" with "suggests."

  d. Replace "other" with "the same."

  e. Replace "benefits" with "advantages."

Use the following passage to answer questions 37 through 40.

(1) Toni Morrison is one of the most renowned and respected writers of our generation. (2) Morrison's visions are as epic and vivid as her social conscience is formidable. (3) She is perhaps best known for her 1977 novel *Song of Solomon* and the 1987 novel *Beloved*, which director Jonathan Demme adapted into a major feature film starring Oprah Winfrey. (4) Then I personally find her most powerful work to be the 1973 novel *Sula*.

    (5) The fictional setting of *Sula*—the African-American section of Medallion, Ohio, a community called "the Bottom"—is a place where people, and even natural things, are apt to go awry, to break from their prescribed boundaries, a place where bizarre and unnatural happenings and strange reversals of the ordinary are commonplace. (6) The very name of the setting of *Sula* is significant; the Bottom is located high up in the hills. (7) The novel is furthermore filled with images of bad stuff, both psychological and physical. (8) A great part of the lives of the characters, therefore, is taken up with making sense of the world, setting boundaries, and devising methods to control what is essentially uncontrollable. (9) One of the major devices used by the people of the Bottom is the seemingly universal one of creating a scapegoat—in this case, the title character *Sula*—upon which to project both the evil they perceive outside themselves and the evil in their own hearts. (10) Essentially, Morrison uses the small community of Sula to convey good insights about our global society.

37. In context, which revision to sentences 3 and 4 (sentences 3 and 4 follow) is most needed?

    She is perhaps best known for her 1977 novel *Song of Solomon* and 1987's *Beloved*, which director Jonathan Demme adapted into a major feature film starring Oprah Winfrey. Then, I personally find her most powerful work to be the 1973 novel *Sula*.

  a. Replace "Then" with "However."

  b. Replace "She" with "Morrison."

  c. Replace "best" with "greatest."

  d. Replace "director" with "filmmaker."

  e. Change "I" to "me."

38. In context, which revision to sentence 5 (sentence 5 follows) is most needed?

> The fictional setting of *Sula*—the African-American section of Medallion, Ohio, a community called "the Bottom"—is a place where people, and even natural things, are apt to go awry, to break from their prescribed boundaries, a place where bizarre and unnatural happenings and strange reversals of the ordinary are commonplace.

a. (As it is now)

b. The fictional setting of *Sula* is the African-American section of Medallion, Ohio, a community called "the Bottom." It is a place where people, and even natural things, are apt to go awry, to break from their prescribed boundaries, a place where bizarre and unnatural happenings and strange reversals of the ordinary are commonplace.

c. The fictional setting of *Sula*—the African-American section of Medallion, Ohio, a community called "the Bottom"—is a place where people, and even natural things, are apt to go awry. They break from their prescribed boundaries.

d. The fictional setting of *Sula*—the African-American section of Medallion, Ohio, a community called "the Bottom"—is a place where people, and even natural things, are apt to go awry.

e. The fictional setting of *Sula* is a place where people, and even natural things, are apt to go awry, to break from their prescribed boundaries, a place where bizarre and unnatural happenings and strange reversals of the ordinary are commonplace.

39. In context, which revision to sentence 7 (sentence 7 follows) is most needed?

> The novel is furthermore filled with images of bad stuff, both psychological and physical.

a. Replace "novel" with "book."

b. Change "bad stuff" to "mutilation."

c. Replace "furthermore" with "not."

d. Change "physical" to "psychological."

e. Replace "is" with "are."

40. In context, which revision to sentence 10 (sentence 10 follows) is most needed?

> Essentially, Morrison uses the small community of Sula to convey profound insights about our global society.

a. Replace "Essentially" with "Incidentally."

b. Change "small" to "pathetic."

c. Replace "good" with "profound."

d. Change "Sula" to "novel."

e. Replace "global" with "worldwide."

Part IIa: Argumentative Essay

Time: 30 Minutes

Carefully read the essay topic that follows. Plan and write an essay that addresses all points in the topic. Make sure that your essay is well organized and that you support your central argument with concrete examples. Allow 30 minutes for your essay.

There are more vegetarians in this country than ever before. Should school and workplace cafeterias accommodate this dietary preference by offering vegetarian selections? Use specific reasons and examples to support your argument.

Part IIb: Source-Based Essay

Time: 30 Minutes
Directions

The following assignment requires you to use information from two sources to discuss the most important concerns that relate to a specific issue. When paraphrasing or quoting from the source, cite each source used by referring to the author's last name, the text's title, or any other clear identifier. Allow 30 minutes for your essay.

Assignment

Read the two passages carefully and then write an essay in which you identify the most important concerns regarding the debates concerning the adoption of the Bill of Rights to the United States Constitution. Your essay must draw on information from both of the sources. In addition, you may draw on your own experiences, observations, or reading. Be sure to cite the sources whether you are paraphrasing or directly quoting.

Source 1

"John DeWitt" (pseudonym), Anti-Federalist Paper #2, Massachusetts, October 27, 1787

That the want of a Bill of Rights to accompany this proposed System, is a solid objection to it, provided there is nothing exceptionable in the System itself, I do not assert. . . . A people, entering into society, surrender such a part of their natural rights, as shall be necessary for the existence of that society. They are so precious in themselves, that they would never be parted with, did not the preservation of the remainder require it. They are entrusted in the hands of those, who are very willing to receive them, who are naturally fond of exercising of them, and whose passions are always striving to make a bad use of them. They are conveyed by a written compact, expressing those which are given up, and the mode in which those reserved shall be secured. Language is so easy of explanation, and so difficult is it by words to convey exact ideas, that the party to be governed cannot be too explicit. The line cannot be drawn with too much precision and accuracy. The necessity of this accuracy and this precision increases in proportion to the greatness of the sacrifice and the numbers who make it. That a Constitution for the United States does not require a Bill of Rights, when it is considered, that a Constitution for an individual State would, I cannot conceive. The difference between them is only in the numbers of the parties concerned they are both a compact between the Governors and Governed the letter of which must be adhered to in discussing their powers. That which is not expressly granted, is of course retained.

The Compact itself is a recital upon paper of that proportion of the subject's natural rights, intended to be parted with, for the benefit of adverting to it in case of dispute. Miserable indeed would be the situation of those individual States who have not prefixed to their Constitutions a Bill of Rights . . . those powers which the people by their Constitutions expressly give them; they enjoy by positive grant, and those remaining ones, which they never meant to give them, and which the Constitutions say nothing about, they enjoy by tacit implication, so that by one means and by the other, they became possessed of the whole. . . . That insatiable thirst for unconditional control over our fellow-creatures, and the facility of sounds to convey essentially different ideas, produced the first Bill of Rights ever prefixed to a Frame of Government. The people, although fully sensible that they reserved every title of power they did not expressly grant away, yet afraid that the words made use of, to express those rights so granted might convey more than they originally intended, they chose at the same moment to express in different language those rights which the agreement did not include, and which they never designed to part with, endeavoring thereby to prevent any cause for future altercation and the intrusion into society of that doctrine of tacit implication which has been the favorite theme of every tyrant from the origin of all governments to the present day.

Source 2

Alexander Hamilton writing as "Publius," Federalist Paper #84, "Certain General and Miscellaneous Objections to the Constitution Considered and Answered" (1788)

It has been several times truly remarked that bills of rights are, in their origin, stipulations between kings and their subjects, abridgements of prerogative in favor of privilege, reservations of rights not surrendered to the prince. . . . It is evident, therefore, that, according to their primitive signification, they have no application to constitutions professedly founded upon the power of the people, and executed by their immediate representatives and servants. Here, in strictness, the people surrender nothing; and as they retain every thing they have no need of particular reservations. . . .

But a minute detail of particular rights is certainly far less applicable to a Constitution like that under consideration, which is merely intended to regulate the general political interests of the nation, than to a constitution which has the regulation of every species of personal and private concerns. If, therefore, the loud clamors against the plan of the convention, on this score, are well founded, no epithets of reprobation will be too strong for the constitution of this State. But the truth is, that both of them contain all which, in relation to their objects, is reasonably to be desired.

I go further, and affirm that bills of rights, in the sense and to the extent in which they are contended for, are not only unnecessary in the proposed Constitution, but would even be dangerous. They would contain various exceptions to powers not granted; and, on this very account, would afford a colorable pretext to claim more than were granted. For why declare that things shall not be done which there is no power to do? Why, for instance, should it be said that the liberty of the press shall not be restrained, when no power is given by which restrictions may be imposed? I will not contend that such a provision would confer a regulating power; but it is evident that it would furnish, to men disposed to usurp, a plausible pretense for claiming that power. They might urge with a semblance of reason, that the Constitution ought not to be charged with the absurdity of providing against the abuse of an authority which was not given, and that the provision against restraining the liberty of the press afforded a clear implication, that a power to prescribe proper regulations concerning it was intended to be vested in the national government. This may serve as a specimen of the numerous handles which would be given to the doctrine of constructive powers, by the indulgence of an injudicious zeal for bills of rights.

Praxis® Core Academic Skills for Educators: Writing Practice Test 1 Answers and Explanations

1. e. Because there are no grammatical, idiomatic, logical, or structural errors in this sentence, choice **e** is the best answer.

2. c. Because the words *but* and *yet* mean the same thing, this sentence contains a redundancy. Either one of these words should be deleted.

3. e. Because there are no grammatical, idiomatic, logical, or structural errors in this sentence, choice **e** is the best answer.

4. a. *Homer's* requires an apostrophe "s" to show possession.

5. d. A comma is needed in this sentence to indicate or set off parenthetical elements. A parenthetical element is segment that can be removed without changing the essential meaning of that sentence.

6. e. Because there are no grammatical, idiomatic, logical, or structural errors in this sentence, choice **e** is the best answer.

7. c. The correct word choice would be *effectively*, meaning "to cause a result." *Affective* refers to "the ability to influence or alter someone's mental state."

8. a. In this comparison, the word *as* should be used instead of *like*. The use of *as* completes the idiom *such as*.

9. b. When two subjects are connected with the conjunction *or*, the subject that is closer to the verb will determine whether the verb is singular or plural. The verb in this sentence should be *is* because *administrator*—the closer subject—is singular.

10. a. This is a grammatical error. Because the word modifies the verb *resemble*, the adverb *closely* should be used instead of the adjective *close*.

11. c. This is an error in sentence construction. For proper parallel construction in the sentence, *must protect* should be changed to *the protection of* to match *the promotion of* and *the assistance of*.

12. a. *Scripps National Spelling Bee* is a proper noun. It is the specific name used to identify a contest, so it must be capitalized.

13. a. This is an error in agreement. The singular noun *one* requires the singular verb *is*. When the subject (in this case *one*) follows the verb, as in a sentence beginning with *here* or *there*, be careful to determine the subject. In this sentence, the subject is not the plural noun *scarves* but the singular *one of the three scarves*.

14. a. In this sentence, the word *good* is being used as an adverb telling how the student thinks he or she will do on the test. Therefore, *good* should be replaced with *well*. This is a word-choice error.

15. b. Using *more* or *most* before an adjective or adverb is an example of a redundancy. In this sentence, just using the word *spicier* is enough to establish the proper comparison between the two dishes of gumbo.

16. d. This is an error of commonly confused homonyms (words that sound alike). The use of the word *illusion* makes this sentence illogical. An illusion is something that is not what it seems. The correct word choice would be *allusion*, which means a reference or hint.

17. c. The word *principle*, meaning rule, can only be used as a noun. *Principal*, meaning leading or main, can be used as a noun or as an adjective. In this sentence, it is clearly an adjective, which rules out choices **a**, **b**, and **e**. Choice **d** incorrectly uses the word *effect*. The verb *affect* means to produce an *effect* (noun) on something.

18. e. This is the only choice that does not contain excessive wordiness and matches the tense of *was* and *had given*. In choice **a**, the phrase *the third of three* is a redundancy. Choice **b** is also repetitive in using both *three* and *third*. Choices **c** and **d**, although constructed differently, make the same error.

19. c. This is the only choice that is grammatically correct in every way. Choice **a** is a double negative using the word *no*. Choice **b** needs an apostrophe in the word *don't*. Choice **d** uses the word *too* when it should be *to*. Choice **e** uses the word *has*, which is the wrong subject/verb agreement.

20. a. When constructing sentences, unnecessary shifts in verb tenses should be avoided. Choice **a** is best because all three verbs in the sentence indicate that the action occurred in the past (*built*, *was given*, and *had deflected*). In choice **b**, there is a shift to the present (*deflect*). Choice **c** begins in the present (*being built*, *is nicknamed*), and then shifts to the past (*had deflected*). Choice **d** starts in the past tense (*built*), shifts to the future (*will be given*), and then reverts back to the past (*had deflected*). Finally, choice **e** shifts from the future (*to be built*) to past tense (*was given*, *had deflected*).

21. a. The clause *who is getting off at the next stop* is a restrictive (essential) clause and should not be set off by commas. Choices **b**, **c**, **d**, and **e** are all punctuated incorrectly. In addition, choice **e** uses the pronoun *whom*, which is the wrong case.

22. e. There are two potential problems in this sentence. One is the possessive form of the word *Atlantic*, and the other is the punctuation between the two clauses. Choice **e** uses the correct possessive form (there is only one Atlantic Ocean), and the correct punctuation (a semicolon should be used between two independent clauses). Choice **a** is incorrect because it creates a comma splice. Choice **b** uses the incorrect possessive form. Choice **c** creates a sentence fragment. Choice **d** creates faulty subordination.

23. b. Choice **b** is correct. This sentence requires a semicolon to separate the independent clauses and subject/verb agreement between *my cousins and I* and *are*.

24. c. The second clause of this sentence requires a parallel construction. Choice **c** is the only one in which all three elements are parallel.

25. b. Choice **b** is correct, as it correctly punctuates this sentence with commas around the parenthetical *his brother*, inserts a semicolon between the independent clauses, and capitalizes *Epimetheus* (as it is a person's name and therefore a proper noun).

26. d. Choice **d** is correctly punctuated with a semicolon between two independent clauses, and there is no shift in person (i.e., everything is in the first person). Choices **a**, **b**, and **e** are incorrect because the sentence shifts from the first person (*we*) to the second person (*you*). Choice **c** uses a semicolon when no punctuation is necessary.

27. b. The original sentence has an error in pronoun case; it requires the nominative pronoun *he* instead of the objective pronoun *him*. Choices **d** and **e** would not be grammatically incorrect if the pronoun did not refer to *my father*, but because the pronoun does refer to *my father*, they are wrong.

28. e. The original sentence contains a misplaced modifier. The phrase *an author of thrilling books for children* modifies *Virginia Hamilton*, so it should be placed directly before or after that name and offset with a comma. Only choice **e** places the modifier correctly. Choice **b** is particularly confusing because it splits up the modifier. Choice **c** mistakenly places the modifier in the middle of the name it modifies. Choice **d** fails to offset the modifier with a comma.

29. a. Books about the causes of World War II might be relevant resources for an essay on that topic, but the fact that such books exist is irrelevant. Choices **b** and **d** pertain directly to the causes of World War II. The date the war began (choice **c**) would certainly be relevant information to include in an essay about the causes of World War II. While the date the war ended (choice **e**) might seem off topic for an essay about the causes of the war, it would likely be more relevant than the fact that World War II has been the topic of many books.

30. e. The fact that many contemporary films include long stretches of silent footage is not particularly relevant to a discussion of silent film. The information in choices **a**, **b**, **c**, and **d** are all more relevant to the topic.

31. b. The title of a book should always be italicized, but this citation fails to italicize the title. The other elements of the citation are all written and formatted correctly.

32. d. When citing a magazine article, it is important to include the page number/numbers on which the article originally appeared immediately after the date of publication. This citation fails to include the page number/numbers. The other elements of the citation are all written and formatted correctly.

33. a. In sentence 4, the writer cites both the CDC and the Surgeon General's 1996 Report on Physical Activity and Health as sources of this information. Although the information in choices **b** and **d** may have come from resources, the writer does not cite them in the passage, so they are not the best answer choices. In sentence 9, the writer states the *opposite* of the conclusion in choice **c**. The writer never explicitly defines the term "couch potato" in the passage, so choice **e** cannot be correct.

34. c. Sentence 3 contains a subject-verb agreement error. The plural subject *habits* needs the plural verb *continue*. Choice **c** corrects this error with the plural verb *continues*. While choice **d** uses the singular verb *continues* with the singular subject *habit*, the subject refers to the plural *couch potatoes*, so it needs to be plural, as well. Choice **e** merely removes the transitional word *Unfortunately* without correcting the subject-verb agreement error.

35. e. As originally written, sentence 6 repeats the phrase *set the stage* from sentence 5. Removing that phrase from sentence 6 makes the sentences less repetitious and monotonous. Choice **e** removes that phrase while remaining grammatically correct. Choice **b** removes the phrase, but it is a fragment because it also removes the subject *exercise*. Choice **c** changes the singular *stage* to the plural *stages*, which makes the sentence awkward and fails to correct the original problem of monotony. Choice **d** removes information arbitrarily (*controlling weight*) and fails to correct the original problem of monotony.

36. b. As it is originally written, sentence 7 is not consistent with the style of the rest of the passage. The majority of the passage is written in the third-person point of view. Sentence 7 switches to the second person by referring to the reader as *you*. Choice **b** corrects this shift in style by removing the phrase *for you*. Choice **c** fails to correct that shift in style and introduces a subject-verb agreement error by changing *suggest* to *suggests*. Choice **d** changes the meaning of the sentence. Choice **e** merely replaced the word *benefits* with the synonym *advantages* without correcting the style-shift error.

37. a. Sentence 4 introduces an idea (*Sula* is Toni Morrison's most powerful novel) that is somewhat contrary to the ideas in sentence 3 (*Song of Solomon* and the 1987 novel *Beloved* are Toni Morrison's best-known novels). Therefore, *However* would be the best transitional word to begin sentence 4, since it indicates a contrary idea. *Then* indicates an idea that follows the previous one without contradicting it. Choice **b** changes a pronoun to a proper name unnecessarily. Choice **c** replaces a word with a synonym that creates an idiom error (*greatest known*). Choice **d** replaces *director* with the synonym *filmmaker* without improving the sentence. Choice **e** makes the sentence grammatically incorrect.

38. a. Although sentence 5 is long and complex, it is grammatically correct, and its length and complexity provides the variety necessary to maintain the reader's interest and prevent the passage from becoming monotonous. Although the other answer choices are all grammatically correct, none of them improves upon sentence 5 as it is now. Choices **c**, **d**, and **e** make cuts that deprive the passage of information.

39. b. The majority of this passage is written for an educated, adult audience. Using the euphemism *bad stuff* does not respect that audience's intelligence. The word *mutilation* is much more precise. Choice **a** replaces *novel* with the synonym *book* without improving the sentence. Choices **c** and **d** change the meaning of the sentence. Choice **e** creates a grammatical error.

40. c. The word *good* is not used incorrectly in this sentence, but it is not a very strong word choice. Replacing it with the stronger word *profound* makes the sentence more effective. Choice **a** changes the sentence's meaning since *Incidentally* has the opposite meaning of *Essentially*. Choice **b** also makes the meaning of the sentence inaccurate. Choice **d** is incorrect because the writer is not using the word *Sula* to mean the novel's title in this sentence; she is referring to the community in the novel. Choice **e** replaces the word *global* with a synonym (*worldwide*) that does not make the sentence incorrect, but does not improve it either.

Sample Responses for the Argumentative Essay

Following are sample criteria for scoring an argumentative essay.

A score 6 writer will

- create an exceptional composition with a clear thesis that appropriately addresses the audience and given task.
- organize ideas effectively and logically, include very strong supporting details, and use smooth transitions.
- present a definitive, focused thesis and clearly support it throughout the composition.

- include vivid, strong details, clear examples, and supporting text to support the key ideas.
- exhibit an exceptional level of skill in the usage of the English language and the capacity to employ an assortment of sentence structures.
- build essentially error-free and varied sentences that accurately convey intended meaning.

A score 5 writer will

- create a commendable composition that appropriately addresses the audience and given task.
- organize ideas, include supporting details, and use smooth transitions.
- present a thesis and support it throughout the composition.
- include details, examples, and supporting text to enhance the themes of the composition.
- generally exhibit a high level of skill in the usage of the English language and the capacity to employ an assortment of sentence structures.
- build mostly error-free sentences that accurately convey intended meaning.

A score 4 writer will

- create a composition that satisfactorily addresses the audience and given task.
- display satisfactory organization of ideas, include adequate supporting details, and generally use smooth transitions.
- present a thesis and mostly support it throughout the composition.
- include some details, examples, and supporting text that typically enhance most themes of the composition.
- exhibit a competent level of skill in the usage of the English language and the general capacity to employ an assortment of sentence structures.
- build sentences with several minor errors that generally do not confuse the intended meaning.

A score 3 writer will

- create an adequate composition that basically addresses the audience and given task.
- display some organization of ideas, include some supporting details, and use mostly logical transitions.
- present a somewhat underdeveloped thesis but attempt to support it throughout the composition.
- exhibit an adequate level of skill in the usage of the English language and a basic capacity to employ an assortment of sentence structures.
- build sentences with some minor and major errors that may obscure the intended meaning.

A score 2 writer will

- create a composition that restrictedly addresses the audience and given task.
- display little organization of ideas, have inconsistent supporting details, and use very few transitions.
- present an unclear or confusing thesis with little support throughout the composition.
- include very few details, examples, and supporting text.
- exhibit a less than adequate level of skill in the usage of the English language and a limited capacity to employ a basic assortment of sentence structures.
- build sentences with a few major errors that may confuse the intended meaning.

A score 1 writer will

- create a composition that has a limited sense of the audience and given task.
- display illogical organization of ideas, include confusing or no supporting details, and lack the ability to effectively use transitions.
- present a minimal or unclear thesis.
- include confusing or irrelevant details and examples, and little or no supporting text.

- exhibit a limited level of skill in the usage of the English language and little or no capacity to employ basic sentence structure.
- build sentences with many major errors that obscure or confuse the intended meaning.

Sample Score 6 Argumentative Essay

It's a fact: more and more people across the United States are vegetarian, and school and workplace cafeterias should be required to provide vegetarian lunch options for them. There are many reasons why vegetarians choose this diet: health concerns, moral issues, and religion among them. Schools and workplaces should honor these reasons by making it easier for vegetarians to purchase healthful, meat-free lunches.

Some vegetarians are responding to the generally unhealthy American diet, which often includes plenty of fast food and processed meats. They prefer salads, vegetables, and protein sources such as beans, soy-based products, and dairy products. However, cafeterias, both in schools and in businesses, tend to resemble fast food restaurants, offering such items as hamburgers, fried chicken, pizza, French fries, and sodas. If they also stocked healthier, meat-free choices, not only would the vegetarians be acommodated, but others would have the opportunity to enjoy healthier options.

It would not be difficult to transform the typical school or workplace cafeteria into a vegetarian-friendly one. Many of the lunch selections currently offered could be made vegetarian with a few simple and inexpensive substitutions. Veggie burgers offered alongside beef burgers, for example, would give vegetarians a satisfactory option. Tacos, burritos, and other Mexican entrees could be made with beans rather than ground beef. A salad bar would serve the dual purpose of providing both vegetarians and others concerned about their health and weight the opportunity for a satisfying meal. These changes, while relatively simple for cafeterias to incorporate, would provide vegetarians with acceptable lunch selections, and in the process, provide all the students or employees they serve with more healthful alternatives.

Comments on the Sample Argumentative Essay That Received a Score of 6

The author has created a solid good argument with a clear thesis that is both definitive and focused. This essay successfully addresses the issue at hand with an effective organization. The supporting details are correct, logical, and relevant. It uses smooth transitions, clear examples, and specific details. The key ideas are readily apparent and explored throughout the essay through varied sentence structures. The author displays a clear mastery of the subject and of the English language.

Sample Score 4 Argumentative Essay

In the United States there are many people who are vegetarian. Many of these people are students or workers who eat lunch at their cafeterias on a daily basis. Surprisingly though, school and workplace cafeterias are not required to provide vegetarian options. That means that most often they don't. That means that vegetarians may be limited to lunches comprised of French fries, or pizza loaded with cheese. While these are vegetarian (non-meat), they are not healthy, especially if they are eaten every day.

Schools and businesses should have a wider variety of vegetarian options. Such as a salad bar, or perhaps even something with tofu. Entrees that use beans or soy-based products instead of meat would also be good. It wouldn't cost cafeterias more money to provide vegetarian lunches. In fact, the ingredients used to make them (like beans) are typically much cheaper than their carnivorous counterparts (like ground beef). Salads require little preparation in comparison with French fries, which could save money on payroll. Also, cafeterias could buy premade vegetarian selections in bulk, just as they do non-vegetarian dishes. These premade foods are becoming more and more popular, and are not more expensive.

While cafeterias can't meet all the demands of those they serve, it is important to offer those committed to a vegetarian lifestyle the choice to eat healthfully and meat-free. Schools should create a menu that offers these options for all students.

Comments on the Sample Argumentative Essay That Received a Score of 4

The author has done a workmanlike job. The essay accomplishes what it sets out to do, addressing the issue at hand. It is fairly well organized and gives reasonable details and arguments. It wants somewhat for style, but displays adequate rhetorical skills and mastery of the English language. For the most part, it is grammatically and orthographically correct.

Sample Score 1 Argumentative Essay

Many people are vegetarian and don't eat meat. This may be because they are afraid of diseases found in meat, such as mad cow disease, salmanella, or avian influenza. Or, they may not eat meat because of their religion. Some care about animal rites, and others are vegetarian because they are concerned about their health. They believe a vegetarian diet will help them lose weight and in general improve their health. But this is not necessarily the case. You could just eat French fries, cold cereal, and pizza every day and be a vegetarian. Vegetarians need to learn about how to eat this diet and make it healthy too. School and workplace cafeterias could help by offering them good selections at lunch.

Comments on the Sample Argumentative Essay That Received a Score of 1

The essay is short, poorly organized, and does not fulfill the requirements. There are a number of grammatical and spelling mistakes, as well poor transitions and weak sentence structure. The argument is not convincing, and the author does not give the appearance of caring much about the subject.

Sample Responses for the Source-Based Essay

Following are sample criteria for scoring a source-based essay.

A score 6 writer will

- create an exceptional composition explaining why the concerns are important and support the explanation with specific references to both sources.
- organize ideas effectively and logically, include well chosen information from both sources, link the two sources in the discussion, and use smooth transitions.
- exhibit an exceptional level of skill in the usage of the English language and the capacity to employ an assortment of sentence structures.
- build essentially error-free and varied sentences that accurately convey intended meaning.
- cite both sources when quoting or paraphrasing.

A score 5 writer will

- create a commendable composition that explains why the concerns are important and supports the explanation with specific references to both sources..
- organize ideas effectively and logically, include information from both sources, link the two sources, and use smooth transitions.
- generally exhibit skill in the usage of the English language and the capacity to employ variety in sentence structures.
- build mostly error-free sentences that accurately convey intended meaning.
- cite both sources when quoting or paraphrasing.

A score 4 writer will

- create a composition that satisfactorily explains why the concerns are important and supports the explanation with specific references to both sources.

- use information from both sources to convey why the concerns discussed in the sources are important.
- display satisfactory organization of ideas, include adequate details, and link the two sources.
- exhibit a competent level of skill in the usage of the English language and the general capacity to employ an assortment of sentence structures.
- build sentences with several minor errors that generally do not confuse the intended meaning.
- cite both sources when quoting or paraphrasing.

A score 3 writer will

- create an adequate composition that basically addresses the audience and given task but conveys the importance of the concerns in only a limited way.
- use information from only one source or inadequately from both sources to convey why the concerns discussed in the sources are important.
- display some organization of ideas and include some supporting details.
- exhibit an adequate level of skill in the usage of the English language and a basic capacity to employ an assortment of sentence structures.
- build sentences with some minor and major errors that may obscure the intended meaning.
- cite sources when quoting or paraphrasing.

A score 2 writer will

- fail to explain why the concerns are important.
- use information from only one source poorly or fail to convey why the concerns discussed in the sources are important.
- display little organization of ideas, have inconsistent supporting details, fail to link the two sources.
- exhibit a less than adequate level of skill in the usage of the English language and a limited capacity to employ a basic assortment of sentence structures.

- build sentences with a few major errors that may confuse the intended meaning.
- fail to cite sources when quoting or paraphrasing.

A score 1 writer will

- display illogical organization of ideas, include confusing or no supporting details, and fail to adequately address the concerns raised by the sources.
- include confusing or irrelevant details and examples, and few or no supporting references.
- exhibit a limited level of skill in the usage of the English language and little or no capacity to employ basic sentence structure.
- build sentences with many major errors that obscure or confuse the intended meaning.

Sample Score 6 Essay

The Bill of Rights—the first ten amendments to the U.S. Constitution—is a part of American jurisprudence that is today often taken for granted. The Bill of Rights grants such fundamental liberties as the freedom of speech, freedom of religion, and protection against unreasonable search and seizure. However, there was a vigorous debate in the early Republic over whether a Bill of Rights should be adopted. Ironically, it was Alexander Hamilton, author of many of the Federalist Papers and proponent of a strong central government—the side eventually victorious—that would argue against the adoption of such a bill.

"John de Witt," speaking for the anti-Federalists, raises sound arguments in favor of a bill of rights. Entering into a form of government, by its nature, entails giving up some of one's natural rights. (This train of thought was in keeping with Enlightenment figures such as John Locke.) These rights are so important and fundamental, that one must carefully delineate what powers are allotted to the government, and which retained, or, as he writes, "The line cannot be drawn with too much precision and accuracy." Furthermore, such legislation would prevent any confusion. Anticipating modern debates over the "original intent" of the

Founding Fathers, "de Witt" points out that "Language is so easy of explanation, and so difficult is it by words to convey exact ideas, that the party to be governed cannot be too explicit." Thus, the new nation needed a bill of rights to eliminate any ambiguity.

One Federalist argument claimed that a constitutional bill of rights was unnecessary owing to the fact that states already had such verbiage affixed to their own constitutions. De Witt counters this by saying that if states had Bills of Rights, why not the Federal government? To do so would be a check on governmental overreach, and reassure people that they retained all rights not specifically allocated to the Federal government.

In rebutting this, Hamilton, writing for the Federalists, deploys two arguments. First, he makes an appeal to the dignity of the new nation: bills of rights were made between rulers and subjects, and are not suited to a free country of free citizens. This, however, is mere rhetoric, and Hamilton proceeds to the meat of the matter. He points out that the central government was intended to be weak, and thus a Bill of Rights is superfluous: "a minute detail of particular rights is certainly far less applicable to a Constitution like that under consideration… than to a constitution which has the regulation of every species of personal and private concerns." Worse, by explicitly mentioning exceptions to powers not even mentioned, they would "afford a colorable pretext to claim more than were granted." Thus, a bill of rights, Hamilton feared, could lead to emboldened citizens seeking to overstep their granted rights.

The debates over the American Bill of Rights are one of the ironies of history. The very statutes that today ensure our liberties—and which have been expanded by judicial opinion to include contingencies that would have been completely foreign to the Founding Fathers like immigration rights and interracial marriage—were once seen as superfluous and even detrimental to a democratic way of life. Ultimately—in this matter, at least—the Anti-Federalists would prevail, and the first ten amendments to the U.S. Constitution stand as one of the foundational documents of the Western concept of freedom and liberty.

Comments on the Sample Source-Based Essay That Received a Score of 6

This is an outstanding essay. The author has clearly explained why the topic is important, making reference to both sources, and clearly, effectively, and logically organized the ideas under discussion. The author has linked these ideas together into a thematic and impartial essay on the subject of the debate over the Bill of Rights. She or he clearly understands the issue, and has additionally brought in a great deal of outside information. The use of the English language is exemplary, with a wide variety of error-free sentences that clearly convey the intended meaning. Both sources are extensively and accurately cited. The author furthermore correctly understands the use of advanced rhetorical techniques like irony and logical fallacies.

Sample Score 4 Essay

From the very beginning, the Bill of Rights, which gives Americans freedom of speech, the freedom of religion, and freedom to own guns has been the subject of the controversy. The two sides of the debate were the Federalists and Anti-Federalists. The Federalists did not want a Bill of Rights, while the Anti-Federalists did.

John de Witt says that when people form governments, they give up some rights. It is therefore important to say which rights are given up, for as he says, "The line cannot be drawn with too much precision and accuracy." He also says that people might be confused as to which rights were given up. A Bill of Rights would help to prevent this confusion. Also, if states had Bills of Rights, why shouldn't the Federal government? This would prevent people from taking too much power, since people naturally want to gain power over other people.

Alexander Hamilton disagrees with this opinion. First, he says that Bills of Rights were made between rulers and subjects. Since Americans are not subjects, they do not need a Bill of Rights. He also says that since the government would not have any powers the Constitution did not grant it, a Bill of Rights is not needed. He *is even afraid that giving a Bill of Rights might make the government think it had more power than it really did.*

Obviously, the Anti-Federalists won this debate. Still, I feel that that people should listen to Alexander Hamilton today. The government has taken too much power. The Bill of Rights is there to stop the government from over-reaching.

Comments on the Sample Source-Based Essay That Received a Score of 4

This composition satisfactorily explains why the concerns in the topic are important and supports the explanation with specific information and references to both sources. However, though the author is able to deploy information from both sources to discuss the source, he or she does not have a deep historical background. The essay is satisfactorily organized and uses adequate details. The use of English is competent, with some variety in sentence structures. Errors are minor, and do not interfere with general understanding. Finally, the essay writer fails to be completely objective.

Sample Score 1 Essay

Today, the government does a lot of things it shouldn't. The government wants to take away guns (2 Amendment) and make us buy health care even if we like the health care we have right now (1 Amendment). Also the CIA and NSA are spying on us and violating our rights against searching and seizing.

The Founding Fathers came up with the best system of government anywhere. They knew what they were ding. In the Bill of Rights to the Constitution, they insured that we would not have our rights taken away. The problem with America today is that people are not listening to what the Founding Fathers said.

I think that we should go back to the original intent of the Founding Fathers. The USA should be One Nation Under God, Indivisible, With Liberty and Justice.

Comments on the Sample Source-Based Essay That Received a Score of 1

This essay displays an illogical organization of ideas and badly mismanages supporting details. The author shows no understanding of the issues. What details it does bring in are completely irrelevant. It also fails to adequately address the concerns raised by the sources. The level of English usage is poor, at best, and confuses the intended meaning. Finally, it fails to deal with the sources objectively.

Praxis® Core Academic Skills for Educators: Mathematics Practice Test 1

Time: 85 Minutes

Directions: Choose the best answer to each of the following questions.

1. Alec needs 432 inches of molding to put along the ceiling of his dining room. How many yards of molding should he buy?
   a. 12
   b. 43.2
   c. 15,552
   d. 36
   e. 440

2. John, Mike, and Dillon are painting a fence. John paints $\frac{1}{4}$ of the fence and Mike paints $\frac{2}{5}$ of the fence. How much of the fence is left to paint for Dillon?

   $$\frac{\boxed{}}{\boxed{}}$$

3. The Andersons went out to dinner Saturday night and had a bill of $190.00. They gave the server a 25% tip. How much money did the Andersons tip their server?
   a. $19
   b. $47.50
   c. $38
   d. $38.50
   e. $47

4. Tanya can pack 4 boxes of fragile dishware in 25 minutes. How many minutes would it take her to pack 28 boxes of fragile dishware?
   a. _____
   b. _____
   c. _____
   d. _____
   e. _____

5. Consider the line in the graph that follows:

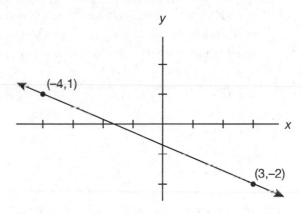

   Which of the following is the equation of this line?
   a. $7x + 3y = 15$
   b. $3x + 7y = -5$
   c. $7x + 3y = 15$
   d. $y + 2 = -(x - 3)$
   e. $y + 4 = -\frac{3}{7}(x - 1)$

6. John must rent vans to take the children from his summer camp on a field trip. There are 34 children, 6 counselors, and 11 assistants who will be going on the trip. If each van can accommodate 9 people, how many vans must John rent?
   a. 9
   b. 51
   c. 6
   d. 5
   e. 7

7. Which of the following is equivalent to $6 \times 7 + 6 \times 9$?
   a. $6(7 + 9)$
   b. $6 + 7 \times 6 + 9$
   c. $(6 \times 7) + 9$
   d. $(6 \times 7) \times (6 \times 9)$
   e. $6(7 \times 9)$

8. Out of 100 workers polled at a local factory, 75 said they would favor being offered a course in management. If there are 25,000 workers, how many would you expect to favor being offered such a course?

   a. 1,875
   b. 18,750
   c. 15,000
   d. 16,000
   e. 19,000

9. Which of the following is equivalent to the expression $xy \cdot yzx^5$?

   a. $5x^2y^2z$
   b. x^5y^2z
   c. $12xyz$
   d. x^6y^2z
   e. $x^6y^6z^5$

10. Jake rents a car for $200 each month, which includes 1,000 miles for the month. He is charged an additional $0.55 for each mile driven over 1,000. If x represents the total mileage Jake drives each month, and if he always drives over 1,000 miles per month, which of the following expressions can be used to calculate his total monthly car rental bill?

    a. $200 + 0.55x$
    b. $200 + 0.55(x - 1,000)$
    c. $200x + 0.55$
    d. $200 \times 0.55x$
    e. $200x + 0.55(x - 1,000)$

11. Suppose $a = -5$, $b = -2$, and $c = -3$. Evaluate $2ac - abc$.

    a. _____
    b. _____
    c. _____
    d. _____
    e. _____

12. Given the equation $y = 7 + 3(2x - 2)$, what is the value of y when $x = 6$?

    a. 14
    b. 21
    c. 25
    d. 35
    e. 37

Use the following chart to answer question 13.

How People Get to Work

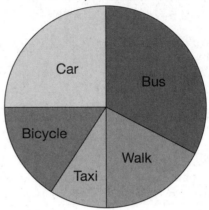

13. What is the total percentage of people who use a car or bicycle to get to work?

    a. 50%
    b. 25%
    c. 80%
    d. 40%
    e. 55%

14. Which of the following fractions is between $\frac{1}{5}$ and $\frac{1}{8}$? Indicate all that apply.

    a. ☐ $\frac{1}{4}$
    b. ☐ $\frac{1}{3}$
    c. ☐ $\frac{1}{7}$
    d. ☐ $\frac{2}{7}$
    e. ☐ $\frac{3}{16}$

15. Jessica received grades of 85, 90, 70, 85, and 100 on her math tests this semester. What grade will she receive in math for the semester?
   a. 70
   b. 85
   c. 86
   d. 90
   e. 100

Use the following figure to answer questions 16 and 17.

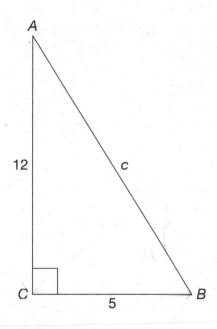

(Numbers indicate miles)

16. Paul drove to work each day using the route *A* to *C* to *B*, which is a total of 17 miles. Recently, a new road was finished that went directly from *A* to *B*. How many fewer miles will Paul be driving each day to work if he uses the new route?
   a. 2 miles
   b. 3 miles
   c. 4 miles
   d. 5 miles
   e. 6 miles

17. If Paul drives to work five days a week using route *A* to *B*, how many fewer miles will he drive than if he used route *A* to *C* to *B* over a period of 3 weeks?
   a. 15 miles
   b. 20 miles
   c. 35 miles
   d. 45 miles
   e. 60 miles

18. Which of the following is the solution of the system: $\begin{cases} x - 4y = 18 \\ 4y + x = 26 \end{cases}$?
   a. $x = 10, y = -2$
   b. $x = 2, y = 6$
   c. $x = 0, y = 0$
   d. $x = 22, y = 1$
   e. no solution

19. Aidan and James sell a total of 48 magazines. If Aidan sells 3 times more magazines than James, how many magazines does James sell?

20. Nella wants to buy wood chips to cover the play area in her backyard. The area is 12 feet long and 6 feet wide. She wants the wood chips to be 3 inches deep. How many cubic inches of wood chips does Nella need to buy?
   a. 216 cubic inches
   b. 500 cubic inches
   c. 2,160 cubic inches
   d. 21,160 cubic inches
   e. 31,104 cubic inches

Use the following dot plot to answer questions 21 and 22.

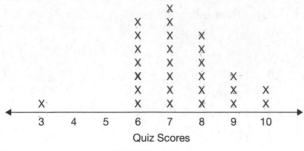

Quiz Scores

KEY: X = 1 Student

21. According to the dot plot, how many students scored at least an 8 on the quiz?

   a. 5

   b. 8

   c. 11

   d. 16

   e. 27

22. What fraction of students earned a 7 or 8 on the quiz?

   a. $\frac{8}{10}$

   b. $\frac{6}{10}$

   c. $\frac{8}{27}$

   d. $\frac{6}{27}$

   e. $\frac{14}{27}$

23. Alexa is making costumes for the school play. She needs 15 yards of fabric to make 3 costumes. How many yards of fabric would she need to make 8 costumes?

   a. 30 yards

   b. 40 yards

   c. 45 yards

   d. 50 yards

   e. 60 yards

24. Mary has exactly 1,560 hours until her vacation begins. How many days are there before her vacation begins?

   a. 30

   b. 50

   c. 65

   d. 75

   e. 37,440

25. A rose garden on a square plot of land has an open wooden fence that is 320 feet long around its perimeter. What is the approximate length of the diagonal of this plot of ground to the nearest foot?

   a. 80 feet

   b. 226 feet

   c. 6,400 feet

   d. 139 feet

   e. 113 feet

Use the following graph to answer questions 26 and 27.

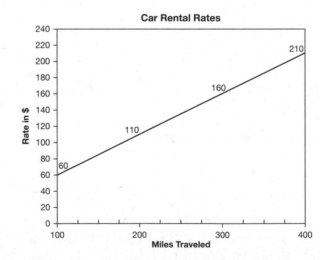

26. Which equation best represents the graph?

   a. $y = 2x$

   b. $y = x - 40$

   c. $y = 2x - 40$

   d. $y = \frac{1}{2}x + 40$

   e. $y = \frac{1}{2}x + 10$

27. If the x-axis is extended, what will y be when $x = 700$?

a. 260

b. 300

c. 310

d. 360

e. 400

28. A factory operates 15 machines that make between 90 and 120 tennis balls per minute. Which of the following could be the number of tennis balls produced in an hour if all 15 machines are working at the same time?

a. 900

b. 1,200

c. 9,000

d. 28,000

e. 90,000

29. The area of Melissa's rectangular garden is 330 square feet. The width of the garden is 15 feet. How many feet of fence does Melissa need to buy to surround the entire garden?

a. 20 feet

b. 34 feet

c. 74 feet

d. 85 feet

e. 94 feet

30. Which of the following numerical expressions is an *irrational* number?

a. $\sqrt{8} \times \sqrt{2}$

b. $\frac{\sqrt{125}}{\sqrt{5}}$

c. $(\sqrt{21})^2$

d. $2 - \sqrt{81}$

e. $\sqrt{169 - 49}$

31. Let $s(x) = \frac{3}{2} - 2x^2 + \frac{1}{3}x^4$ and $r(x) = 5x^2 - 10x^4$. Which of the following is equivalent to $6s(x) - \frac{1}{5}r(x)$?

a. $-11x^2 + 9$

b. $\frac{31}{3}x^4 - 3x^2 + 9$

c. $4x^4 - 13x^2 + 9$

d. $4x^4 - 13x^2$

e. $4x^4 + 13x^2 - 9$

32. Write the following expression as a single decimal: $(2.7 \times 10^{-3}) \div (3.6 \times 10^{-3})$.

a. _____

b. _____

c. _____

d. _____

e. _____

33. For which of the following values of a does the trinomial $x^2 + ax + 24$ factor? Select all that apply.

a. 25

b. −10

c. −11

d. 11

e. 2

34. Patrick has $1,860 saved up from his past five birthdays. He wants to allot himself $75 per week for social activities and $40 per week for gas and food, and wants to keep $400 in the account to avoid monthly maintenance fees. Which of the following inequalities can be used to determine x as the number of weeks he can continue to withdraw from the account?

a. $115x + 1,860 \geq 400$

b. $115 + 1,860x \geq 400$

c. $75x + 1,860 \leq 400$

d. $-115x + 1,860 \geq 400$

e. $1,860 \leq 400 + 115x$

Use the following table to answer questions 35 and 36.

SNOWMOBILE RENTAL RATES	
HOURS OVER 1	RATE
1	$17
2	$24
3	$31
4	$38

35. It costs $250 to rent a snowmobile for the first hour. The chart shows the rates for additional hours. What would be the total cost for Tom and Mary if Tom rented a snowmobile for 4 hours, and Mary rented one for 3 hours?
   a. $281
   b. $288
   c. $560
   d. $569
   e. $622

36. Letting r = rate, and x = number of hours, which equation best represents the data in the chart?
   a. $r = 7x + 10$
   b. $r = 10 + 7$
   c. $r = 5x + 12$
   d. $r = 16x + 1$
   e. $r = 5x + 10$

Use the bar graph below to answer questions 37 and 38.

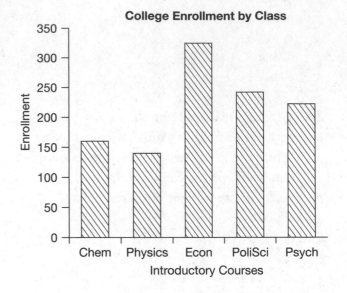

37. According to the chart, what was the approximate total enrollment for the classes shown?
   a. 900
   b. 1,000
   c. 1,025
   d. 1,050
   e. 1,100

38. What is the approximate proportion of students who took PoliSci?
   a. $\frac{1}{2}$
   b. $\frac{1}{4}$
   c. $\frac{1}{3}$
   d. $\frac{2}{3}$
   e. $\frac{3}{4}$

39. The formula for the surface area of a right circular cylinder (including the areas of the two bases) is given by $SA - 2\pi r^2 + 2\pi rh$, where r is the radius of the base and h is the height of the cylinder. If the height equals three times the radius and the surface area is 200π square feet, which of the following is the radius?

  a. 5 feet

  b. $\sqrt{50}$ feet

  c. 25 feet

  d. 15 feet

  e. 5π feet

40. Let $y = f(x)$ be a given function and suppose the point $(2,-3)$ lies on its graph. Consider the translation of this function given by $g(x) = f(x + 4) - 1$. To what point would the given point correspond on the graph of $g(x)$?

  Fill in the blanks: (_____ , _____)

41. Jackie's bank balances were $20 on Monday, $0 on Tuesday, $45 on Wednesday, and $25 on Thursday. What was Jackie's mean balance for the week?

  a. $20.00

  b. $22.50

  c. $25.00

  d. $25.50

  e. $30.00

Use the dot plot to answer questions 42 through 44.

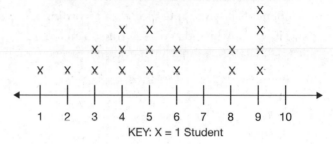

Number of Pencils Each Student Has

KEY: X = 1 Student

42. How many students are surveyed on this dot plot?

  a. 9

  b. 10

  c. 18

  d. 38

  e. 40

43. What is the approximate average number of pencils owned by the students surveyed?

  a. 5.6

  b. 4.5

  c. 10

  d. 6.6

  c. 10.2

44. What is the mode of the data indicated by the dot plot?

  a. 2

  b. 5

  c. 6

  d. 9

  e. 10

45. Neil digitally records birthday parties and charges $120 for the recording. His weekly overhead expenses amount to $390, and he spends $30 on supplies for each recording. How many birthday parties must Neil record each week before he breaks even?

 a. 3

 b. 4

 c. 5

 d. 10

 e. 50

46. Jan and her sister entered a raffle at the football game. Jan put her name on 3 tickets, and her sister put her name on 5 tickets. If there are 100 total tickets and only one winner, what are the chances that Jan or her sister will win the raffle?

 a. 5.0

 b. 0.50

 c. 0.005

 d. 0.8

 e. 0.08

47. Which of the following statements are true? Select all that apply.

 a. All rectangles are rhombi.

 b. There is a rectangle that is not a parallelogram.

 c. Some rhombi are not squares.

 d. A parallelogram is a square.

 e. All squares are rectangles.

Use the chart to answer question 48.

x	y
2	4
4	7
6	10
8	13

48. Which of the following equations best describes the relationship shown in the chart?

 a. $2x = y$

 b. $y = x + 3$

 c. $2x + 3 = y$

 d. $\frac{3x + 2}{2} = y$

 e. $\frac{2x + 3}{2} = y$

49. The ages of the starting lineup for the New York Yankees are as follows:

 26, 29, 35, 29, 22, 31, 35, 21, 27

 What is the median age of the Yankees starting lineup?

 a. 21

 b. 35

 c. 14

 d. 28.5

 e. 29

50. Ellen's square kitchen has a perimeter of 48 feet. What is the area of the kitchen?

 a. 12 square feet

 b. 12 feet

 c. 24 square feet

 d. 560 square feet

 e. 144 square feet

51. Jessica has 3 skirts, 4 shirts, and 2 hats. How many different combinations of skirts, shirts, and hats can she wear?

a. 7

b. 14

c. 24

d. 28

e. 32

52. If p and q are prime numbers, what is the least common multiple of $18p^2$, $30pq^2$, $42pq^3$?

a. $6p$

b. $6p^2q^3$

c. $2p$

d. $630p^2q^3$

e. $22,680p^4q^5$

53. Tom needs to buy paint so that he can paint the emblem on the basketball court. The circular emblem has a diameter of 12 feet. If paint cans come in quarts, and it takes 1 quart to paint 50 square feet, how many quarts of paint will Tom have to buy? Use 3.14 for π.

a. 1

b. 2

c. 3

d. 4

e. 5

54. Consider the two triangles $\triangle ABC$ and $\triangle A'B'C'$ shown below.

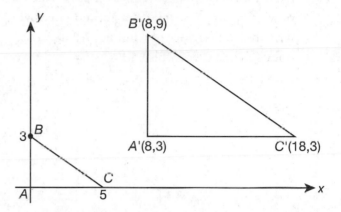

Assume that $\triangle ABC$ can be transformed into $\triangle A'B'C'$ by first translating $\triangle ABC$ and then applying an appropriate dilation centered at the origin. Which of the following translation rule–dilation combination will result in this transformation?

a. Translate using the rule $(x,y) \rightarrow (x - 8, y - 3)$ and then perform a dilation centered at the origin with a scale factor of 2.

b. Translate using the rule $(x,y) \rightarrow (x + 8, y - 3)$ and then perform a dilation centered at the origin with a scale factor of $\frac{1}{2}$.

c. Translate using the rule $(x,y) \rightarrow (x + 8, y + 3)$ and then perform a dilation centered at the origin with a scale factor of $\frac{1}{2}$.

d. Translate using the rule $(x,y) \rightarrow (x + 8, y + 3)$ and then perform a dilation centered at the origin with a scale factor of 3.

e. Translate using the rule $(x,y) \rightarrow (x + 8, y + 3)$ and then perform a dilation centered at the origin with a scale factor of 2.

55. Six students are running for class president. John has a $\frac{1}{8}$ chance of winning. John is half as likely to win as Mike. Kelly has the same chance of winning as Mike. Julie, Kelvin, and Roger all have the same chance of winning. What chance does Kelvin have of winning?

a. $\frac{1}{2}$
b. $\frac{1}{3}$
c. $\frac{1}{4}$
d. $\frac{3}{8}$
e. $\frac{1}{8}$

56. Jason was asked to choose a marble from a bag. If he chose a red marble, he would win a prize. The bag contained 20 blue marbles, 20 black marbles, 20 green marbles, 18 yellow marbles, and 2 red marbles. Which of the following decimals shows Jason's chances of choosing a red marble?

a. 0.025
b. 0.25
c. 0.08
d. 0.8
e. 2.5

Praxis® Core Academic Skills for Educators: Mathematics Practice Test 1 Answers and Explanations

1. a. This is a conversion problem. There are 36 inches in 1 yard. Converting from a smaller unit to a larger unit requires division: $432 \div 36 = 12$. You can also check division with multiplication: $36 \times 12 = 432$.

2. The correct answer is $\frac{7}{20}$. The first step is to rewrite all fractions with a common denominator. The lowest common denominator for $\frac{1}{4}$ and $\frac{2}{5}$ is 20: $\frac{1}{4} \times \frac{5}{5} = \frac{5}{20}$, and $\frac{2}{5} \times \frac{4}{4} = \frac{8}{20}$. These fractions represent portions of the fence that have been painted, so $\frac{5}{20} + \frac{8}{20} = \frac{13}{20}$ of the fence has been painted. Therefore, $1 - \frac{13}{20} = \frac{20}{20} - \frac{13}{20} = \frac{7}{20}$ of the fence is left for Dillon to paint.

3. b. To compute a percent of a number, multiply by the decimal of the percent. The decimal for 25% is 0.25: $0.25 \times \$190 = \$47.50$.

4. **175 minutes.** Let x represent the number of minutes needed to pack 28 boxes of fragile dishware. Set up the following proportion:
$$\frac{4 \text{ boxes}}{25 \text{ minutes}} = \frac{28 \text{ boxes}}{x \text{ minutes}}$$
Cross multiply and solve for x:
$$4x = (25)(28)$$
$$x = 25(7)$$
$$x = 175$$
So, Tanya can pack 28 boxes in 175 minutes.

5. b. We can identify two points on the graph: $(-4,1)$ and $(3,-2)$. The slope of the line containing these two points is $m = \frac{1-(-2)}{-4-3} = -\frac{3}{7}$. Using point-slope form with this slope and the point $(3,-2)$ yields $y - (-2) = -\frac{3}{7}(x-3)$. Now, we simplify as follows:
$$y - (-2) = -\frac{3}{7}(x-3)$$
$$y + 2 = -\frac{3}{7}(x-3)$$
$$7y + 14 = -3(x-3)$$
$$7y + 14 = -3x + 9$$
$$3x + 7y = -5$$

6. c. For this problem, you must first determine how many people will be going on the trip by adding: $34 + 6 + 11 = 51$. Since these people will be splitting into groups of 9, you should divide: 51 total people divided by 9 in each van equals 5 remainder 6. However, the remainder here represents people, so there will be 5 vans with 9 people, and one van with 6 people, for a total of 6 vans.

7. a. This is an example of the distributive property of multiplication over addition. Factor out 6 to get the equivalent expression $6(7 + 9)$.

8. b. 75 out of 100 is 75%. To compute 75% of 25,000, multiply $25,000 \times 0.75 = 18,750$.

9. d. Gather like variables in the product and add their exponents:

$$xy \cdot x^5yz = (x \cdot x^5) \cdot (y \cdot y) \cdot z = x^6y^2z$$

10. b. His rental fee will include the $200 plus $0.55 × the number of miles he drives over 1,000 miles. If x = total miles, then $x - 1,000$ = the total miles driven over 1,000. Therefore, the expression becomes $200 + 0.55(x - 1,000)$.

11. 60. Substitute the values of a, b, and c into the expression and use the order of operations to simplify:

$$2ac - abc = 2(-5)(-3) - (-5)(-2)(-3)$$
$$= 30 - (-30)$$
$$= 30 + 30$$
$$= 60$$

12. e. Substitute $x = 6$ and follow the order of operations (PEMDAS). Multiply inside the parentheses first, and then subtract: $y - 7 + 3(2 \times 6 - 2)$; $y = 7 + 3(12 - 2)$; $y = 7 + 3(10)$. Then, multiply: $y = 7 + 3(10)$; $y = 7 + 30$. Finally, add: $y = 37$.

13. d. Since there are no values given, you must approximate the percentages based on the size of the areas for car and bicycle. It could not be 50%, 55%, or 80% because that would be half the chart or bigger. 25% is $\frac{1}{4}$ of the chart, but this only describes the percentage who take a car to work. 40% is the best choice because it accurately describes how the percentage of people who take a car or bicycle to work is slightly less than half of the graph.

14. c and e. To solve this problem, convert each fraction to a decimal. You are looking for fractions with decimals between $\frac{1}{8} = 0.125$ and $\frac{1}{5} = 0.2$. Of the fractions given, only $\frac{1}{7} \approx 0.1429$ and $\frac{3}{16} = 0.1875$ fall between these two values.

15. c. Jessica's overall grade for the semester will be the average of the grades on her tests. To find the average of a group of numbers, first add the numbers, then divide by the number of numbers: $\frac{85 + 90 + 70 + 85 + 100}{5} = \frac{430}{5} = 86$.

16. c. The new route from A to B represents the hypotenuse of the right triangle. You can find the hypotenuse using the Pythagorean theorem, $a^2 + b^2 = c^2$: $12^2 + 5^2 = c^2$; $144 + 25 = 166$. The square root of $166 = 13$. Subtract the length of the new route from the length of his old route: $17 - 13 = 4$ miles.

17. e. Using the 4 fewer miles that Paul drives each day using this new route, multiply that value by 5 to get 20 miles fewer driven each week. Over a period of 3 weeks, this would be $20 \times 3 = 60$ fewer miles driven.

18. d. The method of elimination is the most efficient one to use here. Add the two equations to cancel the y terms:

$$x - 4y = 18$$
$$+ (x + 4y = 26)$$
$$2x = 44$$
$$x = 22$$

Now, substitute $x = 22$ into the first equation $x - 4y = 18$ to obtain $22 - 4y = 18$. Solving for y then yields $y = 1$. So, the solution of the system is $x = 22$, $y = 1$.

19. The correct answer is **12**. For this problem, use an algebraic equation. Let James be J, and since Aidan sells 3 times more than James, Aidan will be $3J$. The equation becomes $3J + J = 48$. Combine like terms: $4J = 48$. Finally, divide each side by 4: $J = 12$. James sells 12 magazines.

20. e. To correctly solve this problem, it is important to first change the feet to inches. Remember, there are 12 inches in 1 foot: 12 feet is equal to 144 inches, and 6 feet is equal to 72 inches. To find the volume of this rectangular area, multiply length times width times height: $144 \times 72 \times 3 = 31,104$ cubic inches.

21. c. On this dot plot, one X is equal to one student who earned a particular score on the quiz. Looking only at the X's for 8, 9, and 10, add to see that there are 11 students represented.

22. e. Add all the X's on the dot plot to find the total amount of students who took the quiz. There are 27 X's, so this is the denominator of the fraction. The question asks for the fraction of students who scored a 7 or 8, so add the X's for those two scores. There are 14 students who scored either a 7 or 8, so the fraction is $\frac{14}{27}$.

23. b. To solve this problem, set up a proportion and cross-multiply: $\frac{15}{3} = \frac{x}{8}$. Cross-multiply: $15 \times 8 = 3x$; $120 = 3x$. Finally, divide both sides by 3: $x = 40$ yards.

24. c. This problem requires you to convert a smaller unit to a larger unit. To go from a smaller unit to a larger unit, you must divide. Divide 1,560 hours by 24 hours per day to get 65 days.

25. e. Since the garden is a square, each of its four sides has the same length. Since the perimeter is 320 feet, each side has length 80 feet. The diagonal of the garden can be viewed as the hypotenuse h of a right triangle whose legs both have length 80 feet. Using the Pythagorean theorem yields $80^2 + 80^2 = h^2$, which simplifies to $h^2 = 12,800$. So, $h = \sqrt{12,800} \approx 113$ feet.

26. e. Because there are points labeled on the graph, you can use them to find the slope of the line: $m = \frac{160 - 110}{300 - 200} = \frac{50}{100} = \frac{1}{2}$. This eliminates all but 2 of the equations given. To determine which of the two equations is correct, plug an x-value into the equations. The one that produces the correct y-value is the correct equation: $y = \frac{1}{2}(200) + 10$; $y = 100 + 10$; $y = 110$. The point $(200, 100)$ is labeled on the line, so $y = \frac{1}{2}x + 10$ is the correct equation.

27. d. To find the y-value, plug $x = 700$ into the equation of the line: $y = \frac{1}{2}(700) + 10$; $y = 350 + 10$; $y = 360$.

28. e. First, calculate the minimum number of tennis balls that could be produced in an hour by 15 machines: 90 balls per minute $\times$ 60 minutes in an hour $\times$ 15 machines $= 81,000$. Do the same for the maximum number: $120 \times 60 \times 15 = 108,000$. Of the given possible numbers of balls produced, only 90,000 falls within this range.

29. c. To determine how much fencing is needed to go around the entire garden, you need to calculate the perimeter. The perimeter of a rectangle is found by adding twice the length and twice the width. So, you must first find the length of the garden. You are given the area and width of the garden, and remember that the area of a rectangle is found by multiplying length times width. Find the length by dividing: $330 \div 15 = 22$ feet. Now, the perimeter of the garden is $2(22) + 2(15) = 44 + 30 = 74$ feet.

30. c. Observe that $\sqrt{169 - 49} = \sqrt{120}$. Since 120 is not the square of a rational number, this quantity is irrational.

31. c. To compute $6s(x) - \frac{1}{5}r(x)$, first distribute 6 through each term of $s(x)$ and distribute the $-\frac{1}{5}$ through each term of $r(x)$ and then add like terms:

$$6s(x) - \frac{1}{5}r(x) = 6\left(\frac{3}{2} - 2x^2 + \frac{1}{3}x^4\right) - \frac{1}{5}(5x^2 - 10x^4)$$
$$= (9 - 12x^2 + 2x^4) - (x^2 - 2x^4)$$
$$= 9 - 12x^2 + 2x^4 - x^2 + 2x^4$$
$$= 4x^4 - 13x^2 + 9$$

32. **0.75.** Simplify each of the two quantities enclosed within parentheses. Then, divide resulting decimals, as follows:

$$(2.7 \times 10^{-3}) \div (3.6 \times 10^{-3})$$
$$= 0.00027 \div 0.0036 = 27 \div 36 = 0.75$$

33. **a, b, c, d.** For **a**, the trinomial would factor as $(x + 1)(x + 24)$. For **b**, the trinomial would factor as $(x - 4)(x - 6)$. For **c**, the trinomial would factor as $(x - 3)(x - 8)$. For **d**, the trinomial would factor as $(x + 3)(x + 8)$.

34. d. Let x represent the number of weeks he can make withdrawls from the account. Since he withdraws $115 per week (for social activities, gas, and food), the total he withdraws in x weeks is $\$115x$. So, after x weeks, there is $1,860 - 115x$ dollars left in the account. This amount must be greater than or equal to 400 dollars in order to avoid fees. So, the inequality used to model this situation is $-115x + 1,860 \geq 400$.

35. d. Use the table to determine the cost of each person's rental, then add the values. Tom's first hour was $250, and then his 4 additional hours were $38 more: $250 + $38 = $288. Mary's first hour was also $250, and then her 3 additional hours were $31 more: $250 + $31 = $281. Therefore, the total cost is $288 + $281 = $569.

36. a. Use trial and error to find which equation best represents the data in the chart. By plugging the hours in the chart in for x, you see that $r = 7x + 10$ is the equation that shows all the correct values for r.

37. e. The question asks for the approximate total enrollment, so you must round the numbers represented by the bars on the graph. By rounding, represent Chem as 150, Physics as 150, Econ as 325, PoliSci as 250, and Psych as 225: $150 + 150 + 325 + 250 + 225 = 1,100$.

38. b. There are approximately 1,100 total students enrolled, and 250 of them are enrolled in PoliSci. This represented as a fraction would be $\frac{250}{1,100}$. Because the question asks for the approximate fraction, round 1,100 to 1,000 and then reduce: $\frac{250}{1,000} = \frac{1}{4}$.

39. a. Let r represent the radius of the base. Then, the height $h = 3r$. Using the surface area formula for a right circular cylinder yields the following equation that we must solve for r:

$$200\pi = 2\pi r^2 + 2\pi r(3r)$$
$$200\pi = 2\pi r^2 + 6\pi r$$
$$200\pi = 8\pi r^2$$
$$25 = r^2$$
$$5 = r$$

So, the radius is 5 feet.

40. $(-2, -4)$. You need to translate the given point 4 units to the left and 1 unit down. In such case, $(2, -3)$ would become $(2 - 4, -3 - 1) = (-2, -4)$.

41. b. The mean is the same as the average. To find average, add all the values and divide by the total number of values: $\frac{\$20 + \$0 + \$45 + \$25}{4} = \frac{\$90}{4} = \$22.50$.

42. c. On this particular dot plot, one X represents one student. There are a total of 18 X's on the line plot, so there were 18 students surveyed.

43. a. To find the average, add all the values and divide by the total number of values. However, in this situation, the values are the numbers of pencils, not the numbers of students. You must add the amount of each number indicated by the X's, not just the number of X's. For example, 4 students had 9 pencils, so this value in the average would be 4×9. Do this for each column where there are X's, and since there are 18 students, divide this all by 18:

$$\frac{(1\times1)+(2\times1)+(3\times2)+(4\times3)+(5\times3)+(6\times2)+(7\times0)+(8\times2)+(9\times4)+(10\times0)}{18}$$

$$= \frac{1+2+6+12+15+12+0+16+36+0}{18} = \frac{100}{18} = 5.555555\ldots$$
$$\approx 5.6.$$

44. d. The mode is the number that occurs most often. In this case, that would be 9 pencils, which occurs 4 times.

45. c. Neil reaches the break-even point when his sales for a week equal his costs for the week. We know that Neil's weekly overhead expenses are fixed at $390. He also spends $30 on materials for each recording. He then charges $120 for the recording.

46. e. Since Jan *or* her sister are being picked, we must add 3 and 5. There are 100 total tickets, so the chances that Jan or her sister will win is $\frac{8}{100}$. Since the probabilities are written in decimal form, change $\frac{8}{100}$ to the decimal 0.08.

47. c, e. For **c**, any quadrilateral whose opposite sides are parallel and for which all four sides have the same length is a rhombus. If there is no right angle, then it cannot be a square. For **e**, a rectangle must have opposite sides parallel and contain a right angle. Squares satisfy these conditions, as well as having all four sides congruent.

48. d. The easiest way to solve problems like these is to use substitution and the process of elimination. By substituting each x-value into the equations, you find that the only equation that works for every value of x is $y = \frac{3x + 2}{2}$.

49. e. The median is the middle number of a set of data when arranged in increasing order. The given ages in increasing order are 21, 22, 26, 27, 29, 29, 31, 35, 35. The number 29 is in the middle, so it is the medium age for the Yankees starting lineup.

50. e. The kitchen is a square, so its four sides are of equal length. You can find the length of the sides by dividing the perimeter by 4: $48 \div 4 = 12$ feet. Area is then calculated by multiplying length × width: $12 \times 12 = 144$ square feet.

51. c. Each skirt, shirt, and hat can be paired together in any combination, and order doesn't matter. This can be solved using the counting principle and multiplication: $4 \times 3 \times 2 = 24$ combinations.

52. d. The smallest whole number into which all of 18, 30, and 42 divides evenly is 630. Also, the smallest power of p into which each of $18p^2$, $30pq^2$, $42pq^3$ divides is p^2, and the smallest power of q into which each divides is q^3. Hence, the least common multiple of $18p^2$, $30pq^2$, $42pq^3$ is $630p^2q^3$.

53. c. The equation for the area of a circle is $A = \pi r^2$. The diameter of the circle is given as 12 feet, so the radius is 6 feet: $A = \pi(6)^2 = 36\pi \approx 113.04$ square feet. If each quart of paint will cover 50 square feet, then Tom needs to buy 3 cans of paint.

54. e. First, observe that in order to move A to A', we must move the point right 8 units and then up 3 units. This is described by the translation rule $(x,y) \rightarrow (x + 8, y + 3)$. Applying this to all points of the triangle $\triangle ABC$ moves it to a new location in the plane. Now, observe that this triangle is smaller than $\triangle A'B'C'$, so that the scale factor must be greater than 1. Observe that $A'B'$ is twice the length of AB, and $A'C'$ is twice the length of AC. So, the scale factor should be 2.

55. e. The chance of someone winning the election is 1. If John has a $\frac{1}{8}$ chance of winning, and if he is half as likely to win as Mike, that means that Mike has a $\frac{1}{4}$ chance of winning. Since Kelly has the same chance of winning as Mike, she also has a $\frac{1}{4}$ chance. If you add the chances for John, Mike, and Kelly, you get $\frac{5}{8}$, leaving a $\frac{3}{8}$ chance that Julie, Kelvin, or Roger will win. Since they all have the same chance, each has a $\frac{1}{8}$ chance to win. Therefore, Kelvin has a $\frac{1}{8}$ chance of winning.

56. a. First, determine the total number of marbles in the bag by adding the numbers given: $20 + 20 + 20 + 18 + 2 = 80$. Since there are only 2 red marbles, Jason's chances of choosing a red marble are $\frac{2}{80}$. To find the decimal, divide 2 by 80, which is 0.025.

PRAXIS® CORE ACADEMIC SKILLS FOR EDUCATORS: PRACTICE TEST 2

CHAPTER SUMMARY

Here is the final set of full-length tests in this book for each Praxis® Core Academic Skills for Educators test: Reading, Writing, and Mathematics. Now that you have completed the review chapters and taken one full set of practice exams, take these exams to see how much your score has improved.

L ike Chapter 7, this chapter contains three tests that mirror the Reading, Writing, and Mathematics Core tests. Although the actual tests you will take are computer-based, the question types for each test are replicated here for you in the book.

This time, as you take these practice tests, you should simulate the actual test-taking experience as closely as you can. Find a quiet place to work where you won't be disturbed. Follow the time constraints noted at the beginning of each test.

After you finish taking your tests, review the answer explanations. (Each individual test is followed by its own answer explanations.) See **A Note on Scoring** on page 407 to find information on how to score your test.

Good luck!

Praxis® Core Academic Skills for Educators: Reading Practice Test 2

Time: 85 Minutes

Use the following passage to answer questions 1 and 2.

Although it is called Central Park, New York City's great green space has no "center"—no formal walkway down the middle of the park, no central monument or body of water, no sin-
5 gle orienting feature. The paths wind, the landscape constantly shifts and changes, the sections spill into one another in a seemingly random manner. But this "decentering" was precisely the intent of the park's innovative design. Made
10 to look as natural as possible, Frederick Law Olmsted's 1858 plan for Central Park had as its main goal the creation of a democratic playground—a place with many centers to reflect the multiplicity of its uses and users. Olmsted
15 designed the park to allow interaction among the various members of society, without giving preference to one group or class. Thus Olmsted's ideal of a "common-place civilization" could be realized.

1. In the passage, the author describes specific park features in order to
   a. illustrate the centralized nature of Central Park.
   b. suggest the organization of the rest of the passage.
   c. provide evidence that Central Park has no center.
   d. demonstrate how large Central Park is.
   e. show how well the author knows Central Park.

2. The main idea of this passage is that
   a. New York City is a democratic city.
   b. Olmsted was a brilliant designer.
   c. more parks should be designed without centers.
   d. Central Park is poorly laid out.
   e. Central Park is democratic by design.

Use the following passage to answer questions 3 through 5.

O'Connell Street is the main thoroughfare of Dublin City. Although it is not a particularly long street, Dubliners will tell the visitor proudly that it is the widest street in all of
5 Europe. This claim usually meets with protests, especially from French tourists, claiming the Champs Elysees of Paris as Europe's widest street. But the witty Dubliner will not relinquish bragging rights easily and will trump the
10 French visitor with a fine distinction: the Champs Elysees is a boulevard; O'Connell is a street.

3. Which of the following would be the best title for this passage?
   a. "Dublin's Famous Monuments"
   b. "The Irish Take Pride in Their Capital City"
   c. "The Widest Street in Europe"
   d. "Sights and History on Dublin's O'Connell Street"
   e. "Tourism in Dublin"

4. What is the best definition for the word *trump* as it is used in the line 9 of the passage?
   a. to trumpet loudly, to blare or drown out
   b. to trample
   c. to get the better of by using a key or hidden resource
   d. to devise a fraud, to employ trickery
   e. to use a particular suit of cards

5. With which of the following statements about the people of Dublin would the author of the passage most likely agree?
   a. They lack industry.
   b. They are playful and tricky.
   c. They are rebellious and do not like tourists.
   d. They are proud of their city.
   e. They are unaware of their history.

Use the following passage to answer question 6.

Despite what some lawyers might suggest, litigation is not always the only or best way to resolve conflicts. Mediation can be faster, less expensive, and can lead to creative solutions not always possible in a court of law. Additionally, mediation focuses on mutually acceptable solutions, rather than on winning or losing.

6. The author of this passage would most likely agree with which of the following statements?
   a. There is too much reliance on litigation in our society.
   b. Litigation is expensive, slow, and limited by its reliance on following the letter of the law.
   c. Mediation is the best way to resolve a conflict.
   d. Compared to litigation, there is a greater chance that mediation satisfies both parties in a conflict.
   e. Lawyers are overly concerned with their earning potential and not the best interest of their clients.

Use the following passage pair to answer questions 7 through 10.

Passage 1
Far too often artists are pigeonholed into the medium for which they are most famous and the works that are the most lucrative. But for many artists whose talents overflow, it may be

5 the case that no single form can contain their abilities. After all, Pablo Picasso was not only a painter but a sculptor, and Salvador Dali was both a painter and a filmmaker. Emerging artists should never let their output be constrained

10 within a solitary structure, lest their shining brilliance be dulled as a result.

Passage 2
Artists should never be restrained from exploring their creativity, but too much diversifying can degenerate into mere dabbling. Only by specializing can artists truly master their

5 medium. They must study painting for long years of dedicated work before calling themselves painters. Flitting from one medium to another can only dilute that dedication. Only after mastering a medium should artists explore

10 the other mediums available, and they should only do so if ready to commit to the same kind of intense study and dedication. Otherwise, the art world is in danger of being overrun by dilettantes.

7. Which of the following best describes the relationship between Passage 1 and Passage 2?
   a. Passage 1 states a topic and Passage 2 compares it to another topic.
   b. Passage 1 states an opinion and Passage 2 states a contrasting opinion.
   c. Passage 1 makes a general claim and Passage 2 makes a specific claim.
   d. Passage 1 describes a historic event and Passage 2 describes what happened next.
   e. Passage 1 states an opinion and Passage 2 states a fact.

8. In what way is Passage 1 stronger than Passage 2?
a. Passage 1 is written for a more educated audience than Passage 2 is.
b. Passage 1 has a clearer structure than Passage 2 does.
c. Passage 1 mentions more than one artistic medium.
d. Passage 1 backs up the author's claim with specific examples.
e. Passage 1 is written by a professional artist.

9. The primary concern of Passage 1 is
a. describing artists who have found success with a variety of art forms.
b. encouraging artists to experiment beyond their more recognizable media.
c. suggesting that artists disdain the commercial exploits of their artwork.
d. recommending that artists focus on their primary and most profitable art forms.
e. condemning shortsighted people who disregard an artist's secondary works.

10. In Passage 1, the author's ideas could be reinforced with the success of which other artist?
a. Chuck Close, whose paralysis restricts the details of his paintings
b. Samuel Clemens, whose work was attributed to either Clemens or Mark Twain
c. Claude Monet, whose paintings varied in style throughout his career
d. Marc Chagall, whose contributions to art include paintings and stained glass
e. Paul Simon, who wrote songs in a partnership and as a solo artist

Use the following passage to answer questions 11 and 12.

Could good dental hygiene be man's earliest custom? The findings of paleontologist Leslea Hlusko suggest that 1.8 million years ago early hominids used grass stalks to clean their teeth.
5　Many ancient hominid teeth unearthed in archaeological digs have curved grooves near the gumline. Hlusko posited that these grooves were evidence of teeth cleaning by early man. A stalk of grass is also about the same width as
10　the marks found on the ancient teeth. To prove her theory Dr. Hlusko took a baboon tooth and patiently rubbed a grass stalk against it for eight hours. As she suspected, the result was grooves similar to those found on the ancient hominid
15　teeth. She repeated the experiment with a human tooth and found the same result.

It seems that our early human ancestors may have used grass, which was easily found and ready to use, to floss between their teeth. As
20　Hlusko suggests in the journal *Current Anthropology*, "Toothpicking with grass stalks probably represents the most persistent habit documented in human evolution."

11. In the passage, the word *posited* most nearly means
a. insisted.
b. demanded.
c. questioned.
d. suggested.
e. argued.

12. The passage suggests that the theory that early man used grass stalks as toothpicks is
a. a possibility.
b. very probable.
c. absolutely certain.
d. fanciful.
e. uncorroborated.

Use the following passage to answer questions 13 through 15.

The post–World War II era marked a period of unprecedented energy against the second-class citizenship accorded to African Americans in many parts of the nation. Resistance to racial
5 segregation and discrimination with strategies such as civil disobedience, nonviolent resistance, marches, protests, boycotts, freedom rides, and rallies received national attention as newspaper, radio, and television reporters and
10 cameramen documented the struggle to end racial inequality.

When Rosa Parks refused to give up her seat to a white person in Montgomery, Alabama, and was arrested in December 1955, she
15 contributed to a chain of events that generated a momentum the Civil Rights movement had never before experienced. Local civil rights leaders were hoping for such an opportunity to test the city's segregation laws. After deciding to
20 boycott the buses, the African-American community formed a new organization to supervise the boycott, the Montgomery Improvement Association (MIA). The young pastor of the Dexter Avenue Baptist Church, Reverend Mar-
25 tin Luther King, Jr., was chosen as the first MIA leader. The boycott, more successful than anyone hoped, led to a 1956 Supreme Court decision banning segregated buses.

In 1960, four African-American freshmen
30 from North Carolina Agricultural and Technical College in Greensboro strolled into the F. W. Woolworth store and quietly sat down at the lunch counter. They were not served, but they stayed until closing time. The next morning
35 they came with 25 more students. Two weeks later similar demonstrations had spread to several other cities, and within a year similar peaceful demonstrations took place in over a hundred cities in the North and South. At Shaw

40 University in Raleigh, North Carolina, the students formed their own organization, the Student Nonviolent Coordinating Committee (SNCC, pronounced "Snick"). The students' bravery in the face of verbal and physical abuse
45 led to integration in many stores even before the passage of the Civil Rights Act of 1964.

Source: Excerpt from the Library of Congress, "The African American Odyssey: A Quest for Full Citizenship."

13. The passage is primarily concerned with
   a. enumerating the injustices that African Americans faced.
   b. describing the strategies used in the struggle for civil rights.
   c. showing how effective sit-down strikes can be in creating change.
   d. describing the nature of discrimination and second-class citizenship.
   e. recounting the legal successes of the Civil Rights movement.

14. In line 19, the word *test* most nearly means
   a. analyze.
   b. determine.
   c. prove.
   d. quiz.
   e. challenge.

15. The passage suggests that the college students in Greensboro, North Carolina,
   a. were regulars at the Woolworth lunch counter.
   b. wanted to provoke a violent reaction.
   c. were part of an ongoing national movement of lunch-counter demonstrations.
   d. inspired other students to protest peacefully against segregation.
   e. did not plan to create a stir.

Use the following passage to answer questions 16 through 18.

The Environmental Protection Agency (EPA) has published regulations for schools to ensure they are protected against asbestos contamination; the EPA has also provided assistance to
5   help schools meet the requirements of the Asbestos Hazard Emergency Response Act (AHERA). These include: performing an initial inspection for asbestos-containing material and a reinspection every three years; developing,
10   maintaining, and updating an asbestos management plan at the school; providing yearly notification to parent, teacher, and employee organizations regarding the school's asbestos management plan and any asbestos abatement
15   actions taken or planned in the school; designating a contact person to ensure that the responsibilities of the local education agency are properly implemented; performing periodic surveillance of known or suspected asbestos-
20   containing building material; and providing custodial staff with asbestos awareness training.

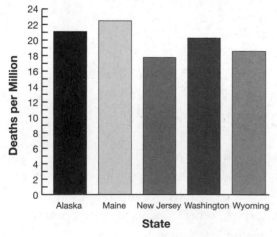

Asbestos-Related Mesothelioma Deaths from 1999–2010: A Sampling of Five U.S. States

16. Based on information in the passage and the graph, which of the following is most likely true?
   a. AHERA regulations are not enforced in Maine.
   b. AHERA has relaxed its regulations in recent years.
   c. AHERA has eliminated asbestos-related deaths in the twenty-first century.
   d. AHERA will reduce the rate of mesothelioma deaths.
   e. AHERA has its central office in New Jersey.

17. Which of the following could be a factor in the difference between the asbestos-related death rates in Maine and Wyoming?
   a. population
   b. climate
   c. geography
   d. education
   e. agriculture

18. The main purpose of this passage is to
   a. teach asbestos awareness in schools.
   b. explain the specifics of the AHERA.
   c. highlight the dangers of asbestos to your health.
   d. provide a list of materials that may include asbestos.
   e. frighten parents.

Use the following passage pair to answer questions 19 through 21.

Passage 1

The ability to defer gratification is an essential skill for negotiating the adult world. In a study of four-year-olds, each child was offered a marshmallow. The child could choose to eat the
5 marshmallow right away or wait 15 minutes to eat the marshmallow and receive another marshmallow as a reward for waiting. Researchers followed the children and found that by high school those children who ate their marsh-
10 mallow right away were more likely to be lonely, more prone to stress, and more easily frustrated. Conversely, the children who demonstrated self-control were outgoing, confident, and dependable.

Passage 2

Being an effective parent requires a tremendous amount of trial and error. My daughter is extremely willful, and it is a quality I admire in her. However, I'm guessing that giving in to that
5 willfulness may not help her to develop into a properly socialized human being. Her willfulness also means that I often have to experiment with several approaches when I want her to do something. For example, she is a fussy eater,
10 and I think it's important that she has a balanced and diverse diet. I have tried bribing her with foods she likes to get her to try new ones, but it was unsuccessful. So I tried pleading with her to appeal to her emotions, but I don't think
15 she's old enough to sympathize. In the end, I tried the most difficult approach by simply withholding other food options until she was hungry enough to try the new food. This has been the most successful with her. I'd imagine it
20 would be very successful with other children too.

19. Which of the following best describes the relationship between Passage 1 and Passage 2?

  a. Passage 1 presents a question and Passage 2 answers it.

  b. Passage 1 describes a method and Passage 2 shows how it is put to use.

  c. Passage 1 presents information that contradicts Passage 2.

  d. Passage 1 discusses a topic objectively and Passage 2 discusses it personally.

  e. Passage 1 describes a specific aspect of Passage 2.

20. Which of the following is a difference between Passage 1 and Passage 2?

  a. Passage 1 is argumentative.

  b. Passage 1 is about children.

  c. Passage 1 is scientific.

  d. Passage 1 is unsupported.

  e. Passage 1 is out of date.

21. Based on the information in Passage 1, one can infer that children who are unable to defer gratification are most unlikely to succeed because

  a. they are unpopular.

  b. they lack empathy.

  c. their parents neglected them.

  d. they are unable to follow directions.

  e. they lack self-discipline.

Use the following passage to answer questions 22 and 23.

The doctrine of judicial review gives the court the authority to declare executive actions and laws invalid if they conflict with the U.S. Constitution.
5   Despite the court's role in interpreting the Constitution, the document itself does not grant this authority to the court. However, it is clear that several of the founding fathers

10 expected the court to act in this way. Alexander
Hamilton and James Madison argued for the
importance of judicial review in the *Federalist
Papers*, a series of 85 political essays that urged
the adoption of the Constitution. Hamilton
15 argued that judicial review protected the will of
the people by making the Constitution supreme
over the legislature, which might only reflect
the temporary will of the people. However, the
practice of judicial review was, and continues to
20 be, a controversial power because it gives jus-
tices—who are appointed, rather than elected
by the people—the authority to void legislation
made by Congress and state lawmakers.

22. The passage suggests that the practice of judicial review allows the court to
a. wield enormous power.
b. determine foreign policy.
c. make laws that reflect the principles of the
Constitution.
d. rewrite laws that are unconstitutional.
e. make amendments to the Constitution.

23. The last sentence in the passage provides
a. a specific example supporting the argument
made earlier.
b. a summary of the points made earlier.
c. an explanation of the positions made earlier.
d. a prediction based on the argument made
earlier.
e. a counterargument to the views referred to
earlier.

*Use the following passage to answer questions 24 and
25.*

If you have ever made a list of pros and cons to
help you make a decision, you have used the
utilitarian method of moral reasoning. One of
the main ethical theories, utilitarianism posits

5 that the key to deciding what makes an act
morally right or wrong is its consequences.
Whether our intentions are good or bad is irrelevant; what matters is whether the *result* of our
actions is good or bad. To utilitarians, happi-
10 ness is the ultimate goal of human beings and
the highest moral good. Thus, if there is great
unhappiness because of an act, then that action
can be said to be morally wrong. Conversely, if
there is great happiness because of an action,
15 then that act can be said to be morally right.
Clearly, utilitarians are the happiest people in
the world.

24. In the passage, the author refers to a list of pros
and cons in order to
a. show that there are both positive and
negative aspects of utilitarianism.
b. suggest that making a list of pros and cons is
not an effective way to make a decision.
c. emphasize that utilitarians consider both the
good and the bad before making a decision.
d. indicate that readers will learn how to make
decisions using pro and con lists.
e. show readers that they are probably already
familiar with the principles of utilitarian
reasoning.

25. The final sentence of the passage makes which
of the following errors in logic?
a. post hoc ergo
b. incomplete comparison
c. hasty generalization
d. fallacy of composition
e. moral equivalence

Use the following passage to answer question 26.

When Maria plays in a softball game for her
company's team, she plays catcher. If she is
unable to attend a game, either Christine or
Thomas plays catcher.

26. Based only on the information in the passage, which of the following is a valid conclusion?

a. Christine and Thomas don't like playing catcher as much as Maria does.

b. Christine and Thomas are equally good softball players.

c. If Maria and Thomas both play in a game, Maria will play catcher.

d. Maria is the best catcher on the team.

e. Maria often misses softball games.

Use the following passage to answer questions 27 through 29.

The Computer Museum of America, in San Diego, California, was founded in 1983 to amass and preserve historic computer equipment, such as calculators, card punches, and typewriters, and owned one of the world's largest collections. In addition, it had archives of computer-related magazines, manuals, and books that were available to students, authors, researchers, and others for historical research. The museum closed in 2005, but it continues to provide exhibits online. Its physical exhibits are now the property of the San Diego State University Library.

COMPUTER INNOVATIONS	
YEAR	**INNOVATION**
1979	MicroPro International releases the first word processor.
1981	IBM introduces the first personal computer.
1983	Apple releases Lisa, the first personal computer with a graphical user interface.
1985	Registration of the first dot-com domain name.
1986	Compaq releases the Deskpro 386 personal computer.
1990	Researcher Tim Berners-Lee develops the computer programming language known as Hyper Text Markup Language (HTML).
1993	Intel introduces the Pentium microprocessor.
1999	Wireless "Wi-Fi" computer networking technology comes into use.
2000	Sony introduces the PlayStation 2.
2003	AMD's Athlon 64 becomes the first 64-bit processor.
2006	Apple releases the MacBook Pro.
2007	Apple releases the iPhone.
2010	Apple releases the iPad.
2015	Apple releases the Apple Watch, a computerized wristwatch.

27. Based on information in the passage and the chart, which of the following could not have been on display in the Computer Museum of America?
   a. a Wi-Fi modem
   b. the PlayStation 2
   c. the MacBook Pro
   d. the Pentium microprocessor
   e. the first personal computer

28. Based on information in the passage and the chart, which of the following was most likely to have been among the first exhibits in the Computer Museum of America?
   a. Lisa
   b. Hyper Text Markup Language
   c. a dot-com domain name
   d. the Deskpro 386
   e. the Apple Watch

29. All the following were probably part of the collection of the Computer Museum of America EXCEPT
   a. adding machines.
   b. old computers.
   c. operation manuals for calculators.
   d. card punch machines.
   e. kitchen scales.

Use the following passage to answer question 30.

Regardless of the claims that may be made by the companies that manufacture them, there are simply no effective boundaries when it comes to pollutants. Studies have shown that toxic insecticides that have been banned in many countries are riding the wind from countries where they remain legal. Compounds such as DDT and toxaphene, used as a pesticide and an insecticide, respectively, for decades before being banned in the United States, have been found in far-flung places like the Yukon and other Arctic regions.

30. Which statement, if it were true, most significantly weakens the argument in the passage?
   a. Few companies continue to claim that their pollutants remain in the same general geographic location.
   b. Depending on the size of compounds and their relative weight, some pollutants are more stationary than others.
   c. Years after the production of some toxic compounds were banned, their presence can be identified in random ocean samplings.
   d. DDT, once considered one of the most environmentally dangerous pesticides, is now not considered nearly as toxic.
   e. The levels of compounds identified in faraway places are low enough to be considered statistically insignificant.

Use the following passage to answer questions 31 through 33.

The forty-three men who have held the title of U.S. president through 2011 have come from a remarkable variety of fields. Before entering politics, these leaders have been schoolteachers
5   (John Adams), tailors (Andrew Johnson), peanut farmers (Jimmy Carter), and even actors (Ronald Reagan). While there are many paths to the presidency, one avenue is less circuitous. Unsurprisingly, most presidents served in the
10 armed forces before becoming commander in chief, including three generals: George Washington, Ulysses S. Grant, and Dwight D. Eisenhower. In fact, only a dozen U.S. presidents never served in uniform. However, voters lately
15 seem to discount the importance of military service; eight of the 12 presidents in the last 100 years, including two of the three presidents

from 1993 to 2012, never served at all. More
important to voters lately is the president's
20   knowledge of the law; half of the presidents
since 1961 have been lawyers at one time,
including two of the last three.

31. Which inference can be made from the
passage?
  a. Regardless of their backgrounds, all
  presidents had some experience in politics
  before attaining the highest office.
  b. Military service is a prerequisite for election
  as U.S. president.
  c. Only Jimmy Carter had a job as a farmer
  before becoming U.S. president.
  d. George H. W. Bush, who served as president
  from 1989–1993, did not serve in the U.S.
  military.
  e. More than thirty U.S. presidents have served
  in the U.S. military in some capacity.

32. According to the passage, which occupation
will the next U.S. president most likely have
had before taking office?
  a. tailor
  b. soldier
  c. lawyer
  d. actor
  e. army general

33. As it is used in the context of the sentence,
which word best describes the meaning of
circuitous (line 8)?
  a. direct
  b. roundabout
  c. mainstream
  d. political
  e. circuslike

*Use the following passage to answer questions 34
through 38.*

The roots of the modern-day sport of lacrosse
are found in tribal stick and ball games developed and played by many native North American tribes dating back as early as the fifteenth
5   century. The Native American names for these
games reflected the bellicose nature of those
early contests, many of which went far beyond
friendly recreational competition. For example,
the Algonquin called their game *Baggattaway*,
10   which meant "they bump hips." The Cherokee
Nation and the Six Tribes of the Iroquois called
their sport *Tewaarathon*, which translated into
"Little Brother of War." Rules and style of play
differed from tribe to tribe and games could be
15   played by as few as 15 to as many as 1,000 men
and women at a time. These matches could last
for three days, beginning at dawn each day and
ending at sunset. The goals could be specific
trees or rocks, and were a few hundred yards to
20   a few miles apart. Despite these differences, the
sole object of every game was the same: to score
goals by any means necessary. Serious injuries
caused by blows from the heavy wooden sticks
used in the games were not uncommon, and
25   often expected. Not surprisingly, the Native
Americans considered these precursors to
today's lacrosse excellent battle preparation for
young warriors, and games were often used to
settle disputes between tribes without resorting
30   to full-blown warfare.

34. The author translates the Native American names for their games in order to
   a. demonstrate a strong knowledge of Native American languages.
   b. highlight the differences between the various tribes.
   c. revive the use of ancient tribal languages.
   d. prove that lacrosse has existed for centuries.
   e. emphasize the warlike aspects of these games.

35. In the second sentence, *bellicose* most closely means
   a. beautiful.
   b. warlike.
   c. peaceful.
   d. family-minded.
   e. clumsy.

36. Which of the following titles would be the most appropriate for this passage?
   a. "Little Brother of War"
   b. "Lacrosse: America's Most Violent Sport"
   c. "The Origins of the Modern Lacrosse Stick"
   d. "The Six Tribes"
   e. "Hockey: The Little Brother of Lacrosse"

37. Near the end of the passage, the author's use of the phrase *by any means necessary* emphasizes
   a. the unpredictable nature of the game.
   b. the mild nature of the game.
   c. the violent nature of the game.
   d. the fact that both women and men participated in the games.
   e. the importance of scoring goals.

38. Which of the following best describes the point of view of the passage?
   a. first person
   b. second person
   c. third person
   d. fourth person
   e. fifth person

Use the following passage to answer questions 39 and 40.

One of the most common fears that people have is that of snakes. However, that fear is not only largely groundless but highly irrational. There are more than 2,500 different species of
5   snakes around the world, but only a small percentage of those species are poisonous. Furthermore, only a few species have venom strong enough to actually kill a human being. Statistically, snakes bite only 1,000 to 2,000 people in
10   the United States each year, and only ten of those bites (that's less than 1%!) result in death. In fact, in this country, more people die from dog bites each year than from snake bites.

39. Based on the information in the passage, which number could best represent the number of unique species of snakes in the world?
   a. 10
   b. 1,100
   c. 2,000
   d. 2,350
   e. 2,700

40. Which sentence from the passage represents an opinion rather than a fact?
   a. "However, that fear . . . highly irrational."
   b. "There are more . . . are poisonous."
   c. "Furthermore, only a . . . human being."
   d. "Statistically, snakes bite . . . in death."
   e. "In fact, in . . . from snake bites."

Use the following passage to answer questions 41 and 42.

Elizabeth Blackwell was the first woman to
receive an M.D. degree since the Renaissance
when she graduated from Geneva Medical College, in New York State, in 1849. She supported
5   women's medical education and helped many
other women's careers. By establishing the New
York Infirmary in 1857, she offered a practical
solution to one of the problems facing women
who were rejected from internships elsewhere
10   but determined to expand their skills as physi-
cians. Dr. Blackwell was initially repelled by the
idea of studying medicine. Instead she went
into teaching, then considered more suitable
for a woman. She claimed that she turned to
15   medicine after a close friend who was dying
suggested she would have been spared her
worst suffering if her physician had been a
woman.

41. The passage is primarily concerned with
a. the breaking down of social barriers for
women.
b. the effect of adversity on a person's life.
c. one woman's determination to open the
field of modern medicine to other women.
d. one woman's desire to gain prestige.
e. the quality of healthcare available in the 1800s.

42. The passage implies that Blackwell's attitude
toward studying and practicing medicine
changed from
a. tenacious to wavering.
b. uninterested to resolute.
c. cynical to committed.
d. idealized to realistic.
e. theoretical to practical.

Use the following passage to answer questions 43 and 44.

After generations of referring to the creature by
its misnomer, marine biologists are now
encouraging people to rename all starfish as sea
stars. The change in name is more than simply
5   a cosmetic alteration. A fish is defined as an
aquatic vertebrate with gills; the marine animals formerly known as starfish are not vertebrates because they have no spine or internal
skeleton. The roughly 2,000 species of sea stars
10   belong to a phylum of marine animals called
echinoderms, and their name should more accurately represent this classification—despite any
complications that some people may have with
the amendment.

43. Which sentence best summarizes the main
point of the passage?
a. Sea stars are not considered vertebrates
because they have no spine or internal
skeleton.
b. It can be difficult, but it is often necessary to
change a creature's name based on scientific
evidence.
c. Starfish are not technically fish and should
therefore be identified as sea stars.
d. A fish is defined as an aquatic vertebrate
with gills.
e. Sea stars belong to a phylum of marine
animals called *echinoderms*.

44. The author of this passage would most likely agree with which of the following statements?
  a. Sea stars are among the most beautiful creatures in the sea.
  b. Sea stars should be considered in the same classification as vertebrates.
  c. It is not worth the trouble to rename an entire class of roughly 2,000 species.
  d. Jellyfish should be given a new name because they do not have a spine.
  e. Sea stars and starfish are synonyms for the same creature and may be used interchangeably.

Use the following passage from Jack London's The Cruise of the Snark *to answer questions 45 through 49.*

[N]ow to the particular physics of surf-riding. Get out on a flat board, six feet long, two feet wide, and roughly oval in shape. Lie down upon it like a small boy on a coaster and paddle
5   with your hands out to deep water, where the waves begin to crest. Lie out there quietly on the board. Sea after sea breaks before, behind, and under and over you, and rushes in to shore, leaving you behind. When a wave crests, it gets
10 steeper. Imagine yourself, on your board, on the face of that steep slope. If it stood still, you would slide down just as a boy slides down a hill on his coaster. "But," you object, "the wave doesn't stand still." Very true, but the water
15 composing the wave stands still, and there you have the secret. If ever you start sliding down the face of that wave, you'll keep on sliding and you'll never reach the bottom. Please don't laugh. The face of that wave may be only six
20 feet, yet you can slide down it a quarter of a mile, or half a mile, and not reach the bottom. For, see, since a wave is only a communicated agitation or impetus, and since the water that composes a wave is changing every instant, new

25 water is rising into the wave as fast as the wave travels. You slide down this new water, and yet remain in your old position on the wave, sliding down the still newer water that is rising and forming the wave.

45. The author compares surfing to
  a. an ever-increasing hole forming in the water.
  b. a chemistry experiment gone wrong.
  c. a boy sledding down a hill on a coaster.
  d. a transformation of time and space.
  e. flying through the air like a bird.

46. As used in the passage, the word *impetus* most nearly means
  a. a moving force.
  b. a serious obstacle.
  c. a slight annoyance.
  d. a slight hindrance.
  e. an area of very warm water.

47. What is the secret referred to in the passage?
  a. A good wave for surfing must be at least six feet tall.
  b. A six-foot wave is between a quarter mile and a half mile in length.
  c. A surfer can slide down a six-foot wave for a quarter of a mile.
  d. The smarter surfers paddle out to the deep water to catch the best waves.
  e. The water that composes a wave remains with the wave until it reaches the shore.

48. What will the writer of this passage most likely explain next?
  a. How to drive a speedboat.
  b. How to disembark from a wave.
  c. How to wait for a wave.
  d. How to choose the right size surfboard.
  e. How to choose the right spot for surfing.

49. Information in this passage can be applied to
   a. a biography of Jack London.
   b. an advertisement for a surf shop.
   c. a skiing handbook.
   d. the history of playground slides.
   e. an essay on the physics of waves.

Use the following passage to answer questions 50 through 53.

The skyline of St. Louis, Missouri, is fairly unremarkable, with one prodigious exception—the Gateway Arch, which stands on the banks of the Mississippi River. Part of the Jefferson
5　National Expansion Memorial, the Arch is an amazing structure built to honor St. Louis's role as the gateway to the West. In 1947 a group of interested citizens known as the Jefferson National Expansion Memorial Association held
10　a nationwide competition to select a design for a new monument that would celebrate the growth of the United States. Other U.S. monuments at the time featured spires, statues, or imposing buildings, but the winner of this con-
15　test was a plan for a completely different type of structure. The man who submitted the winning design, Eero Saarinen, later became a famous architect. In designing the Arch, Saarinen wanted to "create a monument which would
20　have lasting significance and would be a landmark of our time."
　　The Gateway Arch is a masterpiece of engineering, a monument even taller than the Great Pyramid in Egypt. In its own way, the
25　Arch is at least as majestic as the Great Pyramid. The Gateway is shaped as an inverted catenary curve, the same shape that a heavy chain will form if suspended between two points. Covered with a sleek skin of stainless steel, the

30　Arch often reflects dazzling bursts of sunlight. In a beautiful display of symmetry, the height of the arch is the same as the distance between the legs at ground level.

50. Which sentence from the passage contains both a fact and an opinion?
   a. In its own way, the Arch is at least as majestic as the Great Pyramid.
   b. In 1947 a group of interested citizens known as the Jefferson National Expansion Memorial Association held a nationwide competition to select a design for a new monument that would celebrate the growth of the United States.
   c. In designing the Arch, Saarinen wanted to "create a monument which would have lasting significance and would be a landmark of our time."
   d. The Gateway Arch is a masterpiece of engineering, a monument even taller than the Great Pyramid in Egypt.
   e. The Gateway is shaped as an inverted catenary curve, the same shape that a heavy chain will form if suspended between two points.

51. According to the passage, Saarinen's winning design was
   a. modeled after other U.S. monuments.
   b. unlike any other existing monument.
   c. part of a series of monuments.
   d. less expensive to construct than other monuments.
   e. shaped like the Great Pyramid.

52. What was the author's primary purpose in revealing the material of the Gateway Arch's casing?

   a. to provide a comprehensive description of its metallic components

   b. to describe another astounding quality of the monument

   c. to contrast it with the materials of the Great Pyramid

   d. to illustrate the balanced symmetry of the monument

   e. to offer historic context for the construction of the monument

53. As it is used in the context of the sentence, which word best describes the meaning of *prodigious* (line 2)?

   a. commonplace

   b. talented

   c. extraordinary

   d. timely

   e. lackluster

Use the following passage to answer questions 54 through 56.

The atmosphere forms a gaseous, protective envelope around Earth. It protects the planet from the cold of space, from harmful ultraviolet light, and from all but the largest meteors.
5   After traveling over 93 million miles, solar energy strikes the atmosphere and Earth's surface, warming the planet and creating the biosphere, the region of Earth capable of sustaining life. Solar radiation in combination
10   with the planet's rotation causes the atmosphere to circulate. Atmospheric circulation is one important reason that life on Earth can exist at higher latitudes, because equatorial heat is transported poleward, moderating the
15   climate.

The polar regions are the coldest parts of Earth because they receive the least direct and, therefore, the weakest solar radiation. Here, solar radiation strikes at a very oblique angle
20   and thus spreads the same amount of energy over a greater area than in the equatorial regions. A static envelope of air surrounding Earth would produce an extremely hot, uninhabitable equatorial region, while the polar
25   regions would remain inhospitably cold.

54. Which sentence from the passage best supports the author's argument that circulation of the atmosphere is vital to life on Earth?

   a. "[The atmosphere] protects Earth from the cold of space, from harmful ultraviolet light, and from all but the largest meteors."

   b. "Solar radiation in combination with the planet's rotation causes the atmosphere to circulate."

   c. "The polar regions are the coldest parts of Earth because they receive the least direct and, therefore, the weakest solar radiation."

   d. "Here, solar radiation strikes at a very oblique angle and thus spreads the same amount of energy over a greater area than in the equatorial regions."

   e. "A static envelope of air surrounding Earth would produce an extremely hot, uninhabitable equatorial region, while the polar regions would remain inhospitably cold."

55. Which inference about Earth's biosphere can be made from the information provided within the passage?

   a. It operates as the home to human beings.

   b. It is responsible for solar energy in the atmosphere.

   c. It contributes to the circulation of the atmosphere.

   d. It is the uppermost layer of the earth's atmosphere.

   e. It is most susceptible to climate change.

56. The first paragraph of the passage deals mainly with which of the following effects of the atmosphere on Earth?

   a. its sheltering effect

   b. its reviving effect

   c. its invigorating effect

   d. its cleansing effect

   e. its warming effect

Praxis® Core Academic Skills for Educators: Reading Practice Test 2 Answers and Explanations

1. c. The description of the winding paths, shifting landscape, and sections that *spill into one another* supports the assertion that the park lacks a center. It directly contradicts the idea that Central Park has a centralized nature (choice **a**). There's no evidence it suggests the organization of the rest of the passage (choice **b**), that it's designed to persuade a reader that Central Park is large (choice **d**), or (choice **e**) show off the author's knowledge (since the description is general).

2. e. Choice **e** is correct because the passage states that Olmsted wanted to create a *democratic playground*, so he designed the park to have many centers that would *allow interaction among the various members of society*. The information doesn't extend to the nature of New York City (choice **a**), imply Olmsted was a brilliant designer (choice **b**), advocate for more parks to be designed similarly (choice **c**), or suggest that Central Park is poorly laid out (choice **d**).

3. c. Choice **c** is correct because the passage is mainly about how O'Connell Street is the widest street in Europe. Choices **a**, **d**, and **e** are too generalized; choice **b** focuses too narrowly on the Irish residents' feelings about their city.

4. c. Choice **c** is correct; the hidden or key resource mentioned in the passage is the fine distinction between the definitions of street and boulevard, which is used to win the argument with, or get the better of, tourists. Choices **a** and **e** are alternate definitions of *trump* that don't make sense in context. Choices **b** and **d** are misdirections.

5. d. Choice **d** is correct because the author offers an example of how Dubliners are proud of an unimportant but distinctive feature of their city, and they are willing to argue in favor of it. Choices **a**, **b**, **c**, and **e** are not supported by the passage.

6. d. The passage states that mediation *focuses on mutually acceptable solutions*, which suggests that both parties could be satisfied by the resolution of a conflict. Since litigation results in "winning or losing," it is fair to presume that the author would agree with the statement in choice **d**. The statement in choice **a** may be felt by some people, but it is not supported by the passage. It is too broad to be correct. Choice **b** is incorrect; the author states that mediation can be faster, less expensive, and can lead to more creative solutions than litigation. However, that is not the same thing as suggesting that litigation is expensive, slow, and limited by its reliance on following the letter of the law. The author might not agree that litigation is expensive or slow—just that mitigation can be faster and cheaper. Choice **c** might seem attractive, but the passage does not say that mediation is the best way to resolve a conflict—simply that it is an alternative way that might prove effective. The dependent clause that begins the passage hints at the idea that the author thinks that lawyers prefer litigation to resolve conflicts. However, it cannot be deduced from that little information that lawyers are overly concerned with their earning potential; this is beyond the scope of the information provided, making choice **e** incorrect.

7. b. Passage 1 states the opinion that artists should explore diverse artistic mediums to express their full creativity, and Passage 2 contrasts that opinion by claiming that diversifying prevents artists from ever mastering a single medium. There is no comparison between topics across the two passages (choice **a**). Passage 1 is more specific than Passage 2 because it refers to specific artists, so **c** is not the best answer choice. Neither passage describes a historic event (choice **d**). Both passages state opinions and there are no facts in Passage 2, so choice **e** is incorrect.

8. d. Passage 1 backs up its claim that artists should explore diverse artistic mediums by mentioning specific artists who benefitted from this approach (Pablo Picasso and Salvador Dali). Passage 2 mentions no specific artists who benefitted by focusing on a single medium. Both passages are written for an audience of equal education (choice **a**) and structured clearly (choice **b**). While Passage 1 does mention more than one artistic medium, which Passage 2 does not do, this does not necessarily make Passage 1 a stronger passage (choice **c**). There is no way to know if a professional artist wrote either passage (choice **e**).

9. b. The passage focuses on a suggestion that artists should not *let their output be constrained within a solitary structure*, meaning that they should experiment with media other than the one that they're most well known for using. That's choice **b**, and the opposite of choice **d**. The author describes two successful artists, but that is not the primary concern of the passage, so choice **a** is not correct. The focus is also not specifically on the rejection of commercial exploits or on people who disregard artists' non-primary art forms, making choices **c** and **e** incorrect.

10. d. Because the author's primary idea is that talented artists can and should experiment with multiple art forms, the description of Marc Chagall—who paints and creates stained glass—best fits that idea. Nothing about the description of Chuck Close or Samuel Clemens suggests that they've experimented with multiple media, making choices **a** and **b** incorrect. Claude Monet may have experimented with different styles, but those styles were all within the painting medium. Likewise, Paul Simon wrote songs in a partnership and as a solo artist, but that description still limits him to a single art form: songwriting. Therefore, choices **c** and **e** are incorrect.

11. d. Choice **d** is correct because to *posit* means to *suggest*. In this context, Hlusko suggests that grass stalks may have caused the grooves seen on early hominid teeth. The passage doesn't provide evidence that she *insisted*, *demanded*, or *argued* her point (choices **a**, **b**, and **e**), or that she *questioned* the discovery (choice **c**) since she's venturing it forth herself.

12. b. Choice **b** is correct because in the passage, the author states, *It seems that our early human ancestors may have used grass, which was easily found and ready to use, to floss between their teeth.* The use of *may* indicates that the author is not absolutely certain (choice **c**), but as the author does not suggest anything to contradict Dr. Hlusko's findings, we can conclude that the author finds her theory very probable (definitely not *fanciful* or *uncorroborated*, choices **d** and **e**).

13. b. Choice **b** is correct because the passage illustrates several protest strategies used in the Civil Rights movement. Choices **c** and **e** are true statements but are too specific to be the primary focus of the passage. Choices **a** and **d** are not described in detail in the passage.

14. e. Choice **e** is correct because in this context, *test* refers to putting something to a test or challenging something. Although one meaning of *to test* is to apply a test as a means of analysis or diagnosis, that's not how it's used in this passage. *Determine* (choice **b**), *prove* (choice **c**), and *quiz* (choice **d**) are other alternate definitions of *test* that are not the best fit in this context.

15. d. Choice **d** is correct because the protest at the Greensboro Woolworth lunch counter inspired others. The passage states *two weeks later similar demonstrations had spread to several other cities, and within a year similar peaceful demonstrations took place in over a hundred cities in the North and South.* Nowhere in the passage does the author suggest that the students were regulars (choice **a**), that they wanted to provoke violence (choice **b**), that there was an ongoing movement in progress (choice **c**), or that they did not plan to create a stir (choice **e**).

16. d. According to the passage, the EPA has published regulations in accordance with AHERA to reduce asbestos-related hazards, and the graph indicates that asbestos causes a disease called mesothelioma. Therefore, it is logical to conclude that EPA regulations will reduce the rate of mesothelioma deaths. Although Maine has a higher rate of asbestos-related deaths than the other states on the graph, choice **a** is still an extreme conclusion to draw. There is no evidence in the passage or the graph to support choice **b**, and the graph contradicts choice **c** completely. Although New Jersey has the lowest rate of asbestos-related deaths of all the states included in the graph, there is no evidence to suggest that AHERA has its central office in New Jersey or that having its central office there would reduce local asbestos-related deaths (choice **e**).

17. a. A state with a larger population than another is likelier to have more deaths, and in fact, Maine does have a larger population than Wyoming. There is no information in either the passage or the graph to support the idea that climate (**b**), geography (**c**), education (**d**), or agriculture (**e**) account for the difference between the asbestos-related death rates in Maine and Wyoming.

18. a. Choice **a** is correct. While the passage does include the other choices (except choice **e**), the overall purpose of the passage is to teach asbestos awareness in schools. It doesn't go into details of the *AHERA* (choice **b**), highlight any specific health risks of asbestos (choice **c**), provide a list of contaminated materials (choice **d**), or contain language designed to frighten parents (choice **e**).

19. d. Passage 1 is written from an objective point of view: the reader does not know who is discussing child behavior. Passage 2 is written from a personal point of view: the reader knows the writer is a parent, and that parent discusses his own experiences with child behavior. Passage 2 does not answer a question posed in Passage 1 (choice **a**). The passages discuss different aspects of child behavior (Passage 1 is about how children react to deferred gratification; Passage 2 is about child eating habits), so choices **b**, **c**, and **e** do not apply.

20. c. Passage 1 discusses a scientific research study, but Passage 2 discusses a parent's experiences with his own child and reaches a conclusion the writer fails to support scientifically. Passage 1 is informational, not argumentative (choice **a**). Both passages are about children, so choice **b** does not answer the question correctly. Passage 1 supports its claim that deferred gratification is an essential skill with evidence from a scientific study, so choice **d** is incorrect. There is no evidence to support the conclusion that Passage 1 is out of date (choice **e**).

21. e. Choice **e** is correct. This passage links the ability to defer gratification with self-control. Hence, children who are unable to defer gratification are unlikely to succeed because they lack self-discipline, or self-control. Nowhere in the passage is it suggested that the children are unpopular (choice **a**), lack empathy (choice **b**), have been neglected (choice **c**), or were unable to follow directions (choice **d**)—they simply chose not to.

22. a. Choice **a** is correct. The fact that judicial review can override decisions made by the legislative and executive branches implies that it gives the court great authority. The passage doesn't suggest judicial review grants any of the powers given by the other answer choices.

23. e. Choice **e** is correct. The last sentence offers a counterargument to the points made earlier in the passage supporting the Supreme Court's power to interpret the Constitution. It is not a specific example (choice **a**), a summary (choice **b**), an explanation (choice **c**), or a prediction (choice **d**).

24. e. Choice **e** is correct. The opening sentence tells readers that making a list of pros and cons is a technique of utilitarian reasoning. Thus, readers who have used this technique will realize they are already familiar with the basic principles of utilitarianism. The author clearly does not think list making indicates there are negative aspects of utilitarianism (choice **a**), or want to suggest that making a list of pros and cons is not an effective way to make a decision (choice **b**). The passage doesn't appear to be preparing to teach its readers to make decisions (choice **d**). Choice **c**, emphasizing that utilitarians consider both the good and the bad, is not the best answer because the author is actually emphasizing that utilitarians focus on the consequences of their actions in decision making.

25. c. A hasty generalization is a thoughtless jump to a conclusion. The final sentence of the passage makes the hasty generalization that utilitarians are clearly "the happiest people in the world" based on the fact that utilitarians believe that "happiness is the ultimate goal of human beings." Simply holding this belief does not guarantee that utilitarians are happier than every one else in the world. The final sentence of the passage does not make any of the logical errors in the other answer choices.

26. c. Choice **c** is correct. This is the only conclusion that is supported by information in the passage, which doesn't mention how much any of the players like softball (choices **a** and **b**), or how good they are at it (choice **d**). There is no implication that Maria misses games particularly often (choice **e**).

27. c. According to the passage, the museum closed in 2005, and according to the chart, Apple did not release the MacBook Pro until 2006. The items in the other answer choices all existed before the museum closed.

28. a. According to the passage, the Computer Museum of America opened in 1983, and according to the chart, Apple released Lisa, the first personal computer with a graphical user interface, that same year. So it could have been included among the museum's first exhibits. Choice **b** is a language and choice **c** is a name, neither of which are physical objects that can be exhibited in a museum. According to the chart, Compaq did not release the Deskpro 386 personal computer until 1986, which was three years after the museum opened, so **d** is not the best answer choice. Choice **e**, the Apple Watch, was not released until ten years after the museum closed.

29. e. Choice **e** is correct The passage mentions choices **a** through **d**: adding machines, computers, card punches, and manuals. The only item not mentioned is *kitchen scales*.

30. e. The main argument of the passage is that there are no boundaries when it comes to pollutants. Only the statement in choice **e** weakens the argument by suggesting that the levels of the pollutants found are so low as to be "statistically insignificant." That doesn't mean that the compounds aren't there at all, but that the levels are so low that the argument is weakened. The statements in the other answer choices do not significantly weaken the argument. For choice **a**, the main argument of the passage is not about the companies' claims about their pollutants. Whether or not companies make claims about them, the author's main argument— that there are no boundaries when it comes to pollutants—is not weakened. The statement in choice **b** would suggest that some compounds travel better than others. That doesn't necessarily weaken the main argument that pollutants are not constrained by boundaries, however. If the sentence in choice **c** were true, the author's argument would be *strengthened,* not *weakened.* This is suggesting that even years after a compound stops being created, it can be found throughout the planet's oceans. The statement in choice **d** would weaken the author's argument if the chief argument were that DDT causes significant damage. However, the chief argument is simply that there are no boundaries when it comes to pollutants. This statement, even if it were true, does not address that issue.

31. e. The passage states that all but a dozen U.S. presidents served in uniform. That means that 31 presidents have served in some capacity, making choice **e** correct. The fact that twelve men become president with no military experience also means that choice **b** cannot be correct. The statements in choices **a, c,** and **d** are neither confirmed nor denied based on the information in the passage; therefore, they are not correct.

32. c. The end of the passage states that voters are most concerned now with their presidents' knowledge of the law. Therefore, based on the passage, a lawyer is the best prediction for the next president's former occupation (choice **c**). The passage mentions that at least one president was a tailor, choice **a**, and one was an actor, choice **d**, but there is nothing to indicate that that is the most likely occupation of the next U.S. president. While many presidents were previously soldiers, not as many lately have served in the military, so choice **b** is not the best answer. Only three presidents were generals, so choice **e** is not the best answer either.

33. b. The passage mentions that the U.S. presidents have had a variety of occupations before holding the highest office. To contrast those varying paths to the presidency, the passage mentions the clearer path from the U.S. military to the presidency. Therefore, the path was being described as indirect, or *roundabout* (choice **b**). *Direct*, choice **a**, has the opposite meaning of *circuitous*. Similarly, *mainstream* (choice **c**) could also be considered an antonym of *circuitous*. There is nothing in the passage to suggest that the route would be *political* or *circuslike*, so choices **d** and **e** are not correct either.

34. e. Choice **e** is correct. The Native American names for their games, "they bump hips" and "Little Brother of War," indicate that these games *went far beyond friendly recreational competition*, and at the end of the passage the author further says that Native Americans viewed these games as *excellent battle preparation* for the young. The author does not appear to have any particular knowledge of Native American languages (choice **a**), nor does he spend time focusing on the difference between various tribes in any area other than these games (choice **b**). Since he is translating the languages into English, he's actually doing the opposite of reviving ancient tribal languages (choice **c**), and though he is proving that lacrosse (or a variation of it) has existed for centuries (choice **d**), the translation from native languages doesn't contribute to that argument.

35. b. Choice **b** is correct. *Bellicose* most closely means *warlike*. There are two major clues in this passage to help you answer this question. The first clue lies in the translation of the name *Tewaarathon*, meaning "Little Brother of War." Another clue lies in the line where the author states that these games were *excellent battle preparation for young warriors*. The other answer choices do not make sense in this context.

36. a. Choice **a** is correct. "Little Brother of War" is the best choice for the title of this passage because the games are described as fierce and warlike, and the entire passage is devoted to discussing the game play. Since the passage is describing forerunners of lacrosse, and not the modern game, choice **b** is incorrect. Choice **d** is incorrect because it describes only a minor detail of the passage. Choices **c** and **e** are not discussed in the passage.

37. c. Choice **c** is correct. The answer can be found in the two sentences that follow the phrase *by any means necessary*. The passage states that the games were often high-stakes substitutes for war, and it was not uncommon for players to suffer serious injuries at the hands (and sticks) of others. These statements describe the fierce nature of the games and suggest that players would not hesitate to resort to violent tactics to score, *by any means necessary*. Choices **a**, **d**, and **e** are true and mentioned or implied in the passage, but they do not fit in context with the phrase. The game is by no means mild (choice **b**).

38. c. Choice **c** is correct. *Third person point of view* is the phrase for a narrator of a story who is not present in the story. Choice **a**, first person point of view, is when the narrator speaks as an "I" within the story. Choice **b**, second person point of view, is when the narrator addresses the reader with "you." Choices **d** and **e** do not exist.

39. e. There are several numbers given in this passage, but the only one that matters for this question is that there are *more than 2,500 difference species of snakes around the world*; therefore, choice **e** is correct. Choice **a** refers to the approximate number of snake bite fatalities in the United States each year, so it is not correct. Choices **b** and **c** could refer to the number of annual snake bites in the United States, so they are not correct. Choice **d** is less than 2,500, so it cannot be correct either.

40. a. An opinion cannot be proven with facts or statistics. The statement in the second sentence, choice **a**, cannot be proven because there is no way to show definitively whether someone is or is not irrational. The statements in choices **b**, **c**, **d**, and **e** each contain statements that can be verified—making them statements of fact rather than opinion. Therefore, those answer choices cannot be correct.

41. c. Choice **c** is correct The focus of the passage is Blackwell's efforts to open the profession of medicine to women. The first paragraph states that Blackwell *supported women's medical education and helped many other women's careers*. There is no mention in the passage of other social barriers for women breaking down (choice **a**), or of the effect of adversity (choice **b**). There's nothing to indicate Blackwell sought prestige (choice **d**) and no specific details about the quality of healthcare available in the 1880s (choice **e**).

42. b. Choice **b** is correct. Initially Blackwell was interested in teaching (and *uninterested* in medicine). However, she was inspired by her dying friend and went on to become not only the first woman doctor since the Renaissance, but also a *resolute* supporter of medical education for women. None of the other answer choices accurately reflect the change in her attitude.

43. c. The passage begins with the proposed name change from starfish to sea stars, and then the rest of the passage provides support for this change. Therefore, the statement in choice **c** best summarizes the passage. The statements in choices **a**, **d**, and **e** are all correct, but they act as supporting details that reinforce the main point of the idea: that the name should be changed. The statement in choice **b** is also correct, but the main idea of the passage is not the difficulties in changing a name but how and why the starfish should be changed to the sea star specifically. Therefore, there is a better choice than choice **b**.

44. d. The author makes it clear that the name *starfish* is factually incorrect and should therefore be revised to something more scientifically accurate. Given that information, it would also make sense that the author would agree that jellyfish should also have their name changed if they are also not technically fish (choice **d**). The author may agree that sea stars are beautiful, choice **a**, but that cannot be verified from any information in the passage; the author is interested in naming the marine creatures appropriately, but that does not necessarily mean that he or she finds them attractive. The author would likely disagree with the statements in choices **b**, **c**, and **e** since he or she clearly states that sea stars are *not* vertebrates, and they should therefore not be referred to as "fish"—and it *is* worth the trouble to rename them.

45. c. Choice **c** is correct. In the passage, the author states a surfer should lie upon a surfboard *like a small boy on a coaster*, and then goes on to say that the surfer slides down a wave *just as a boy slides down a hill on his coaster*. The other choices aren't supported by evidence from the passage.

46. a. Choice **a** is correct. As it is used in the passage, *impetus* most nearly means *a moving force* because a wave is a moving force through the water. If you did not know the correct definition, the best way to answer this question would be to replace *impetus* in the sentence with each of the given answer choices to see which one makes the most sense in context. The wave is not likely to be a serious obstacle (choice **b**), a slight annoyance (choice **c**), a slight hindrance (choice **d**) or an area of very warm water (choice **e**).

47. c. Choice **c** is correct. The secret of the passage is that a surfer can slide down a six-foot wave for more than a quarter of a mile without ever reaching the bottom. This is possible because new water is rising into the wave as fast as the wave travels, preventing the surfer from reaching the bottom. It's not necessary or true that the wave should be six feet tall (choice **a**), that it always be a quarter mile in length (choice **b**), that a surfer should paddle to deeper water (choice **d**), or that the same water stays with the wave (choice **e**).

48. b. This passage explains how to surf, focusing on the best way to get onto a wave and ride it. However, a surfer cannot ride a single wave forever and needs to know the best way to disembark from that wave. Therefore, it is most likely the writer will explain how to do this next. There is no reason to believe the writer will next switch to a totally different topic, even if it is also related to water activities (choice **a**). The writer already explained how to wait for a wave (choice **c**) and how to choose the right size surfboard (choice **d**), and there is no reason to believe he will repeat either of those details next. Choosing the right spot for surfing is the kind of information that should be explained before a discussion of how to surf in such a spot, so **e** is not the best answer choice.

49. e. The passage is mainly about how to surf, but it also includes information about the physics of ocean waves, specifically that a wave is an agitation that can allow for a slide much longer than its physical height. Although Jack London wrote this passage, its specific explanation of how to surf is not the kind of personal information that would usually appear in a biography (choice **a**). The passage is too detailed and specific to apply to an advertisement (choice **b**), which is usually short on technical details. Although surfing and skiing are both sports, surfing is very different from skiing, and the information in this passage would be of little use in a skiing handbook (choice **c**). Although the author discusses sliding down a wave, he does not mention anything related to playground slides (choice **d**).

50. d. Calling a monument a masterpiece is an opinion because it cannot be verified with facts or statistics; whether it is taller than a pyramid, however, is a fact because it can be verified with measurements. Therefore, choice **d** contains both a fact and an opinion. The statement in choice **a** contains only an opinion and no verifiable facts. The statements in choices **b** and **e** contain only facts and no opinions, so they are not correct either. The quote in choice **c** is a fact because it can be proven that Saarinen said those words, and it does not contain the author's opinion.

51. b. The passage states that the winner of the contest was a plan for a completely different type of structure. Therefore, this describes a design that was unlike any other existing monument (choice **b**). This is the opposite of the statement in choice **a**, so that choice is not correct. There is no evidence in the passage that Saarinen's design was part of a series of monuments or less expensive than other monuments, making choices **c** and **d** incorrect. The shape of the arch is considerably different from the shape of the Great Pyramid, so choice **e** is not correct.

52. b. The author in the passage reveals the material of the Arch's casing by saying that it is stainless steel. As a result, *the Arch often reflects dazzling bursts of sunlight*. Therefore, the purpose of including this information was to describe another astounding quality of the monument (choice **b**). No other information about the metallic components of the Arch is given, so choice **a** is not correct. Similarly, no materials are listed for the Great Pyramid, so choice **c** cannot be correct. The following sentence in the passage describes the Arch's symmetry, but the information about the stainless steel skin does nothing to illustrate the symmetry; therefore, choice **d** is incorrect. The information also does not provide any historical context for the monument, meaning that choice **e** is incorrect as well.

53. c. The initial sentence of the passage describes the skyline of St. Louis as *unremarkable with one prodigious exception*. The word *prodigious* must therefore have the opposite meaning as unremarkable. The best choice is *extraordinary* (choice **c**). *Commonplace* and *lackluster*, choices **a** and **e**, have similar meanings as unremarkable, so they cannot be correct. The exception is not being described as *talented* or *timely*, so choices **b** and **d** are incorrect as well.

54. e. The sentence in choice **e** explains that conditions would be inhospitable at the equator and the polar regions without the circulation of the atmosphere; therefore, it is the best choice to support the author's argument that circulation of the atmosphere is vital to life on Earth. The sentence in choice **a** describes how the atmosphere protects Earth, but it does not speak of the circulation of the atmosphere; therefore, it cannot be correct. The sentences in choices **b** and **c** deal with solar radiation, not with circulation of the atmosphere, so they are incorrect. The fact that solar radiation is spread over a greater area, choice **d**, does not directly explain how the circulation of the atmosphere is vital to life on Earth; a different sentence better makes the connection to the author's argument.

55. a. The passage states that the biosphere is the region of Earth capable of sustaining life. Therefore, you can infer that human beings must live within the biosphere, making choice **a** correct. If you read the passage carefully, you will see that it is the solar energy that is responsible for the creation of the biosphere, not the other way around. Therefore, choice **b** cannot be correct. According to the passage, a combination of Earth's rotation and solar radiation causes the atmosphere to circulate. Because the passage does not mention the atmosphere as one of the causes, you can eliminate choice **c**. There is no indication in the passage that the biosphere is the uppermost layer of Earth's atmosphere or the most susceptible to climate change, so choices **d** and **e** are incorrect.

56. a. The very first sentence of the first paragraph sums up the main effect of the atmosphere on Earth—to create a *protective envelope around Earth*. This can be described as a sheltering effect because it shelters Earth from most dangers other than large meteors. There is no mention in the first paragraph of any *reviving* or *cleansing* effect of the atmosphere on Earth. Therefore, choices **b** and **d** are not correct. In a sense, enabling Earth to sustain life is *invigorating*; however, there is a better choice than choice **c** because the first two sentences talk about how the atmosphere specifically *protects* Earth from harmful forces. The first paragraph mentions ways in which the solar energy warms the planet, not the atmosphere itself. The heat in the atmosphere may be spread across Earth through circulation, but that is not the same as suggesting that the focus of the paragraph is the atmosphere's warming effect on Earth; therefore, choice **e** is incorrect.

Praxis® Core Academic Skills for Educators: Writing Practice Test 2

Part I: Multiple-Choice
Time: 40 Minutes

Directions: Choose the letter for the underlined portion that contains a grammatical error. If there is no error in the sentence, choose **e**.

1. Pressed <u>sailors</u>[a] in the time of <u>Lord Nelson</u>[b] lived in cramped quarters, fought battles <u>on the high</u>[c] seas, <u>and learn to</u>[d] understand the blessings of a mariner's life. <u>No error</u>[e]

2. My <u>Father</u>[a] is a good <u>cook</u>[b]<u>; he</u>[c] makes dinners as well as <u>desserts.</u>[d] <u>No error</u>[e]

3. Ernest Hemingway <u>and fellow</u>[a] writer F. Scott Fitzgerald met as <u>expatriates</u>[b] in Paris during the 1920s; <u>he</u>[c] was the first of the two to move <u>there</u>[d] in 1921. <u>No error</u>[e]

4. Did those <u>dogs</u>[a] wag <u>they're</u>[b] tails when <u>Dalia</u>[c] gave them leftovers? <u>No error</u>[d][e]

5. We all <u>agreed</u> that the quick action of the
       a

security <u>officers'</u> thwarted the robbery attempt
       b

<u>yesterday</u> at the <u>bank</u>. <u>No error</u>
   c   d   e

6. <u>Too</u> <u>teachers</u> and a student <u>are</u> speaking to
   a   b   c

the class today about <u>studying</u> for the
              d

standardized tests. <u>No error</u>
           e

7. <u>During</u> the summer season, boat owners should
   a

replace <u>their</u> oil filters at least once <u>a month; a</u>
      b   c

dirty filter <u>reduce</u> engine efficiency. <u>No error</u>
        d   e

8. The Rolling Stones, <u>one of</u> the most influential
             a

<u>British</u> rock bands, they released their first
 c

album <u>in</u> 1964. <u>No error</u>
     d   e

9. Our Russian <u>teacher</u> was born in <u>Moscow, he</u>
        a   b c

came to the <u>United States</u> when he was very
          d

young. <u>No error</u>
     e

10. The freshwater source of the Hudson <u>River</u> can
                        a

be found in the Adirondack <u>Mountains</u>; it's a
                 b

small lake <u>on</u> Mount <u>Marcy</u> <u>known</u> as Lake
       c   d

Tear of the Clouds. <u>No error</u>
            e

11. The basketball <u>magically</u> fell <u>threw</u> the <u>hoop</u>
            a   b   c

in the last few seconds <u>of</u> the game. <u>No error</u>
              d   e

12. The <u>aorta</u> is the largest artery in the
     a

<u>human body</u>; it receives <u>oxygen-rich</u> blood
  b   c

from the <u>heart and</u> carries it to the rest of the
        d

body. <u>No error</u>
     e

13. <u>Were</u> you planning on spending
   a

<u>Easter</u> <u>Vacation</u> with your cousins? <u>No error</u>
   b   c   d   e

14. <u>Considering</u> the <u>principal</u> believed in school
    a   b

<u>uniforms</u>, so he implemented a new rule in the
  c

<u>high school</u>. <u>No error</u>
    d   e

15. The network, which <u>produces</u> family
        a   b

<u>specials</u> for TV, <u>are</u> owned by the millionaire.
 c   d

<u>No error</u>
 e

16. The lifeguard staff at the <u>public</u> beach <u>deserve</u>
                a   b

recognition for <u>winning</u> the annual
          c

<u>"safest waters"</u> award. <u>No error</u>
   d   e

Directions: Choose the best replacement for the underlined portion of the sentence. If no revision is necessary, choose **a**, which always repeats the original phrasing.

17. My favorite subjects <u>are gym and calculus, my second semester electives are Italian and physics.</u>
    a. are gym and calculus, my second semester electives are Italian and physics.
    b. are gym, and calculus; my second semester electives are Italian, and physics.
    c. are gym and calculus; my second semester electives are Italian and physics.
    d. are gym and calculus; my second semester electives are italian and physics.
    e. are gym, and calculus, my second semester electives are Italian, and physics.

18. <u>The Mississippi River, it originates in Minnesota,</u> empties into the Gulf of Mexico.
    a. The Mississippi River, it originates in Minnesota,
    b. The Mississippi River, that originates in Minnesota,
    c. The Mississippi River, who originates in Minnesota,
    d. The Mississippi River, which originates in Minnesota,
    e. The Mississippi River, whose originates in Minnesota,

19. <u>When twins have the same DNA, it is said to be identical.</u>
    a. When twins have the same DNA, it is said to be identical.
    b. When twins has the same DNA, it is said to be identical.
    c. Twins with the same DNA is said to be identical.
    d. They are identical when the said twins has the same DNA.
    e. When twins have the same DNA, they are said to be identical.

20. Angela's <u>dog Pepper can sit up, come when called, and sometimes roll over.</u>
    a. dog Pepper can sit up, come when called, and sometimes roll over.
    b. dog Pepper, can sit up, come when called, and some times roll over.
    c. dog , Pepper, can sit up, come when called, and sometimes roll over.
    d. dog Pepper, can sit up, come when called and sometimes roll over.
    e. dog Pepper can sit up come when called and sometimes roll over.

21. <u>Because the economy is improving,</u> there are still many people who are unemployed.
    a. Because the economy is improving,
    b. Because the economy was improving,
    c. The economy is improving,
    d. Although the economy is improving,
    e. Although the economy is improving;

22. <u>The fictional film version of the actual story is never not accurate.</u>
   a. The fictional film version of the actual story is never not accurate.
   b. The fictional film version of the story isn't never not accurate.
   c. The fictional film version of the story is never accurate.
   d. The fictional film version of the actual story are never not accurate.
   e. The fictional film version of the story are never not accurate.

23. A number of skeptics don't believe in the <u>effects of global warming on the earths climate.</u>
   a. effects of global warming on the earths climate.
   b. effects' of global warming on the earth's climate.
   c. effect's of global warming on the earths climate.
   d. effect's of global warming on the earths' climate.
   e. effects of global warming on the earth's climate.

24. <u>She sold her patent to a company in Delaware, the product then became a common household item.</u>
   a. She sold her patent to a company in Delaware, the product then became a common household item.
   b. She sold her patent to a company in Delaware; the product then became a common household item.
   c. She sold her patent to a company in Delaware the product then became a common household item.
   d. She sold her patent to a company in Delaware, the product then become a common household item.
   e. She sold her patent to a company in Delaware, the product than became a common household item.

25. <u>I look forward to speaking with you and having</u> the opportunity to explain my views on the subject.
   a. I look forward to speaking with you and having
   b. I will look forward to our speaking and having
   c. As I look forward to our speaking and to have
   d. I look forward to speaking with you and have
   e. Looking forward to our speaking and hoping to have

26. Nobody on the team <u>skates more graceful than me.</u>
   a. skates more graceful than me.
   b. skates more gracefully than I do.
   c. skates gracefuller than I do.
   d. skates more graceful than I do.
   e. skates more gracefully than me.

27. It snowed; so I tried to shovel the driveway.
   a. It snowed; so I tried to shovel the driveway.
   b. It snowed, so I tried to shovel the driveway.
   c. It snowed, I tried to shovel the driveway.
   d. It's snowing, I tried to shovel the driveway.
   e. It will snow, so I tried to shovel the driveway.

28. Would you like to come to the park with Sherine and I?
   a. park with Sherine and I
   b. park with Sherine and me
   c. park with Sherine and myself
   d. park with Sherine and we
   e. park with Sherine and they

29. Of the two new cars, it is the safer one.
   a. it is the safer one
   b. the newer model is the safer one
   c. they are the safest ones
   d. it is the safest one
   e. it is the safe one

30. Both my family or my friends enjoy going to the movies.
   a. Both my family or my friends enjoy
   b. Both my family and my friends enjoy
   c. Either my family and my friends enjoy
   d. Whether my family and my friends enjoy
   e. Neither my family and my friends enjoy

Directions: *Choose the letter for the underlined portion of the citations that contains an error. If there is no error in the citation, choose **e**.*

31. Journal citation:
   Pridi, Saumia. Habits of the Hyena.
   ㅤㅤㅤㅤㅤㅤㅤㅤㅤ a

   Bi-annual Science and Nature Journal
   volume 73. Issue 2 (2013): 11–16. Print.
   ㅤㅤa ㅤㅤㅤㅤ b ㅤㅤㅤㅤ c
   No error.
   ㅤd

32. Newspaper citation:
   Harrison, Lauren R. "Plans for Smithtown
   ㅤㅤㅤㅤ a ㅤㅤㅤㅤㅤㅤㅤㅤㅤㅤㅤㅤㅤ b

   assisted living center to move forward as town,
   developer end dispute." *Newsday* June 16, 2015:
   ㅤㅤㅤㅤㅤㅤㅤㅤㅤㅤㅤㅤㅤㅤㅤㅤㅤㅤㅤㅤㅤㅤ c

   42–43. No error.
   ㅤd ㅤㅤ e

Use the following passage to answer questions 33 through 36.

(**1**) In space flight there are the obvious hazards of meteors, debris, and radiation. (**2**) However, astronauts must also deal with two vexing physiological foes—muscle atrophy and bone loss. (**3**) Space shuttle astronauts, because they spend only about a week in space, undergo just a teensy bit of wasting of bone and muscle. (**4**) But when longer stays in microgravity or zero gravity are contemplated, as with the International Space Station or a two-year round-trip voyage to Mars, these problems are of particular concern because they could become acute.

(**5**) Some studies show that it can be kept largely at bay with appropriate exercise, but bone loss caused by reduced gravity cannot. (**6**) Scientists can measure certain flight-related hormonal changes. (**7**) Scientists obtain animal bone biopsies immediately after flights. (**8**) Scientists do not completely understand how gravity affects the bones or what happens at the cellular level.

(**9**) Even pounding the bones or wearing a suspenderlike pressure device does nothing to avert loss of calcium from bones. (**10**) Researcher Dr. Lisa Ruml says that after a three-month or longer stay in space, much of the profound bone loss may be irreversible, a claim backed by a similar study published in *The Journal of Sports Science & Medicine*. (**11**) Some argue that protracted missions should be curtailed.

(12) They are conducting a search for the molecular mechanisms behind bone loss, and they hope these studies will help develop a prevention strategy to control tissue loss associated not only with weightlessness but also with prolonged bed rest.

33. In context, which revision to sentence 3 (sentence 3 follows) is most needed?

> Space shuttle astronauts, because they spend only about a week in space, undergo just a teensy bit of wasting of bone and muscle.

a. Replace "a week" with "seven days."
b. Change "they" to "he."
c. Replace "just a teensy bit" with "minimal."
d. Change "wasting" to "waste."
e. Change "muscle" to "muscles."

34. In context, which revision to sentence 5 (sentence 5 follows) is most needed?

> Some studies show that it can be kept largely at bay with appropriate exercise, but bone loss caused by reduced gravity cannot.

a. Replace "it" with "muscle atrophy."
b. Replace "Some studies" with "They."
c. Change "largely" to "largest."
d. Replace "exercise" with "it."
e. Change "cannot" to "can't."

35. In context, which revision to sentences 6 through 8 (sentences 6 through 8 follow) is most needed?

> Scientists can measure certain flight-related hormonal changes. Scientists obtain animal bone biopsies immediately after flights. Scientists do not completely understand how gravity affects the bones or what happens at the cellular level.

a. (As it is now)
b. Scientists can measure certain flight-related hormonal changes and obtain animal bone biopsies immediately after flights, but they do not completely understand how gravity affects the bones or what happens at the cellular level.
c. Scientists can measure certain flight-related hormonal changes; scientists obtain animal bone biopsies immediately after flights; scientists do not completely understand how gravity affects the bones or what happens at the cellular level.
d. Scientists can measure certain flight-related hormonal changes, and they do not completely understand how gravity affects the bones or what happens at the cellular level.
e. Can measure certain flight-related hormonal changes. Scientists obtain animal bone biopsies immediately after flights. Scientists do not completely understand how gravity affects the bones or what happens at the cellular level.

36. For which conclusion does the writer cite multiple resources?
   a. Space shuttle astronauts lose little bone and muscle after a week in space.
   b. The muscle loss of astronauts can be kept at bay with appropriate exercise.
   c. Scientists can measure certain flight-related hormonal changes.
   d. Profound bone loss may be irreversible after three months in space.
   e. Protracted space shuttle missions should be curtailed.

Use the following passage to answer questions 37 through 40.

(1) Taking your child to the library can be a harrowing experience when books with hastily written, lazy text litter the shelves. (2) Too many children's books take the easy route by conveying dull messages that display little respect for how keenly children are aware of the subtleties of life and how strongly they respond to beautifully crafted writing. (3) Seeing the way my son has taken to the books of Dr. Seuss made this entirely clear.

   (4) One reason kids love Dr. Seuss is his stories deal with matters of great human importance. (5) Not surprisingly, he based a number of his works on actual historical events, such as the rise of Hitler in *Yertle the Turtle*, the arms race in *The Butter Battle Book*, and what happened in Hiroshima and Nagasaki in *Horton Hears a Who*. (6) These matters of global significance still have relevance to children as they boil down to simple lessons: abusing power is wrong, violence solves nothing, etc. (7) The depth of their messages and Seuss's beautiful writing ensures that parents such as myself do not mind reading these books over and over and over again. (8) I'm certain my son detects my own enthusiasm for these books, and that has rubbed off on him. (9) However, parents who find those library visits daunting would be doing their children—and themselves—a favor by locating the Dr. Seuss shelf.

37. In context, which revision to sentence 2 (sentence 2 follows) is most needed?
   Too many children's books take the easy route by conveying dull messages that display little respect for how keenly children are aware of the subtleties of life and how strongly they respond to beautifully crafted writing.
   a. (As it is now)
   b. Too many children's books take the easy route by conveying dull messages that display little respect for children.
   c. Too many children's books take the easy route by conveying dull messages—you know the kind I'm talking about— that display little respect for how keenly children are aware of the subtleties of life and how strongly they respond to beautifully crafted writing.
   d. Too many children's books convey dull messages that display little respect for how keenly children are aware of the subtleties of life and how strongly they respond to beautifully crafted writing.
   e. Too many children's books take the easy route by conveying dull messages—be nice to Mom and Dad, drink your milk, learning is fun, etc.—that display little respect for how keenly children are aware of the subtleties of life and how strongly they respond to beautifully crafted writing.

38. In context, which revision to sentence 4 (sentence 4 follows) is most needed?

> One reason kids love Dr. Seuss is his stories deal with matters of great human importance.

a. (As it is now)

b. One reason kids love good ol' Dr. Seuss is his stories deal with matters of great human importance.

c. One reason kids love Dr. Seuss is his tales deal with matters of great human importance.

d. One reason kids love Dr. Seuss is his stories deal with matters of great importance to them.

e. A reason kids love Dr. Seuss is his stories deal with matters of great human importance.

39. In context, which revision to sentence 5 (sentence 5 follows) is most needed?

> Not surprisingly, he based a number of his works on actual historical events, such as the rise of Hitler in *Yertle the Turtle*, the arms race in *The Butter Battle Book*, and what happened in Hiroshima and Nagasaki in *Horton Hears a Who*.

a. (As it is now)

b. Not surprisingly, he based a number of his works on actual historical events, such as the rise of evil in *Yertle the Turtle*, conflict in *The Butter Battle Book*, and what happened in Hiroshima and Nagasaki in *Horton Hears a Who*.

c. Not surprisingly, he based a number of his works on actual historical events, such as the rise of Hitler in *Yertle the Turtle*, the arms race in *The Butter Battle Book*, and the U.S. bombing of Hiroshima and Nagasaki in *Horton Hears a Who*.

d. Not surprisingly, he based a number of his works on actual historical events, such as the rise of Hitler, the arms race, and what happened in Hiroshima and Nagasaki.

e. Not surprisingly, he based a number of his works on actual events, such as the rise of Hitler in *Yertle the Turtle*, the arms race in *The Butter Battle Book*, and what happened in Hiroshima and Nagasaki in *Horton Hears a Who*.

40. In context, which revision to sentences 8 and 9 (sentences 8 and 9 follow) is most needed?

> I'm certain my son detects my own enthusiasm for these books, and that has rubbed off on him. However, parents who find those library visits daunting would be doing their children—and themselves—a favor by locating the Dr. Seuss shelf.

a. Change "I'm" to "I am."

b. Replace "However" with "So."

c. Change "who" to "whom."

d. Replace "daunting" with "off-putting."

e. Change "shelf" to "shelves."

Part IIa: Argumentative Essay

Time: 30 Minutes

Carefully read the essay-writing topic that follows. Plan and write an essay that addresses all points in the topic. Make sure that your essay is well organized and that you support your central argument with concrete examples. Allow 30 minutes for your essay.

Many people would say that the Internet has become an indispensable aspect of our lives, affecting our work, our school, and our modes of communication. Write an essay in which you show how important or not the Internet is to modern life.

Part IIb: Source-Based Essay

Time: 30 Minutes
Directions

The following assignment requires you to use information from two sources to discuss the most important concerns that relate to a specific issue. When paraphrasing or quoting from the source, cite each source by referring to the author's last name, the text's title, or any other clear identifier. Allow 30 minutes for your essay.

Assignment

Read the two passages carefully and then write an essay in which you identify the most important concerns regarding the debates concerning stem cell research. Your essay must draw on information from both of the sources. In addition, you may draw on your own experiences, observations, or reading. Be sure to cite the sources whether you are paraphrasing or directly quoting.

Source 1

An Analysis of Stem Cell Research

Stem cell research is research using embryonic and "somatic" or "adult" stem cells for the purpose of advancing medicine. This research has been in existence since the beginning of the 20th century, and over the years many breakthroughs have come from it. In 1998, scientists discovered methods to derive stem cells from human embryos. In 2006, researchers made another breakthrough, which involved reprogramming some adult cells in certain conditions to assume a stem cell-like state. Stem cells themselves are useful in medical research because they are at the early state of reproduction, where the cell can either remain a stem cell or become a cell that would be involved in the formation of bones, brain cells, skin, the nervous system, organs, muscles and every other part of the body.

Benefits of Stem Cell Research

Theoretically, research points to stem cell research being of great value in medical advancement. At this time, it is not yet clear how much can be done with stem cell research, and the possible benefits are incalculable. It could lead to cures for diabetes or heart disease. It is also seen as a potential resource to help cure cancer, Parkinson 's disease, or even to regenerate a severed spinal cord and allow someone to walk who has been confined to a wheel chair. Although this sounds miraculous, it will not happen without extensive work and time.

Currently, adult stem cell therapies are used in the form of bone marrow transplants for treating leukemia. In 2006, researchers created artificial liver cells from umbilical cord blood stem cells. And in 2008, a study was published of the first successful cartilage regeneration in a human knee using adult stem cells. The variety of ways in which stem cell research could aid in curing many diseases has just begun to be explored.

continues

While there are questions regarding human embryo stem cells for research, there are a variety of ways to acquire stem cells. As noted in a 2008 Stanford publication, regarding human embryo stem cell research specifically, a majority of the researchers are not actually touching newly derived stem cells, but are instead using the lineage and data of stem cells that have already been researched by other scientists. They have made these cell lines available for others to work with and learn from. Along with advances regarding adult stem cell research, this could be a fruitful direction for medical inquiry to go.

Source 2

Arguments against Stem Cell Research

Stem cell research is a risky endeavor that does not have clear cut benefits and a lot of moral questions are involved. While it seems clear that certain diseases are being treated by stem cell therapies, there are too many questions regarding further study and use.

With human embryo stem cells, a major concern is where they are coming from. One suggestion is for these stem cells to be taken from embryos that have been created for reproduction via *inÁ vitro* fertilization. These embryos could be donated for scientific research after it is confirmed that they are not going to be used for reproduction. While this seems like a simple solution, there's also the question of the actual usefulness of those stem cells. With all stem cell therapies, in 2010, *ConsumerÁReports* noted the concern regarding transplanted cells forming tumors and becoming cancerous if the cell's division continued uncontrollably. There are also concerns of immune rejection by the patient being treated. While immunosuppressant drugs are used in organ transplant surgery, would this work on a body with new cells injected into it? There's also the additional question of whether the correct cell types can be induced in the stem cells, since the stem cells themselves are undifferentiated and can become many different kinds of cells.

While certain therapies have been successfully created, this research is still very untested. More conversations and clear education of the public is needed regarding this controversial form of medical therapy and the research behind it.

Praxis® Core Academic Skills for Educators: Writing Practice Test 2 Answers and Explanations

1. d. There are three items in a series in this sentence: *lived in cramped quarters*, *fought battles*, and *learn to understand the blessings*. To make these three items parallel, the word *learn* should be changed to *learned*.

2. a. The word *father* in this sentence is not being used as a proper or common noun; therefore, it should not be capitalized.

3. c. The pronoun *he* does not have a definitive antecedent; it could be referring to either writer. Replacing *he* with *Hemingway* would make this sentence grammatically (and factually) correct.

4. b. The word *they're*, a contraction meaning they are, should be replaced by the word *their* showing possession.

5. b. The apostrophe at the end of the word *officers* is incorrect and should be deleted. In this sentence, *officers* is not possessive.

6. a. This sentence contains the incorrect usage of the homophones too and two. *Too* is a modifier, and *two* is a number. This sentence calls for the use of the number two.

7. d. The subject of the second independent clause is *dirty filter*, a singular noun. Therefore, the singular form of the verb should be used. The verb *reduce* should be replaced by the verb *reduces*.

8. c. There are two subjects that mean the same thing: *Rolling Stones* and *they*. To correct this problem, the word *they* should be deleted from the sentence.

9. b. This sentence contains a punctuation error. It should have a semicolon to link the two independent clauses, not a comma.

10. e. Because there are no grammatical, idiomatic, logical, or structural errors in this sentence, choice **e** is the best answer.

11. b. The correct word for this sentence is *through*, which is used in reference to a movement or passage that proceeds it. *Through*, an adverb, means from one point to its end. The word *threw* is the past tense of *throw*, which means to toss or to fling.

12. e. Because there are no grammatical, idiomatic, logical, or structural errors in this sentence, choice **e** is the best answer.

13. c. The word *vacation* in this sentence is not being used as a proper or common noun; therefore, it should not be capitalized.

14. a. Starting the sentence with the conjunction *considering* is a subordination error because it creates two dependent clauses in this sentence. It should be deleted to make the sentence grammatically correct.

15. d. This choice is correct because a singular subject takes a singular verb. Therefore, because *network* is singular, the correct choice in this sentence should be *is*, not *are*.

16. b. The singular collective noun *staff* requires a singular verb form. Therefore, the plural form *deserve* should be replaced with the singular *deserves*.

17. c. This is the only choice that uses correct punctuation and contains no capitalization errors. Choice **d** uses correct punctuation, but *Italian* should be capitalized. Two independent clauses should be joined by a semicolon or a coordinating conjunction, not a comma, so choice **a** is incorrect. Choices **b** and **e** are incorrect because no commas are necessary when two items are linked by a conjunction (*gym and calculus*; *Italian and physics*).

18. d. This is the only choice that uses the correct pronoun, *which*. Use *which* when introducing clauses that are not essential to the information in the sentence, unless they refer to people (then use *who*). The second clause in choice **c** refers to a river, not a person, so the use of *who* is incorrect.

19. e. This is the only sentence to have agreement between the subject and the verb and between the pronoun and its antecedent. *It* sounds like the DNA is the subject that's considered identical. It is, but the sentence is referring to the twins.

20. c. This is the only choice that is correct because the other sentences are missing commas after *called* and *dog*. *Sometimes* should be one word.

21. d. This is the only choice that employs the correct conjunction *although* and uses the proper punctuation between the two clauses. The use of the conjunction *because* in choices **a** and **b** sets up faulty coordination between the two clauses. In addition, the use of *was* in choice **b** is a verb-tense error that creates a nonparallel sentence. Choice **c** lacks a proper conjunction. Choice **e** is properly coordinated, but the incorrect use of a semicolon instead of a comma creates a punctuation error.

22. c. This is the only sentence to have agreement between the subject and the verb. The other sentences contain multiple negation, which is the more general term referring to the occurrence of more than one negative in a clause.

23. e. This is the only choice that contains the correct plural form of *effect* and the correct possessive form of *the earth*. To form the possessive case of a singular noun, add *'s*.

24. b. This is the correct choice because a semicolon is needed to link these two independent clauses. The use of a comma in this sentence is incorrect and considered a comma splice. This sentence has the correct subject and verb agreement.

25. a. This sentence requires parallelism between the verbs *speak* and *have*, and choice **a** is the only choice that does this (*speaking* and *having*).

26. b. This is the only choice that uses the adverb correctly and establishes the appropriate comparison. Choices **a**, **c**, and **d** are incorrect because an adverb (*gracefully*) is required to modify the verb *skates*. Choice **e** correctly uses the adverb, but it contains a comparison error: When the conjunction *than* is used to indicate a comparison, it should be followed by the nominative case, *I*.

27. b. The most common way to join two independent clauses is with a comma and a coordinating conjunction. The only sentence that does both correctly is choice **b**. Two closely related independent clauses can also be linked by a semicolon, but for choice **a** to be correct, the coordinating conjunction *so* needs to be deleted. Choice **d** lacks a proper coordinating conjunction and has faulty parallelism. Choice **e** contains a verb tense error.

28. b. The original sentence contains a pronoun case error. Since the pronoun *I* takes the place of the object in this sentence, it should be in the objective case, and the sentence should read, *Would you like to come to the park with Sherine and me?* For sentences such as this one with a compound object (*Sherine and me*), just try saying the sentence without the first part of the compound object (*Would you like to come to the park with I?*) because it will probably sound wrong without the correct pronoun case. Choice **c** uses the intensive pronoun incorrectly. Choices **d** and **e** use nominative pronouns incorrectly.

29. b. The original sentence is unclear because of the vague pronoun *it*, which could refer to either of the two cars. By using the descriptive phrase *the newer model*, choice **b** clarifies which car is safer than the other. None of the other answer choices corrects the vague pronoun.

30. b. The original sentence is grammatically incorrect because it needs the correlative conjunction pair *both/and*. There is no such correlative conjunction pair as *both/or* because *both* indicates a couple not a choice. Similarly, *either* (choice **c**), and *whether* (choice **d**) indicate a choice, so they should not be used with *and*. *Neither* is a negative conjunction that needs to be paired with *nor*, not *and* (choice **e**).

31. a. The title of a journal article needs to be placed within quotation marks. The other elements of this citation are all written and formatted correctly.

32. d. MLA citation guidelines now require the publication's medium to indicate if the source appeared in print or online. This citation fails to include the source's medium, which should appear after the page numbers. Those page numbers indicate that this was a print source. The other elements of this citation are all written and formatted correctly.

33. c. The language used in the majority of this passage indicates that it was written for an educated, adult audience. The phrase *just a teensy bit* is too childish for this passage. Changing that phrase to *minimal* maintains the passage's sophisticated style. Choice **a** replaces *week* with a phrase that has the same exact meaning and fails to correct the stylistic error. Choices **b** and **d** introduce grammatical errors to the sentence.

34. a. As originally written, this sentence is unclear because the pronoun *it* is too vague. Replacing *it* with the term that pronoun replaces (*muscle atrophy*) clarifies the sentence's meaning. Choices **b** and **d** each introduce new vague pronouns to the sentence, making it even less clear than it originally was. Choice **c** introduces a grammatical error to the sentence. Choice **e** changes *cannot* to its contraction without correcting the original vague pronoun error.

35. b. As originally written, sentences 6 through 8 lack variety; each sentence begins with the word *Scientists*. Choice **b** corrects this problem by joining the three sentences into a single one. Although the sentence is long, it is grammatically correct, and its length provides some welcome variety from the shorter sentences placed before and after it. Choice **c** is not grammatically incorrect, but it does not correct the original problem of repetitiousness. Choice **d** corrects that repetitiousness, but it also removes important information from the sentence (*Scientists obtain animal bone biopsies immediately after flights*). Choice **e** makes sentence 6 grammatically incorrect by removing its subject (*Scientists*).

36. d. The writer cites a study by Dr. Lisa Ruml and a similar one that appeared in *The Journal of Sports Science & Medicine* as the sources of her claim that profound bone loss may be irreversible after three months in space (sentence 10). Choices **a** and **c** make claims that the writer does not support at all. The writer uses the vague terms "some studies show" and "some claim" to validate the claims in choices **b** and **e**, respectively; however, more specific citation is needed.

37. e. Choice **e** improves the original sentence by providing some examples of the kinds of "dull messages" children's books often convey. This information strengthens the writer's argument in favor of Dr. Seuss by specifying the kinds of simplistic messages Seuss does not convey. Choice **b** removes important information from the sentence. The phrase *you know the kind I'm talking about* used in choice **c** is a lazy way to avoid providing specific examples of the kinds of

dull messages the writer means. Choice **d** merely removes the phrase *take the easy route* without improving the original sentence at all.

38. a. Sentence 4 is perfectly clear and grammatically correct as it is originally written. None of the answer choices improve the sentence.

39. c. Although this passage deals with the topic of children's books, it is written for an adult audience that does not need to be protected from the reality of what the United States did to Hiroshima and Nagasaki. Choice **c** replaces the euphemism *what happened* with specific wording more respectful of an adult audience. Choice **b** makes the matter worse by introducing additional euphemisms (*evil*; *conflict*) to sentence 5. Choice **d** removes important information—the titles of Dr. Seuss's books that deal with the matters of great importance—from sentence 5. Choice **e** merely removes the word *historical*, which does not make the sentence grammatically incorrect, but does not improve it either.

40. b. As originally written, sentence 9 begins with the wrong transitional word because *However* suggests a contradiction, yet sentence 9 follows sentence 8 without contradicting it. Therefore, a better transitional word is *So*. Choice **a** replaces a contraction without correcting the organizational error. Choice **c** introduces a grammatical error to the sentence. Choice **d** replaces *daunting* with a synonym that does not correct the original error. Choice **e** does not correct that error either.

Sample Responses for the Argumentative Essay

Following are sample criteria for scoring an argumentative essay.

A score 6 writer will

- create an exceptional composition with a clear thesis that appropriately addresses the audience and given task.
- organize ideas effectively and logically, include very strong supporting details, and use smooth transitions.
- present a definitive, focused thesis and clearly support it throughout the composition.
- include vivid, strong details, clear examples, and supporting text to support the key ideas.
- exhibit an exceptional level of skill in the usage of the English language and the capacity to employ an assortment of sentence structures.
- build essentially error-free and varied sentences that accurately convey intended meaning.

A score 5 writer will

- create a commendable composition that appropriately addresses the audience and given task.
- organize ideas, include supporting details, and use smooth transitions.
- present a thesis and support it throughout the composition.
- include details, examples, and supporting text to enhance the themes of the composition.
- generally exhibit a high level of skill in the usage of the English language and the capacity to employ an assortment of sentence structures.
- build mostly error-free sentences that accurately convey intended meaning.

A score 4 writer will

- create a composition that satisfactorily addresses the audience and given task.

- display satisfactory organization of ideas, include adequate supporting details, and generally use smooth transitions.
- present a thesis and mostly support it throughout the composition.
- include some details, examples, and supporting text that typically enhance most themes of the composition.
- exhibit a competent level of skill in the usage of the English language and the general capacity to employ an assortment of sentence structures.
- build sentences with several minor errors that generally do not confuse the intended meaning.

A score 3 writer will

- create an adequate composition that basically addresses the audience and given task.
- present a somewhat underdeveloped thesis but attempt to support it throughout the composition.
- display limited organization of ideas, have some inconsistent supporting details, and use few transitions.
- exhibit an adequate level of skill in the usage of the English language and a basic capacity to employ an assortment of sentence structures.
- build sentences with some minor and major errors that may obscure the intended meaning.

A score 2 writer will

- create a composition that weakly addresses the audience and given task.
- display little organization of ideas, have inconsistent supporting details, and use very few transitions.
- present an unclear or confusing thesis with little support throughout the composition.
- include very few details, examples, and supporting text.
- exhibit a less than adequate level of skill in the usage of the English language and a limited

capacity to employ a basic assortment of sentence structures.

■ build sentences with a few major errors that may confuse the intended meaning.

A score 1 writer will

■ create a composition that has a limited sense of the audience and given task.

■ display illogical organization of ideas, include confusing or no supporting details, and lack the ability to effectively use transitions.

■ present a minimal or unclear thesis.

■ include confusing or irrelevant details and examples, and little or no supporting text.

■ exhibit a limited level of skill in the usage of the English language and little or no capacity to employ basic sentence structure.

■ build sentences with many major errors that obscure or confuse the intended meaning.

Sample Score 6 Argumentative Essay

In the twenty-first century, the first place people turn to when there is a question to be answered, information to be located, or people to be contacted, is often the Internet. The Internet has supplanted the traditional encyclopedia, as well as a number of other reference sources, such as phone books and travel agents. Online, one can make reservations, plan vacations, play interactive games, learn a language, listen to music or radio, watch TV shows, read the newspaper, and research about a medical condition.

There is no limit to the subject matter that can be found on the Internet. Search engines like Google can summon links to more sources than one could imagine. The Internet allows those at home in front of their computers to shop and socialize without coming face-to-face with another person. Clearly, the Internet is an invaluable tool in modern life.

If, however, one wishes to speak directly to another person, email and social networks provide that connection. You can find groups of people conversing with one another on any topic under the sun—politics, sports, health, pop culture, travel, food, and more. Social networks like Twitter and Facebook can be a place to meet people, exchange ideas, or learn a new skill. Emailing and instant messaging let you talk to anyone anywhere as long as there is an internet connection. In a world where people frequently travel, and where family members do not necessarily live in the same state, email is a means of making simple, inexpensive, immediate contact. Digital cameras and the rise of smart phones allow images to spread online as quickly as words do.

Unfortunately, there are individuals who subvert the opportunities offered by these technologies. They are less than honest, disguise their identity, lure people into financial scams, and entice the unsuspecting, including children, into giving them personal information. It's up to each individual user to protect their data and their identity with the most up-to-date spyware protection and exercise personal caution when corresponding with strangers.

Of course, every company with a web presence is still in business to make a profit, so sites from the New York Times to Amazon sell ad space to companies who want to reach their readers. Some are easy to ignore, such as banners at the top and bottom of the screen. However, some advertising comes in the form of pop-ups that require the user to stop and respond, either positively or negatively, to the ads.

When one considers that, among other things, you can visit a museum and view its contents, visit the websites of numerous individuals and organizations, play a game with a whole community of players, and pay your bills, it becomes obvious that the uses of the Internet are too vast for a short list. Most would agree that much has been added to people's lives by connecting them to the Internet, and that we probably cannot anticipate what new purposes will be explored in the future.

Comments on the Sample Argumentative Essay That Received a Score of 6

The author has created an informative essay with a clear thesis. It answers the question and has a smooth, logical organization. Stylistically, it uses smooth transitions and relevant and correct examples. The key ideas are readily apparent and explored throughout the essay through well-written and varied sentences.

Sample Score 4 Argumentative Essay

The Internet has many important purposes. It has connected people all over the world in a way that has never been done before. You can send and receive email from friends and colleagues whenever you want. You can also meet people through the Internet, and make friends. These facts prove the importance of the Internet in people's daily lives.

The internet is also good for research. If you want to get information about just about any topic, you can look it up. You don't have to go to the library. You can also use the Internet for recreation purposes. There are also good games and music that you can download, often for free.

Shopping may also be done on the Internet. You can buy things at home, without having to go the store.

For providers, the internet is a way for them to make money. They sell subscriptions, and also sell advertising space. Some provide good service, while others seem to want to make the most profit, and don't hire many technical people to help when there is a problem.

While the internet has its downside, such as identity theft problems and stalkers, these problems are found off the internet, too. You just have to be careful when using the internet, and you can enjoy the countless ways in which it has improved our lives.

Comments on the Sample Argumentative Essay That Received a Score of 4

The author has created a serviceable composition. The thesis is readily perceived and adequately, if not spectacularly, defended. Details are correct, if vague. Stylistically, it is rather stilted. However, the author displays adequate knowledge of the subject and sufficient command of the English language; the essay is grammatically and orthographically correct, even if it is not scintillating.

Sample Score 1 Argumentative Essay

The Internet has lots of purposes. It has been around for about ten years and it has really taken off. Most people have at least one computer in their house most of them have an internet connection. If you ask them why they have it they will probably tell you about the useful purposes.

One of the best things you can do on the Internet is play games, such as chess and backgammon, with people you don't even know. Sometimes you have to pay for the games, and sometimes they are free. Sometimes you play against a really tough opponent, and sometimes you can win every game. I perfer the latter. Its also fun to listen to music on the internet. You can find just about any kind you like. These are some purposes of the Internet.

Comments on the Sample Argumentative Essay That Received a Score of 1

The author neither understands the subject, nor expresses an opinion in a clear and coherent manner. The author furthermore focuses on his or her experience with online gaming, not with the more general benefits of the Internet. There are grammatical and spelling errors, and the essay neither develops in a clear way, nor has very much to say.

Sample Responses for the Source-Based Essay

Following are sample criteria for scoring a source-based essay.

A score 6 writer will

- create an exceptional composition explaining why the concerns are important and support the explanation with specific references to both sources.
- organize ideas effectively and logically, include well chosen information from both sources, and link the two sources in the discussion.

- exhibit an exceptional level of skill in the usage of the English language and the capacity to employ an assortment of sentence structures.
- build essentially error-free and varied sentences that accurately convey intended meaning.
- cite both sources when quoting or paraphrasing.

A score 5 writer will

- create a commendable composition that explains why the concerns are important and supports the explanation with specific references to both sources..
- organize ideas effectively and logically, include information from both sources, link the two sources, and use smooth transitions.
- generally exhibit skill in the usage of the English language and the capacity to employ variety in sentence structures.
- build mostly error-free sentences that accurately convey intended meaning.
- cite both sources when quoting or paraphrasing.

A score 4 writer will

- create a composition that satisfactorily explains why the concerns are important and supports the explanation with specific references to both sources.
- display satisfactory organization of ideas, include adequate details, and link the two sources.
- exhibit a competent level of skill in the usage of the English language and the general capacity to employ an assortment of sentence structures.
- build sentences with several minor errors that generally do not confuse the intended meaning.
- cite both sources when quoting or paraphrasing.

A score 3 writer will

- create an adequate composition that basically addresses the audience and given task but conveys the importance of the concerns in only a limited way.

- display some organization of ideas and include some supporting details.
- exhibit an adequate level of skill in the usage of the English language and a basic capacity to employ an assortment of sentence structures.
- build sentences with some minor and major errors that may obscure the intended meaning.
- cite sources when quoting or paraphrasing.

A score 2 writer will

- use information from only one source poorly or fail to convey why the concerns discussed in the sources are important.
- display little organization of ideas, have inconsistent supporting details, and fail to link the two sources.
- include very few details, examples, and supporting text.
- exhibit a less than adequate level of skill in the usage of the English language and a limited capacity to employ a basic assortment of sentence structures.
- build sentences with a few major errors that may confuse the intended meaning.

A score 1 writer will

- display illogical organization of ideas, include confusing or no supporting details, and fail to adequately address the concerns raised by the sources.
- include confusing or irrelevant details and examples, and few or no supporting references.
- exhibit a limited level of skill in the usage of the English language and little or no capacity to employ basic sentence structure.
- build sentences with many major errors that obscure or confuse the intended meaning.

Sample Score 6 Essay

Stem cell research is a complicated topic to evaluate. While it is noted as having a lot of potential with regard to medical advancements, there are several elements of it that can cause moral quandaries, such as the use of human embryos in the research. At the same time, it is providing valuable therapies for diseases such as leukemia and could treat diseases like diabetes and heart disease. With that in mind and on reviewing the two passages, I find that I must argue in favor of stem cell research.

Since the passage against stem cell research makes several valid points, especially questioning the source of the stem cells used in the research, this is sure to inspire many readers to question the morality of the supporting argument. This concern does not actually have any evidence behind it, saying that only human embryo stem cells are being used, so it is difficult to know where this concern came from. In addition, the particular evidence noting that stem cell research itself is potentially harmful has no scientific basis and was simply based on concerns from the populace, as noted by Consumer Reports, than actual research. At the end of the third paragraph, this passage even questions whether scientists could differentiate the cells properly to make them become what is needed for that specific stem cell therapy. Would the stem cells become an actual brain cell or would it just become a bunch of organ cells and cause a tumorous growth? This is stated without any evidence to back up the concern at all. While it is clear that the reason stem cell research is interesting in any form is that the cells themselves can be formed into any other cell needed, this worry about differentiation seems to be idle speculation rather than something that would legitimately make this research impossible.

In contrast, the passage supporting stem cell research is full of dates and specific examples. While the against passage only notes an article from Consumer Reports, this passage notes research done in the 1900s, all the way through 2008. It points out some of the current research and medical benefits of stem cell research being used right now, including bone marrow transfu-

sions to treat leukemia and the generation of artificial liver cells just in 2006. It also notes that the major concern regarding the source of the stem cells should be less of a concern due to a report from Stanford, a major research institute, about how researchers acquire the data of human embryo stem cells. It appears that not every single researcher is getting a new set of embryo stem cells to work off of. Instead, the information about one set is shared among all of the researchers. Also, the passage pointed to a 2008 article about medical advancements using adult stem cells. If stem cell research should be argued against, there needs to be more thorough and specific evidence provided to support that argument.

It is clear that the arguments against stem cell research are antiquated and have been addressed by the medical community. Perhaps there is research regarding why stem cell research should not be pursued, but it is unspecified in these passages. Overall, while the supporting passage addresses many of the same concerns as the "against" passage, it is better organized and supported throughout with actual referenced research.

Comments on the Sample Source-Based Essay That Received a Score of 6

This is an outstanding essay. This response evaluates the arguments in the source text, develops an effective position supported by the text, and fulfills the criteria to earn a top score. This response establishes its stance at the conclusion of the first paragraph (*I find that I must argue in favor of stem cell research*) and provides a summary of support for that stance in the second and third paragraphs. In the second paragraph, the writer also weighs the validity of the evidence in the "against" argument, for example: "*the particular evidence noting that stem cell research itself is potentially harmful has no scientific basis and was simply based on concerns from the populace, as noted by Consumer Reports, than actual research.*"

The essay is well organized, opens with a definitive stance, offers a discussion of the pros and cons of stem cell research and the evidence provided, and then provides a summary in support of the chosen stance. The writer provides multiple, specific examples and then elaborates on them, using an appropriately formal tone throughout. In addition, the writer adheres to proper grammar and usage.

Sample Score 4 Essay

It seems clear that we must not allow stem cell research. It may have been around since the early 1900s, but that does not outweigh the moral questions it raises.

I am against stem cell research for mainly the same reasons stated in the passage. Since stem cell research has been around, there is no clear answer regarding where the human embryo stem cells come from. This was not answered in the supporting passage.

What's more, I also think the possibility that the cells could form tumors and become cancerous, as noted in the against passage, is pretty worrying. At the very least, more education and research into the risks of stem cells is very necessary.

Finally, while it may be true that the arguments for stem cell research list many favorable benefits, and those aspects of stem cell research seem intriguing, the arguments against the research are better than the ones for it. At the very least there needs to be more education on the dangers.

Comments on the Sample Source-Based Essay That Received a Score of 4

This response makes a simple argument, supports it with some evidence from the source text, and offers a partial analysis of the opposing argument.

The writer generates an argument against stem cell research and makes a clear statement of her position in the first paragraph (*It seems clear that we must not allow stem cell research*), in the second paragraph (*I am against stem cell research for mainly the same reasons*), and final paragraph (*the arguments against the research are better than the ones for it*). The writer does cite some evidence from the source text to support her position (*Since stem cell research has been*

around, *there is no clear answer regarding where the human embryo stem cells come from*). The writer offers a partial analysis of the issue (*At the very least, more education and research into the risks of stem cells is very necessary*) and (*It's true; there are arguments for stem cell research that list a lot of favorable benefits*); however, this analysis is simplistic and limited.

In addition, in the second paragraph the writer offers a partial evaluation of the validity of the "for" arguments (*there is no clear answer regarding where the human embryo stem cells come from. This was not answered in the supporting passage*).

Although this response has a general organization and focus, the supporting ideas are developed unevenly. The second and third paragraphs focus on the troubling aspects of stem cell research, and the writer offers a clear progression of ideas. Her main points are clear but not sufficiently elaborated upon. Her argument is based solely on what is offered in the passage (*I am against stem cell research for mainly the same reasons stated in the passage*).

The concluding paragraph offers a very basic comparison of the "for" and "against" arguments, but not much development is offered.

In addition, the writer adheres to proper grammar and usage.

Sample Score 1 Essay

Stem cell research is way too confusing and disturbing for a lot of people. While these scientists think that listing all of the accomplishemtns will mean that stem cell research should continue it's not clear at all whether that's true. If perhaps you had loukemia, then it would be ok for it to continue.

Also we don't know where the human embryo stem cells come from also some of them could become cancerous and that isn't a good idea either I thought Loukemia was some kind of cancer, that makes it even more confusing. Also the differentiation of cells. If you can't get the right kind of cells for your therapy, then those cells are useless and are a waste.

I think it's a better idea to not have stem cell research until we know more about what it could do. There are too many factors that seem harmful or dangerous in some way.

Comments on the Sample Source-Based Essay That Received a Score of 1

In general, this response provides a minimal summary of the source text and lacks insight and topic analysis. The writer fails to summarize source texts in a coherent and organized structure. Although this response addresses the source material, the writer fails to cite evidence to support any arguments and does not take a firm stance until the final paragraph (*I think it's a better idea to not have stem cell research until we know more about what it could do*). She also seems to flip-flop on her stance (*While these scientists think that listing all of the accomplishemtns will mean that stem cell research should continue it's not clear at all whether that's true. If perhaps you had loukemia, then it would be ok for it to continue*).

Overall, the response is poorly developed, disorganized, and lacks any clear progression of ideas. The writer uses informal and colloquial language (*Stem cell research is way too confusing and disturbing for a lot of people*) and fails to demonstrate awareness of audience and purpose. The response lacks organizational structure and a clear progression of ideas.

Many sentences lack sense and fluency and are incorrect and awkward. The writer misuses and confuses words, punctuation, and usage as well as the conventions of English in general, making the response almost incomprehensible. This short response shows flawed sentence structure, including run-on sentences (*Also we don't know where the human embryo stem cells come from also some of them could become cancerous and that isn't a good idea either I thought Loukemia was some kind of cancer, that makes it even more confusing. . . .*) and fragments (*Also the differentiation of cells*).

Praxis® Core Academic Skills for Educators: Mathematics Practice Test 2

Time: 85 Minutes

Directions: Choose the best answer to each of the following questions.

Use the following information to answer questions 1 and 2.

Tickets to the school play cost $7.50 for adults and $5 for children ages 12 and under. On Saturday and Sunday afternoon, there is a special matinee price: $5.50 for adults and $3 for children ages 12 and under. Special group discounts are available for groups of 30 or more people.

1. Which of the following can be determined from the information given in the passage?
   a. how much it will cost a family of four to buy tickets to the school play on Saturday afternoon
   b. the difference between the cost of two tickets to the school play on Tuesday night and the cost of one ticket on Sunday afternoon
   c. how much tickets to the school play will cost each person if he or she is part of a group of 40 people
   d. the difference between the cost of a ticket to the school play for an adult on Friday night and a ticket to the school play for a 13-year-old on Saturday afternoon
   e. the total amount of money saved by a group of 35

2. Using the information in the passage, how can you find the difference in price between a ticket to the school play for an adult and a ticket for a child under the age of 12 if they are attending the show on Saturday afternoon?

a. subtract $3.00 from $7.50
b. subtract $3.00 from $5.50
c. subtract $5.00 from $7.50
d. subtract $7.50 from $5.50
e. add $5.50 and $3.00 and divide by 2

3. One thousand students are participating in the regional math competition. An equal number of teams of five students are placed into four different gymnasiums. Each team has one adult coach. To find the total number of people (students and coaches) in each gymnasium, you could

a. divide 1,000 by 4, divide that result by 5, and then add that result and 1,000.
b. divide 1,000 by 5, add that result to 1,000, and then divide that result by 4.
c. divide 1,000 by 4, divide that result by 4, and then add that result and 1,000.
d. divide 1,000 by 5, divide that result by 4, and then add that result and 50.
e. divide 1,000 by 4, add 50 to that result, and then divide that result by 5.

4. Out of 100 students polled at a local university, 80 said they would favor being offered a course in web page development. If there are 30,000 students enrolled at this university, how many would you expect to favor being offered such a course?

a. 2,400
b. 6,000
c. 16,000
d. 22,000
e. 24,000

5. Marvin wrapped a gift that is in a box that is a perfect cube with each side measuring d inches. Maya arrives with a gift that is also in a box that is a perfect cube, but the edge length of each side of her gift is twice as long as Marvin's gift. How many square inches of wrapping paper, in terms of d, did Maya need to wrap her gift?

a. $6d^2$
b. $12d^2$
c. $24d^2$
d. $2d^3$
e. $12d^3$

6. A factory operates 20 machines that make granola bars. Each machine can make between 80 and 100 granola bars per minute. Which of the following could be the number of granola bars produced per hour if all 20 machines are working at the same time? Choose *all* that apply.

a. ☐ 1,800
b. ☐ 5,000
c. ☐ 18,000
d. ☐ 100,000
e. ☐ 119,500

7. Jesse ate $\frac{1}{2}$ of a pizza and left the other half in his dorm room. Dennis came by and ate $\frac{1}{4}$ of what was left there. How much of the original pie did Dennis eat?

a. $\frac{1}{16}$
b. $\frac{1}{6}$
c. $\frac{1}{4}$
d. $\frac{1}{8}$
e. $\frac{3}{4}$

8. Solve for x in the following equation:

$2x - 3(x - 1) = -12$

a. 11

b. 15

c. −11

d. 9

e. −15

9. Belicia drives a compact car that gets, on average, 28 miles for every gallon of gas. If she must drive 364 miles from Los Angeles to San Francisco, and gas costs on average $4.85 per gallon, approximately how much will she spend on gas?

a. $63

b. $75

c. $73

d. $136

e. $65

10. Consider the following scatterplot:

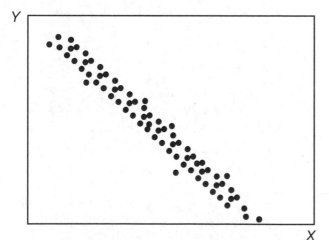

Which of the following is the most reasonable correlation coefficient for this bivariate data set?

a. 0.95

b. 0.60

c. 0.10

d. −0.59

e. −0.91

11. Harold has two containers that he has filled with water. One is a rectangular plastic box with a base of 16 square inches, and the other is a cylindrical container with a base radius of 2 inches and a height of 11 inches. If the rectangular box is filled with water 9 inches from the bottom, and Harold pours the water into the cylinder without spilling, which of the following will be true?

a. The cylinder will overflow.

b. The cylinder will be exactly full.

c. The cylinder will be filled to an approximate level of 10 inches.

d. The cylinder will be filled to an approximate level of 8 inches.

e. The cylinder will be filled to an approximate level of 6 inches.

12. There were 504 candies in a jar. Between 8 o'clock and 9 o'clock, $\frac{1}{8}$ of the candies were given out. Between 9 o'clock and 10 o'clock, $\frac{2}{9}$ of the remaining candies were handed out. In the following hour, $\frac{1}{7}$ of the remaining candies are distributed. How many candies are left?

13. Nyaah's bank balance was $40 on Monday, $10 on Tuesday, $65 on Wednesday, and $25 on Thursday. What was Nyaah's mean balance for the week?

a. $140.00

b. $22.50

c. $35.00

d. $25.50

e. $30.00

14. Suppose you spend $903 on a one-time cost for materials necessary to start a snow removal business. For each driveway you clear of snow, you earn $40, but it costs $5.25 in gas for each job. Determine the number of driveways you must clear order to break even.

a. 20
b. 25
c. 26
d. 52
e. 23

15. Consider the following distribution:

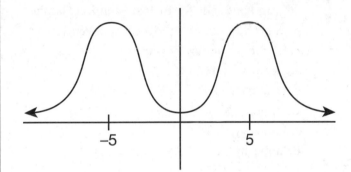

Select all of the following statements that are true.

a. The distribution is symmetric.
b. The distribution is bimodal.
c. The distribution is skewed left.
d. The mean of this distribution is positive.
e. The median is larger than the mean.

16. Lucinda is at the grocery store. If her purchases are a total of $30 or less, she will pay with cash. If she spends an amount between $30 and $70, she will pay with a check. If she spends $70 or more, she will use a credit card. If Lucinda recently paid for her grocery bill using a check, which of the following statements could be true?

a. The bill was $20.
b. The bill was $80.
c. If the bill was $20 more, she would have paid with cash.
d. The bill was at least $70.
e. The bill was more than $35.

The following graph shows the yearly electricity usage for Finnigan Engineering Inc. over the course of three years for three departments. Use it to answer question 17.

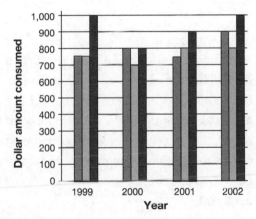

■ Engineering Dept. ▦ Customer Service ▨ Sales Dept.

17. What was the percent decrease in cost of electricity usage from 1999 to 2000 for the Engineering Department?

a. 25%
b. 20%
c. 12.5%
d. 10%
e. 0%

18. The sequence of numbers 0, 2, 2, 4, 6, 10, 16 follows a pattern. Using this pattern, which of the following is the next number in the sequence?
   a. 16
   b. 20
   c. 22
   d. 26
   e. 32

19. Thirty percent of the students at a high school are involved in the vocal and instrumental music programs. If 15% of the musicians are in the choir, what percentage of the whole school is in the choir?
   a. 4.5%
   b. 9.0%
   c. 15%
   d. 30%
   e. 45%

20. Zelda wants to invite the employees of her small business for a springtime picnic that will be held on her family's farm. The amount of land is 45,000 square feet. In order for her guests to be comfortable, she doesn't want the population density to exceed 0.03 people per square foot. What is the maximum number of guests she should invite?
   a. 45,000
   b. 4,500
   c. 135
   d. 450
   e. 1,350

21. Which of the following has the greatest value?
   a. $4\frac{3}{4}\%$
   b. 4.09%
   c. $\frac{47}{1,000}$
   d. $\frac{23}{500}$
   e. 0.0408

22. Consider the triangle $\triangle ABC$ with vertices $A(-11,3)$, $B(-11,14)$, and $C(-21,5)$. If $\triangle ABC$ is reflected over the line $x = 2$, what are the coordinates of the image of vertex B?
   a. $(-11,-10)$
   b. $(15,14)$
   c. $(14,-11)$
   d. $(15,27)$
   e. $(-14,11)$

23. At a baseball game, Deanna bought the following food for herself and her sister Jamie: one jumbo box of popcorn to share at $7 a box, two hot dogs for each of them (four total) at $3 a dog, and one soda for each at $4 apiece. Jamie paid for their tickets at $13 a ticket. Who spent more money and by how much?
   a. Deanna, by $1
   b. Deanna, by $3
   c. Jamie, by $1
   d. Jamie, by $2
   e. Jamie, by $4

24. Ryan and Kimberly spend a combined total of 12 hours to begin the spring landscaping for a friend. The next week Jaime and Janet spend another 18 hours to finish the landscaping job. If Ryan worked three times as many hours as Kimberly, and Jaime worked five more hours than Ryan worked, how many hours did Janet spend on the landscaping?
   a. 3
   b. 9
   c. 14
   d. 4
   e. 7

25. Select the sentence below that best describes the following scatterplot:

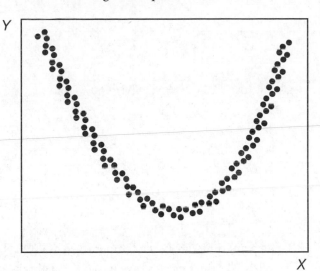

a. These data have a strong positive correlation.

b. The correlation is weak.

c. There is a moderate negative correlation between the variables.

d. There is a strong nonlinear relationship between the two variables.

e. There is no relationship between the data.

Use the following table to answer question 26.

TRAIN SCHEDULE		
DESTINATION	DEPARTURE	ARRIVAL
1	7:55	8:35
2	8:40	9:50
3	8:45	10:25
4	9:05	10:25
5	10:00	11:15
6	11:35	12:15

26. According to the table, which destination takes the longest time to reach?

a. 1

b. 2

c. 3

d. 4

e. 6

27. During her shift at a busy restaurant, a chef uses $2\frac{1}{4}$ pounds of flour the first hour, $4\frac{5}{8}$ pounds of flour the second hour, and $\frac{1}{2}$ pound of flour the third hour. How many pounds of flour does the chef use during these three hours?

a. $6\frac{3}{8}$

b. $6\frac{7}{8}$

c. $7\frac{1}{4}$

d. $7\frac{3}{8}$

e. $7\frac{3}{4}$

28. If a, b, and c represent nonzero real numbers, which of the following statements are equivalent?

    I. $a + (b + c)$

    II. $(a + b) + (a + c)$

    III. $(a + b) + c$

a. I and II

b. I and III

c. II and III

d. I, II, and III

e. None of the statements is equivalent.

Use the following table to answer question 29.

DISTANCE TRAVELED FROM CHICAGO WITH RESPECT TO TIME	
TIME (HOURS)	DISTANCE FROM CHICAGO (MILES)
1	60
2	120
3	180
4	240

29. A train moving at a constant speed of 60 miles per hour leaves Chicago for Los Angeles at time $t = 0$. If Los Angeles is 2,000 miles from Chicago, which of the following equations describes the distance the train is from Los Angeles at any time t?
 a. $D(t) = 60t - 2,000$
 b. $D(t) = 60t$
 c. $D(t) = 2,000 - 60t$
 d. $D(t) = -2,000 - 60t$
 e. $D(t) = 2,000 + 60t$

Use the following information to answer question 30.

A grocery store has a total of 55 different varieties of candy bars. Twelve are made of milk chocolate, 5 are made of white chocolate, and 15 are made of dark chocolate. The candy bars are made by three different companies: Hometown Confections, Cocoa Inc., and Taste of Chocolate.

30. Which of the following can be determined from the information given?
 a. the number of candy bars made by Hometown Confections
 b. the ratio of milk chocolate candy bars to white chocolate candy bars
 c. the number of toffee candy bars
 d. the cost of a milk chocolate candy bar made by Cocoa Inc.
 e. the ratio of milk chocolate peanut butter candy bars to dark chocolate candy bars with nuts

31. Vic and Dahlia go to eat sushi together. He likes sea urchin, which costs $3 apiece. She likes eel, at $2.25 per. The bill without tax, drinks, or tip comes to $36, and each owes half. How many eel pieces did Dahlia order?
 a. 20
 b. 15
 c. 8
 d. 6
 e. 7

32. What is the median of the data set represented by this box-and-whisker plot?

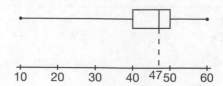

 a. 35
 b. 40
 c. 47
 d. 50
 e. 60

33. A springtime day had a temperature of 40°C. What was the temperature in degrees Fahrenheit? The formula for converting Celsius to Fahrenheit is $F = \frac{9}{5}C + 32$.
 a. 100°F
 b. 101°F
 c. 102°F
 d. 103°F
 e. 104°F

34. An aquarium has a base length of 12 inches and a width of 5 inches. If the aquarium is 10 inches tall, what is its total volume?
 a. 480 cubic inches
 b. 540 cubic inches
 c. 600 cubic inches
 d. 720 cubic inches
 e. 1,200 cubic inches

35. A floor rug in the shape of a circle has a diameter of 152 cm. What is the approximate area of the rug?
 1 cm = 0.39 inches
 a. 878.53π in.²
 b. 360π in.²
 c. 3,514.12π in.²
 d. 2,252.64π in.²
 e. 5,776π in.²

36. Given the equation $y = 5 + 4x$, what is the value of y when $x - 3$?

37. Donut Store

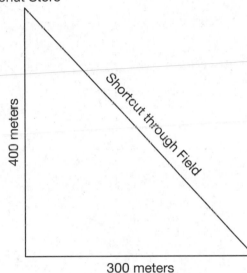

400 meters

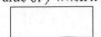

300 meters

Daphne and Margaret get a text from a friend that their favorite donut shop is down to its last raspberry-custard donut. They race for it. Both run at an average 5 meters per second. If Daphne cuts through a field instead of following the lanes, as shown in the diagram above, by how many seconds will she beat Margaret to the store?

a. 200

b. 25

c. 100

d. 500

e. 40

38. A circle drawn on a gymnasium floor for a basketball court has an area of 78.5 square feet. What is the length of the diameter of this circle? Use $\pi = 3.14$.

a. 25 feet

b. 15 feet

c. 12.5 feet

d. 10 feet

e. 5 feet

39. Byron keeps a drawer of unmatched blue socks and brown socks. He keeps 11 blue socks and 10 brown socks. What is the percent likelihood that the second sock he pulls is a match if he draws blue first?

a. 5

b. 10

c. 50

d. 7

e. 8

40. The average high temperature for the first five days in July was 90°. If the temperatures for the first four days were 95°, 85°, 88°, and 84°, respectively, what was the temperature on the fifth day?

a. 90°

b. 92°

c. 94°

d. 96°

e. 98°

41. A triangle has two sides that measure 14 cm and 17 cm, respectively. Which of the following could be the length of the triangle's third side? Choose all that apply.

a. □ 3 cm

b. □ 16 cm

c. □ 25 cm

d. □ 28 cm

e. □ 31 cm

42. Which of the following fractions is between $\frac{1}{3}$ and $\frac{1}{4}$?

a. $\frac{1}{2}$

b. $\frac{1}{5}$

c. $\frac{2}{3}$

d. $\frac{2}{5}$

e. $\frac{2}{7}$

43. Ezra is purchasing sunscreen. The only bottle size available is 25ml. The instructions say that 5ml cover 288 square inches. His body surface is 20 square feet. How many bottles does he need to purchase to cover himself?

a. 1
b. 2
c. 3
d. 4
e. 5

44. Which of the following distributions has a nonpositive mean? Select all that apply.

a.

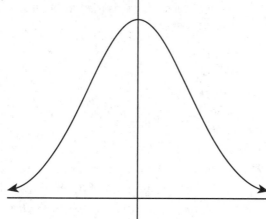

b.

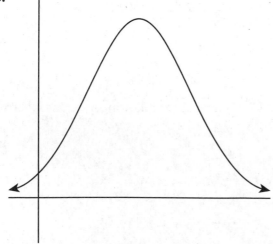

c.

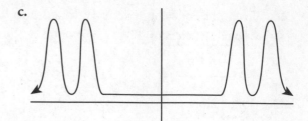

d.

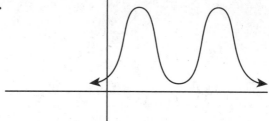

e.

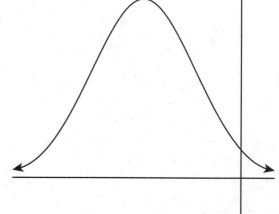

45. Eva has exactly 1,632 hours until her vacation begins. How many days are there before her vacation begins?

   a. 30

   b. 50

   c. 68

   d. 75

   e. 37,440

46. If a function is defined as $f(x) = 3x^2 - \frac{1}{2}x + 7$, what is $f(\frac{1}{2})$?

   a. $\frac{15}{2}$

   b. $-\frac{15}{2}$

   c. 8

   d. $\frac{17}{2}$

   e. $-\frac{17}{2}$

47. The Astoria Main Street Fair is raffling off a weeklong stay at a summer art camp. Sohail buys 4 raffle tickets for his son, Asad, and three times as many raffle tickets for his daughter, Amara. If a total of 80 raffle tickets are sold for the art camp, what is the probability that Asad or Amara will win?

   a. 0.05

   b. 0.15

   c. 0.20

   d. 0.25

   e. 0.09

48. A rectangle is divided into six congruent squares, as shown in the following figure.

If the area of one of the squares is 9 square units, what is the perimeter of the rectangle?

   a. 30 units

   b. 24 units

   c. 36 units

   d. 15 units

   e. 72 units

49. Which of the following fractions are in order from greatest to least?

   a. $\frac{1}{2}, \frac{6}{11}, \frac{3}{5}, \frac{5}{8}$

   b. $\frac{3}{5}, \frac{6}{11}, \frac{1}{2}, \frac{5}{8}$

   c. $\frac{5}{8}, \frac{6}{11}, \frac{3}{5}, \frac{1}{2}$

   d. $\frac{5}{8}, \frac{3}{5}, \frac{6}{11}, \frac{1}{2}$

   e. $\frac{3}{5}, \frac{1}{2}, \frac{5}{8}, \frac{6}{11}$

50. A jar of coins contains 8 dimes, 10 quarters, 3 nickels, and 9 pennies. What is the probability of selecting either a nickel or a penny if you draw one coin from the jar?

   a. $\frac{1}{10}$

   b. $\frac{2}{5}$

   c. $\frac{4}{15}$

   d. $\frac{3}{10}$

   e. $\frac{1}{3}$

51. First-year members of an auto club have to purchase the membership at the full price of $84.50, but those who were also members last year get a 15% discount. Those who have been members for at least three years get an additional 10% off the discounted price. How much does a person who has been a member for at least three years have to pay for his or her membership?
a. $63.38
b. $64.64
c. $65.78
d. $71.83
e. $72.05

52. Given a polygon with four congruent sides, which of the following does NOT contradict the statement, "If a polygon has four congruent sides, then the polygon is a square"?
a. The polygon has five congruent sides.
b. The polygon does not have four congruent sides.
c. The polygon has exactly one pair of parallel sides.
d. The polygon is a triangle.
e. The polygon is also a rhombus.

53. A sixth-grade teacher would like to select a student to serve as this month's hall monitor. To do this, he randomly selects a letter from the alphabet and then chooses the first student in his roster whose last name begins with that letter. Which statement below is true?
a. This would be fair for a class of 50, but not for a class of 20.
b. The selection is unfair because there may not be an equal number of students for each letter.
c. The selection is fair because students with an uncommon last name will not be singled out.
d. The selection is fair because each letter has an equal chance of being selected.
e. The selection is unfair because she did a random selection of letters instead of numbers.

54. One hundred male and female college freshmen were asked if they intended to transfer to another university for their sophomore year. The responses are tabulated in the following table:

	MALE	FEMALE
Yes	8	21
No	16	20
Maybe	22	13

What is the probability that the student is male given that the answer is YES?
a. 29/100
b. 46/100
c. 8/100
d. 21/29
e. 8/29

55. The height of the right circular cone shown is twice the diameter of the base. If the diameter of the base of the cone is 20 inches, what is its volume?

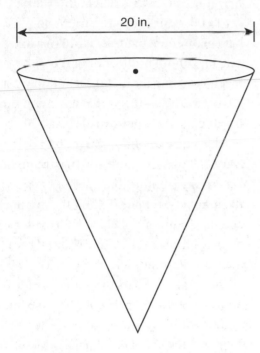

20 in.

a. $4,000\pi$ in.^{3}

b. $\frac{400\pi}{3}$ in.^{3}

c. $\frac{4,000\pi}{3}$ in.^{3}

d. $\frac{16,000\pi}{3}$ in.^{3}

e. 40π in.^{3}

56. Given the equation $14x + 2(x + 1) = 34$, each of the following steps would most likely be used to solve the problem EXCEPT

a. subtract 2 from each side of the equation.

b. divide each side of the equation by 16.

c. combine $14x$ and $2x$.

d. add 2 to each side of the equation.

e. use the distributive property to multiply $2 \times (x + 1)$.

Praxis® Core Academic Skills for Educators: Mathematics Practice Test 2 Answers and Explanations

1. d. Read the paragraph carefully to determine what information you are actually given. The actual discount given to groups of 30 or more people is not given, so choices **c** and **e** can be eliminated. Choices **a** and **b** can also be ruled out because you are not told how many tickets are for adults and how many are for children.

2. b. The adult price on Saturday afternoon is $5.50, and the child's price is $3.00. Find the difference in price by subtracting $3.00 from $5.50.

3. b. Because there are 1,000 students and there are five students on a team, $1,000 \div 5 = 200$ teams. Therefore, there are a total of $1,000 + 200 = 1,200$ people involved (because each of the 200 teams has one adult coach). 1,200 people $\div$ 4 gymnasiums = 300 people in each gym.

4. e. 80 students out of the 100 polled would prefer this class, and 80 out of 100 is 80%. To find 80% of 30,000, multiply: $0.80 \times 30,000 = 24,000$.

5. c. The concepts to be considered here are area and surface area. The amount of paper needed to cover a cube is equivalent to the surface area of a cube. The surface area of a cube is the area of each face $(d \times d) \times 6$, which is $6d^2$ (incorrect choice **a**). Although it is tempting to just double $6d^2$ to $12d^2$ (incorrect choice **b**), that will not work because it doesn't take into consideration that *each* side length has doubled. Instead, you must consider that Maya's gift has a side length of $2d$, which will, in turn, have 6 faces that are each $4d^2$ in area. The total surface area of Maya's gift will be $6 \times 4d^2 = 24d^2$. Choice **d**, $2d^3$, is a mistake made by taking the volume, $l \times w \times h$, of Marvin's gift and doubling that. Choice **e**, $12d^3$, comes from a combination of errors made by confusing volume, surface area, and how the doubling of an edge length affects either of these measures.

6. d and e. First, calculate the minimum number and the maximum number of granola bars that the 20 machines can make per minute. Because the minimum number of bars each machine can make is 80, multiply 80×20 to get 1,600—this is the minimum number of bars per minute made by all 20 machines. The maximum number of bars each machine can make is 100, so multiply 100×20 to get 2,000—this is the maximum number of bars per minute made by all 20 machines. Be careful—you're still not finished. These minimum and maximum numbers are per minute; the question asks for the number *per hour*. To find the minimum and maximum numbers of bars made per hour, multiply both numbers by 60 because there are 60 minutes in an hour. The minimum number of bars that can be made per hour = $1,600 \times 60 = 96,000$. The maximum number of bars that can be made per hour = $2,000 \times 60 = 120,000$. 100,000 and 119,500 are the only numbers listed between 96,000 and 120,000.

7. d. The question being asked here is "What is $\frac{1}{4}$ of $\frac{1}{2}$?" The word *of* in math is normally an indication that multiplication is required. To multiply fractions, multiply straight across their numerators and straight across their denominators: $\frac{1}{4} \times \frac{1}{2} = \frac{1}{8}$.

8. b. First, eliminate the parentheses on the left side of the equation using the distributive property: $2x - 3x + 3 = -12$. Combine like terms on the left side of the equal sign: $-x + 3 = -12$. Subtract 3 from both sides of the equal sign: $-x + 3 - 3 = -12 - 3$. Simplify: $-x = -15$. Divide each side of the equal sign by -1 to get $x = 15$.

9. a. The first calculation needed is how many gallons of gas Belicia's car will consume on the 364-mile trip. Because her car gets 28 miles for every gallon of gas, divide 364 by 28: 364 miles ÷ 28 miles per gallon = 13 gallons of gas needed. Because gas costs $4.85 per gallon, calculate the total cost by multiplying 13 gallons of gas by $4.85: 13 × $4.85 = $63.05.

10. e. This suggests a strong negative trend, which is what is illustrated in this scatterplot.

11. a. First, determine the amount of water that can be held in each container by finding the volume of each. The volume of the water poured into the rectangular box is found by multiplying the area of the base by the height of the water: $V = 16$ in.$^2 \times 9$ in. $= 144$ in.^{3} The total volume of the cylindrical container can be found by using the formula $V = \pi r^2 h$, where r = the radius of the base, h = the height of the container, and $\pi = 3.14$: $V = (3.14)(2)^2(11) = (3.14)(4)(11) = 138.16$ in.^{3} Because there is more water in the rectangular box, the cylinder will overflow when all the water is poured in.

12. The correct answer is **294**. Remember that when taking a fraction *of* some number, you are actually *multiplying* that number by the fraction. Let's look at what happens hour by hour, starting with 504 candies:

TIME	CANDIES GIVEN OUT	CANDIES REMAINING
8–9 o'clock	$\frac{1}{8} \times 504 = 63$	504 – 63 = 441
9–10 o'clock	$\frac{2}{9} \times 441 = 98$	441 – 98 = 343
10–11 o'clock	$\frac{1}{7} \times 343 = 49$	343 – 49 = 294

13. c. The mean is the average balance. To find the average, add all the values and divide by the number of values: $\frac{\$40 + \$10 + \$65 + \$25}{4} = \frac{\$140}{4} = \$35.00$.

14. c. We must express profit as a function of the number of driveways cleared of snow. So, the $903 spent on materials yields *negative profit* and so we express it as –903 in our function. Next, since we earn $40 per driveway, and it costs $5.25 per job, our net gain per job is $40 – $5.25 = $34.75. This is constant and so the profit gained from clearing x driveways is 34.75x$. So, the function describing our profit is $P(x) = 34.75x - 903$. Computing the break-even point is an inverse problem. We know the output (namely profit), but need to determine the input (number of driveways cleared) that will yield it. We must solve the equation $0 = 34.75x - 903$. We do so as follows:

$$0 = 34.75x - 903$$
$$903 = 34.75x$$
$$x \approx 25,986$$

So, you must round up and conclude that you will break even after clearing 26 driveways.

15. **a, b.** For **a**, if you fold the distribution over the y-axis, the graph lines up perfectly, which implies that it is symmetric. For **b**, the fact that there are two identical peaks in the distribution implies it is bimodal.

16. e. Because Lucinda pays with a check only if an item costs more than $30, the item must have cost more than $35. Choice **a** is incorrect because if the bill was $20, she would have paid with cash. Choice **b** is incorrect because if the bill was $80, she would have used her credit card to pay. Choice **c** is incorrect because she pays cash only for bills less than $30; if she has paid with a check, you can assume that the bill is already greater than this. Choice **d** is incorrect because if the bill was at least $70, she would have used her credit card.

17. b. The Engineering Department's electricity usage decreased $200, from $1,000 to $800, in the period from 1999 to 2000. To calculate the percentage decrease between two numbers, divide the difference between the two numbers by the original number. So $\frac{\$200}{\$1,000} = \frac{20}{100}$, which is 20%.

18. d. After the first two terms, each term is obtained by adding the preceding two terms in the sequence. Following this pattern, the next term would be $10 + 16 = 26$.

19. a. You are being asked to find 15% of the 30% of students who are in the music program. To find 15% of 30%, first change the percentages to decimal form: 30% = 0.30 and 15% = 0.15. Then, multiply: $(0.30)(0.15) = 0.045$. This is equivalent to 4.5%.

20. e. Multiply the square footage times the density to obtain $45,000 \cdot 0.03 = 1,350$.

21. d. In order to compare percentages, fractions, and decimals it is easiest to convert them all into decimals. The $\frac{3}{4}$ in choice a is equivalent to 0.75, so $4\frac{3}{4}\%$ is the same as 4.75%. When working with percentages, remember that they mean "out of 100." Therefore, in order to turn them into decimals you need to divide them by 100, which simply moves the decimal point two places to the left. So in this case, 4.75% is the same as 0.0475. Next, convert choice **b** into a decimal the same way: 4.09% becomes 0.0409. Choice **c**, $\frac{47}{1,000}$, is equivalent to 0.047 (move the decimal three times to the left). Choice **d**, $\frac{23}{500}$, is the same as $\frac{46}{1,000}$ or 0.0460. Choice **e** is already in decimal form for us, 0.0408. Once they are all in decimal form and you are looking for the largest value, follow these steps: compare the numbers' tenths place, looking for the highest number. If all the numbers have the same value in the tenths place, then move to the hundredths place and exclude any decimals whose value in the hundredths place is smaller than the rest. Next move to the thousandths place, still looking for the largest number, and so on. Of all these choices, **a** has the largest value.

22. b. When reflecting a point across the line $x = 2$, the y-coordinate will stay the same, but the x-coordinate will change. You subtract $2 - (-11) = 13$ and *add* this to 2 to get the new x-coordinate. So, the image of vertex B is (15,14).

23. a. This problem has multiple steps. First, determine what Deanna spent: $7 for popcorn, 2 hot dogs × 2 girls × $3 each = $12, and 2 sodas × $4 = $8, for a total of $7 + $12 + $8 = $27. Next, determine what Jamie spent: $13 × 2 = $26. Finally, subtract the two numbers: $27 − $26 = $1. Deanna spent $1 more.

24. d. First, represent the number of hours Kimberly worked as k and Ryan's hours as $3k$. Their combined work would be represented as $3k + k = 12$. So $4k = 12$ and $k = 3$. Therefore Kimberly worked 3 hours (which is the incorrect choice **a**), and Ryan worked $3k$, or 9 hours (which is the incorrect choice **b**). If Jaime worked 5 more hours than Ryan, that means he worked 14 hours (which is the incorrect choice **c**). Because Jaime and Janet worked a total of 18 hours, that means that Janet worked 4 hours. Choice **e**, 7, is the answer when subtracting the 5 more hours that Jaime worked from the 12 total hours that Ryan and Kimberly worked, which does not show how many hours Janet worked.

25. d. The points are closely packed together, so the correlation is strong. And, a parabola describes the relationship, which is nonlinear.

26. c. By figuring travel times in minutes, it becomes apparent that destination 3 takes the longest to reach: 100 minutes. Choice **a**, destination 1, is a 40-minute trip. Choice **b**, destination 2, is a 50-minute trip. Choices **d** and **e**, destinations 4 and 6, respectively, take 80 minutes and 40 minutes to reach.

27. d. First, convert the two mixed numbers to improper fractions: $2\frac{1}{4} = \frac{9}{4}$, and $4\frac{5}{8} = \frac{37}{8}$. Then, rewrite $\frac{1}{2}$ as $\frac{4}{8}$ and $\frac{9}{4}$ as $\frac{18}{8}$ so that all fractions have a common denominator. Add the fractions: $\frac{37}{8} + \frac{18}{8} + \frac{4}{8} = \frac{59}{8}$. Because the answer choices are presented as mixed numbers, rewrite $\frac{59}{8}$ as the mixed number $7\frac{3}{8}$.

28. b. Statements I and III illustrate the associative property of addition. In this property the association, or grouping, of the numbers changes, but the result is the same.

29. c. The speed of the train is 60 miles per hour, so as each hour increases by one, the number of miles traveled increases by 60. Therefore, the distance the train is from Chicago would equal $60t$ because distance – rate × time. However, as the train moves on, the distance from Los Angeles decreases (because the train is moving *toward* Los Angeles), so there must be a function of $-60t$ in the equation. At time $t = 0$, the distance the train is from Los Angeles is 2,000 miles, so the function is $2,000 - 60t$.

30. b. Because the only categories quantified are the types of chocolate in the candy bars, only the ratio of milk chocolate candy bars to white chocolate candy bars can be found. You would need additional information to determine any of the other choices.

31. c. The key to this question is that the bill is even, so the answer choice will be a number that when multiplied by 2.25, the eel price, yields a product of 18, half the bill. It is also helpful with this question to recognize that the sea urchin costs exactly one third more than the eel. Since the bill divides evenly, the number of sea urchin pieces will be an integer that can be formed by adding one-third to another integer. Choice **c**, 8, is one-third more than 6. No other answer choice is exactly one-third more than any integer.

32. c. The median is depicted in a box-and-whisker plot as the vertical line segment occurring within the box portion of the plot itself. Here, that line occurs at the value 47. So, the median of the data set is 47.

33. e. Substitute the value of 40 for C into the given formula: $F = \frac{9}{5}(40) + 32 = 72 + 32 = 104$. Therefore, 40° Celsius is equal to 104° Fahrenheit.

34. c. The volume of the aquarium, which is a rectangular prism, can be found by using the formula $V = l \times w \times h$. Because the length is 12 inches, the width is 5 inches, and the height is 10 inches, multiply $V = 12 \times 5 \times 10$ to get a volume of 600 cubic inches.

35. a. The formula for the area of a circle is $A = \pi r^2$, where r = the radius of the circle. Because each answer choice is in terms of π, do not bother to substitute anything for this symbol—just leave it in your answer. The diameter of the rug is 152 cm, so the radius, which is half of the diameter, must be 76 cm. Substitute into the area formula: $A = \pi(76)^2 = 5{,}776\pi$ cm^2. However, notice that the answer choices are given in square inches, not square centimeters. You are told that 1 cm = 0.39 in., so 1 cm^2 = 0.1521 in.^{2} Multiply the area by 0.1521 to convert cm^2 to in.^{2}: $5{,}776\pi \times 0.1521 = 878.53\pi$ in.^{2}

36. The correct answer is **17**. Substitute $x = 3$ into the equation $y = 5 + 4x$. Thus, $y = 5 + 4(3)$. Multiply first, and then add: $y = 5 + 12$, so $y = 17$.

37. e. Daphne's route is the hypotenuse. Solve for distance and divide by the rate to see how much sooner Daphne arrives. With legs of 300 and 400 meters, the triangle's hypotenuse will be 500 meters. Subtracting 500 from 700 (the sum of the lengths of the two legs) gives 200, which is then divided by 5 meters per second to give 40. Daphne arrives 40 seconds sooner.

38. d. The area of a circle can be found using the formula $A = \pi r^2$, where r is the radius of the circle. Because the area of 78.5 square feet is given, substitute $A = 78.5$ and $\pi = 3.14$ into the formula: $78.5 = 3.14r^2$. Divide each side of the equation by 3.14 to get $25 = r^2$. Take the square root of each side to get $r = 5$ feet. The diameter is twice the radius, so in this case, it is 10 feet.

39. c. This is a probability question with a percent conversion. First, there are 21 socks in all; after pulling one blue, there are an even number of blue socks and brown socks left in the drawer. The percent likelihood, then, is a conversion of the fraction $\frac{10}{20}$, or 50 percent.

40. e. To find the average of the numbers, divide the sum of the numbers by the number of terms being averaged. In this case, let x represent the temperature on the fifth day and set the expression equal to the average temperature for the five days, which was 90: $90 = \frac{95 + 85 + 88 + 84 + x}{5} = \frac{352 + x}{5}$. Cross-multiply to get $450 = 352 + x$. Subtract 352 from each side to get $x = 98$.

41. b, c, and d. The length of the third side of the triangle must be less than the sum of the other two sides (17 + 14) and greater than their difference (17 − 14). This means that the third side must be less than 31 and greater than 3. It could be 16, 25, or 28 cm long.

42. e. You can use the decimal equivalents to compare the numbers. Since $\frac{1}{4} = 0.25$ and $\frac{1}{3} = 0.3333\ldots$, look for the fraction that will fall between those values when written as a decimal: $\frac{1}{2} = 0.50$ (too large); $\frac{1}{5} = 0.20$ (too small); $\frac{2}{3} = 0.6\overline{6}$ (too large); $\frac{2}{5} = 0.40$ (too large). $\frac{2}{7} = 0.29$, which falls between 0.25 and 0.3333. . . .

43. b. For this problem it is important to first convert square inches to square feet. 288 square inches is 2 square feet (twice the product of 12 inches by 12 inches). Then determine how many 5 ml applications are in a single bottle: 5. Therefore, one bottle covers 10 square feet. Two bottles will exactly cover Ezra's 20-square-foot body surface area.

44. **a, c, e.** For **a** and **c**, the mean of the distribution is zero, which is nonpositive. For E, the mean of the distribution is negative.

45. **c.** This problem requires you to convert a smaller unit to a larger unit, which is done by dividing: 1,632 hours ÷ 24 hours per day = 68 days.

46. **a.** Substitute the value of $\frac{1}{2}$ in for each x in the function: $f(\frac{1}{2}) = 3(\frac{1}{2})^2 - \frac{1}{2}(\frac{1}{2}) + 7 = 3(\frac{1}{4}) - \frac{1}{4} + 7 = \frac{3}{4} - \frac{1}{4} + \frac{28}{4} = \frac{30}{4} = \frac{15}{2}$.

47. **c.** Because Sohail bought 4 raffle tickets for Asad and three times that for Amara, he bought $4 \times 3 = 12$ tickets for Amara, which means there were 16 tickets in total between the two of them. To find the probability of an event happening, the number of desired events must be put over the total number of events. In this case, there are 16 "desired events" (tickets belonging to Asad or Amara) and 80 total events (total number of tickets). Probability can be written as a fraction or as a decimal (between 0 and 1). In this case all the answers are given in decimal form, so $\frac{16}{80}$ must be turned into a decimal. Using long division to do this, 0.20 is the correct quotient.

48. **a.** If the area of one square is 9 square units, then each side has length $\sqrt{9} = 3$ units. Using how the rectangle is subdivided into squares as shown above, we multiply 3 by 2 to get 6 units as the width of the rectangle, and then multiply 3 by 3 to get 9 units as the length of the rectangle. Then, to get the perimeter, compute $2(6) + 2(9) = 30$ units.

49. **d.** A way to order the fractions is to change each to its decimal form and compare the values. Change a fraction to a decimal by dividing the numerator (top number) by the denominator (bottom number): $\frac{1}{2} = 0.5$; $\frac{6}{11} \approx 0.545$; $\frac{3}{5} = 0.6$; $\frac{5}{8} = 0.625$. To compare decimals, add zeroes to the end so that each decimal has the same number of digits after the decimal point: 0.500, 0.545, 0.600, 0.625. In order from greatest to least: 0.625, 0.6, 0.545, 0.5 – or $\frac{5}{8}$, $\frac{3}{5}$, $\frac{6}{11}$, $\frac{1}{2}$.

50. **b.** The probability of selecting a nickel or a penny is equal to the number of nickels and pennies in the jar divided by the total number of coins in the jar. There are 3 nickels and 9 pennies in the jar, so the number in the numerator (or top) of the fraction is 12. There are a total of 30 coins in the jar, so the probability is $\frac{12}{30}$, which reduces to $\frac{2}{5}$.

51. **b.** Take caution in percent problems, especially when the percent is taken off of two different amounts. First, find 15% off $84.50, and then find 10% off the membership price *after* the 15% discount: 15% of $84.50 = $0.15 \times \$84.50$ = $12.68; $84.50 – $12.68 = $71.82. Now, calculate 90% of $71.82 (remember, if you save 10%, you need to pay 90%): $0.90 \times \$71.82$ = $64.64.

52. **e.** The only statement that does not contradict the original statement is choice **e** because a square is a special rhombus.

53. b. The correct answer is **b**. A fair selection would result in each student having an equal chance of being selected. However, if 5 students have last names starting with the letter *S*, while 10 have last names starting with the letter *D*, then the students do not have an equal chance of being selected.

54. e. This is a conditional probability. Let A be the event that the student is male, and B the event that the answer is YES. We are asked to compute P(A|B). This is computed as follows:

$$P(A \mid B) = \frac{P(A \cap B)}{P(B)} = \frac{\frac{8}{100}}{\frac{29}{100}} = \frac{8}{29}$$

55. b. The correct answer is C. The height is 2(20 in.) = 40 in. and the radius is $\frac{1}{2}$(20 in.) = 10 in. So, the volume of the cone is $V = \frac{1}{3}\pi r^2 h$ = $\frac{1}{3}\pi(10 \text{ in.})^2(40 \text{ in.}) = \frac{4,000}{3} \text{in.}^3$

56. d. In order to solve the equation $14x + 2(x + 1) = 34$, first use the distributive property to eliminate the parentheses: $14x + 2x + 2 = 34$. Then, combine the like terms of $14x$ and $2x$: $16x + 2 = 34$. Subtract 2 from each side of the equation: $16x + 2 - 2 = 34 - 2$; $16x = 32$. Divide each side of the equation by 16: $x = 2$. The only step not useful in solving this equation was choice **d**.

A NOTE ON SCORING ▶

In order to evaluate how you did on the Praxis Core diagnostic and practice tests, first count the number of questions you answered correctly on each test. You will recall that your scores on the multiple-choice and fill-in segments of the tests are only based on the number of questions you answered correctly; there is no guessing penalty or penalty for unanswered questions. You will also recall that the Educational Testing Service has not set passing scores for these tests; this is left up to the institutions, state agencies, and associations that utilize the tests. Therefore, the interpretation of your score depends on the purpose for which you are taking the test.

If you are unsure of the passing score you will need, you can set yourself a goal of at least 70% of the answers right on each multiple-choice/fill-in section of the Praxis Core. To find the percent of questions you answered correctly, add up the number of correct answers and then divide by the total number of questions to find your percentage.

Even if you have scored well on the Reading test, the Mathematics test, and the multiple-choice subsections of the Writing test, don't forget that you must receive a passing score on the essay portion of the Praxis Core Writing test. On this portion, your essay will be scored by at least two writing experts, and their combined score will be used to evaluate how you did. The scoring criteria are outlined in detail in the answer explanations. The best way to see how you did on the essay portion of the exam is to give your essay and the scoring criteria to a teacher or other reader whom you trust to see what scores he or she would assign.

- If you scored below 60% on any subject, you should seriously consider whether you are ready for the Praxis Core test in this subject at this time. A good idea would be to take some brush-up courses, either at a university or community college nearby or through correspondence, in the areas you feel less sure of. If you don't have time for a course, you might try private tutoring.
- If your score is in the 60 to 70% range, you need to work as hard as you can to improve your skills. Also, reread and pay close attention to all the advice in Chapters 2, 4, 5, and 6 of this book in order to improve

your score. It might also be helpful to ask friends and family to make up mock test questions and quiz you on them.

- If your score is between 70% and 90%, you could still benefit from additional work by going back to Chapters 4, 5, and 6 and brushing up your reading, writing, and general math skills before the exam.
- If you scored above 90%, that's great! This kind of score should make you a success in the academic program of your choice or in a teaching position.

Once you have honed your test-taking skills, go back to the review chapters and study again the areas that gave you the most trouble. The key to success in almost any pursuit is to prepare for all you are worth. By taking the practice tests in this book, you have made yourself better prepared than other people who may be taking the test with you. You have diagnosed where your strengths and weaknesses lie and learned how to deal with the various kinds of questions that will appear on the test. So go into the tests with confidence, knowing that you're ready and equipped to do your best!

Using the codes below, you'll be able to log in and access additional online practice materials!

Your free online practice access codes are:

FVES55TCQF67LN1OQDO6

FVE6J14I1VWMFEB4XEDQ

FVEST2M8GG774LTYTWYL

Follow these simple steps to redeem your code:

- Go to **www.learningexpresshub.com/affiliate** and have your access code handy.

If you're a new user:

- Click the **New user? Register here** button and complete the registration form to create your account and access your products.
- Be sure to enter your unique access code only once. If you have multiple access codes, you can enter them all—just use a comma to separate each code.
- The next time you visit, simply click the **Returning user? Sign in** button and enter your username and password.
- Do not re-enter previously redeemed access codes. Any products you previously accessed are saved in the **My Account** section on the site. Entering a previously redeemed access code will result in an error message.

If you're a returning user:

- Click the **Returning user? Sign in** button, enter your username and password, and click **Sign In**.
- You will automatically be brought to the **My Account** page to access your products.
- Do not re-enter previously redeemed access codes. Any products you previously accessed are saved in the **My Account** section on the site. Entering a previously redeemed access code will result in an error message.

If you're a returning user with a new access code:

- Click the **Returning user? Sign in** button, enter your username, password, and new access code, and click **Sign In**.
- If you have multiple access codes, you can enter them all—just use a comma to separate each code.
- Do not re-enter previously redeemed access codes. Any products you previously accessed are saved in the **My Account** section on the site. Entering a previously redeemed access code will result in an error message.

If you have any questions, please contact Customer Support at Support@ebsco.com. All inquiries will be responded to within a 24-hour period during our normal business hours: 9:00 A.M.–5:00 P.M. Eastern Time. Thank you!